The 1968 Project

The Intersection of History and Music in 1968

Gregory L. Seltzer

This book is dedicated to my wonderful wife, Jenn, my two amazing sons, Max and Nate, to my loving and supportive parents, Karen and Steven, my brother, Mark, and his wife, Becca, and their two boys, Zack and Danny. Thanks to my dear friend, Jane, for her effort and counsel. Credit and thanks to the talented Hannah Westerman for the cover design.

Prologue

"When the Movement is Strong, the Music is Strong"

– Harry Belafonte

The United States was at peace in 1964. No soldiers in Vietnam. No active foreign conflict. The global economy was robust, both domestic and abroad. The United States government enacted sweeping legislation to address racial injustice, including The Civil Rights Act of 1964. The legislation led to productive discussions regarding racial equality and the hope of eliminating discrimination. The streets lacked hostility in 1964. Likewise, the music created in 1964 lacked hostility.

The Beach Boys and The Beatles dominated the charts in 1964, offering bright, simple and safe songs. Each focused on love, adolescence and well, cars. Then, as the United States commenced an aggressive bombing campaign in Vietnam in February 1965 – followed by deadly race riots in Selma, Alabama in March 1965, a certain spirit awoke. Evil emerged and unconscionably spread.

The bombing campaign led to American ground troops deployed to Vietnam later in 1965, then even deadlier race riots in the Watts neighborhood of Los Angeles in August 1965. Not entirely unhinged, but by the end of 1965, a wicked dark cloud cloaked the hearts, minds and culture of the United States. A movement was born.

Contemporaneous with the shift in political and cultural disposition, the music created in 1965 went from light to dark. By mid-1965, musicians reacted to the aggression of the American government by embracing an equally aggressive, darker version of Rock. Perhaps most importantly, musicians began using lyrics as a mechanism to express substantive messages in Pop music. The trajectory of music was influenced and affected by the trajectory of history.

In 1966, history and music maintained a similar continuum, as the music of 1966 echoed the attributes germinated in 1965. Merely a continuation, though – rather than a further shift in style and context. The next dramatic shift occurred in 1967. However, the musical shift in 1967 was not sparked by historical events. Rather, the shift manifested from a cultural phenomenon – the liberalization of American society.

Drugs, sex and freedom of expression fueled a devout and sweeping progressiveness. The children of World War II, or baby boomers, dominated the economics of American society – populating universities in record numbers, buying consumer goods and – yes, supporting the music industry. The Vietnam War still raged, even escalated in 1967 and racial instability continued to exist – yet, in 1967, a distinct haze hovered over the intuition of reasonable minds. A velvet curtain covered the wounds of American society.

Corporations embraced the liberal trends and musicians capitalized on the economic opportunity. In 1967, music was colorful, creative and bright. Arrangements became downright silly and alarmingly theatrical. Lyrics were abstract, devoid of message and, in many cases, meaning. Record covers depicted bands in costumes, drenched in concept rather than content. The music of 1967 anesthetized the pain of existing tragedies.

The 1968 Project is the story of the slow unveil. The painful realization that the United States was not on a course towards disaster, it was immersed in disaster. Like having a bloody, deep, open wound – visible to anyone that cared to look, but painless to the wounded. The pain was masked by bright colors, cool new sounds, smiling musicians, sexy actors and actresses, color television, the American space program – and, no doubt – drugs and alcohol.

No event from 1967 had the strength to rip off the veil and expose the tragic condition of America. This changed immediately in 1968. Irreversible tragedy occurred nearly every month in 1968. In January, the Tet Offensive by the North Vietnamese woke the American

realization that, "we are losing the war." In February, Walter
Cronkite turned on the Johnson Administration, swaying millions of
Americans towards the anti-war movement. The protective veil of
1967 started to fray.

Sensing the shift, musicians gradually began to modify their
expression. Early releases in 1968 by the Velvet Underground (*White
Light/White Heat*) and Singles by Cream ("Sunshine of Your Love")
and Steppenwolf ("Born to Be Wild") espoused and advocated a more
aggressive, violent version of Rock. Devoid of silliness, devoid of
color. The movement was coalescing. No longer would psychedelic
excess be tolerated. No longer could musicians make music without
contemplating their surroundings. Anger surfaced and spread. As the
tragedies of 1968 mounted, the musical consequence was
unavoidable. Death ignited an uncontrollable blaze of emotion.

Martin Luther King, Jr. was assassinated in April. Robert F. Kennedy
was murdered in June. In August, millions witnessed television
images of young demonstrators beaten and bloodied by police in
Chicago. No longer could Americans embrace yellow, blue and red –
expression was officially black. Laughing was replaced with crying.
Smiles turned to tears. Violence was no longer limited to Vietnam.
War raged in the streets of the United States. America became
unhinged.

As musicians digested and incorporated the tragedies of early-1968,
the reaction flooded the new music recorded and released in late-
1968. Definitive statements from Pink Floyd, The Doors, Buffalo
Springfield, then The Band released the seminal *Music From Big
Pink.* Classics by Cream, Jimi Hendrix, Janis Joplin, The Grateful
Dead. *Astral Weeks* by Van Morrison and then legendary releases by
The Beatles with *The White Album* and The Rolling Stones with
Beggar's Banquet and its opening track, "Sympathy for the Devil."

Music is often the byproduct of difficult times – and there may not
have been a more difficult time in American history than 1968.
Accordingly, there may not be a single year that produced better

6

music than 1968. However, please understand – that is not the premise of this book – that 1968 is the "greatest year in music."

Rather, the thesis of this book is to illustrate the manner in which history intersected with and influenced music in 1968. As the movement strengthened, the music strengthened. But, 1968 is unique – the influence became cyclical. While history is often the catalyst for a shift in musical style and content, in 1968 – history and music influenced each other, offering a revolving mutually impactful sea change of consequence.

January

January

HISTORY

The State of the Union
The Tet Offensive

MUSIC

The Woody Guthrie Memorial Concert at Carnegie Hall
Cream – "Sunshine of Your Love"
Steppenwolf – "Born to Be Wild"
The Velvet Underground – *White Light/White Heat*
Aretha Franklin – *Lady Soul*
Simon and Garfunkel – *The Graduate*

The downward spiral of the United States was set in motion in January 1968. The first thirty-one days of 1968 started an irreversible chain reaction. The freedom and psychedelic haze of 1967 masked a depression that existed in the hearts and minds of the American people. In just one month, the citizens of the United States lost faith in their President and alarmingly realized that their beloved country was not militarily invincible.

These two dramatic jarring emotional realizations exposed the depression. The free and jovial spirit of 1967, instilled and aided by music, film and drugs, seemed trivial and immature. However, the reaction of the American people was not sadness – the reaction was anger. Throughout 1968, this anger materialized in the streets – and eventually, in the studio.

HISTORY

The State of the Union

The chasm between government statements about The Vietnam War and the actual reality of the loss of life and, most stunningly, our loss of the war – the gap was massive, and an outright fraud perpetrated on the American people by senior governmental and military officials, including the President of the United States. In 1968, mainstream journalists began to travel abroad to cover the military conflict in Vietnam, however, the journalists would generally stay in the confines of United States or South Vietnam controlled city centers, such as Saigon. The journalists received information directly through briefings by military officials. So, the information reported by the media was generally filtered through governmental channels – essentially, domestic propaganda. Naively, the citizens of the United States (and the media) trusted their government. Yes, people actually used to trust the government.

On January 17, President Lyndon B. Johnson delivered his fifth (and final) Annual Message to the Congress on the State of the Union. Johnson broached the topic of the Vietnam War in his first sentence:

10

"I report to you that our country is challenged, at home and abroad."
Now, the President of the United States doesn't always (or need to)
covet the support of the citizens when determining whether to engage
in and continue foreign conflict. Unless, however, the citizens of the
United States are "voters." And, in 1968, the citizens of the United
States were voters in the upcoming Presidential election in November.
Johnson knew that he needed to gain the support of the people for the
war effort in order to be successful in the upcoming November
election.

Strategically, President Johnson positioned the Vietnam War as a
battle of *purpose*, not *fortitude*. In his opening remark, Johnson
stated, "it is our will that is being tried, not our strength…we have the
strength to meet our every challenge; the physical strength to hold the
course of decency and compassion at home; and the moral strength to
support the cause of peace in the world." You see, in 1968 it was
unfathomable that any nation, especially a small Asian country, could
test the strength, or fortitude, of the United States. So, Johnson was
asking – pleading – with the American people to support the war.
Reinforcing the premise, "Our patience and our perseverance will
match our power."

Johnson reported that "the enemy has been defeated in battle after
battle." This very statement would soon be viewed as misleading, or
in some circles, an outright lie. Johnson used the statement as a ploy
to convey strength and summon support. However, this statement
would essentially mark the demise of Johnson's candidacy for
reelection, as just 13 days after the State of the Union speech, after
Johnson insisted the United States was more powerful and winning
each battle, the American people witnessed the Tet Offensive and
realized that the North Vietnamese were not being defeated in "battle
after battle." In fact, it sure as heck looked on television like the
United States was being defeated. The people of the United States –
the voters – immediately lost trust in their Commander in Chief.

Perhaps the most accurate statement in Johnson's speech on January
17 was uttered at the conclusion of his remarks: "Aggression will

never prevail." Of course Johnson was referring to the North Vietnamese as the "Aggressor", but ironically, the American voters would soon consider President Johnson to be the "Aggressor" and ensured that he "would not prevail" in the upcoming election.

The Tet Offensive

The Vietnam War did not begin in 1968, but it most certainly began to end. After commencing a massive bombing campaign (Operation Rolling Thunder) in 1965 and dispatching the first cavalry of ground troops, also in 1965, the United States slowly entered into a comprehensive battle throughout 1966 and 1967. Opposition to the Vietnam War existed in 1966 and 1967, and was growing, but the thought, or fear, of actually losing the Vietnam War did not exist in 1966 and 1967.

The notion of losing the Vietnam War became a reality on January 31, 1968. Ultimately, the importance of the Tet Offensive was not the military losses experienced, but rather the change in mood and tone of the domestic opposition effort. Protests that had previously been peaceful, yet passionate, became dangerous and without order. The level of violence in the streets of the United States would soon echo the horrific scenes of violence in Vietnam. The Tet Offensive brought the war home.

What exactly was the Tet Offensive? The Tet Offensive was a highly coordinated, simultaneous series of attacks on over 100 cities, towns and villages in South Vietnam, including military installations and, shockingly, the United States Embassy in Saigon. The execution and strategy of the North Vietnamese attack was nothing short of impressive. Through the element of surprise and clever deception, the North Vietnamese changed the course of the Vietnam War, and the course of American politics.

The North and South Vietnamese, having been engaged in military conflict for decades, had long established a truce on the most important holiday on the Vietnamese calendar, Tet. Leading up to the

12

celebration of Tet in 1968, both the North and South Vietnamese made announcements that 1968 would be no different – the war would cease on Tet for the celebration of the Lunar New Year. Despite the mutual declaration, only one side would obey. Tactical or deceptive? Does it matter? It's war.

On January 21, prior to the celebration of Tet on January 31, the North Vietnamese Army launched a massive attack on the United States Marine installation at Khe Sanh. The attack on Khe Sanh was larger in scope than prior attempts to destroy United States garrisons and most certainly drew the attention of the most senior officials in the United States military regime, including General William Westmoreland, Commander in Chief of the Vietnam Military Forces, and President Johnson. Westmoreland authorized the mobilization of ground, air and naval units to converge on Khe Sanh and defeat the North Vietnamese attack. As the United States took the bait and engaged by committing a large number of troops and resources to protecting Khe Sanh, the North Vietnamese covertly commenced their primary objective.

The North Vietnamese had been preparing for the Tet Offensive in the months, maybe years, prior to January 31 by infiltrating and assimilating in major cities and provincial capitals in South Vietnam, hiding in warehouses and the homes of North Vietnamese supporters, stockpiling secret reserves of weapons and ammunition – waiting for orders. During the celebration of Tet, the streets of most South Vietnamese cities were crowded with jubilant citizens, providing the perfect cover for the hiding North Vietnamese guerilla forces to emerge undetected.

After sun down on January 31, the celebration of Tet commenced peacefully. The North Vietnamese soldiers fighting at Khe Sanh respected the truce and ceased fighting, further enhancing the element of surprise and deception. Amid the festivities, simultaneously, the North Vietnamese commenced a coordinated attack on over 100 cities in South Vietnam, using the guerilla forces within the cities, but also dispatching hundreds of thousands of North Vietnamese soldiers that

13

were lying in wait, undetected outside of the South Vietnamese cities. While the scale and ferocity of the attacks stunned United States military leaders, the television images resulted in downright outrage and fear on the part of the American people.

Television cameras were plentiful on January 31, as reporters were covering the celebration of Tet. As North Vietnamese soldiers slaughtered innocent South Vietnamese civilians in Saigon, a small group of North Vietnamese soldiers took aim at the United States Embassy, traditionally a sacred acreage in Saigon. Television cameras captured images of the North Vietnamese forces killing five United States guards, then filing onto the perimeter grounds of the embassy. Surrounding the embassy, the North Vietnamese attempted to breach the building entrance with anti-tank rockets. Eventually, United States troops engaged the North Vietnamese and after a bloody firefight, the United States defeated the North Vietnamese insurgency, protecting the embassy from further breach.

However, the images of North Vietnamese soldiers entering the front gate of the United States Embassy projected the impression of a North Vietnamese occupation of the United States Embassy. Just days later, video and still photographs famously depicted a South Vietnamese army officer executing a North Vietnamese soldier by shooting the soldier in his head while the soldier was on his knees, apparently begging for mercy. The image was so vivid and so abhorrent that it became cemented in the psyche of the American people as a microcosm of the brutality of the Vietnam War. The narrative immediately changed from "we are opposed to the Vietnam War" to "we are opposed to the government of the United States."

The government could no longer penetrate the minds and opinions of American citizens by *telling* them about the war. The American citizens could now *see* the war. "For the first time in a major war, the power of television became apparent. Fifty million people watched the destruction brought on by the war. The moment Vietnamese commandos penetrated the American Embassy in Saigon, all the official propaganda crumbled to dust" (Woods, Alan, Marxist.com 2008).

Eventually, President Johnson was correct – the strength and fortitude of the United States military overcame the Tet Offensive and pushed the North Vietnamese forces out of South Vietnamese territories (death tolls were approximately 45,000 dead North Vietnamese and 6,000 dead South Vietnamese and Americans). Johnson and Westmoreland claimed victory. But, the damage was irreversible. The Tet Offensive convinced the American people to abandon their President, fueling fierce demonstrations and dramatically affecting the course of politics for decades. Perhaps more impactful, the desire for peace abroad turned to violence at home.

MUSIC

The Woody Guthrie Memorial Concert at Carnegie Hall

After being the central figure of Folk music in the early-1960s and then the central figure of Rock music in the mid-1960s, Bob Dylan disappeared. Dylan's disappearance in 1966 coincided with the industry's shift from Blues Rock to Psychedelic Rock and, ultimately, Psychedelic Pop in 1967. However, Dylan's disappearance was not a consequence of the shift towards an aesthetic for which he did not approve. Dylan's disappearance was due to good old fashioned exhaustion.

After a controversial concert tour in 1966, where Dylan played an acoustic set to a loving, warm audience and then an electric set of Rock music to the same audience, which became pugnacious and aggressive in their disapproval, Dylan returned home to Woodstock, NY. After resisting several attempts by his manager (Albert Grossman) to book another World Tour, Dylan was coincidentally involved in a motorcycle accident. No injuries, not even a hospital visit, but an accident nonetheless and an excuse to remain in Woodstock, indefinitely (for a more detailed account of Dylan's rise and his impact and influence, along with a dissection of his lyrics and their effect on other musicians in 1965 and thereafter, please check out The 1965 Project, as the March, July and August chapters feature Dylan).

After the motorcycle accident, Dylan did not appear in public for 18 months. Dylan's reclusion was difficult for the music community on several levels. Dylan was an influencer. He started trends and ended trends. He was the hippest, coolest guy on the scene. After two classic releases, both in 1965, *Bringing It All Back Home* and *Highway 61 Revisited*, the community craved more music, but more so, the community craved his words.

Dylan, whether intentionally or unintentionally (we say intentionally, he says unintentionally), provided the soundtrack to political events such as the Cuban Missile Crisis and the seemingly unavoidable impending nuclear war ("A Hard Rain Is Gonna Fall"), the early machinations of the Vietnam War ("Masters of War") and, possibly more important, the racial discrimination and plight of African Americans in the United States (there are too many to list, but how about "John Birch Society Blues", "Hattie Carroll", "Blowin' in the Wind" and "Times They Are A-Changing"). As the world sank deeper into war and injustice, the community searched for Dylan's voice, the community looked to Dylan for answers. To no avail. Dylan essentially sat out the second half of 1966 and 1967.

So, upon the announcement of Dylan's appearance at a Woody Guthrie Memorial Concert on January 20 at Carnegie Hall in New York, tickets sold out immediately. In a *Rolling Stone* review after the concert, it was noted that tickets were being sold for as high as $25 (adjusting for inflation, $487 in 2016). People swarmed the theatre, "begging" for extra tickets.

Woody Guthrie died on October 3, 1967 after a long battle with Huntington's disease, a degenerative neurological disorder. Guthrie, a singer and songwriter, introduced the notion of message in song, usually politics and race. Guthrie had been (and by all accounts, remains) Dylan's hero, ever since a college classmate gave Dylan a copy of Guthrie's autobiography, *Bound For Glory*. Mythically, Dylan left his hometown of Hibbing, MN in search of Woody Guthrie, locating and visiting Woody at Greystone Park Psychiatric hospital in New Jersey.

As unpredictable as Dylan was and has since proven to be, Dylan has consistently remained loyal and respectful to those that came before him. So, if there was going to be a Woody Guthrie Memorial Concert – seclusion or no seclusion – Dylan would be there.

The format for the memorial concert was fairly traditional: several well-known artists would perform Woody Guthrie songs, usually solo acoustic or accompanied by another musician on acoustic guitar. In addition to Dylan, the lineup included Pete Seeger, Judy Collins, Ramblin' Jack Elliott, Odetta and Richie Havens. After several performances, Dylan took the stage wearing a gun metal grey silk mohair suit, blue shirt with green jewel cufflinks and black suede boots. His hair was long and he had a beard. Loyal and respectful, but never a conformist, Dylan played an acoustic guitar, but was accompanied by an amplified acoustic guitarist, an electric bass player and a drummer.

Dylan played three Guthrie songs: "Grand Coulee", "Mrs. Roosevelt" and "I Ain't Got No Home." The performance has since been released, so you can check it out, but musically – it's not remarkable. The import of the performance was Dylan's actual appearance, or existence. Was he back? Would he comment on the society that he motivated, then left behind? Does he have new music about the Vietnam War? Can he help us?

After Dylan's performance, the musicians took a bow and left the stage. The crowd, though, couldn't contain themselves – chants of "We Want Dylan" raged. As only Pete Seeger could do, he walked to the front of the stage and reminded the audience that the evening was about Woody, stating "Woody wants to say to you to take this music to the world, because if you do, maybe we won't have any more fascists."

17

And, that was it. Dylan remained in seclusion throughout the rest of 1968, playing with The Band in the basement of Big Pink (a house rented by The Band in Woodstock) and jamming with George Harrison twice at Dylan's home (other than the Guthrie concert, these are the only reported musical activities by Dylan in 1968).

The seclusion would last until May 1, 1969, when Dylan appeared on television with his good friend, Johnny Cash, on Johnny's new show, *The Johnny Cash Show* (recorded at the Ryman Auditorium in Nashville, TN). Despite occasional studio recording sessions between 1969 and 1973, and the release of three studio albums, Dylan would not perform in concert until a tour with The Band in 1974. Then, from that point on, he hasn't stopped touring. Dylan has been on the road, playing shows and on tour every year since 1974, except 1977 and 1982. They don't call it "The Never Ending Tour" for nothing.

Unlike The Beatles, The Rolling Stones and Jimi Hendrix, the foremost musical figure of the decade, Bob Dylan, is ominously absent in 1968. Perhaps he had nothing to say? Or perhaps he had shown others how to say?

Cream – "Sunshine of Your Love"

In 1968, Singles were typically released just prior to the release of a full LP. Some artists, though, including The Beatles, would not include Singles on their forthcoming LP ("Hey Jude", "Lady Madonna", for example). "Sunshine of Your Love" was a departure from both strategies, as "Sunshine of Your Love" was released as a Single three months *after* the release of *Disraeli Gears*, which featured "Sunshine of Your Love" as the second track. Why did Cream employ such a strategy?

Cream formed in 1966 and is widely considered the first "supergroup" (pre-dating Crosby, Stills and Nash). Eric Clapton was the most talented electric guitarist in London in 1965 and early-1966, after stints in The Yardbirds and then with John Mayall and the Bluesbreakers. Jack Bruce (bass) and Ginger Baker (drums) were members of the Graham Bond Organization, a popular London band that achieved short-lived international success. Baker was widely considered the premier drummer in the Rock scene (despite being trained as a Jazz drummer) and Bruce was known for his lead vocal ability, creative bass playing and songwriting talent.

Cream's first release in 1966, *Fresh Cream*, was popular, but not a hit. *Fresh Cream* concentrated more on psychedelic elements rather than Hard Rock, the band's eventual hallmark. Psychedelic music was sweeping across the musical underground and starting to surface in Pop. The track "I Feel Fine" is an example of Cream's version of Psychedelic Rock/Pop. The sound is okay, but does not take advantage of the band's strengths. A return to Rock would be the soundtrack of 1968 – and this new, or old, brand of Rock was much harder than its predecessors. Disengaged delirium migrated to chaotic violence. "Sunshine of Your Love" was at the dawn of the shift.

"Sunshine of Your Love" possessed a bright and sunny title, but any notion of a bright and sunny track was immediately erased by the crunchy intro electric guitar riff by Clapton. Bruce and Clapton then alternate vocals over the main riff, leading to a dual vocal chorus and raunchy power chords. The drumming is punchy, yet seems a bit in the background. The highlight, though, is clearly Clapton's guitar.

We'll explore Cream's music in more detail later in 1968, with the release of *Wheels of Fire*, but at this point, focus on the instrumentation. Cream was a three piece Rock band – guitar, bass and drums. Popular in Jazz, the trio format was not common or widely accepted in Rock. After Cream, several famous bands embraced the format, including The Jimi Hendrix experience, the Police, Rush, and later, Nirvana and Green Day.

Bruce wrote the riff and melody for "Sunshine of Your Love" after witnessing a Jimi Hendrix concert for the first time on January 29, 1967 in London. Commenting on the concert, Clapton stated, "Hendrix played this gig that was blinding. I don't think Jack had really taken him in before...and when he did see it that night, he went home and came up with the riff" (*Rolling Stone*).

So, why was "Sunshine of Your Love" released as a single after *Disraeli Gears*? The reason is because famed producers Ahmet Ertegun and Jerry Wexler preferred "Strange Brew" and "Tales of Brave Ulysses", as those tracks possessed the mainstream Psychedelic Rock sound that was topping the charts. Both Singles sold poorly and therefore *Disraeli Gears* experienced a sluggish start. Upon the suggestion of Booker T. Jones and Otis Redding, Ertegun and Wexler released "Sunshine of Your Love" as a Single. Ertegun later admitted that he couldn't process "Sunshine of Your Love" when he heard it in the studio due to the volume at which Cream played the track (Cream used multiple 100 watt amplifiers in the studio, whereas most musicians used one 20 watt amplifier).

After its release on January 6, 1968, "Sunshine of Your Love" reached #6 on the *Billboard* Hot 100 Singles chart and ended the year in the same slot. The track was clearly popular among non-musicians (let's call them fans), but musicians began to take note of the heavy, Hard Rock element and crunch of Clapton's guitar. Many musicians point to "Sunshine of Your Love" as the touchstone for the return of Rock – after the psychedelic excess of the Summer of Love in 1967.

Birth of Heavy Metal: Steppenwolf – "Born to Be Wild"

"Born to Be Wild" was the lead Single released in advance of Steppenwolf's self-titled debut album, *Steppenwolf*. Evoking (and in some cases, promoting) revolt, "Born to Be Wild" reached #2 on the *Billboard* Hot 100 Singles Chart in 1968. Famously, "Born to Be Wild" appeared in the 1969 hit film, *Easy Rider*, cementing the song as an anthem of counterculture and havoc.

The genre of Hard Rock had been established in late-1965 with the evolution of the Yardbirds, from Eric Clapton to Jeff Beck, but the emergence of Jimi Hendrix and Cream in 1966 and 1967 – Hard Rock became downright popular. Steppenwolf had something else, though

20

– outright recklessness and a certain toughness in tone and lyrics. Steppenwolf romanticized biker culture and raw spirit.

Before examining "Born to Be Wild", let's first consider the B-side, a power ballad titled, "Desperation." The song begins with a familiar sound – yes, The Who's guitar intro to "Pinball Wizard." However, "Pinball Wizard" wasn't released until 1969. So, maybe Townsend borrowed from Steppenwolf? Take a listen and you be the judge.

"Desperation" is a brooding ballad. With a sound that foreshadows classic early-1970s Lynyrd Skynyrd ("Tuesday's Gone"), the lyrics convey depression and helplessness, but also contain the optimism and hope that still existed in late-1967.

> *When rain drops fall and you feel low*
> *Ah, do you ever think it's useless*
> *Do you feel like letting go*
> *Do you ever sit and do you wonder*
> *Will the world ever change*
> *And just how long will it take*
> *To have it all rearranged*
>
> *Take my hand if you don't know where you're goin'*
> *I'll understand, I've lost the way myself*
> *Oh, don't take that old road it leads to nowhere*

"Desperation" is a simple song – basic power chords (C/G/F) and a short, direct guitar solo – but for a band that specialized in heavy, Hard Rock, "Desperation" is an exhale, an important glimpse into the mindset of youth – "I've lost the way myself" and "Don't take the old road, it leads to nowhere." As the flip side to "Born to Be Wild', "Desperation" provides context and ultimately underscores the ferocity and raw power of "Born to Be Wild."

Historians credit the beatnik author William Burroughs with the first use of the word "heavy metal" in the 1962 novel, *The Soft Machine*. Burroughs, a renowned author of Beat literature and a notorious drug addict, created a character known as "Uranium Willy, The Heavy Metal Kid" (a reference to Uranium being a "heavy" metal). Steppenwolf, though, is credited for being the first artist to use the term "heavy metal" in a song lyric, without reference to the attributes of metal:

> *I like smoke and lightning*
> *Heavy metal thunder*
> *Racin' with the wind*
> *And the feeling that I'm under*

The lasting value or element of the song is its chorus, "Born to be wi-i-i-ild, Born to be wi-i-i-ild" (you know what I'm talking about), a refrain that would resonate throughout the streets in 1968. You are hard pressed to find a documentary chronicling the violence of 1968 that doesn't make use of "Born to Be Wild." It incited riot by its mere reference. *Urban Dictionary* defines "Born to Be Wild" as "Steppenwolf's most famous song which kicks ass."

The Velvet Underground – *White Light/White Heat*

White Light/White Heat is the second album released by The Velvet Underground, released on January 30. *White Light/White Heat* is the follow-up to the band's debut, *Velvet Underground & Nico*, released in 1967 (and, of course, famously according to Brian Eno, the debut album caused the very small audience that actually heard the record to each start a band of their own, paraphrasing). *White Light/White Heat* marks the last studio recording with original bassist, John Cale.

The Velvet Underground blazed their own path. The band influenced others more than it was influenced *by* others. In response to lackluster sales of its first release, The Velvet Underground decided to make and release a record even less accessible. Not surprisingly, it sold even less than their debut. *White Light/White Heat* includes six tracks, four on Side A and two on Side B. The album was experimental in 1968 and still sounds experimental today.

The chaos and turbulence in The United States had yet to materialize in January, however, The Velvet Underground resided in New York City, amidst an underground scene unlike any other prior to its existence. Drugs, sex, experimental film. The current of rebellion already existed in New York City in 1968. Turbulence was a way of life. The Velvet Underground were amongst chaos and transmitted such chaos through their music. According to Sterling Morrison (electric guitar and backing vocals), "we were all pulling in the same direction. We may have been dragging each other off a cliff, but we were all definitely going in the same direction. [O]ur lives were chaos. That's what's reflected on *White Light/White Heat*.

The motivation or intention of the record is not exactly clear, but based on interviews, *White Light/White Heat* is regarded as an "assault on the Pop sensibilities of the time." The Velvet Underground despised the hippie culture of 1967 and were revolting against the scene through music that lacked optimism, was devoid of hooks and appealed to very few. Case in point – the production and sound of the record is lo-fi, before lo-fi really existed and the cover photo is blurry and bleak, in contrast to the colors and clarity of psychedelic records.

The Velvet Underground were ahead. Always ahead of the rest. There is no evidence that The Velvet Underground participated in peace protests. The Velvet Underground innately sensed that the only way to stop the violence was to get violent. That was the band's DNA. Such an attitude would eventually become the mainstream sentiment later in 1968. The Velvet Underground set the tone.

The opening track, "White Light/White Heat" is perhaps the most straight-forward and contained song on the album. Sure, the guitar is distorted and there's an aural cacophony, but the song has rhythm, piano exists and the vocals are simple. Contrary to many of the other tracks on *White Light/White Heat*, the title track is actually a "song."

The second track, "The Gift", erased all notions or suggestions of normalcy. "The Gift" is a nine minute short story, read word for word over a screeching lead electric guitar. The track is mixed such that the narration of the short story is heard in the left stereo channel, while the instrumental/experimental Rock is heard in the right channel. The story, read by John Cale and written by Lou Reed, is bizarre.

Contemporary in prose, "The Gift" tells the story of Waldo Jeffers, a recent college graduate, and his girlfriend, Marsha Bronson. After graduation from college, Waldo and Marsha returned to their respective hometowns. Fearful and paranoid about Marsha's potential unfaithfulness, Waldo mails himself to Marsha in a large cardboard box. Upon receipt of the box, Marsha and her friend, Sheila, are unable to open the box. Grabbing a sheet metal cutter, Sheila "plunged the long blade through the middle of the package, through the masking tape, through the cardboard, through the cushioning and right through the center of Waldo Jeffers head which split slightly and caused little rhythmic arcs of red to pulsate gently in the morning sun."

That's how the story, and the song, ends. It's a harrowing tale, no doubt. Imagine placing the vinyl record on the turntable and hearing this story emanate. Imagine what parents must have thought?

Would a cathartic song follow "The Gift?" Plainly, no. "Lady Godiva's Operation" follows and extends the bizarre. The song is about a botched surgical operation featuring Cale's plain spoken vocals and Cale and Reed alternating verses in the second half of the song. The musical template is equally as dark as "The Gift", but never really gels with the lyrical narrative. "Godiva" also does not possess the level of creative writing and production as "The Gift."

As "Godiva" gives way to "Here She Comes Now", we're immediately reminded of talent. The talent of Lou Reed. Whether "Here She Comes Now" is about a female orgasm, or more likely, related to drugs – the interesting aspect is that the song is a reprieve – a two minute and four second reprieve from the shred and shriek and gore of the three previous songs. "Here She Comes Now" is accessible and possesses a lo-fi pop quality illustrating Reed's ability to compose and write likeable songs, a skill he would master as a solo artist. "Here She Comes Now" is both an outlier and a conformist (to popular music) and remains the best track on *White Light/White Heat*. Each of Nirvana and Galaxie 500 have covered the track, with the latter being a personal favorite that accentuates the melodic quality of Reed's composition.

Side 2 of *White Light/White Heat* is dominated by the seventeen minute, two chord track, "Sister Ray." Recorded in one take, "Sister Ray" is the story of a transvestite drug dealer, Sister Ray, and seven other characters, all participating in a drug-induced orgy that results in death and decay. Yes, you read that correctly. "Sister Ray" is still today considered provocative – imagine how it was perceived in early-1968? The story contains far less compelling prose than "The Gift", but the music is wonderfully potent – containing a highly improvised cathartic chaos that at times serves as a soundtrack to tragedy.

It's difficult to assess the impact of *White Light/White Heat*, as it is well documented that the record was not widely purchased. Did *White Light/White Heat* affect and influence other artists? Evidence of such influence is not readily apparent, as I failed to find artists citing or commenting on or about *White Light/White Heat* in 1968. What is apparent, though – is that the feelings borne by Reed and Cale and The Velvet Underground – the feelings of action and rage and violence – would be felt by a cavalry of young people and musicians later in 1968. In a couple months, the rage and chaos expressed by The Velvet Underground was pervasive. The Velvet Underground were always ahead.

As for the legacy of *White Light/White Heat*, like each record in the catalog of the Velvet Underground, *White Light/White Heat* has aged very, very well. *Pitchfork* stated that *White Light/White Heat* "clung to the bottom of the album chart for two weeks, disappeared, and went on to become the glorious, tainted fountain from which all scuzz flows." Perfectly stated.

Aretha Franklin – *Lady Soul*

Released on January 22, *Lady Soul* is the fourteenth studio album by Aretha Franklin. *Lady Soul* was a hit, reaching #1 on the *Billboard* R&B Album Chart and #2 on the *Billboard* Pop Album Chart. Unlike many of the most popular African American artists of her generation, Aretha did not record at Motown. Similar to Ray Charles, Sam Cooke and Otis Redding, Aretha was signed very early to a major label (Columbia, then Atlantic). Typically, African American artists signed to Motown after the major labels passed. Why was Aretha signed early, in the class of Ray, Otis and Sam? Cleary, her voice. It's uncommon, unparalleled and unavoidably compelling.

Lady Soul contains three Top Ten hits: "Chain of Fools" (#2), "(You Make Me Feel Like) A Natural Woman" (#8) and "Since You've Been Gone" (#5). The record is extremely accessible from an instrumentation perspective and although the lyrical substance avoids political themes, the message is wonderfully feminist. Aretha released her cover version of the Otis Redding song, "Respect" in 1967, establishing Aretha as a dominant voice in the burgeoning feminist movement. The songs on *Lady Soul* echo the message of "Respect" and led to a slot at the Newport Folk Festival in July (along with Janis Joplin).

Notably, and with all due respect to the Funk Brothers (the venerable and highly accomplished backing band for most of the Motown artists), the skill of the musicians in Aretha's band on *Lady Soul* is stunning. Aretha is backed by Bobby Womack on guitar, Spooner Oldham on organ, King Curtis on tenor saxophone and Roger Hawkins on drums. A collection of the best session players in music at the time. Start to finish, *Lady Soul* just cooks and would become the template for all female vocal recordings thereafter. After *Lady Soul*, Aretha became Soul.

Simon and Garfunkel – *The Graduate*

The Graduate is a film directed by Mike Nichols, released on December 20, 1967. Based on a novel written by Charles Webb published in 1963, *The Graduate* tells the story of Benjamin Braddock (Dustin Hoffman), a recent college graduate that has returned home after graduation to live with his parents in order to "figure out" what he will do with the rest of his life. Braddock certainly lacks ambition, but more so, he is aimless.

Dustin Hoffman was a relatively unknown actor when he auditioned for the role of Benjamin Braddock, but Nichols chose Hoffman for the part due in large part to his eyes and his facial expression. Hoffman's somewhat bewildered expression and demeanor define Benjamin Braddock – and Benjamin Braddock defined an entire generation of young people in 1967 and 1968. Unwilling to adhere to the direction and will of their parents, but yet unclear as to the meaning or direction of their life. Outwardly aloof, and inwardly focused, but focused on confusion.

The plot is centered on Braddock's seduction by Mrs. Robinson (Anne Bancroft), the wife of Braddock's father's law partner (aptly named, Mr. Robinson). At first, the seduction is awkward – or, Braddock's reaction to the seduction is awkward. The film focuses entirely on Braddock, but ultimately, the more interesting character is Mrs. Robinson. At the core of the film, the viewer sees that not only young people are depressed and lost, but even the wealthy wife of a law partner was depressed and lost.

The cinematography is a bit dated in terms of montages, close-ups and wide angle shots, but the film amazingly has the feel of a modern "indie movie." The dialogue is quick, witty and smart. The story arc is character-driven, similar to movies by Wes Anderson and the Coen brothers. Perhaps the main similarity between *The Graduate* and recent indie movies is the role of the film's soundtrack. Music had been used in films for decades before *The Graduate*, dating back to *Gone With The Wind*, *The Wizard of Oz* and *The Sound of Music*, but

The Graduate was one of the first movies to incorporate music into the direction of the film and use contemporary, popular music, largely by one artist.

Simon & Garfunkel formed in 1964, but struggled. Eventually breaking up, Paul Simon moved to London in 1965 and wrote and released *The Paul Simon Songbook* in August 1965. A few of the tracks from *Songbook*, including "The Sound of Silence", received radio play. The radio play elevated the interest in the first Simon & Garfunkel release, *Wednesday Morning 3 AM*. In light of the renewed attention, CBS (record label and owner of *Wednesday Morning 3 AM*) unilaterally re-mixed "The Sound of Silence" and included a jangly electric guitar, drums and bass (capitalizing on the Folk Rock style invented and popularized by The Byrds in 1965).

The consequence was a Folk Rock hit that reached #1 on the *Billboard* Hot 100 Singles chart. Despite hating the re-mix, Simon & Garfunkel welcomed the accolade and released two records in 1966: *Sound of Silence* and *Parsley, Sage, Rosemary and Thyme*. Both records were hits, with Simon's poetic lyrics and phrasing echoing Dylan at a time when Dylan was noticeably absent.

In early-1967, director and writer Mike Nichols was obsessed with both 1966 releases by Simon & Garfunkel. Nichols reportedly listened to both records before and after filming scenes of *The Graduate*. Initially seeking to engage Crosby, Stills & Nash to license certain songs for inclusion in *The Graduate*, Nichols changed gears and approached Clive Davis at CBS to ask about a license to "The Sound of Silence", "Scarborough Fair" and inquired about the possibility of Paul Simon writing a couple new songs for the soundtrack. Nichols was successful in obtaining the support of Davis and CBS, but Paul Simon rejected the notion of his music being used in a film, feeling as though it was "selling out." CBS suggested that Simon meet with Nichols and perhaps read *The Graduate* script. Simon agreed to meet and read the script.

The two apparently hit it off immediately and Simon agreed to see a couple rough cut movie scenes. Simon reportedly found the script incredibly well written and liked Nichols' directorial style. Simon agreed to the license of his music and agreed to write a couple new songs specifically for *The Graduate*. Simon wrote "Punky's Dilemma" and "Overs", but Nichols didn't feel that either song was a fit. Simon then played Nichols a rough cut of another song he was working on – and Nichols immediately loved it. The song would eventually be titled, "Mrs. Robinson" (early versions by Simon were titled "Mrs. Roosevelt").

Famously, *The Graduate* opens with Benjamin Braddock on an airport moving sidewalk, with a zoomed in shot of Benjamin's emotion-less face and "The Sound of Silence" playing in the background, yet very much in the foreground. It's a dramatic use of the song and sets the tone for the entire film. "The Sound of Silence" is used three times throughout the movie, weaved into and between scenes perfectly. "Scarborough Fair" is also used multiple times throughout the film and serves as the soundtrack to a few montage scenes that propel the narrative while preserving consistency by refraining the song's theme.

Teased instrumentally early in the film with acoustic guitar strums, the first full version of "Mrs. Robinson" was not used until later in the film. While *The Graduate*, as a whole, attempts to abstractly capture the mood of youth in 1967 and the perception of youth by the traditional adult community, "Mrs. Robinson" states it explicitly. Religion. Politics. Culture. In that order.

> *And here's to you, Mrs. Robinson*
> *Jesus loves you more than you will know*
> *God bless you, please Mrs. Robinson*
> *Heaven holds a place for those who pray*

Many young folks in 1968 associated religion with their parents and in 1968, young folks wanted anything but the traditions of their parents. Support for religion was waning in favor of rebellion, drugs, sex and living a free and open life, while still pursuing causes. Mrs. Robinson, a smoker, a drinker, a provocatively dressed adult – cheating on her husband with a 21 year old – this is not conduct that would be embraced by the church, or any religion for that matter. Nichols and Simon were aligned in their contempt for religion (as discussed below, the film ends with Braddock barging into a church and, ultimately barring the doors with an enormous cross).

Simon wastes no time, referencing Jesus in the second line of the song and, speaking to Mrs. Robinson, tells her that Jesus still loves her and that she can still make it to heaven despite her horrible conduct, so long as she prays. It's an indictment of religion – that such a contemptible being could still find salvation. The next topic: Politics.

> *Sitting on a sofa on a Sunday afternoon*
> *Going to the candidates' debate*
> *Laugh about it, shout about it*
> *When you've got to choose*
> *Every way you look at this you lose*

Simon's ability to foreshadow the events of the 1968 election cycle are frightening, but in this one verse, Simon nails it. In subsequent chapters of this book, we'll cover the election primaries and then the general election in November, but basically – the candidates were "laughable" and people most certainly "shouted about it." But, when it came time to vote – he was right, everyone "lost." Simon suggests an apathy certainly present in 1967, but the inclusion of politics also suggests the importance and stature that politics held in the public's conscious. The next verse attacks Culture and in my view, is sheer brilliance.

> *Where have you gone, Joe DiMaggio*
> *Our nation turns its lonely eyes to you*
> *What's that you say, Mrs. Robinson*
> *Joltin' Joe has left and gone away*

What a verse – memorable, meaningful and, ultimately, metaphorical. Joe DiMaggio, the Hall of Fame centerfielder for the New York Yankees, retired in 1951. Seventeen years prior. In many respects, DiMaggio represented everything great about America. DiMaggio represented the "Greatest Generation." Not only was he a wonderfully successful professional athlete, but he served in World War II (in the middle of his Major League Baseball career), he was politically conservative and socially liberal (at one time, married to Marilyn Monroe). DiMaggio exuded loyalty – to his friends, his family, his team and his country (famously, upon Monroe's death, DiMaggio claimed her body in Los Angeles, orchestrated her funeral and had a half dozen roses sent to Monroe's gravesite three times a week for 20 years).

So, why the lyrical reference to DiMaggio? Despite retiring in 1951, DiMaggio was not out of the public eye – he was the spokesperson for Mr. Coffee and Bowery Bank, in addition to his highly public social relationships. By asking "where has Joe DiMaggio gone" Simon is really asking "where have Joe DiMaggio's values gone", and "where has Joe DiMaggio's generation gone?" Maybe, "where has America gone?"

Simon doesn't answer the question, maybe suggesting that nobody quite knows where they've gone, but clearly – they're gone. Simon refers to the mood of the country as having "lonely eyes." Simon then affirmatively states that Joltin' Joe (or his values) have "left and gone away." It's somber and clearly metaphorical, but not dispositive. What is going to happen? Simon doesn't quite endorse the values of the new generation, but simply announces the change.

If you feel that the song's nexus to the plot of the movie is somewhat lacking, you're not alone. Simon acknowledged that the song is "not for the movie…it's a song about times past." The song not only worked great in the movie, "Mrs. Robinson" was a hit, reaching #1 on the *Billboard* Hot 100 Singles chart and winning the Grammy Award for Record of the Year (surprisingly, the first Rock song to win the Grammy Award for Record of the Year).

31

The ending of *The Graduate* is highly relevant to the months ahead in 1968. Born out of the freedom of experience in 1967, rebellion was beginning to coalesce, but there existed a sentiment of "is this really the right direction, what do we really want?" Ultimately, the malaise of youth and indecision morphed into action throughout 1968, but in late-1967 and early-1968, the time *The Graduate* was filmed and released, there remained a sense of uncertainty.

At the end of *The Graduate*, after Benjamin Braddock endures a series of embarrassing circumstances, finally tracking down the woman he loves (Elaine Robinson, Mrs. Robinson's daughter), the young couple run away just before Elaine was to marry another man, with Benjamin breaking into the church and barring the door with a large cross. The two formerly docile, drifting, but now action-driven kids boarded a public bus and meandered excitedly to the back seat.

With the camera zoomed in on just the two of them, their joy is so present, smiling, happy and energized – free from their parents and societal norms, finally on their own. Then slowly, their facial expressions fade to plain. Not upset or anxious, not sad or violent – just plain – a return to the exact same malaise and adrift expression that we witnessed in the first scene of the movie as Benjamin coasted on the airport moving sidewalk. "The Sound of Silence" plays again as the two stare into the unknown, and the credits roll. Absolutely brilliant. Symmetrical, yet irregular. Magic.

February

February

HISTORY

Nixon Enters the Race for President of the United States
Martin Luther King, Jr. and the Speech That Would Became His
Eulogy
The Most Trusted Man in America

MUSIC

Louis Armstrong – "What A Wonderful World"
Otis Redding – *(Sittin' On) The Dock of the Bay*
Fleetwood Mac – *Fleetwood Mac*

HISTORY

Nixon Enters the Race for President of the United States

On February 1, just days after the dramatic and incendiary Tet Offensive horrified the American people, Richard M. Nixon announced his candidacy for President of the United States. With Nixon's announcement, the United States would embark on a political course of irreparable harm, concluding in 1974 with Nixon's resignation – the only President in the history of the United States to resign.

In 1968, Nixon was not a symbol of evil or corruption. A career politician, Nixon was elected to Congress as a representative for California's 12th District in 1946. In 1950, Nixon was elected to the Senate as a representative of California, winning the election by over twenty percentage points. Nixon, a Republican, ran on a conservative platform and waged a tactical campaign against his opponent (Helen Douglas), arguing that his opponent possessed liberal views and a liberal voting record. Such negative campaign messages and strategies were uncommon in 1950, earning Nixon the nickname "Tricky Dick."

In 1952, Dwight D. Eisenhower won the Republican nomination for President. The Republicans had not held the Oval Office since 1932 (Herbert Hoover). As a running mate, Eisenhower sought youth and sought a Vice President that could carry a large, typically liberal state. A 39 year old Senator from California was the perfect choice. Eisenhower and Nixon beat Adlai Stevenson and John Sparkman in a landslide (over 11 percentage points).

Nixon served two terms as Vice President and then declared his candidacy for President in 1960. Nixon won the primary easily and faced a young and savvy Senator from Massachusetts in the general election – John F. Kennedy. A heavy favorite, Nixon possessed considerably more political experience than Kennedy. Early polls indicated an advantage for Nixon. However, the United States was amidst a recession dating back to 1957 and the economy became a significant talking point. Nixon had considerable experience in foreign affairs, but Kennedy, a Harvard graduate, held the edge in economics. This edge would be the second most important aspect of the election – the first being, of course – television.

The Presidential election of 1960 was not only the first election that featured televised debates, it was the first Presidential election that featured organized debates. Consequently, the first of four debates in 1960 attracted massive television viewership. The candidates approached the debate quite differently. Nixon resisted makeup and insisted on campaigning right up until the start of the televised debate. Looking pale and tired, and wholly unfamiliar with how to make eye contact with the television cameras, Nixon's appearance was a disaster.

At one point, sweat from the lights was clearly visible on his face and in conjunction with Nixon's scattered and fleeting eye contact, he looked stunningly overmatched standing next to the handsome, polished, seasoned and experienced celebrity of John F. Kennedy (the Kennedy family had been in the political and tabloid spotlight for decades). Kennedy wore make up and rehearsed for the debate, with a focus on appearance, disposition and character.

Interestingly, immediately after the debate, the electorate was split as to who "won" the debate. Those watching on television insisted that Nixon lost the debate, as he looked "old and untrustworthy", while those listening on the radio insisted that Nixon won the debate, sounding more experienced on each and every issue. Ultimately, this first Nixon-Kennedy debate was the birth of politics as we know it today – fixated on glamour and "electability", rather than economic plans, vision, social beliefs and policy. The American people flocked to Kennedy. People wanted a better America, people wanted to be like the Kennedys.

Kennedy beat Nixon in the general election by a mere 112,000 votes, or 0.02% of the popular vote. Nixon actually won more states, 26-22, but the Electoral College count favored Kennedy, 303-129. Nixon was devastated. A career politician, eight years in the White House as Vice President – and he lost to a first term Senator from Massachusetts, yielding the White House to the Democrats.

Nixon retreated to California, vowing retirement from politics. However, in 1962, the Republican Party convinced Nixon to run for Governor of California, providing significant financial support to the Nixon campaign. Nixon ran against the incumbent Governor, Pat Brown. Initially favored, Nixon lost to Brown by more than five percentage points. Once again, Nixon's political career was dead.

After the assassination of Kennedy, and Lyndon Johnson's widely heralded first full term as President from 1964 to 1968, the notion of a Republican contending for the White House in 1968 was outlandish. But, as we started to see in 1965 – the Vietnam War changed the course of the United States, from a political perspective, sure, but as we'll explore throughout this book – from a cultural and social perspective, with music being the output – the most visible product of distress.

In early 1968, as unbridled, and to many conservatives, offensive levels of freedom of expression, dominated the cultural landscape, combined with increasingly larger and louder anti-Vietnam War protests, the Republicans sensed an opening. The Republicans yearned for a conservative candidate with foreign affairs experience and a strong sense of "law and order" to thwart the insurgence of liberals and the youth of America. Nixon was the perfect candidate and was embraced by not only the right wing of the Republican Party, but Nixon was strong with moderates.

It became official on February 1, Nixon was a factor. Formerly maligned, Nixon found himself embraced – a candidate that could restore the traditions of the United States. Arguably, Nixon would soon do just that – restoring the American traditions of greed, corruption, misdirection and tragedy.

Martin Luther King, Jr. and the Speech Became His Eulogy

Exactly two months before his assassination in Memphis, Martin Luther King, Jr. (MLK) told his congregation what he would like said at his funeral. As an aside, imagine if you could script what would be said at your funeral. Would you craft the words? Would you most certainly not? Would you care? I mean, you're dead. Does it matter? Martin Luther King, Jr. thought it mattered. He said, "I'd like for somebody to say that day that Martin Luther King, Jr. tried to love somebody." Now, whatever you just thought of to be said at your funeral – it ain't as poetic and special and cool as that.

MLK was a wonderful speaker (an understatement), and supposedly he wrote much of what he preached. Many of his speeches and quotes are facially insightful, not unduly abstract or indirect. So, when MLK announced what he would like said about him at his funeral, people paid attention. And, surprisingly, MLK seemed somber, almost expecting death.

The basis of MLK's sermon on February 4 at the Ebenezer Baptist Church in Atlanta (MLK's home congregation) was an adaptation of the 1952 homily, "Drum-Major Instincts", originally written by J. Wallace Hamilton, a liberal white Methodist preacher. The "Drum-Major Instinct" tells the story of James and John, both of whom ask Jesus for the most prominent seats in heaven. The homily goes on at length, but the core reason for James and John wanting the prime seats in heaven is their desire to lead, a desire to be in front, to be the drum major.

Diverting to race, MLK stated, "Do you know that a lot of the race problem grows out of the drum major instinct? A need that some people have to feel superior…and to feel that their white skin ordained them to be first." MLK then relayed that Jesus responded to James and John by telling them to "Keep feeling the need for being first. But I want you to be first in love." When interpreting MLK's desired eulogy – it seems as though MLK wanted to be remembered not as a leader, not as a drum major, but as someone that tried to love. MLK sensed his mortality and wanted his congregation to understand that he, the drum major, is not the most important factor in the cause for racial equality – the key factor is love – and if MLK were not to exist, if the African American community could love – they could continue the fight. Love. A hallmark of 1967. "All You Need Is Love" – MLK connected people – he related to the youth and to the elders. MLK was a magician, a savant, a once in a generation talent.

MLK ended the sermon by again imagining his own funeral. MLK urged the congregation to not dwell on his life. An odd thing to convey when you are 39 years old. He asked to be remembered as someone who "tried to give his life serving others." Then, he refrained the "Drum-Major Instinct" and echoed realism – "Yes, if you want to say that I was a drum major, say that I was a drum major for justice. Say that I was a drum major for peace. I was a drum major for righteousness."

These final thoughts are more functionally accurate. MLK was most definitely a drum major. He was perhaps the greatest drum major of the 20th Century. Check that – eternity. However, he seemed to be readying his followers for his passing, for a life without him. The effort was admirable, but ultimately, not successful. In exactly two short months, the nation would mourn. MLK's followers would take to the streets in retaliation. Can you blame them? I would have taken to the streets. MLK pleaded for love, but people embraced rage. And, rightfully so, as rage was becoming the pulse of society in 1968.

39

The Most Trusted Man in America

Walter Cronkite, the host of *CBS Evening News* from 1962 to 1981, was widely considered and often called, the "most trusted man in America." Television had recently become the dominant medium for news and entertainment. Cronkite typically reported facts – news reports about domestic and world events, rather than reacting with his own opinions. Cronkite relayed election results, but rarely commented on elections. Cronkite reported on divisive social issues, but rarely discussed race. Cronkite routinely reported on the Vietnam War, but didn't publicly support or condemn the war. Editorials and opinions remained creatures of newspapers and magazines, not television.

Many Americans interpreted Cronkite's demeanor as loyal – not to a political party, but loyal to the American people. Cronkite dictated public opinion without giving his own. No event underscores the relationship between Cronkite and his viewers more so than his coverage of the assassination of John F. Kennedy in November 1963.

For millions, Cronkite broke the story, interrupting *As the World Turns* to break the news of a shooting in Dallas. Not many evening news anchors were on set to break news in the middle of the afternoon, but Cronkite religiously hung around the newsroom. Once the initial report came across the wire about a shooting involving the President, Cronkite immediately demanded to be on the air.

Cronkite proceeded to read, verbatim, the news bulletins as they arrived in the newsroom. This was one of the first instances, if not the first, of breaking news broadcasted live on the air. Viewers rushed to television sets to not *watch* the news, but to *get* the news.

The viewers sat, stared and prayed – hoping that Cronkite would deliver a glimmer of hope. Then, famously taking off his glasses, Cronkite uttered:

"President Kennedy died at 1 p.m. Central Standard Time (glancing at a clock on the newsroom wall), 2 o'clock Eastern Standard Time, some 38 minutes ago."

Putting his glasses back on, eyes visibly watering, Cronkite swallowed hard and stated:

"Vice President Johnson has left the hospital in Dallas, but we do not know to where he has proceeded; presumably he will be taking the oath of office shortly and become the 36th President of the United States."

Walter Cronkite just told the country that their beloved President had been assassinated. Walter Cronkite also told the nation how to respond. But, he did so with his actions and emotions, not his opinion or words. Cronkite set the tone for the nation. Viewers witnessed a deeply saddened Walter Cronkite. Noticeably devastated and in disbelief. Sad, but not angry. Overcome with grief, but not rage. Devastated, but alive. The American people would respond in kind (other than, Jack Ruby, I guess), embracing depression and sadness, instead of taking to the streets and expressing anger. Walter Cronkite was the pulse and heartbeat of the American people.

In 1968, Cronkite turned 52 years old. Removed from any visceral youthful passion, but also fully entrenched and secure in his role as anchor of the most watched evening news program on television.

The method of reporting news abroad in 1968 was still somewhat primitive. Reporters generally remained confined to a secure, designated area (such as a military base or embassy). This allowed the government to control the message.

After the horrors of the Tet Offensive in January, Cronkite decided and convinced Ernest Leister, the Executive Producer of *CBS Evening*

News, that both he and Leister must travel to Vietnam to discern exactly what was transpiring.

Upon his return, Cronkite prepared a written report and on February 27, Cronkite closed the *CBS Evening News* with the following remarks (my commentary would pale in comparison to the eloquence of Cronkite, so please read the exact text of his remarks):

> *"We have been too often disappointed by the optimism of the American leaders, both in Vietnam and Washington, to have faith any longer in the silver linings they find in the darkest clouds. They may be right, that Hanoi's winter-spring offensive has been forced by the Communist realization that they could not win the longer war of attrition, and that the Communists hope that any success in the offensive will improve their position for eventual negotiations. It would improve their position, and it would also require our realization, that we should have had all along, that any negotiations must be that – negotiations, not the dictation of peace terms. For it seems now more certain than ever that the bloody experience of Vietnam is to end in a stalemate. This summer's almost certain standoff will either end in real give-and-take negotiations or terrible escalation; and for every means we have to escalate, the enemy can match us, and that applies to invasion of the North, the use of nuclear weapons, or the mere commitment of one hundred, or two hundred, or three hundred thousand more American troops to the battle. And with each escalation, the world comes closer to the brink of cosmic disaster.*

> *To say that we are closer to victory today is to believe, in the face of the evidence, the optimists who have been wrong in the past. To suggest we are on the edge of defeat is to yield to unreasonable pessimism. To say that we are mired in stalemate seems the only realistic, yet unsatisfactory,*

conclusion. On the off chance that military and political analysts are right, in the next few months we must test the enemy's intentions, in case this is indeed his last big gasp before negotiations. But it is increasingly clear to this reporter that the only rational way out then will be to negotiate, not as victors, but as an honorable people who lived up to their pledge to defend democracy, and did the best they could."

Today, these comments may not seem remarkable or noteworthy, but in 1968, coming from Walter Cronkite on national television – there was nothing more remarkable or noteworthy. The headline or takeaway after these remarks was clearly Cronkite's use of the word "stalemate." Following Cronkite's remarks on February 27, President Johnson stated in confidence, "If I've lost Cronkite, I've lost Middle America" (whether or not President Johnson made this remark is debated, but several sources confirm the statement). Cronkite provided immediate credibility to the anti-war effort and swayed millions of viewers (and soon-to-be voters) towards opposing the war.

The most trusted man in American had lost faith in the President of the United States of America. Therefore, the American people lost faith in the President. Just four weeks after Cronkite's comments, President Johnson announced in a televised address to the American people that he would not seek reelection. Sure, other factors were at play, which we'll cover next month, mainly the results of the New Hampshire Primary, but undoubtedly, when President Johnson lost Cronkite, he lost the election.

MUSIC

Louis Armstrong – "What A Wonderful World"

Louis Armstrong contended for his entire life that he was born in New Orleans on July 4, 1900. After his death in 1971, upon biographers

43

researching Armstrong's early life, baptism documentation conclusively indicated that he was actually born on August 4, 1901. The notion of Louis Armstrong entering the world on America's birthday at the turn of the 20th Century – it's an intoxicating narrative that I wish was true. Few individuals have lived a life worthy of such a meaningful birthday. Louis Armstrong lived the American Dream.

Born into extreme poverty in a New Orleans neighborhood referred to as the "Battlefield", Armstrong was raised by his grandmother after his mother left home (his father had left a few years prior). Armstrong dropped out of school at age 11, turning to the streets in order to make a living. He performed odd jobs, sang in a quartet and, eventually, started blowing a horn (a cornet).

After months of homelessness, Armstrong was taken in by a Lithuanian-Jewish immigrant family, the Karnofskys. The Karnofskys owned a junk hauling business in New Orleans and supported Armstrong by paying him to do odd jobs for the business. Armstrong became a part of the family. Ultimately, the Karnofskys encouraged Armstrong to pursue his interest in music.

In his autobiography, Armstrong noted the influence of the Karnofskys and described his disbelief in discovering that the Karnofskys experienced a similar discrimination that Armstrong himself had experienced in the South. Armstrong was astonished that the Karnofskys were treated so poorly by "other White people." Armstrong described the discrimination the Karnofskys endured as "ungodly treatment." Later, upon saving enough money, Armstrong purchased a gold Star of David necklace in honor of the Karnofskys – a necklace Armstrong wore for the entirety of his life. When asked about his religion, Armstrong would answer, "I was raised Baptist, always wear a Star of David and I'm friends with the Pope."

Armstrong escaped the extreme and violent discrimination in the South by hitchhiking to Chicago in pursuit of one of the few music forms open to African Americans in the 1920s – Jazz. The Big Band style of Jazz dominated the genre in the 1920s, especially in Chicago. The Big Bands consisted of as many as 20 horn players, providing ample opportunities for young musicians.

Armstrong had natural talent, but in the Big Band format, he was an ensemble player, a sideman – not a soloist. After a move to Manhattan, Armstrong began to play in smaller bands and eventually became known as an ace sideman in the late 1920s (usually, with a saxophone or piano player as the lead musician). Then, in 1929, just as Armstrong started to emerge as a soloist, the United States fell into the Great Depression.

The Great Depression had an enormous effect on Jazz, essentially changing the style of the genre. Concert promoters and labels could no longer afford to pay all of the members in a Big Band, therefore Jazz ensembles contracted and eventually became quartets and quintets (even trios). Armstrong shined in the smaller format, dominating small clubs in Chicago and New York throughout the 1930s (playing close to 300 shows a year). Armstrong established himself as the preeminent trumpet player in Jazz.

Despite racial tensions in the late-1940s and early-1950s, leading to desegregation in 1954, Armstrong was fiercely apolitical. He didn't speak out against racism, he didn't attend marches or protests. Armstrong had an enormous smile and, frankly, appealed to White audiences. Armstrong became one of the wealthiest African Americans in the United States.

Armstrong maintained that he led by example, hard work and determination. Armstrong seemed to believe he could help other African Americans by showing them the success they could achieve in a divisive environment. Such an attitude appealed to the masses, but his political absence made him a target of liberal, African American leaders of the Civil Rights Movement.

Louis Armstrong's popularity, however, was not in doubt – he was arguably the most famous African American entertainer of the 1940s, 1950s and 1960s. In 1964, Armstrong made music history – but, not with his trumpet – he made history with his voice. Armstrong had incorporated vocals into his music four years prior, but as Armstrong aged, so did his voice – resulting in a raspy, charred and wonderfully eccentric tone that was the antithesis to Armstrong's sweet, soft trumpet sound. The vocal tracks also broadened his audience base, allowing Armstrong to play more diverse venues (lounges, hotels, concert halls – as opposed to only Jazz clubs).

In 1964, Armstrong released "Hello Dolly" and the track charted on the *Billboard* Hot 100 for 22 weeks (longer than any other record in 1964) and eventually hit #1, making Armstrong the oldest artist with a #1 song on the *Billboard* Hot 100. More amazing than the feat of age, Armstrong's chart topping track displaced The Beatles, who dominated 1964 with a string of three tracks that topped the *Billboard* Hot 100 for 14 consecutive weeks.

Despite a more limited touring schedule in 1966 and 1967, Armstrong had one more career highlight. "What A Wonderful World" was written by Bob Thiele and originally offered to Tony Bennett, despite Thiele swearing he wrote the track for Louis Armstrong. Bennett turned down the song, but Armstrong appreciated the song's optimism at a time when the world was filled with negativity.

The lyrics reference race and the instability of society in 1968 (with a rare subtlety). As stated, Armstrong was fiercely apolitical, but – perhaps the United States had become so fractured and so dissident that Armstrong finally believed he needed to intervene? Regardless of the intent, "What A Wonderful World" is that rare perfect track.

The beauty and legacy of "What a Wonderful World" is Armstrong's voice and delivery, but the lyrics are important. In the opening verse,

Armstrong makes it clear that the natural beauty of the world is for ***all*** to enjoy:

> *I see trees of green,*
> *Red roses too*
> *I see them bloom,*
> *For me and you*

The notion of color is introduced immediately (green and red), but again – the reference to race in the last line is subtle – rather than stating "everyone should be able to enjoy the trees and roses", he sings "for me and you." Armstrong invokes color again in the next verse, but more overtly relates the reference to race.

> *The colors of the rainbow,*
> *So pretty in the sky*
> *Are also on the faces*
> *Of people going by*
> *I see friends shaking hands.*
> *Saying, "How do you do?"*
> *They're really saying,*
> *"I love you"*

Juxtaposing the colors of the rainbow to the colors of faces – it's a brilliant piece of lyrical craftsmanship (by Thiele). Armstrong's delivery suggests a depressive quality, acknowledging the racial divide, but a palpable optimism exists. "Friends shaking hands", but really saying "I love you" – well, that's a little dose of 1967 (the Summer of Love and the thought that the cure for all problems was, of course, love). By marrying racism and love in a single verse, as well as pronouncing the world to be "Wonderful" – this track is Armstrong's plea for peace and equality.

"What A Wonderful World" was a #1 hit in the United Kingdom, but only reached #116 in the United States. It's hard to determine why the

47

track didn't achieve more chart success, but given the chaos and violence percolating in the United States, I suspect the American people were not ready, or maybe unwilling to accept, an optimistic view. The American people in 1968 seemed to embrace the chaos – almost cherish it. The tumult and instability was the heartbeat of society – the fuel used to achieve political and social change. Americans probably didn't want to spin "What a Wonderful World", they wanted "Born to Be Wild", and later, "Helter Skelter" and "Sympathy for the Devil."

"What A Wonderful World" would have its day, though. In 1987, "What a Wonderful World" was used in the film *Good Morning, Vietnam*. *Good Morning, Vietnam* was directed by Barry Levinson and starred Robin Williams. Williams played a DJ in Saigon and, largely through improvisation, played several records on camera throughout the movie, interjecting comedy and sensitivity. The soundtrack is quite good, but only one track charted as a result of the film: "What a Wonderful World." Twenty years after its release, "What a Wonderful World" reached #32 on the *Billboard* Top 40 (the successor to the Hot 100). The real beauty of the rebirth of "What a Wonderful World" is that future generations will continue to be exposed to Louis Armstrong.

Otis Redding – *(Sittin' On) The Dock of the Bay*

Several musicians have been taken from us way too early. The list is, quite frankly, endless – and endlessly sad. The following are just some of the musicians that died at the age of 27 (the so-called "27 Club"): Robert Johnson, Joe Henderson (legendary saxophonist), Brian Jones (founder, guitarist of The Rolling Stones), Jimi Hendrix, Janis Joplin, Jim Morrison, Ron "Pigpen" McKernan (founder, vocalist of The Grateful Dead), Chris Bell (founder, guitarist of Big Star), Kurt Cobain and Amy Winehouse. A staggering dreadful and amazing list.

Fortunately, Otis Redding is not on that list. Unfortunately, we lost Otis Redding even earlier – at age 26. Otis Redding died in a plane crash on December 10, 1967. Not quite "The Day the Music Died", but damn near close.

Redding's first single was released in 1962 and his first full LP, *Pain in My Heart*, was released in 1964. Then, two classic albums in 1965 (*The Great Otis Redding Sings Soul Ballads* and *Otis Blue*). These recordings, along with two records in 1966 and one in 1967, represent the entirety of Redding's music released during his lifetime. Thankfully, a plethora of material existed from studio sessions during the making of the above records, which has been released posthumously. Redding was also recording new material throughout 1967, right up until his death.

Otis Redding was born in rural Georgia in 1941, his father a sharecropper, Redding had five siblings and in 1944, Redding's family moved to a public housing project in Macon, Georgia. At age 10, Redding was introduced to music through services at the family's Baptist church in Macon. Redding took drum lessons, but ultimately gravitated towards singing – emulating his heroes: Little Richard and Sam Cooke.

Redding was forced to drop out of high school at age 15 to help his father support the family. Otis dug wells for a construction company and worked as a gas station attendant. These day jobs allowed for time in the evening – which he spent playing in various local bands, mostly Soul and early Rock and Roll. Redding's "break" came in 1958 after an appearance at a local talent show. Redding performed and won the talent show (earning the first place prize of $5.00), but more importantly, impressing Johnny Jenkins.

Jenkins was a locally known lead guitarist, but Jenkins had decent contacts in the music industry. After witnessing Redding in the talent show, Jenkins encouraged Redding to commit to music and introduced Redding to the vibrant Atlanta music scene. Redding sang lead in local bands and improved his timing. Redding's next big break was actually Jenkins' big break. Jenkins was summoned to Stax Records in Memphis to cut a record with Booker T. & the M.G.'s. Jenkins didn't have a driver's license, so he asked Otis to drive him to Memphis. A chance to watch a session at Stax with Booker T. & the M.G.'s? A no-brainer "yes" for Otis.

The session with Jenkins was dragging a bit, so the session producer, Jim Stewart, told the musicians to end early. Typically, a short session was a license for the musicians to head to a bar, but on this day – a couple of the musicians stuck around, including drummer Al Jackson and Steve Cropper, guitarist and lead arranger for Booker T. & the M.G.'s. With Jenkins on piano, the trio jammed for a bit, then invited Otis to sing lead on a couple tracks. The first track was "Hey Hey Baby"… the second track launched Redding's career.

After the run through "Hey Hey Baby", Jim Stewart, who was packing up and getting ready to leave the studio, commented that Redding had some talent, but "sounded too much like Little Richard." Ah, the old "sounds like" game. The classic utterance of a listener that hears something of interest, but is dismissive of its originality, relating the music to subjective experience. I'm guilty of the "sounds like" mentality at times, but I've been trying really hard to kick the habit.

Anyway, the course of music was changed by Jim Stewart not packing up quickly enough, as Redding, Jenkins, Jackson and Cropper shifted to a minor key, dropped into a down-tempo time signature and allowed Otis Redding to introduce a ballad he wrote, "These Arms of Mine."

As quickly as Stewart, a veteran producer, dismissed "Hey Hey Baby" as nothing special, he embraced "These Arms of Mine." Stewart later stated, "We were fixin' to go home, but [t]here was something different about [the ballad]. He really poured his soul into it." It's not clear whether Stewart signed Redding immediately after the session or shortly thereafter, but Stewart recorded, produced and released the Single "These Arms of Mine" in 1962, with "Hey Hey Baby" as the B-Side. In March 1963, "These Arms of Mine" peaked at #65 on the *Billboard* Hot 100 and #20 on the *Billboard* R&B chart, eventually selling more than 800,000 copies. "These Arms of Mine" was included on Redding's first LP, *Pain in My Heart*, released on January 1, 1964 (by Stax on the Volt label).

Invoke the cliché, "the rest was history." However, in this case, history was a short, but momentous, three years. African American popular music in 1964 and 1965 was dominated by two genres: Blues and Motown (yes, I consider the Motown sound to be a genre). Soul music existed, but it was not yet a recognized genre. Soul music fused traditional Gospel with R&B – initially, focused on ballads, the genre would incorporate horn sections in the 1970s and borrow a poignancy from Funk to create a spirited and emotionally charged style.

After a string of Top 100 hits, including "Chained and Bound", "Come to Me" and "That's How Strong My Love Is", Otis Redding released *Otis Blue* in 1965. *Otis Blue* largely consisted of covers, as Redding tackled The Rolling Stones and Sam Cooke, but *Otis Blue* also contained the Redding original, "Respect" (later covered by Aretha Franklin). The impact of *Otis Blue* cannot be overstated. By covering popular songs, Redding appealed – whether intentionally or unintentionally – to White audiences. He "crossed over." You see, Otis Redding's voice was undeniable. His charisma was addictive. Such talents were unseen in an artist of his vintage. Race was finally irrelevant, as talent obscured color.

On April 6, 1966, Otis Redding performed at the famed Whisky A-Go-Go in Los Angeles. The buzz surrounding the performance was tangible, yet still underground. Bob Dylan attended the gig (he was not yet in seclusion), as did other musicians from Los Angeles and New York. Redding blew away the (mostly White) audience. The *Los Angeles Times* wrote an incredibly favorable review and launched Redding into the national spotlight.

The attention and intrigue surrounding Redding culminated in May 1967 with Redding's performance at the Monterey Pop Festival in California. With a lineup that included Jimi Hendrix, The Who, The Grateful Dead, Janis Joplin, Jefferson Airplane and The Animals, Redding was given the headlining slot on Saturday night (the infamous Hendrix burning of the guitar took place on Sunday night). Backed by Booker T. & the M.G.'s, Otis crushed.

The set opened with "Shake" by Sam Cooke, a featured tracks on *Otis Blue*. After a run through "Respect" and a few other classics, Otis closed the set with "I've Been Loving You" and "Try A Little Tenderness." The crowd was enamored. Reports indicated that Hendrix and Brian Jones were transfixed with Redding's performance.

When I listen to Redding's set at Monterey (portions were released later on a compilation record), it sounds terrific, but not revolutionary. Or, not other-worldly (listening to Hendrix in 1968 evokes each of those adjectives). However, when you watch video clips of Redding's performance – the impact is apparent (similar to the visual impact of television on the Kennedy-Nixon debate in 1960). Otis was not only a Soul singer, he sang with his soul. His emotion touched the audience while his charisma torched the audience.

On December 10, 1967, Redding and his bandmates boarded a private jet in Cleveland, en route to Madison, Wisconsin for their next show. Four miles from Madison, the pilot radioed for assistance, citing poor visibility. The plane crashed moments later into Lake Monona, killing all passengers except Ben Cauley.

Unbelievably, just three days before the plane crash, Redding recorded his most famous song, "(Sittin' On) The Dock of the Bay." Redding wrote the lyrics about his time living in Sausalito, CA and shared the words with Steve Cropper. When you listen to "(Sittin' On) The Dock of the Bay", you hear Redding's voice and you hear his soul, but the song probably doesn't evoke Soul, as in the genre. The song evokes "Otis Redding."

When comparing Redding's pre-"(Sittin' On) The Dock of the Bay" material to "(Sittin' On) The Dock of the Bay", the difference is readily apparent. "(Sittin' On) The Dock of the Bay" is decidedly a Pop song. Redding typically specialized in tender ballads, but "(Sittin' On) The Dock of the Bay" was different – it flowed, bouncing ever so slightly between mid-tempo and ballad. Lacking horns and the punch that even Redding's ballads possessed, the most dramatic Pop aspect of "(Sittin' On) The Dock of the Bay" was the lyrics. Introspective and clearly first person narration.

When Redding presented the song to studio executives, he received a reaction of trepidation. Even the musicians at Stax feared that the Pop sound would injure Stax's swampy, crunchy, Blues and R&B reputation. However, as usual, Cropper was Redding's most important ally. Cropper backed Redding and pushed Stax to record the track. Redding supposedly predicted that the track would be a #1 hit on the *Billboard* Hot 100. Otis didn't live to see it, but he was absolutely right.

After the release of the album *The Dock of the Bay* in February 1968, on March 16 "(Sittin' On) The Dock of the Bay" became the first posthumous song to reach #1 on the *Billboard* Hot 100. The song reached #3 in the UK. Redding's catalog contains some of the best Soul and R&B ever recorded, yet a little Pop song that Otis wrote and recorded just three days before his death remains his most successful and recognizable song. Soak in the final verse and chorus:

Sittin' here resting my bones
And this loneliness won't leave me alone
Two thousand miles I roam
Just to make this dock my home

I'm just gonna sit at the dock of the bay
Watchin' the tide roll away
Sittin' on the dock of the bay
Wastin' time

During the recording sessions, as Redding was explaining his vision for the song, he suggested (or demanded) that the track begin with the sound of waves. Otis wanted the listener to hear what he heard when he wrote the song. Redding also wanted the song to fade out with whistling over the chords to the chorus.

As Cropper finalized the recording, despite objection from "pretty much everyone" he included the crashing waves intro per Redding's request, but he decided not to include Redding's whistling. Now, of course, there is whistling at the end of the track – but, that whistling is the work of Sam "Bluzman" Taylor. Cropper was so committed to making the track a #1 hit, he just couldn't bring himself to include the whistling by Otis, which even to my ear – was not very good and not in the correct key (you can find the first couple takes that include Redding's whistling on YouTube).

The song should have provided some levity and optimism in early 1968, but given Redding's death, the song carried a somber, even depressive character. Seemed like everything 1968 touched turned to sadness.

In addition to "(Sittin' On) The Dock of the Bay", *The Dock of the Bay* album included some of Redding's strongest material. "Don't Mess With Cupid" stands out as a strong indication of what would have been – the track starts with Cropper's guitar and then Redding

54

just dominates. The chorus includes a vocal inflection that is a hook unto itself (in between "with" and "cupid"). The horns provide a punch and the rhythm is driving – distinctly not Motown. The fade out on "Don't Mess with Cupid" is classic Otis – just riffing, rapping – whatever you want to call it – just pure emotion. Listen to him sing the words "home" and "wasting time." It's essential.

"The Glory of Love" (no, not the Peter Cetera classic from the *Karate Kid*) is a perfect example of the difference between a typical Redding Soul ballad and "(Sittin' On) The Dock of the Bay." "Glory of Love" opens with horns, then downshifts into somber crooning with repeating electric guitar notes and sprinkled piano flourishes – all hallmarks of a traditional Soul ballad. Contrasted with "(Sittin' On) The Dock of the Bay" which makes certain that the lyrics are the main event – a simple drum back beat in 4/4 time, guitar licks are original, not necessarily tracking the melody, then a classic Pop bridge (right out of the Lennon/McCartney repertoire) – no horns, no organ – slow, but not somber.

"Let Me Come On Home" depicts Redding in a Blues style, but ultimately – the track shows off the guitar tone of Steve Cropper. The horns are a bit too upfront in the mix for me, and a bit too prevalent in occurrence – I would have preferred more Cropper – but, the track moves, that's for sure. The album then ends wonderfully with a cover of Jimmy Cox's "Nobody Knows You (When You're Down and Out)" and the Redding original "Ole Man Trouble."

"Nobody Knows You" is a wonderful listen, but this track has been recorded by so many that it's tough to discern its merit. Of course, Redding's voice is suited perfectly for the slow Blues standard, but I find the arrangement a bit sluggish. However, every time that thought pops into my head while listening, Otis obliterates the last verse and chorus – just classic – and then I find myself considering that this might be the definitive version of the song. Redding's vocal fade outs are untouchable. Seriously, nobody has better vocal fade out rants than Otis. He's the master.

"Ole Man Trouble", a track that Otis originally released on *Otis Blue*, was included as the final track on *The Dock of the Bay*. Such inclusion (likely by Cropper) was no accident. The song was an ode to Otis – a farewell of sorts – a message from Cropper and the folks at Stax. "Ole Man Trouble" ends with the following:

> *Ole man trouble, leave me alone*
> *Go find you someone else to pick on*
> *I live my life now you see*
> *Ole man trouble*
> *Please stay away from me, oh no*
>
> *Oh, I look like I'm down on my luck*
> *Please send faith to just help pick me up*
> *I've lived this way so many years, now*
> *Ole man trouble*
> *Please wash away all my fears, oh no*
> *Good God Almighty, help me*

A heart-breaking end to a heart-warming artist. Later in 1968, *The Immortal Otis Redding* was released, followed by *Love Man* in 1969 and *Tell the Truth* in 1970. Each record contained unreleased material, but eventually – all unreleased tracks were unearthed and only compilations and live recordings would be released, including the excellent *Remember Me* in 1992.

Fleetwood Mac – *Fleetwood Mac*

Before you flip the page, please wait – just hear me out – this record isn't what you might have already conjured in your head. Remember, this is 1968, not 1978 – when *Rumours* dominated the radio, dominated the Grammy Awards and became the 8th highest grossing album of all-time.

A slight digression, but if you're curious about #'s 1 through 7, they are as follows: *Thriller* (Michael Jackson), *Back In Black* (AC/DC), *Dark Side of the Moon* (Pink Floyd), *The Bodyguard* (Whitney Houston), *Bat Out of Hell* (Meatloaf), *Their Greatest Hits (1971-1975)* (The Eagles) and *Saturday Night Fever* (The Bee Gees).

Maybe I'm alone, but that list isn't that impressive. Of course, it's not a list of the "best" albums ever produced, it's a list of the "best-selling" albums ever produced. The most popular.

So, if you immediately think of the Soft Rock and Pop of Fleetwood Mac's "Dreams", "Go Your Own Way", "Songbird" or "Don't Stop" – I really can't blame you. The thing is – there were two distinct chapters of Fleetwood Mac. Well, maybe not chapters – kind of like a short story followed by a novel. Our focus is on the short story.

Fleetwood Mac was formed in London in 1967 by Mick Fleetwood, John McVie and Peter Green. Fleetwood and McVie are characters in the short story as well as central figures in the novel. Green is the distinguishing factor, or character. Green stars in the short story, but is absent from the novel.

Peter Green was the ace Blues guitarist that replaced Eric Clapton in John Mayall and the Bluesbreakers when Clapton left Mayall's band to form Cream. Green's guitar playing was quite different than Clapton's. Clapton had always been a traditionalist, focusing more on melody than poignancy, but in 1967, Clapton evolved further. Playing with Ginger Baker and Jack Bruce, both of whom possessed training in Jazz, Clapton's tone became quite fluid. Clapton stated in a 1967 interview that "I am playing more smoothly now. I'm developing what I call my 'woman tone.' It's a sweet sound"

(Oxman). Clapton's tone was further described as "overdriven, yet smooth, distorted yet creamy" (Dregni).

Green's playing, despite the same genre, was trending in the opposite direction. Overdrive and piercing, not smooth. Distorted and acidic, not creamy. Green channeled Mike Bloomfield and Jimi Hendrix more so than Clapton's heroes, Muddy Waters and B.B. King. Green's first album with John Mayall and the Bluesbreakers, *A Hard Road* (February 1967) received, and still receives, critical acclaim. Given that John Mayall's band tended to be a training ground, or launching pad, for musicians (much like The Yardbirds), the lineup was constantly changing. After *A Hard Road*, Green became the leader of Mayall's band and suggested that Mick Fleetwood replace Aynsley Dunbar on drums (Green had played with Fleetwood in a band called Shotgun Express, which featured a very young Rod Stewart on vocals). John McVie played bass in Mayall's band at this time.

Several articles describe Peter Green as the classic "musician's musician." I've always found that term interesting. A "musician's musician" is generally an artist that is respected by peer musicians, and imitated, but usually the musician's musician is not a well-known or commercially successful musician. I've always wanted to analyze these musicians and try to figure out why the musician's musicians never achieved commercial success, yet were adored by those who achieved commercial success. Names that come to mind: J.J. Cale in Rock, Art Tatum in Jazz and John Fahey in Folk.

Green apparently lived at the recording studio, jamming for hours with anyone, and sometimes nobody. In 1967, the Mayall band was a four piece, with Mayall on vocals, organ and rhythm guitar, along with Green, Fleetwood and McVie. John Mayall was 35 years old in 1968, while Green, Fleetwood and McVie were 22, 21 and 23, respectively. Mayall would leave the studio at a reasonable hour and return to his family while Green, Fleetwood and McVie would jam until sunrise.

Green, Fleetwood and McVie recorded five tracks at Mayall's studio. With no Mayall, Green handled the vocals, but no vocals were needed on the fifth track recorded – an instrumental that Green titled, "Fleetwood Mac", after the driving rhythm section. Ecstatic with the quality of the recordings, Green and Fleetwood decided to leave Mayall and form a new band. McVie decided to stay with Mayall, however, after seeing Green and Fleetwood's new band play a show on August 12, 1967, McVie informed Mayall that he was joining Green and Fleetwood.

Using pieces of the tracks recorded in Mayall's studio (with Mayall's permission), Green, Fleetwood and McVie, along with slide guitarist Jeremy Spencer, recorded the tracks that appear on the band's debut album, *Fleetwood Mac*. Note that the band was named after the instrumental recorded in Mayall's studio, but Green and Fleetwood have admitted to using the title to entice McVie to join the band when he was still with Mayall. McVie doesn't seem to agree that the naming rights were a factor in the decision (and with the drama and strife that would surround Fleetwood Mac in the late-1970s, the naming issue is a minor concern).

Fleetwood Mac was not only a Blues album, it was an extremely popular Blues album. *Fleetwood Mac* reached #4 on the UK chart, at a time when Pop/Rock dominated the charts. The relevance of a traditional Blues album charting so high was not likely viewed as a trend in February 1968, however, it's one of the first signs of the musical shift. A shift away from Pop/Rock. A shift back to Rock, and more specifically, Hard Rock – emulating the hardening of society and a loss of patience that manifested in violence.

Fleetwood Mac opens with "My Heart Beat Like a Hammer." The track has a raunchy guitar intro that not only echoes Hendrix's "Foxy

59

Lady", but kind of outright rips it off (in Green's defense, a lot of people were ripping Hendrix off in 1968). The intro gives way to a thick Blues jam and vocals that sound like a British kid imitating an African American man. Again, in Green's defense, that's what British kids (and American kids) did in the late-1960s (and arguably are still doing today).

As "Merry Go Round" and "Long Grey Mare" unfold, the record starts to sound more like a "session" than a production. At a time when sound effects and studio pageantry dominated the music landscape, a few kids playing the Blues must have been refreshing. But, that undersells this record. The music has immediacy and, while not necessarily asserting a substantive message, the instrumentation and delivery confers the notion that the Blues are alive and well and still subject to interpretation.

Case in point, "Shake Your Moneymaker." Several bands have covered the track, but this version by Fleetwood Mac injects youth and fuzz. Green's vocals are a bit thin, but his axe is the star. His tone is pure and his licks incredibly natural. Whereas Mike Bloomfield, a young Blues guitarist from Chicago that played an important role in The 1965 Project, both in the Butterfield Blues Band and Bob Dylan's electric arrangements, plays fast – Bloomfield fits an unreal amount of notes into each bar – Green's playing is more emotive. Not melodic and sweet, but you can feel him channeling passion through each note.

On "I Loved Another Woman", Green switched to a minor key Blues and increased the reverb, resulting in a swanky, sway-worthy canvas, but a rustic vibe is retained, rather than a softer edge. The production on *Fleetwood Mac* is a bit rough, which can be heard at the end of this track – a veteran producer might have incorporated an organ, or another guitar solo, but instead the track abruptly ends.

After another slower tempo song ("Cold Black Night"), the album concludes with two tracks that seem juxtaposed for a reason, at least in name. "The World Keep on Turning" is a solo acoustic track by Green, reminiscent of a Hendrix constructed acoustic Blues, but despite lacking substance, the star is again Green's guitar. The verses are accompanied by a chugging, heavy rhythm, foreshadowing the way Neil Young plays rhythm – hitting the low E string on each strum. The substance, or meaning, of the track never really hits home, but darkness exists.

The album closes with "Got To Move", a Blues standard, with context derived from the Bible, made popular by Fred McDowell in 1965. Again, the track is cut short, just as you think Green's guitar solo is about to lift off – a tough end to a surprisingly great album.

I can't help but conclude that the music scene was eager to move on from psychedelia, and get back to Rock. Just seems as though every influential musician, every artist on the cutting edge or in the underground scene – these essential pieces of the puzzle all gravitated abruptly back to Rock. The musicians discussed in the early chapters of this book ignited a fire that became a tremendous blaze in August.

We'll hear from Fleetwood Mac again later in <u>The 1968 Project</u> and when that happens, maybe you won't approach the passage with such disdain. I know you did. I did as well. It's okay – forget about it. But, please do check out *Fleetwood Mac*, it's a really solid listen.

March

March

HISTORY

The New Hampshire Primary
Robert F. Kennedy Announces Candidacy for President
President Johnson Announces He Will Not Seek Reelection
My Lai Massacre

MUSIC

Johnny Cash Marries June Carter Cash
The Fillmore East Opens in New York
The Beatles – "Lady Madonna"
The Mothers of Invention – *We're Only in it For the Money*
(Frank Zappa)
Miles Davis – *Miles in the Sky*
James Brown – *I Can't Stand Myself (When You Touch Me)*

HISTORY

The thesis of The 1968 Project is to illustrate the manner in which historical events influenced the music created immediately thereafter. Whereas in 1965 historical events had a more immediate, linear and direct influence on music, the historical events of 1968 seemed to aggregate in a cauldron, with each month dripping more and more hot, dark, toxic liquid into an already simmering stew. Some musicians recognized the rapidly filling cauldron, but most musicians in early-1968 still maintained the lunacy, freedom, optimism and "love" of 1967.

Many argue that the turning point, the moment that the cauldron boiled over, was the assassinations of Martin Luther King, Jr. (April) and Robert F. Kennedy (June). While those events may have tipped the cauldron, remember – the cauldron was already full of disasters – political instability, the horrors of the Vietnam War, civilian unrest – and once toppled, all of these disasters spilled out – in plain sight.

Why was the music scene slow to react? Maybe it was the haze of narcotics or new-found freedom of expression borne in 1967 (or at least commercialized in 1967). Maybe it was the homogenization of the music industry. Whatever the reason, the point is that very few realized the apathy, naivety and immaturity, of 1967. However, in March, Frank Zappa and his band, The Mothers of Invention, through satire, exposed the fallacies of 1967 and the obstructed view of youth.

After death and sadness in April and June, musicians will finally react – and so will we.

The New Hampshire Primary

Prior to 1968 only two incumbent Presidents in the history of the United States (post-1900 electoral system) lost a reelection campaign (William Taft lost to Woodrow Wilson in 1912 and Herbert Hoover lost to Franklin D. Roosevelt in 1932). President Johnson was embattled, but a political stalwart with massive support in the South and the Rust Belt (Michigan, Ohio and Pennsylvania). Such was typically enough for an incumbent to win the general election and assume the Presidency.

The results of the New Hampshire Primary in 1968 changed the course of American politics. An overstatement? You decide. On November 30, 1967, Eugene McCarthy, a Senator from Minnesota, declared his intention to contest President Johnson in the Democratic primary and run for President of the United States. McCarthy stated, "There comes a time when an honorable man simply has to raise the flag." Did the statement insinuate that President Johnson was not an honorable man? Did the statement suggest that our soldiers in Vietnam need to retreat, or raise the flag? A savvy orator and poet, McCarthy likely intended all of the above.

Throughout the end of 1967 and the beginning of 1968, affiliating with Eugene McCarthy was a vote against the Vietnam War. McCarthy attracted young voters and liberal celebrities, the veneer of the Democratic Party. President Johnson was still an overwhelming favorite, despite focusing less on reelection and more on the Vietnam War. As with each election since 1912, the New Hampshire primary was the first state primary election. A steady barometer for the pulse of the nation, McCarthy campaigned long and hard in New Hampshire, while President Johnson, as a result of being either over-confident or ignorant, failed to submit his election paperwork and therefore was not even listed on the New Hampshire primary ballot, requiring voters to write in the President's name.

Eugene McCarthy earned 42% of the vote, while President Johnson received 48% of the vote. President Johnson won by just 230 votes.

Sure, President Johnson won the primary and the delegates, but the New Hampshire primary was a referendum on President Johnson and a referendum on the Vietnam War, which were inextricably linked.

Ultimately, Eugene McCarthy is a political footnote. His performance in the New Hampshire primary, though, set in motion a staggering series of events. These events are causally connected. In short, McCarthy's strong showing in New Hampshire proved to Robert F. Kennedy that opportunity existed to unseat President Johnson, resulting in Kennedy entering the Democratic race days after the New Hampshire primary. Kennedy entering the race and the ensuing swoon of Democratic public support resulted in President Johnson's surprising announcement just two weeks later that he would not seek reelection, ceding the Presidency to Kennedy. When Kennedy was assassinated in June, the path was clear for Richard Nixon to assume the Presidency of the United States. Nixon would scale the Vietnam War throughout the early-1970s and ultimately embroil the United States in the worst political corruption in modern history.

So yes, the results of the New Hampshire Primary changed the course of American politics.

Robert F. Kennedy Announces Candidacy for President

On March 16, just days after the shocking results of the New Hampshire primary, Robert F. Kennedy declared his bid for the Presidency. Maybe you are wondering why Kennedy was not already in the race? Kennedy's relationship with President Johnson was widely known to be hostile, bordering on hatred. Kennedy was certainly a noted champion of civil rights, which aligned with President Johnson, but Kennedy was also publicly critical of the Vietnam War. Kennedy, though, was a politician. Some may say he had respect for the political system and was reluctant to challenge his party's incumbent – others questioned whether Kennedy thought he could win.

After seeing a relatively unknown political commodity, Eugene McCarthy, obtain 42% of the vote in New Hampshire, Kennedy, at the time the junior Senator from New York, quickly activated his base. In announcing his candidacy, Kennedy stated, "I am today announcing my candidacy for the President of the United States. I do not run for the Presidency merely to oppose one man, but to propose new policies. I run because I am convinced that this country is on a perilous course and because I have such strong feelings about what must be done, and I feel that I'm obliged to do all I can." Kennedy made the announcement from the exact same spot in the Senate Caucus Room that his brother, John F. Kennedy, announced his candidacy in 1960.

Kennedy's objective was to defeat McCarthy and become the sole alternative to President Johnson. McCarthy ran on a single issue platform – immediate withdrawal from Vietnam. Kennedy, however, was an adept politician and outlined a cadre of social programs that extended the racial equality programs advocated by his brother and aggressively pursued by President Johnson (before he set the "Great Society" aside in favor of the Vietnam War).

Kennedy's campaign was initially a grass roots effort, consisting of young intellectuals and minority leaders, but within thirty days of his announcement, Kennedy put together a formidable campaign team, targeting the Indiana primary. In addition to an intense political savvy, Kennedy exhibited a certain charm – no Jack Kennedy, but still – he was a Kennedy. Asked at a student rally in Indiana at the Indiana School of Medicine, "Where are you going to get the money to pay for all these new programs you're proposing?" Kennedy replied to the medical student, "from you." More serious, during a rally at Ball State University in Indiana, Kennedy predicted that the 1968 election would "determine the direction that the United States [will] move [in]." He could see it. He knew the magnitude.

On May 7, voters in Indiana went to the polls and the political landscape experienced the inevitable shift towards Kennedy. Kennedy received 42% of the vote, while McCarthy received just

27%. Next up was Nebraska on May 14, another Midwest state that typically would reject a Northeast liberal and rather vote for a Senator from Minnesota. Kennedy won Nebraska in a landslide, receiving 52% of the vote, to McCarthy's 31%.

Kennedy had acquired the requisite momentum. He was the favorite to win the Democratic nomination for President and the favorite to beat Richard Nixon in the general election. He obtained the appropriate endorsements within the Senate and the House of Representatives. The only remaining task was to secure the necessary delegates with a win in California on June 4. Just after midnight on June 5, Kennedy won the California primary, moments later he lost his life.

President Johnson Announces He Will Not Seek Reelection

On March 31, President Johnson alerted news outlets that he would address the nation, live on television. President Johnson reportedly would discuss and outline steps to "limit the war in Vietnam." Remember, prior to March 31, President Johnson was still running for reelection. He had beaten McCarthy in New Hampshire, albeit by a narrow margin, and Robert F. Kennedy had entered the race to great fanfare but the subsequent primaries had not yet taken place. The prevailing political sentiment was that if President Johnson catered to the anti-Vietnam War movement, his path to the White House was clear and likely.

President Johnson opened his address with the following statement, "Tonight I want to speak to you of peace in Vietnam and Southeast Asia." Political rhetoric of the highest degree. Johnson continued, "No other question so preoccupies our people...No other goal motivates American policy." Arriving at what was thought to be the crux, or purpose, of Johnson's remarks, "Tonight, I renew the offer I made last August – to stop the bombardment of North Vietnam. We ask that talks begin promptly, that they be serious talks on the substance of peace."

After President Johnson's poor showing in New Hampshire, viewers expected Johnson to advance a strategy of negotiated peace. McCarthy polled well in New Hampshire behind an immediate withdrawal platform – but, McCarthy's success was thought to be neutralized if President Johnson declared a rededication to peace talks. The narrative and political strategy was unfolding systematically as Johnson declared, "I have ordered our aircrafts and our naval vessels to make no attacks on North Vietnam...[so long as] our restraint is matched by restraint in Hanoi."

After a (very) lengthy digression into the specifics of the Vietnam War, which likely lulled viewers to sleep a bit, Johnson arrived at a rather unusual statement of reflection. "Fifty-two months and 10 days ago, in a moment of tragedy and trauma, the duties of this office fell upon me. I asked then for your help and God's, that we might continue America on its course, binding up our wounds, healing our history, moving forward in new unity, to clear the American agenda and to keep the American commitment for all of our people. United we have kept that commitment."

President Johnson further stated, "What we won when all of our people united must not now be lost in suspicion, distrust, selfishness and politics among any of our people." This comment on its own was classic Lyndon B. Johnson. A statement surely meant to combat the public's perception of his Administration. President Johnson was assuredly demanding respect from the American people and would subsequently reinvigorate his pursuit of the Presidency. Right?

Not so. President Johnson continued, "Believing this as I do, I have concluded that I should not permit the Presidency to become involved in the partisan divisions that are developing in this political year." What? A curious comment from a politician. Politicians, and yes even the President of the United States, are intimately involved in partisan divisions. It is the job of a politician to work through the partisan divide and achieve progress in the name of the American people. This statement, more than any other in Johnson's speech, depicted the immense pressure and darkness that had beset the President.

Stunning the nation, Johnson announced, "I do not believe that I should devote an hour or a day of my time to any partisan causes or to any duties other than the awesome duties of this office – the Presidency of your country. Accordingly, I shall not seek, and I will not accept, the nomination of my party for another term as your President."

The nation was shocked. Not exactly a resignation, but certainly close. President Johnson's announcement shook the political landscape, especially in the Democratic National Party. While President Johnson attempted to appear contrite and purposeful by placing the nation above his personal political success, Johnson's decision not to run for reelection was perceived as weak. At a time of considerable instability, America craved a leader.

My Lai Massacre

There were countless tragedies of the Vietnam War. There are countless tragedies in every war. Senseless death. Unclear purpose. No consequence. No resolution. Destruction of families. Destruction of property. Destruction of culture. But, nothing – nothing worse than senseless death. Perhaps, no death makes sense? Is all death senseless? Maybe – but, certain deaths are absolutely and utterly without purpose, without reason. Certain deaths are unlawful, intentional, willful and premeditated. These deaths are commonly referred to as – murder.

When an American soldier kills an "enemy" soldier in combat, is that murder? What is considered murder in the arena of war? Treatises exist to deal with that question. Tribunals and courtrooms have considered the question for centuries. There are most certainly laws of war, such as the Geneva Convention, but only lawful nations follow the laws of war. In many respects, the laws are a disadvantage for the law-following nations, as the law-following nations abide by

70

the laws, while non-law following nations engage in behavioral atrocities, ignoring the laws of war.

How do the laws of the United States intersect and interact with the laws of war? When do the laws of war supersede the laws of the United States? Are certain killings justified?

In the United States, murder is a crime, punishable by a prison sentence and, in some states, death. However, under the laws of the United States, certain defenses exist that exculpate a killer – one of which is "justification." If a killing is justified, then the killing is not a crime, the killer is not a murderer. The most frequent example of a justified killing is a killing due to self-defense. Person A is being attacked by Person B and Person A believes that her life is in danger, Person A can justifiably kill Person B. Similarly, Person A sees Person B trying to kill Person C, Person A can justifiably kill Person B.

When the United States is at war, is killing the enemy justified? Is killing enemy civilians justified? What is an "enemy civilian"? The answer to these questions may be a matter of international law, or the laws of war, but irrespective of what the laws of war dictate, the citizens of the United States have their own rules, their own moral code – the rule of decency and the rule of respect. While the Tet Offensive in January terrified the American people, threatening the strength of the United States, the My Lai Massacre outraged the American people, threatening the decency of the United States.

The remainder of this section will recount the events of the My Lai Massacre. Consider the context, though – consider that the soldiers are young men, fighting for their lives, fighting a war of unclear purpose, fighting an elusive enemy that has killed countless American soldiers – friends and relatives, consider the responsibility of a soldier – strict compliance with orders and unwavering support of authority, a focus on command – but, most of all – consider what it means to be an American and what it means to be decent – and, finally, consider the law against murder and the defense of justification.

71

On March 15, Army Captain Ernest Medina held a briefing with Company C, a rifle company of the 11th Brigade (Charlie Company). Captain Medina explained that a search and destroy mission had been ordered, with the purpose of eliminating North Vietnamese soldiers from certain villages, securing more territory and pushing the enemy away from Saigon. The order included an instruction to kill all North Vietnamese soldiers. Whether Captain Medina ordered the killing of civilian men, woman and children and the burning of villages and pollution of wells – that fact remains unclear.

At 7:30 in the morning on March 16, Charlie Company was split into three platoons. Landing via helicopter just outside of My Lai, the 1st Platoon, led by Second Lieutenant William Calley, immediately killed a group of North Vietnamese men that appeared to be farming (wearing no uniforms and carrying no weaponry). Second Lieutenant Calley then ordered his platoon to enter the village of My Lai. Private Harry Stanley, a machine gunner in the 1st Platoon, testified that "without warning", immediately upon entering My Lai, an American soldier stabbed a "villager" with a bayonet, pushed the villager into a well and threw a grenade into the well.

Private Stanley testified further that he saw a group of woman and children, gathered on their knees outside a temple, burning incense and praying. He witnessed American soldiers under Calley's command shoot each civilian in the head at close range.

Second Lieutenant Calley ordered the platoon to gather all of the North Vietnamese villagers in sight, reportedly 70-80 unarmed civilians. Calley instructed that the villagers be lined up and led to an irrigation ditch. Testimony indicated that Calley ordered the villagers to be pushed into the irrigation ditch and shot. The platoon followed the order of their commanding officer. Reports indicated that Calley not only gave the order, but he participated by pushing the villagers and firing at the villagers in the irrigation ditch. The group of villagers included several women, children and even babies, with the women reportedly screaming, "no VC, no VC" (not Viet Cong, not enemy soldiers or supporters). Private First Class Dennis Konti testified that during the incident, women were laying on top of their children and babies, shielding them from the gunfire. Konti reported that after the shooting ceased, certain of the children were still alive and got up to run away, only to be shot by Calley.

Private First Class Michael Bernhardt witnessed American soldiers setting fire to North Vietnamese straw huts, and when the villagers fled from the burning home, they were shot by American soldiers, many shot in the back. Bernhardt recalls a scene of fire and "piles of people all through the village...all over." Bernhardt ended his remarks by emphasizing that the American soldiers "met no resistance...had no casualties. As a matter of fact, I don't remember seeing one military-age male in the entire place, dead or alive."

More accounts could be set forth, and maybe should be, but for purposes of this book – the point is that our military, our American soldiers, were engaging in abhorrent behavior. A product of war, yes – but, also a reflection of the chaos and instability existent in American government in 1968. Such behavior would spill into American society in just a few months. A complete lack of control, lack of discipline and lack of direction – unhinged aggression rather than calculated protectionism. The actions of the soldiers at My Lai were a reflection of the United States.

Would the American soldiers and officers be held accountable for their actions, or would such actions? Did the soldiers commit murder? Or would such actions be characterized as justifiable killings in the theater of war?

Upon learning of the American soldier conduct at My Lai, Lieutenant Colonel Frank Barker, commander of the My Lai operation, contacted Captain Medina to understand the status of the operation. It is not clear what Medina reported to Barker, but after speaking with Barker, Medina ordered Charlie Company to "knock off the killing." An immediate investigation was conducted by Colonel Oran Henderson, commander of the 11th Infantry Brigade (which controlled all of the units in question). After his inquiry, Henderson took two actions.

Henderson ordered Barker to cancel all scheduled search and destroy operations. Henderson then issued a Letter of Commendation to Captain Medina on March 27, citing his actions at My Lai. Barker submitted a Combat Action Report that described the operation in My Lai as "a success." After reports surfaced, indicating that the My Lai operation resulted in 128 Viet Cong and 22 civilian deaths (numbers that were fabricated), General William Westmoreland, the most senior and decorated officer in the United States Army during the Vietnam War, congratulated Charlie Company on an "outstanding job."

Six months after the initial report and investigation by Colonel Henderson, Tom Glen, a 21-year old soldier from the 11th Light Infantry Brigade, wrote a letter to General Creighton Abrams, a Four Star General in the United States Army and the newly appointed commander of the Military Assistance Command Vietnam (after Westmoreland had been demoted). Glen described an "ongoing and routine brutality against Vietnamese civilians" that he personally witnessed, and the letter specifically mentioned the incident at My Lai. A letter of this sort from a United States soldier to the supreme commander of Vietnamese military operations – well, it was, and remains, highly unusual.

General Abrams reacted by appointing Colin Powell, then a 31-year old Major of the United States Army, to investigate the letter and the assertions therein. Yes, that Colin Powell – the future Four Star General in the United States Army and later, United States Secretary of State.

As a quick aside, as of this writing, there have been 204 officers of the United States Army to achieve the rank of Four Star General, including George Washington, Ulysses Grant, George Patton, the aforementioned Westmoreland and Abrams, and more recently, Norman Schwarzkopf and Powell. The list is quite impressive, and certainly elite, but not as exclusive as the list of Five Star Generals in the United States Army. That list includes only George Marshall, Douglas MacArthur, Dwight Eisenhower and Omar Bradley.

Colin Powell thoroughly investigated the matter, reviewing documents and interviewing soldiers. Powell concluded in a written report that, "In direct refutation of this portrayal is the fact that relations between American Division soldiers and the Vietnamese people are excellent." Powell determined no wrongdoing had occurred and recommended no further action. Not surprising, but certainly unfortunate.

On November 12, 1969, based on extensive research and interviews, independent investigative journalist, Seymour Hersh, published a report about the killings at My Lai with the Associated Press. Immediately, *Time*, *Life*, *Newsweek* and *CBS* covered the story and further investigated the massacre. The news coverage included photographs of stacked bodies, dead women and children and videos of soldiers burning homes. Outraged, the American people and news media urged Congress to act – and Congress responded by ordering an inquiry into the events at My Lai.

After a thorough investigation by Congress and military officials, Colonel Henderson, Captain Medina and Second Lieutenant Calley (among others) were charged in a court-martial for their conduct at My Lai. Henderson was charged with covering up the My Lai massacre, while Medina was charged with command responsibility, essentially – he was charged with being responsible for the conduct of his unit. Calley, however, was charged with first degree, premeditated murder.

Henderson was acquitted on December 17, 1971, found not guilty on all charges. Medina denied giving the order to kill innocent North Vietnamese civilians and denied fabricating reports to senior officers. Medina was acquitted, found not guilty on all charges. Medina later admitted that he lied to Henderson about the magnitude of death at My Lai and suppressed evidence at his trial. Medina did face new charges, but was again acquitted and discharged from the Army, without punishment.

Calley's trial lasted four months. Calley repeatedly insisted that he was following direct orders from Medina and should not be held accountable for following the command of a superior officer. In essence, Calley contended his conduct was justified. A jury of his peers did not agree. Calley was convicted of first degree murder, found guilty in the deaths of at least 20 innocent Vietnamese civilians (he was charged with the murder of 102 civilians). Calley was sentenced to life in prison on March 29, 1971 and remanded to a Federal prison.

Two days later – just two days later – President Richard Nixon ordered that Calley be released from Federal prison and transferred to house arrest at Fort Benning, pending appeal of his sentence. On appeal, Calley's sentence was reduced from life in prison to twenty years in prison. After serving three years of house arrest at Fort Benning, Calley was ordered to serve the remaining sixteen and a half years in Federal prison. However, right after Calley lost his final appeal in 1974, Calley was paroled by Secretary of the Army Howard Callaway and then pardoned by Richard Nixon. Calley immediately became a free man.

The My Lai Massacre is a permanent stain. The United States Army has admitted to the deaths of 347 unarmed civilians at My Lai, many of which were women and children. The North Vietnamese government insists that 504 civilians were killed on March 16 at My Lai. There is no appropriate way to sum up the impact and tragedy of the My Lai Massacre. The facts speak for themselves.

In 2004, during an interview with Larry King on CNN, then Secretary of State, Colin Powell stated in response to a question from King regarding his investigation and report on My Lai in 1968, "in war, these sorts of horrible things happen every now and again, but they are still to be deplored." I can't stand that statement. Part indirect apology and part Jack Nicholson portraying Colonel Nathan Jessup in *A Few Good Men* ("you're damn right I ordered the Code Red"). The death at My Lai is not justifiable. The death at My Lai cannot and should not be tolerated. Herman Melville described the actors of war:

"War being the greatest of evils, all its accessories necessarily partake of the same character." Everyone is guilty.

Perhaps, a more apt quote about war to close this section, a comment made by Albert Einstein: "I do not know with what weapons World War III will be fought, but I do know that World War IV will be fought with rocks."

MUSIC

Once an underground sound, psychedelic music became ubiquitous in 1967, referred to herein as "Psychedelic Pop." Psychedelic Pop was a creation by studio technicians and record label executives. Fashion and marketing were essential attributes of the genre. Psychedelic Pop was created for profit rather than for experience. Psychedelia became a fad, and in music – fads often die a very embarrassing death.

Frank Zappa exposed the idiocy and hypocrisy of Psychedelic Pop, but Zappa and The Mothers of Invention were an offbeat, underground phenomena – hardly noticed by the mainstream they ridiculed. The mainstream, however, would come around in 1968. The mainstream would abandon the nuisance of Psychedelic Pop and return to Rock, channeling an omnipresent evil.

Johnny Cash Marries June Carter Cash

Somehow, Country music has a way of remaining isolated, or insulated, from the political and cultural demise of America. The 1965 Project illustrated how and why Motown and other African American labels and artists chose not to comment on the Vietnam War or racial discrimination during 1965. Racial overtones and outright discrimination forced African American musicians – if they wanted to sell records – to conform to the expectations of white audiences, and not "threaten" young white teenagers (or their parents). Essentially, racial discrimination deprived African Americans of their freedom of speech and expression.

Also, in <u>The 1965 Project</u>, we examined Country music and noted that Country music was also devoid of substantive social commentary (Folk, Rock and Jazz all contained dramatic levels of social commentary and expression). Why did Country musicians avoid political and racial expression? The answer is not exactly clear. A guess would be that Country music is a more traditional, more specific style or genre of music? Or, possibly that Country musicians largely were raised in the South, which tended to be more conservative and was on the wrong side of racial segregation? Maybe Country musicians knew that their audience had no tolerance for political and social commentary, that they just wanted entertainment? Each of those hypotheses is fraught with stereotypes and generalizations.

On March 1, 1968, just nine days after he proposed, Johnny Cash and June Carter Cash were married in Franklin, TN. The love story of Johnny Cash and June Carter Cash is well documented, most recently and vividly in the movie, *Walk The Line*. The couple met in 1956 at the Grand Ole Opry in Nashville, TN. By 1968, Johnny Cash had "crossed over", his music known to fans of both Pop and Rock. Cash became adored for his accessible version of Country music that included his distinct, raspy, deep voice and his penchant for rebellion, instability, substance abuse and forays with law enforcement.

On March 1, Johnny Cash and June Carter Cash became music royalty. Their marriage received national public attention, aided by the narrative that June Carter Cash had helped Johnny to kick his amphetamine habit and become sober.

With June Carter Cash in a light blue dress and matching blue flowers in her hair, the couple were wed at a small ceremony, followed by an alcohol-free wedding at their home in Hendersonville, TN. Johnny Cash and June Carter Cash remained married for 35 years, until June's death in 2003. Johnny died four months later. We'll focus on Cash's legendary recording, *At Folsom Prison*, in the May chapter.

The Fillmore East Opens in New York

On March 8, Bill Graham opened the Fillmore East, a Rock music venue on Second Avenue and 6th Street in New York (East Village). Bill Graham was an incredibly influential concert promoter (and character). Born in Berlin in 1931, Graham escaped the Holocaust, fleeing from Germany to France in 1939. At age 10, after his parents were killed in the Holocaust, Graham was sent by his aunt to the United States, settling with foster parents in the Bronx, NY.

In 1961, Graham moved to San Francisco. After many odd jobs, some related to entertainment, music and theater, but some completely unrelated, Graham began to manage the San Francisco Mime Troupe in 1965, a locally famous group of comics and provocateurs. In 1966, Graham teamed up with Chet Helms to produce and promote benefit concerts in Golden Gate Park and the Family Dog, a venue owned by Helms. The experience of promoting benefit concerts taught Graham the value of a lean production budget and ensuring the musicians were always content, despite maybe not being paid as much as they normally would at a for-profit show.

In late-1965, seeking to promote his own concerts, Graham approached Charles Sullivan, a San Francisco businessman and owner of the Fillmore Auditorium. Graham secured a lease to the Fillmore Auditorium and ownership of the "Fillmore" trademark. On August 2, 1965, Sullivan was found murdered, shot to death in his home. The Sullivan murder remains unsolved. Graham considered Sullivan the unsung hero of the San Francisco music scene and routinely credited Sullivan with Graham's future success.

Under Graham's operation, the Fillmore Auditorium in San Francisco, commonly referred to as the Fillmore West, hosted the burgeoning local music community, including early iterations of Jefferson Airplane, The Grateful Dead and Quicksilver Messenger Service, later Big Brother and the Holding Company featuring Janis Joplin. Graham then began to attract national acts, such as the Paul Butterfield Blues Band, Jimi Hendrix, The Doors, Buffalo

Springfield, Miles Davis, Muddy Waters and B.B. King. The Fillmore West became the mecca of improvisational music, Psychedelic Rock and Blues.

In late-1968, Bill Graham began to experience financial difficulties as the San Francisco scene began to crumble, giving way to the economic underperformance of Woodstock in 1969 and the tragic Altamont Motor Speedway concert featuring The Rolling Stones that ended in the beating and death of a fan at the hands of the Hells Angels. Always a visionary though – Graham sensed it was time to move on – or move away.

Originally a Yiddish theater, Graham was obsessed with the medieval design of a 2,700 seat theater in the East Village neighborhood formerly known as the "Jewish Rialto." Before falling into disrepair, the theater had been used as a movie theater. Graham purchased the rights to the theater in 1967 and renovated the facility to accommodate Rock concerts, retaining the historic medieval beauty.

Named the Fillmore East, the venue became the sister venue to Graham's Fillmore West in San Francisco. The savvy Graham would take advantage of his bi-coastal operation, structuring contracts that brought acts to each of San Francisco and New York (not exactly two for the price of one, but not too far off). After the decline of the San Francisco scene, New York became the center of attention for Rock in the United States – and the Fillmore East was known as "The Church of Rock & Roll." The list of bands that graced the stage at the Fillmore East is unimaginable. Instead of listing all of the bands that played the Fillmore East, the following is a list of just *some* of the released live records recorded at the Fillmore East:

The Allman Brothers – *At Fillmore East, February 1970*
Miles Davis – *Live at the Fillmore East, March 7, 1970*
Derek and the Dominos – *Live at the Fillmore*
The Grateful Dead – *Ladies and Gentlemen*
Jimi Hendrix – *Band of Gypsys*
Jefferson Airplane – *Live at the Fillmore East*

King Crimson – *Live at Fillmore East*
John Lennon and Yoko Ono – *Live Jam*
Al Kooper and Mike Bloomfield – *Fillmore East: The Lost Concert Tapes*
John Mayall – *The Turning Point*
Quicksilver Messenger Service – *Happy Trails*
Sly and the Family Stone – *Live at the Fillmore East*
Traffic – *John Barleycorn Must Die, Live Disc*
Neil Young & Crazy Horse – *Live at the Fillmore East*
Frank Zappa and the Mothers of Invention – *Freaks and Motherfu*#@%!*

In 1971, the short life of the Fillmore East came to an end (as did the life of the Fillmore West). Citing "changes in the music industry", Graham closed both of his venues. Interestingly, "changes in the music industry" related to two main concepts: (1) money and profit moving away from concert promoters and towards record labels and album sales and (2) large scale, stadium tours as opposed to smaller, club shows. The interesting part of that is that the music industry today has shifted back to the original model – the profit residing with concert promoters and venues, as opposed to record labels and album sales and smaller clubs and theatres becoming more popular than large arena shows.

Don't feel bad for Bill Graham though. Bill Graham went on to be the greatest concert promoter in the history of Rock. He promoted a concert at Watkins Glen (NY) in 1973 that featured The Band, The Grateful Dead and the Allman Brothers that attracted over 600,000 attendees. He promoted Led Zeppelin's first shows in California, organized and promoted the first arena/stadium tour by a Rock band (Crosby, Stills, Nash and Young in 1974) and handled the return of Bob Dylan in 1974 playing stadium shows with The Band. Graham also promoted *The Last Waltz* and handled almost all aspects of Live Aid (the event at JFK Stadium in Philadelphia, PA).

Today, Bill Graham Presents is a national concert promotion company, based in San Francisco. In addition to promoting concerts and tours, the company operates venues in various cities. Not surprisingly, each venue is called, The Fillmore.

Go learn about Bill Graham. He was a fantastically revered man throughout the music scene, until his death in 1991 (helicopter crash). Graham promoted just about every major concert event between 1966 and 1991.

The Beatles – "Lady Madonna"

As mentioned, typically a Single was released as a strategy to promote an upcoming full length album. For example, "Light My Fire" was released by The Doors in January 1967, just prior to the release of their self-titled debut album, *The Doors*. "Light My Fire" reached #1 on the *Billboard* Hot 100 and remained in the top slot for three weeks, fueling the commercial success of *The Doors*.

In the early years of their career, The Beatles employed the same strategy. The Beatles released "Ticket to Ride" and "Help!" as Singles prior to the release of *Help!* in 1965. Similarly, "Eleanor Rigby" was released as a Single in 1966 prior to *Revolver*. However, beginning in 1967, with the release of *Sgt. Pepper's Lonely Hearts Club Band*, The Beatles shifted focus to the album as an art form, resulting in no Singles.

In five years, The Beatles went from a teen Pop/Rock band in 1963 and 1964, to an experimental and pre-Psychedelic Rock band in 1966, to a full-fledged Psychedelic Pop concept band in 1967. Add drugs and Eastern philosophy to the mix, along with global instability and dissent. The result? Lady Madonna?

After releasing multiple studio albums each year in 1963, 1964 and 1965, The Beatles released only *Revolver* in 1966, although, *Yesterday and Today* was released in the US in 1966, but other than "Yesterday", the album contained previously released material. In 1967, the band released the aforementioned *Sgt. Pepper's* and *Magical Mystery Tour*, with no accompanying Singles. In order to understand why The Beatles released two Singles in 1968 that would *not* appear on a studio album, a quick study of prior Beatles album release dates is in order.

The Beatles commenced a pattern in 1964 whereby the band released two albums per year, one approximately in the middle of the year and the other at the end of the year, capitalizing on the holiday season. The Beatles were a sensation, the most popular band in the world. It was important for The Beatles to stay current, stay in the public's conscious and, in some respects, stay relevant. In 1964, The Beatles released *A Hard Day's Night* in June and then *Beatles For Sale* in December. In 1965, The Beatles released *Help!* in August and *Rubber Soul* in December. In 1966, The Beatles released *Yesterday and Today* in June and *Revolver* in August. In 1967, *Sgt. Pepper's* was released in June and *Magical Mystery Tour* in November. That is a pattern.

In 1968, The Beatles would release only one full length album (albeit a "double" album). *The Beatles* (typically referred to as "*The White Album*") was released in November, marking a full year between studio releases. How would The Beatles (and their label) stay in the public's conscious? Strategically, The Beatles released the Single "Lady Madonna" in March and then "Hey Jude" in August.

"Lady Madonna" is both unremarkable and remarkably important. The song is a traditional Blues template, leaning towards a boogie vibe, driven by piano and a saxophone solo. The lyrics were written predominantly by McCartney, but as usual, credited to "Lennon/McCartney." Lennon later remarked, "Maybe I helped him on some of the lyrics, but I'm not proud of them either way."

The lyrics suggest an attempt by McCartney to make a social statement, or at least, a social observation – but, the narrative about a single, working mother (Lady Madonna) falls well short. Moreover, McCartney's lead vocal sounds odd, with one critic wondering why "Paul's singing sounds like Ringo" – the essence of unremarkable. So, why is "Lady Madonna" remarkably important? "Lady

Madonna" is a reversion to the Blues and a drastic diversion from the psychedelic canvas The Beatles had been painting the prior two years.

"Lady Madonna" is an early glimpse at the musical trend stemming from recent historical events. After the theatrics of *Magical Mystery Tour* in late-1967, The Beatles signaled a departure from the psychedelic trivialness and a return to Earth. In the shadow of the Vietnam War and unprecedented political instability in both the United States and Europe, The Beatles expressed distance from the wayward, care-free aloofness of 1967. No longer could The Beatles dress up in costumes and pretend as though life is wonderful. "Lady Madonna" is the first step by The Beatles backwards towards Rock.

"Lady Madonna" debuted on the *Billboard* Hot 100 at #23 and peaked at #4, making "Lady Madonna" the first Single since "Eleanor Rigby" in 1966 that failed to reach the #1 slot (after a string of six straight #1 Singles in 1966 and 1967). Perhaps, "Lady Madonna" is not a #1 hit in terms of quality. However, "Baby, You're a Rich Man" and "Hello, Goodbye" from *Magical Mystery Tour* both hit #1. "Lady Madonna" is a better track than each of those. "Lady Madonna" did not become a #1 track because it was seen as an outlier, an abrupt departure from the themes promoted on the beloved *Sgt. Pepper* and *Magical Mystery Tour* records.

The Beatles didn't formally or explicitly announce the end of their overt, outlandish Psychedelic Pop experiment. Rather, The Beatles simply released a short, traditional Blues boogie track and then left for India. More on that later.

The Mothers of Invention – *We're Only in it For the Money*

We're Only in it For the Money solidifies the premise of a musical sea change in 1968. Whereas the Velvet Underground's *White Light/White Heat* was an instrumental assault on Pop and psychedelic sensibilities and "Sunshine of Your Love" by Cream was a gravitational reversion to Hard Rock, *We're Only in it For the Money* is a direct attack on popular culture, societal norms, materialism and, ultimately, The Beatles.

The Mothers of Invention were the backing band for Frank Zappa, a highly skilled guitarist and vocalist, but an even more talented lyricist and creator. Based in California, the Mothers of Invention released their first album, *Freak Out!* in 1966. *Freak Out!* garnered critical acclaim, but failed to achieve commercial traction. Set to a complicated instrumentation of chord charts, Zappa's lyrics embraced non-conformity and rebellion, advocated for the disparagement of authority, shunned materialism and exuded creativity. Initially, Zappa embraced the ideals of the counterculture, or hippie, movement – but, once he explored the community and investigated the intentions of its inhabitants, he was underwhelmed (to say the least).

In 1967, as the flower power movement engaged in the Summer of Love, Frank Zappa and the Mothers of Invention relocated to New York. Projecting the attributes of New York, the band embraced a grungier underworld – a stark contrast to the bright, colorful template in California. The dirt and grunge ended up suiting Zappa well, as the environment fueled his disdain for the mainstream and his hatred of commercial influence.

From late-1965 through early-1967, the hippie scene was relatively small and located mainly in and around San Francisco. Hippies generally lived communally, in a rented house. Hippies loved music and many had visions of "starting a band." Women wore flowing Indian dresses with beads around their neck and flowers in their hair. Men wore ripped jeans and t-shirts. Most everyone looked dirty. Almost everyone smoked a lot of marijuana. Some took LSD. But, everyone was respectful, idealistic, docile and principled.

On June 1, 1967, The Beatles released *Sgt. Pepper's Lonely Hearts Club Band* and the hippie culture immediately became popular. The Beatles made a Psychedelic Pop album that was clearly influenced by drug use (the third track on the album was titled, "Lucy in the Sky with Diamonds", or LSD). Through the use of primary colors,

85

outrageous costumes and cutting edge studio equipment, The Beatles promoted the physical, tangible elements of hippie culture.

However, the ideals and principles ingrained in the hippie culture were lost on the masses. The Beatles focused more on promotion and revenue. The hippies were unabashedly non-violent yet demanded equal rights. The hippies required anti-authoritarianism yet fostered a vigorous work ethic, holding down jobs and paying taxes. The hippies loved to have fun, listen to music and take drugs, yet ascribed to unwritten rules of safety and care for fellow hippies. The hippies were generally apolitical, but leaned socialist from an economic perspective – skeptical of wealth and allergic to materialism. Mainstream hippies put these attributes aside, in favor of fun and irresponsibility.

Amidst the bliss of 1967, very few people noticed the fallacy. But, Frank Zappa noticed it immediately. Zappa was less appalled at the mainstream's embrace of the hippie movement as he was amused. In researching Frank Zappa, articles exist that proclaim Zappa the greatest choreographer of Rock music. Other articles declare Zappa the premier lyricist of the late-1960s (remember, Dylan was in seclusion). One article simply announces that Zappa is "a supreme genius of American music." Avoiding further superlatives, my view is that Zappa's greatest strength was as a satirist. The music equivalent of Mark Twain.

For example, The Velvet Underground reacted to the psychedelic excess of 1967 and the chaos of Vietnam and American politics by creating a wildly experimental and highly inaccessible Rock record, *White Light/White Heat*. Frank Zappa responded to the psychedelic excess of 1967 and the undercurrent of turmoil by waging war on the exploding mainstream hippie culture. Zappa crafted an album that ridiculed hippie culture. The lyrics are priceless and the sarcasm is a work of art. Before detailing some of the more hysterical lyrics, a quick note on the cover photo for *We're Only in it For the Money*.

Not willing to rely on the interpretation of his words as satire, Zappa sought an outright parody. Zappa's idea was to recreate the cover of *Sgt. Pepper's*, but completely invert the concept – for example, Zappa replaced the blue sky with dark clouds and a thunderstorm. Jimi Hendrix, a supporter and fan of Zappa, appears on the cover of *We're Only in it For the Money*, standing in the spot occupied by a statue of Sonny Liston on the *Sgt. Pepper's* cover. The drum kit on the album cover donned the album name, "We're Only in it For the Money", replacing "Sgt. Pepper's Lonely Hearts Club Band", driving home the anti-materialistic theme and taking direct aim at the commercialism of The Beatles.

Zappa did reach out to Paul McCartney and asked permission to release the album cover parody. McCartney reportedly valued the satiric effort, but indicated that his management would not allow the image. Zappa responded by reminding McCartney that artists are supposed to make decisions, not management. Verve, Zappa's label, decided to go forward with the release, but switched the parody cover photo to inside the record sleeve and used an alternative image as the album cover.

Zappa was incensed, but ultimately – the album cover parody paled in comparison to the vitriol and disdain set forth in Zappa's lyrics. The album begins with "Are You Hung Up", which is less a song and more a studio creation of weird noises, nonsensical vocals and irritating editing – all of which are intended to irritate, of course. If the parody was lost on any listener, after the next track, "Who Needs the Peace Corps?" the message was quite clear. The following is an excerpt of the lyrics:

> *Think I'll just DROP OUT*
> *I'll go to Frisco*
> *Buy a wig & sleep*
> *On Owsley's floor*
>
> *Walked past the wig store*
> *Danced at the Fillmore*

I'm completely stoned
I'm hippy and I'm trippy
I'm a gypsy on my own
I'll stay a week and get the crabs and
Take a bus back home
I'm really just a phony
But forgive me
'Cause I'm stoned

Every town must have a place
Where phony hippies meet
Psychedelic dungeons
Popping up on every street
GO TO SAN FRANCISCO . . .

Oh, my hair is getting good in the back!

First I'll buy some beads
And then perhaps a leather band
To go around my head
Some feathers and bells
And a book of Indian lore
I will ask the Chamber of Commerce
How to get to Haight Street
And smoke an awful lot of dope
I will wander around barefoot
I will have a psychedelic gleam in my eye at all times
I will love everyone
I will love the police as they kick the shit out of me on the
street
I will sleep . . .
I will, I will go to a house
That's, that's what I will do
I will go to a house
Where there's a Rock & Roll band
'Cause the groups all live together
And I will join a Rock & Roll band
I will be their road manager

And I will stay there with them
And I will get the crabs
But I won't care
Because . . .

While the lyrics are priceless, the song itself is not really listenable. The music is well executed and quite complicated in structure, but like most songs on *We're Only in it For the Money*, the song lacks melody and is devoid of rhythm. But, remember – that's the point.

In "Harry, You're a Beast", the insults continue:

I'm gonna tell you the way it is
And I'm not gonna be kind or easy
Your whole attitude stinks, I say
And the life you lead is completely empty
You paint your head
Your mind is dead
You don't even know what I just said

Beginning with a guitar lick that utilizes a wah pedal, the following lyrics from "Flower Punk" are spoken more than sung, but the vocals are also sped up, resulting in a higher pitched, almost "chipmunk" sounding pitch from Zappa:

Hey Punk, where you goin' with that flower in your hand?
Well, I'm goin' up to Frisco to join a psychedelic band.
I'm goin' up to Frisco to join a psychedelic band.

I'm goin' to the love-in to sit and play my bongos in the dirt.
Hey Punk, where you goin' with that hair on your head?

I'm goin' to the dance to get some action, then I'm goin' home to bed.
Hey Punk, where you goin' with those beads around your neck?

I'm goin' to the shrink so he can help me be a nervous wreck

After the above rather humorous lines, the track drips into a psychedelic mash up of noises, voices, scratching sounds – it's pretty awful, but the song finishes with the following lyrics:

> *When do we get paid for this?*
> *Stop sloppy Rock & Roll*
> *One more time!*
> *Stop sloppy Rock & Roll*

There are other examples – frankly, every track is an illustration of Zappa's objection to the corporatization of youth. Zappa's indictment of The Beatles seems more of a vessel to release his message, as Zappa actually embraced many of the recording innovations of The Beatles – not only on *We're Only in it For the Money*, but on *Freak Out!* and *Absolutely Free* and each release thereafter. The ironic result, though, was that listeners actually enjoyed *We're Only in it For the Money*. Even the mainstream hippie culture that Zappa ridiculed – they seemed to think it was funny.

We're Only in it For the Money peaked at #30 on the *Billboard* Top 200 Albums chart. In an April 6, 1968 review by *Rolling Stone*, Barret Hansen characterized *We're Only in it For the Money* as "the most advanced work to be heard in Rock today." Hansen continued, "his lyrics contain the most brilliant satire in the whole Pop world." While those comments are typical album reviewer fodder, Hansen's next quote is the key: "Suddenly, The Beatles look much too pretty, and not a little bit plastic in all those satin uniforms."

Zappa exposed the lunacy of mainstream youth and the corporate machine that fueled the lunacy. Zappa brutally exposed the irrelevance of hippie culture and the Psychedelic Pop genre. Hansen appropriately declared *We're Only in it For the Money* a "message album." It's a perfect description, as the message is the lasting quality. In fact, Hansen predicted the fate of *We're Only in it For the*

Money: "In a day when the term is tossed around very lightly, this album will assuredly and genuinely "blow your mind." The long-range effects, however, may not be quite as strong, [the album] depend[s] an awful lot on shock value, and after 20 listens, there isn't so much shock value anymore."

The decorated music critic, Robert Christgua, also gave the album an "A" and wrote: "With bohemia permanent and changed utterly, this early attack on its massification hasn't so much dated as found its context. Cheap sarcasm is forever." Oscar Wilde notably stated that "imitation is the greatest form of flattery" – but, what is parody? Zappa is certainly not *imitating* The Beatles and the many, many other Psychedelic Pop bands. Zappa uses the parody as a vehicle to criticize the underlying motivations of record labels and corporations. Pointing out to fans, and the bands, that they are being taken advantage of – that they are being capitalized, even securitized.

Zappa cleverly presented musical arrangements that initially conveyed familiarity to the listener, dragging the listener into the songs, then bludgeoning the listener with message, disgust and noise. Many of Zappa's lyrics on *We're Only in it For the Money* are sophomoric. Basic in word choice and mundane in phrasing. The lyrical simplicity, I believe, was by design – to engage the average music listener.

On *Freak Out!* and *Absolutely Free*, Zappa proved his intelligence through incredibly experimental arrangements and wildly complicated and vivid composition. Zappa's intended audience for *Freak Out* and *Absolutely Free* were avant-garde, progressive listeners. His intended audience for *We're Only in it For the Money*, though, was mainstream youth. Zappa therefore utilized a voice his targets could understand. For example, taking aim at the parents of the aimless youth Zappa parodied, on "Mom & Dad", Zappa utilizes a ballad format to convey "Ever wonder why your daughter looks so sad?/It's such a drag to have to love a plastic Mom and Dad." No humor there, just a skewer through the heart of the American institution of family.

Zappa centered The Beatles and the hippie movement in his scope and pulled the trigger, but after reading his lyrics several times, I believe his true objective was to motivate the youth, encourage the youth to wake up and engage. Zappa saw a generation adrift, affected by drugs and apathy. Zappa perhaps sensed the instability and chaos on the horizon and knew the youth were an integral part of social change.

The legacy of *We're Only in it For the Money* is its role as a change agent in 1968. Zappa was respected as a musician in 1968 and admired by musicians as an eccentric forward thinker. When Zappa abused and ridiculed the scene, the scene changed. The Beatles took notice. Zappa was ahead of the change, but more likely – Zappa incited the change. The Beatles would certainly not appear in costume on the cover of their next release.

Miles Davis – *Miles in the Sky*

Miles Davis evolved over the course of his career, but Miles was fiercely apolitical and alarmingly absent from the Civil Rights Movement. Notwithstanding a reluctance to infuse music with elements of social discourse, the evolution or shift in his music from traditional Jazz to Fusion (or Jazz Rock) tracked the shift in society from traditional to experimental. *Miles in the Sky* is the change album – the first album on which Miles used electric instruments (electric piano, electric guitar and electric bass). Subsequent Miles Davis releases receive more critical acclaim, such as *In A Silent Way*, *Tribute to Jack Johnson* and *Bitches Brew*, but without question, those masterpieces are direct descendants of *Miles in the Sky*.

Before providing some quick background information on the career of Miles Davis, I should disclose that *Miles in the Sky* has always held a very important spot in my heart, or my musical education. Growing up on Rock and Pop, I only started listening to Jazz in college. Not only did Jazz seem cool, but I found it relaxing at a time of uncertainty and stress. Initially, I listened to the classics – John Coltrane's early records, Art Blakey, Miles' early stuff, Horace

Silver, Thelonious Monk, Dave Brubeck, Jimmy Smith, Charles Mingus and Lee Morgan.

Everything blended together a bit – same instruments, same bop style, with a bit of Blues from Jimmy Smith and a Latin flare from Horace Silver. I was exposed to Free Jazz, through the music of Ornette Coleman and Eric Dolphy, but it was quite chaotic and unsteady. Then, sometime in my Junior year, I went to Arboria Records in State College, PA and bought *Miles in the Sky*. That record never left my six disc changer. That record altered my perception of Jazz and allowed for a deeper understanding of music. We'll get to some thoughts on why *Miles in the Sky* had such an impact, but first – Miles Davis.

Born in 1926, Miles Davis was raised in Alton, IL and then East St. Louis, IL. Hailing from an affluent African American family, Miles' father was a dentist and the family owned a second home, a ranch outside of Pine Bluff, AS. In addition to stressing academics, Miles was urged to play the piano. Miles obliged, but was not intrigued by music until his father brought home a trumpet. Miles was immediately obsessed with the instrument and began a rigorous study through lessons focusing both on playing and theory.

At age 16, Miles was being asked to play in local ensembles – at community centers and local Jazz clubs. At 17, Miles played in a band led by Eddie Randle, which included a future saxophone legend, Sonny Stitt. Sonny was leaving Randle's band and urged Miles to join him on tour with Tiny Bradshaw's band, a regionally noteworthy band. Miles initially agreed, but his mother forced him to remain home and finish high school.

In Miles' senior year at Lincoln High School in 1944, Billy Eckstine's band stopped in East St. Louis for a string of shows. Eckstine's band was the hottest Jazz band in America at the time, featuring Dizzy Gillespie on trumpet and Charlie Parker on saxophone. As luck would have it, Eckstine's third trumpet player, Buddy Anderson, was ill and Miles was asked to fill the slot for the three shows in East St.

Louis. Impressing Eckstine, Miles was offered the third trumpet position permanently, but again – Miles' parents forced Miles to finish high school.

As soon as Miles graduated high school in 1944 he immediately moved to New York, attending the Julliard School of Music. Despite being devoted to his studies at Julliard, Miles was intent on finding Charlie Parker. Locating Parker at a club, Minton's in Harlem, Davis was invited to sit in on jam sessions featuring Parker, Thelonious Monk, Kenny Clarke, Coleman Hawkins, J.J. Johnson and several other Jazz legends. At this time, Parker was playing in a band co-led by he and Gillespie. When Parker and Gillespie parted ways, Davis became Parker's full-time lead trumpeter in his Charlie Parker Quintet.

Davis toured with Parker throughout the late-1940s. Due in large part to a notorious drug addiction, Parker's behavior became increasingly erratic and unprofessional. Upon Parker's second drug rehab stint and one trip to a mental institution in Los Angeles, Miles Davis parted ways with Parker, embarking on a period of session work and a crack at leader, but mostly just sitting in with many of the leading Jazz musicians in the country, including Monk, Charles Mingus and Max Roach.

Not being attached to a specific band afforded Miles the ability to learn many different styles of Jazz and experiment without fear of being labeled. Such an embrace of change fostered a career-long obsession with being at the forefront of Jazz's evolution. In 1954, the first major shift in Jazz style occurred, moving from Bop (or Bebop) and Cool Jazz to Hard Bop. Hard Bop involved a slower tempo, with less emphasis on structure and more emphasis on rhythm and melody. Hard Bop derives several attributes from the Blues, including an affinity for minor key compositions and a smoother, less angular, approach.

Still a free agent, meaning – not tied to a particular band or regularly leading the same musicians – Miles was invited to perform at the

Newport Jazz Festival in 1955. The Newport Jazz Festival was founded in 1954 by Elaine and Louis Lorillard and produced by George Wein (the legendary festival producer). The Newport Jazz Festival was the marquee showcase for Jazz talent, with an all-star cast of performers, and replete with a throng of record label executives and concert tour promoters (searching for the next big Jazz talent). The performance by Miles Davis at the Newport Jazz Festival would become massively important. The audience was reportedly floored by the imagination and tone of the set. Likewise, the record executives were salivating at the prospect of profit.

After the set, Miles was approached by George Avakian, a respected label executive from Columbia Records. Avakian offered Miles a lucrative record contract, with one condition: Miles must put together a regular ensemble. Columbia Records recognized that Jazz fans sought consistency and gravitated towards a strong leader with an up and coming ensemble. That's the formula that sold records for Duke Ellington, Charlie Parker, Louis Armstrong, Chet Baker, Dizzy and then, Art Blakey and the Jazz Messengers.

Miles agreed and formed a group that would become known as The First Great Quintet, featuring John Coltrane on saxophone, Red Garland on piano, Paul Chambers on bass and Philly Joe Jones on drums. The First Great Quintet recorded *Round About Midnight*, *Milestones* and the highly regarded series of records that included *Relaxin'*, *Cookin'*, *Workin'* and, my favorite of the series, *Steamin'*. In 1958, Davis added Cannonball Adderly on alto saxophone and Bill Evans replaced Red Garland on piano. The sextet proceeded to record the critically acclaimed, *Kind of Blue*, in 1959. The unprecedented run of classics ended with Coltrane leaving the group in 1960 to pursue a career as a leader.

After Coltrane's departure, Miles experimented with several musicians, but more impactful, Miles started to gravitate towards a different sound, a modal style that facilitated and encouraged improvisation, which attracted younger musicians, and younger fans. Miles settled on what is known as The Second Great Quintet. Miles recruited four of the brightest young stars on the Jazz scene: Herbie Hancock on piano, Wayne Shorter on saxophone, Ron Carter on bass and Tony Williams on drums. If there was a Hall of Fame for Jazz, each of these musicians would be first ballot inductees.

In the years between The First Great Quintet and The Second Great Quintet, Jazz changed dramatically. Musicians such as Ornette Coleman, Eric Dolphy, Albert Ayers and, to some extent, John Coltrane, developed and promoted a style of Jazz known as Free Jazz. Free Jazz was devoid of structure and time and, to most critics and musicians, simply noise. Free Jazz musicians improvised obsessively. Not just the soloists (horns and piano), as the bass and drums would also improvise throughout a song, resulting in a cacophony of experimentation.

When it worked, it was sublime – but, at the outset of Free Jazz, before the musicians were acquainted with the style, the product was difficult to process and uneven. Miles Davis was critical of Free Jazz in 1960 and the years shortly thereafter. Miles was famously a proficient technician and a student of structure and theory (as opposed to a player like Ornette Coleman, who lacked technical music education, relying mostly on instinct and ear).

In 1964 and 1965, as Free Jazz became more popular and more listenable, Miles began to embrace the style, or at least, his version of Free Jazz. Davis referred to the style of The Second Great Quintet as "time, no structure" (a reference to Thelonious Monk's classic Jazz standard, "Straight, No Chaser"). The sound of The Second Great Quintet embraced certain elements of Free Jazz without completely surrendering to the prohibition of composition. Many critics suggest that Miles' work with The Second Great Quintet adopted the best elements of Free Jazz, while discarding its worst attributes, resulting in the pinnacle of Jazz recordings. Miles encouraged each musician to improvise, facilitating a full band approach, rather than roles as a leader, soloists and rhythm section.

The sound of The Second Great Quintet is stunning. Tangible elements exist, but the glue that holds the tangible elements together is loose, allowing for a certain floating or levitation. Instead of breezy, quick solos, the tempo is slower and paced, allowing the listener to focus on each musician simultaneously. In succession, The Second Great Quintet released: *E.S.P.* (1965), *Miles Smiles* (1966), *Sorcerer* and *Nefertiti* (both in 1967) and *Miles in the Sky* and *Filles de Kilimanjaro* (both in 1968). Of the pre-1968 releases, *Miles Smiles* is clearly the standout. Wayne Shorter steps out as a star and Herbie Hancock demands attention. But, the lead is Miles and he delivers a tone that remains uncompromised and uncontested. As we'll highlight throughout this book, 1968 facilitated, and in many respects caused, change. *Miles Smiles* is an incredible record, but 1968 urged Miles to change – accordingly, Miles adopted a new sound.

The departure from acoustic Jazz (no electric instruments) got the headlines, and in my view, obscured the greatness of *Miles in the Sky*. Of course, fifty years later, the sound of electric piano, electric bass and electric guitar in the context of Jazz – it sounds at home, normal, but in 1968, it was antithetical to the culture and vaunted history of Jazz.

Miles in the Sky consists of four tracks, two on Side 1 and two on Side 2. The shortest track is "Black Comedy" at 7:38, followed by "Paraphernalia" at 12:38, "Country Son" at 13:52 and the album opener, "Stuff" at 17:00. "Stuff" and "Country Son" were written by Miles Davis, while "Paraphernalia" was written by Wayne Shorter and "Black Comedy" by Tony Williams.

Picking up *Miles in the Sky*, the first thing one notices is the record cover. Even in 1968, art rarely graced the cover of Jazz records, with the notable exception of *Time Out* by The Dave Brubeck Quartet in 1959 (however, *Time Out* also included a dominant header featuring the album title and a text banner for the lead Single ("Take Five") and the band's name, all in large block text). *Miles in the Sky* consisted of a psychedelic image of an eye, with various colors accentuating the different layers of the lens and pupil. The only text on the cover is "miles davis" (in lowercase) and "MILES IN THE SKY" (in uppercase). The font is a thin, white font at the top center of the album cover. It's an awesome image that certainly makes a statement about Jazz in 1968. But, as is usually the case with Miles Davis, the music is the show.

The opening track, "Stuff", begins with a quick drum roll and cymbal ride by Williams that leads into an electric piano riff by Hancock. The intro feeds into a trumpet sequence by Miles at 0:30 that establishes the melody for the track. The playing by Miles seems traditional, or at least consistent with prior efforts as his notes build to a peak at 1:53, at which point the band drops back into the intro and melody. I recall listening to that intro sequence at 19 years old and thinking that it just made sense. Nothing more elaborate or intellectual than that – just that this track seemed to make sense to me, like I could predict the timing of various solos and the return to a familiar melody.

Little did I know, and make no mistake, I certainly knew very little at 19 years old, the reason I understood *Miles in the Sky* had nothing to do with electric instruments, a cool album cover or a familiar melodic composition. *Miles in the Sky* made sense to me because it was in 4/4 time – the standard time signature for pretty much every Rock and Pop song I'd ever heard prior to *Miles in the Sky*. The entirety of *Miles in the Sky* is in 4/4 time, the first such Jazz album to accomplish that feat (or defeat, depending on your opinion).

"Stuff" remains one of the most influential tracks in early Jazz Fusion, paving the way and establishing a formula to combine attributes of Rock and Jazz. At 5:55, after a refrain of the melody/theme, a brief pause by Miles leads into a soaring trumpet solo – announcing that the track, and the session, would not be just a groovy excursion, *Miles in the Sky* would be an adventure.

I'm not going to detail each track, but I'd be negligent to not highlight the second track, "Paraphernalia." As mentioned, the track was written by Wayne Shorter, a soon to be revered composer. The track embraced the same qualities as "Stuff", but the overwhelming characteristic that set "Paraphernalia" apart was the inclusion of George Benson on electric guitar. Beginning with Miles and Shorter taking huge, incredibly moving solos, the track breaks down a bit around 7:01 and then the faint first notes of Benson's guitar trickle in at 7:10. Sounding initially like it could be a bass solo, Benson proceeds to run through a few scales and then, with only Williams backing him on drums with mostly snare, Benson solos for a few minutes, leading to an improvised solo by Hancock on electric piano.

The inclusion of the guitar cannot be understated. A track entitled "Paraphernalia" that included an electric guitar? Miles was speaking to a younger generation. Whether Miles was appealing to the mainstream – or gravitating in that direction – it's unclear, but it's undeniable that the use of electric instruments, along with the artwork on the album cover and the use of an electric guitar, resulted in Miles Davis becoming a cross-over superstar. Just 18 months after the release of *Miles in the Sky*, Bill Graham booked Miles at the Fillmore West, opening for The Grateful Dead. Miles would go on to play several shows at the Fillmore West and then the Fillmore East, attracting massive audiences.

While *Miles in the Sky* is considered a bit of a gateway drug in the catalog of Miles Davis, leading to *In A Silent Way* and *Bitches Brew*, not to mention the equally incredible *Tribute to Jack Johnson* and *On the Corner*, after experiencing these later masterpieces, *Miles in the Sky* seems to get a bit lost. However, *Miles in the Sky* might just be the most listenable of Miles' later work. Not as creative, not as distant, not as elaborate – but, *Miles in the Sky* strikes the perfect balance of traditional Jazz and Rock.

Please give it a listen – and to truly understand its significance, listen to *Miles Smiles* and then listen to *Miles in the Sky* then spin *Bitches Brew*. You will then understand the significance of *Miles in the Sky*.

James Brown – *I Can't Stand Myself (When You Touch Me)*

I Can't Stand Myself (When You Touch Me) was the 22nd album by James Brown, released in March 1968 on King Records. Inventing the genre of Funk in late-1965 with the album *Papa's Got a Brand New Bag*, James Brown continued to push R&B and Soul towards Funk in 1966 and 1967. The instrument arrangement in Brown's backing band stayed fairly consistent between 1965 and 1967, as Brown utilized a horn section, electric bass and organ to infuse each track with vigor.

Subsequent to *Papa's Got a Brand New Bag*, Brown released several heralded records, including *I Got You (I Feel Good)*, *It's a Man's Man's World* and *Handful of Soul* in 1966 and *James Brown Sings Raw Soul*, *James Brown Plays the Real Thing* and *Cold Sweat* in 1967. Each of these releases indeed featured a large band arrangement, including a horn section. Brown's vocal approach on the releases leans R&B/Soul.

Ultimately, the key to Funk was not so much the instruments as it was the timing. James Brown generally defined Funk as music "on the one." Meaning, the punch or the beat is on the first note in a four note bar. Traditionally, R&B and Rock & Roll were "on the two and four." After *Papa's Got a Brand New Bag*, everything James touched was "on the one."

The beauty of *Can't Stand Myself* is the lack of beauty. On the first track, "I Can't Stand Myself (When You Touch Me)", an experienced listener and fan of James Brown immediately realizes what he or she does not hear: horns. Not only is the track stripped-down, featuring only Brown on vocals, along with electric bass, organ, electric guitar and drums, the production is borderline lo-fi. The recording has a primitive and simple essence compared to the elaborately arranged and produced predecessor records.

It's hard to describe any musician other than James Brown as being featured on a James Brown record, but on *Can't Stand Myself*, to my ear, the star of the session is "Fat Eddie" Setser on electric guitar. James Brown had utilized electric guitarists in his ensemble for years, but the instrument was merely a rhythm participant, not a feature – not a creator of melody. On the album opener "I Can't Stand Myself (When You Touch Me)", Setser leads with a guitar riff that repeats throughout. The next track, "There Was a Time", also features Setser's guitar – not only the classic, scratchy, choppy Funk chords, but also picked riffs on the turnaround between bars.

Many of the tracks on *Can't Stand Myself* are – just average James Brown – but, average James Brown in 1968 remains some of the best R&B/Funk in any canon. That line of thought reminds me of a comment from John Fishman of Phish describing, in a self-deprecating manner, his band's performance at a festival in Maine, stating that Phish was as "funky as James Brown on his worst night."

I suggest focusing on a couple tracks. The first two tracks are great and then "Get It Together, Pt. 2" and maybe the slow Blues "Need Your Love So Bad", an interesting palate for Brown that works really well. "You've Got to Change Your Mind" is a sweet, simple R&B track that might feel at home on the Motown label, but Brown's delivery has just enough rasp and energy – and along with Setser's clean, chord driven guitar playing – the track has more depth and truth than most of the Motown records released in 1968.

The core of *Can't Stand Myself* is the stripped-down brand of Funk that Brown would perfect over the next seven years. The harder version of Funk that would dominate the "Godfather of Soul" period of Brown's career (1970-1975) got its start on *Can't Stand Myself*. The smaller ensemble and stripped-down session illuminates and accentuates James Brown's talent as a singer.

Finally, as stated earlier, *Can't Stand Myself* contains no substantive message and does not refer to political or social causes or concerns. One might have expected the brash James Brown to have spoken out against racism and war. Not so in March 1968. However, James

Brown would find himself at the vortex of racial discord just one month later.

April

April

HISTORY

Assassination of Martin Luther King, Jr.
The Godfather of Soul Saves Boston

MUSIC

Simon & Garfunkel – *Bookends*
Sly & the Family Stone – *Dance to the Music*
The Zombies – *Odessey and Oracle*
2001 – A Space Odyssey

HISTORY

Assassination of Martin Luther King, Jr.

Only one historical event will be covered in this chapter. Only one historical event mattered. While opposition to a senseless war penetrated the fabric of American culture, racial discrimination was adrift from the white conscious. Whereas the young, liberal generation had previously galvanized behind integration and the eradication of racism, the "cause" shifted to the anti-war effort, leaving the discriminated minority to fight alone. Commenting on the "Great Society", a series of legislative social programs created and promoted by President Johnson in 1964 to eliminate poverty and racial inequality, Martin Luther King, Jr. (MLK) stated in 1967 that, "the promises of the Great Society have been shot down on the battlefield of Vietnam."

As discussed in the February chapter, MLK sensed his death was near. Why would a 39 year old man firmly believe that he was about to die? Sure, he was weathered and likely tired from a relentless travel schedule and the weight of a movement – but, death?

In 1956, MLK's house was bombed with a small explosive. Nobody was injured. In 1957, a shotgun was fired at the front door of MLK's home in Birmingham, Alabama. Again, nobody was injured, but this second attack prompted MLK to heighten his vigilance and security. Just five weeks after the shotgun incident, MLK found twelve sticks of dynamite on his front porch. Fortunately, a defective fuse prevented detonation. Then, at an event in Harlem in 1958, a woman approached MLK and stabbed him in the chest with a letter opener. The blade narrowly missed his aorta. In 1962, a member of the American Nazi party was able to penetrate security and physically assault MLK, punching him several times in the face (Kaiser).

Why did MLK fear that his death was near? MLK feared for his life because he lived in fear. Not simply the fear of physical violence – possibly more sacred, he feared the daunting realization that his efforts were falling short – or, not materializing quickly enough for his increasingly impatient movement.

MLK advocated for non-violence. MLK demanded non-violence. Non-violence was the core of his message and the essence of his strategy. As the United States scaled its war effort in Vietnam, young African Americans began to scale the war effort at home. The African American base was fracturing, along with the country. MLK's movement of non-violent protest was losing resonance. The Black Power movement was more synonymous with the culture of America.

Prior to 1967, MLK avoided commenting about the Vietnam War, separating his plight for equality from his views on geopolitics. But in 1967 and 1968, MLK spoke out against the Vietnam War. For a man that required interaction with politicians in order to advance his cause, publicly denouncing the Vietnam War was significant.

Astutely, MLK analogized the violence against the North Vietnamese with the violence against African Americans. MLK declared that "the greatest purveyor of violence in the world today – [is] my government." Such a stance was not only derided by politicians, but the mainstream media was outraged – in my opinion, exhibiting racism in their criticism.

The Washington Post stated that MLK had done "a grave injury to those who are his natural allies" and "many who have listened to him with respect will never again accord him the same confidence." Even the normally passive *Life* magazine called MLK's comments "demagogic slander", even stating that MLK "goes beyond his personal right to dissent when he connects progress in civil rights here with a proposal that amounts to abject surrender in Vietnam." Is the author of that comment suggesting that African Americans have fewer personal rights than white Americans? Just a despicable comment. Finally, the routinely liberal *New York Times* stated that MLK's "outspoken stand…has dampened his prospects for becoming the Negro leader who might be able to get the nation 'moving again' on civil rights." Again, appalling.

The country was entrenched in violence. Violence conveyed strength and strength seemed necessary to defeat the opposition. MLK's message of non-violence suddenly conveyed weakness. Nonetheless, MLK tirelessly promoted his message and vision for progress – traveling to Memphis in late-March 1968.

MLK focused on Memphis in support of a group of African American sanitation workers that decided to strike due to unequal wages and hazardous working conditions. The City of Memphis paid African American workers less than white workers and required African American, not white, workers to perform certain dangerous tasks, resulting in the death of several African Americans.

MLK organized a demonstration, a march, on Beale Street to support the sanitation worker strike and appeal to the local, white politicians through a peaceful, non-violent protest. His goal, as always, was to depict the African American community as intelligent, principled, calm and communal. However, for the first time, a demonstration organized by MLK turned violent.

One of the demonstrators smashed the plate glass front window of a white merchant, setting off a barrage of similar activity, followed by rampant looting. The Memphis police force engaged, using tear gas and clubs. The disruption turned deadly when a police officer shot and killed an unarmed sixteen year-old boy (for looting). Sixty others were injured, two hundred arrested.

MLK was anguished. He remarked to his chief aide, Ralph Abernathy, "Maybe we just have to admit that the day of violence is here…maybe we have to just give up and let violence take its course." This comment, along with the comments from February that foreshadowed his death, illustrate the dark cloud under which MLK existed in 1968. MLK returned to his home in Atlanta on March 30, reportedly lost and uncertain.

On April 1, MLK woke to the news of President Johnson not running for reelection. Given MLK's lack of progress with the Johnson Administration, MLK was immediately reenergized by the possibility of another, more racially sensitive and focused candidate. MLK summoned Abernathy and put in motion arrangements for MLK to return to Memphis. MLK sought redemption and was energized to promote his strategy of non-violence.

Landing in Memphis on April 2, MLK gathered support and prepared for a public address. On April 3, MLK delivered a speech at the Mason Temple in Memphis. The speech would become known as the "I've Been to the Mountaintop" address, but the speech would also become known as MLK's final speech. He stated:

> *"Well, I don't know what will happen now. We've got some difficult days ahead. But, it doesn't matter with me now. Because I've been to the mountaintop. And I don't mind. Like anybody, I would like to live a long life. Longevity has its place. But I'm not concerned about that now. I just want to do God's will. And He's allowed me to go up to the mountain. And I've looked over. And I've seen the promised land. I may not get there with you. But I want you to know tonight, that we, as a people, will get to the promised land! And so I'm happy, tonight. I'm not worried about anything. I'm not fearing any man. My eyes have seen the glory of the coming of the Lord!"*

Chills. Just chills. It is incredibly difficult to set aside the sadness inherent in that passage and realize the beauty of his words – but, please try. MLK's prescience is startling. MLK had a gift. He could see what very few could see. He seemed to understand that his legacy was more important than his life.

After the near-death experiences noted above, and the assassination of Malcolm X in 1965, MLK implemented a security detail in 1968. However, MLK made a fatal mistake in Memphis. MLK insisted on staying in the same second floor room at the same motel. Room 306 at the Lorraine Motel. The room was known to locals as the "King-Abernathy Suite."

At 6:01 pm on Thursday, April 4, after preparing to attend a meeting of supporters, MLK walked out onto the balcony of Room 306. Just prior to stepping out on the balcony, MLK remarked to his friend and musician Ben Branch, "Ben, make sure you play 'Take My Hand, Precious Lord' in the meeting tonight. Play it real pretty." Such would be MLK's last words. He was struck by a single bullet fired from a Remington Model 760. The bullet entered MLK's right cheek and severed his jugular vein. MLK fell to the ground, unconscious. He was rushed to St. Joseph's Hospital where doctors operated on MLK, attempting to remove the bullet and resuscitate. MLK never regained consciousness and was pronounced dead at 7:05 pm.

Witnesses reportedly saw a man fleeing a rooming house across the street from the Lorraine Motel. Shortly thereafter, Memphis police found a package dumped in a nearby alley that contained a rifle and binoculars. Fingerprints on the rifle and binoculars matched fingerprints in a room in the rooming house. The FBI confirmed that the fingerprints belonged to a recently escaped convict, James Earl Ray.

After an international manhunt, Ray was arrested at Heathrow Airport in London, en route to Angola or Rhodesia. Ray was immediately extradited to Tennessee and charged with murder. To avoid the death penalty, Ray pleaded guilty, confessing to the assassination on March 10, 1969. Ray was convicted and sentenced to 99 years in prison. He died in 1998 from kidney and liver failure. Ray was 70.

A bit of controversy does exist as to the guilt of James Earl Ray. Covering the controversy does not comport with the motive of this book, but many significant figures in the Civil Rights Movement believed – and still believe – that Ray was either innocent or did not act alone, with most theories concluding that the government of the United States was somehow complicit in the killing of MLK. I have reviewed several of the assertions and have read various court documents, as well as a report prepared by the Department of Justice in 2000. While several interesting, and to some extent realistic, theories exist, for me – the fingerprint evidence is overwhelming and, despite the lack of a credible eyewitness, I am comfortable concluding that Ray was the killer, acting alone. The esteemed Jesse Jackson, however, disagrees.

In 2004, Jesse Jackson stated, "I will never believe that James Earl Ray had the motive, the money and the mobility to have done it himself. Our government was involved in setting the stage for and I think the escape route for James Earl Ray." James Bevel, MLK's friend and colleague, put it plainly: "There is no way a ten-cent white boy could develop a plan to kill a million-dollar black man."

While the manhunt for James Earl Ray consumed the nation for months after the assassination, and conspiracy theories surfaced in the decades after, what exactly transpired in the days after the assassination? Not surprisingly, the aftermath tracked the reactionary theme of 1968 – VIOLENCE. The precise reaction that MLK feared and detested.

As news of MLK's death spread, African Americans took to the streets. Many expressed sadness through candlelight vigils. But, sadness was secondary to outrage. In Washington D.C., several hundred demonstrators gathered at 14th and U. Initially peaceful, the crowd began approaching white-owned restaurants and shops, demanding that the businesses close out of respect. When the businesses resisted, the demonstration turned violent. By 11:00 pm, demonstrators were smashing windows, looting shops and burning vehicles in the street. As word spread through other African American neighborhoods in Washington, D.C., a crowd of close to 20,000 overwhelmed the city's 3,100 officer police force.

The city was on fire. Historians consider the Washington D.C. riot of 1968 to be the first occupation of a United States city since the Civil War. Charles Kaiser noted that the fires in Washington, D.C. were the worst since the British burned the White House in 1814.

110

President Johnson dispatched 13,600 federal troops and 1,750 members of the National Guard to regain control. Marines armed with machine guns were able to contain the crowds and, with force, quell the insurgency.

The damage was immense. An estimated 1,200 buildings had been burned and completely destroyed, including over 900 retail stores, totaling approximately $27 million in damages. Thousands of jobs were lost due to the retail destruction and insurance rates in the District surged. Several blocks remained rubble for decades. Images of Washington D.C. on April 5, 1968 look eerily similar to images of Saigon under siege during the Tet Offensive. War abroad, war at home.

In Chicago, violence erupted on the West side of the city, gradually expanding to West Madison Street. At its peak, the rioting, looting and violence engulfed a 28-block portion of downtown Chicago. Close to 10,500 local police officers were engaged, along with 6,700 from the Illinois National Guard. As it became clear more support was needed, President Johnson sent 5,000 soldiers from the 1st Armored and 5th Infantry. Soldiers, not National Guard. Soldiers. Mayor Richard Daley (who we will hear from again later in 1968) instructed Chicago police officers to "shoot to kill any arsonist or anyone with a Molotov cocktail in his hand…and…to shoot to maim or cripple anyone looting any stores in our city." Quite the pacifist.

Order was restored in Chicago on April 7, but not before 11 people were killed, 500 injured and 2,150 arrested – an estimated $10 million in damages. More of the same in Baltimore. Local law enforcement was overwhelmed as a result of violent demonstrations, leading Governor Spiro Agnew to request support from President Johnson. Stretched thin, President Johnson did not immediately provide the requested support. As reports of civilian deaths surfaced, President Johnson sent 5,000 soldiers from the XVIII Airborne Corps at Fort Bragg. Two days later, order was restored. Two days later, six deaths, 700 injured, 4,500 arrested and $13.5 million in damages.

Riots in Kansas City resulted in five deaths. Riots in Cincinnati resulted in two deaths. Riots in Detroit and Pittsburgh each resulted in one death. There were riots in over 100 cities across the United States. The period of time between April 4 and April 8 is regarded as the "greatest wave of social unrest the United States has experienced since the Civil War." (Peter B. Levy)

When the rioting finally subsided, nationally – 39 people were dead – 34 of which were African American, with 15 victims less than 21 years old. Over 20,000 arrests were made – the damage to property was close to $100 million. The magnitude of the reaction is a testament to the significance of MLK's life, but the reaction itself was antithetical to the life of MLK.

MLK was buried on April 9 in Atlanta. Over 20,000 people attended, including celebrities such as Jackie Robinson, Aretha Franklin, Richard Nixon, Stevie Wonder, Eugene McCarthy, Bobby Kennedy, Jackie Kennedy, Marlon Brando and Nelson Rockefeller. President Johnson did not attend. Rockefeller subsidized the entire funeral.

Who, though, would eulogize MLK? MLK's wife, Coretta King decided that only one man's words could justify the life of her husband. And that man was her husband. Loudspeakers were stationed throughout the funeral hall and outside the Ebenezer Baptist Church to accommodate thousands of attendees. MLK's remarks from two months prior overwhelmed the masses:

"If any of you are around when I have to meet my day. I don't want a long funeral. And if you get somebody to deliver the eulogy, tell him not to talk too long." He continued, "I want you to be able to say that day that I did try to feed the hungry. I want you to be able to say that day that I did try in my life to clothe the naked. I want you to say on that day that I did try in my life to visit those who were in prison. And I want you to say that I tried to love and serve humanity."

MLK is still inspiring millions of people today. He may just be the single most influential person in the history of the United States.

The Godfather of Soul Saves Boston

The premise, or motive, of this book is to bind historical events with music. After detailing the sadness and horror of the assassination of MLK, analyzing the albums released in April 1968 seems inconsequential. Fortunately, James Brown has provided a segue.

As chaos engulfed every major city in the United States, Boston was quiet. Believe it or not, credit for Boston's peace has been attributed not to a politician or activist, but to James Brown. Brown was scheduled to play a sold-out show at the Boston Garden on April 5. The Boston Garden was located in downtown Boston, an overwhelmingly white community. In 1968, African Americans mostly lived and stayed in a neighborhood called Roxbury. Boston was very much a racially divided climate. That said, for a James Brown concert – the African American community was most certainly going to travel downtown to attend the show.

Fearing an uprising, Mayor Kevin White considered canceling the concert. As word quickly spread about the possibility of a cancelation, an African American City Council member, Thomas Atkins, argued that "if the black community hears that the city stopped James Brown from performing, all hell will break loose." An interesting dilemma.

Ultimately, a relatively decent compromise was reached. Mayor White held a press conference and informed the people of Boston that the James Brown concert at the Boston Garden would take place and it would be broadcasted live on television. Mayor White encouraged the people of Boston to stay inside and watch.

James Brown was an ardent supporter of MLK and his position of non-violence. The events of 1968 would indeed change James Brown, but on April 5, Brown was a man that sought peace and advocated for integration. Brown was also notoriously committed to earning a buck, so he likely was motivated to react in a manner that would not result in a cancelation.

At 9:00 pm, James Brown walked on stage alongside Mayor White. Mayor White addressed the attendees and the television audience. He stated, "This is our city, and our future is in our hands – today, tomorrow, and the days that follow. So all I ask you tonight is this: look at each other, and pledge that no matter what any other community might do, here in Boston, we will honor Dr. King's legacy in peace." James Brown, dressed in all black, grabbed the microphone and kicked off the show.

Running through a set list that included "Kansas City", "Mustang Sally", "It's a Man's Man's World" and "Chain of Fools" – James Brown was killing it. Tom Vickers, a music journalist, was 18-years old at the time, and recalled watching the broadcast in Boston with his family. Vickers stated, "that night, there was an emotional edge to it. He seemed totally present, in the moment, and giving 110 percent." The strategy seemed to be working. The crowd was calm, enjoying the show and scores of people at home were watching the broadcast on television. Boston was quiet.

Then, a young African American man jumped on the stage during Brown's performance. A white police officer grabbed the man and threw him back into the crowd. No arrest, but the moment seemed to stop time. The image echoed the violent images of riots in Washington, Chicago and Baltimore. The band stopped playing and the crowd became restless. Additional young men jumped on stage and were instantly grabbed by police and thrown back into the audience. Not only was a riot brewing at the Boston Garden, the riot would be witnessed by the entire city of Boston and most certainly bleed into the streets. The fate of Boston was in the hands of James Brown.

Brown took control and politely asked the police officers to leave the stage. He engaged the young men that had jumped on stage, shaking their hands. Suddenly, fans swarmed the stage and surrounded James Brown. He continued to shake hands and stay calm. Brown then picked up the microphone and addressed the arena – and the City of Boston. He stated, "You're making me look bad...You're not being fair to yourself or your own race. I asked the police to step back because I figured I could get some respect from my own people. It doesn't make sense. Now, are we together or we ain't?" He paused, gained the assent and support of the audience, and cleared the fans off the stage in an orderly fashion. He then said, "Hit the thing, man…one-two-three."

The band kicked back in and Brown finished the set, without a single disturbance. James Brown featured "I Heard It Through the Grapevine", "When a Man Loves a Woman", "Cold Sweat", "I Got You (I Feel Good)" and closed the show with the recently released, "I Can't Stand Myself (When You Touch Me)." Brown's statement to the audience and the people of Boston was interesting. Not political and not overly intellectual. Brown expressed his view in a way that "his" people could understand. He made it clear he didn't approve of the unrest. He used respect as an instrument to suppress violence.

Despite being a severely racially divided community, Boston experienced no deaths, no injuries, no arrests and no material damage after the assassination of MLK. Undeniably, Brown's handling of the crowd, his direct message to the people, along with the very notion that most African Americans stayed home to watch the concert, were at the heart of Boston's passivity. A recording of the concert was released in 2008, titled *Live at the Boston Garden: April 5, 1968*, in conjunction with a PBS documentary titled, *The Night James Brown Saved Boston*.

James Brown's advocacy of non-violent protest may have saved Boston on April 5, but Brown would soon shed his affinity for non-violence and embrace the Black Power movement, which entailed a louder, more direct voice against racism. Brown's shift would, of course, take place later in 1968, with the release of "Say it Loud – I'm Black and I'm Proud."

MUSIC

Three important albums were released in April, along with a classic movie that contained an equally famous music score. It is critical to again note the aspect of timing. The music released in April 1968 was largely recorded in late-1967 and the first two months of 1968. The chaos and tragedy unfolding in March and April had not yet impacted the mainstream creative process. The music released in April is not necessarily bright and optimistic, but reaction to losing the Vietnam War, a President stepping down and the assassination of the most revered civil leader in America would not surface generally in music until July.

Simon & Garfunkel – *Bookends*

Bookends was released in the United States on April 3, the day prior to the assassination of MLK. After a sluggish first week of sales, the album reached #1 on the *Billboard* Top 200 Albums chart and remained at #1 for seven non-consecutive weeks, charting for a total of 66 weeks.

Released by Columbia Records, *Bookends* was the fourth studio album by Simon & Garfunkel (not including *The Graduate* soundtrack). Simon & Garfunkel were incredibly popular in 1968, after the success of *Sounds of Silence* (1966) and *Parsley, Sage, Rosemary and Thyme* (1966), not to mention the adulation received after the release of *The Graduate*.

Known primarily as a "Folk Duo", Simon & Garfunkel also embraced the Folk Rock genre invented by The Byrds in 1965. However, the duo never sunk into the psychedelic atmospherics of 1967. That said, *Bookends* is a concept album. Well, kind of – the record is only 29 minutes and 51 seconds and the "concept" portion of the album is contained solely on Side 1. So it might be a concept album, but it's an awfully short concept.

Side 1 of *Bookends* is intended to present the journey from childhood to old age. Side 2 is essentially a combination of tracks that were either not used on *The Graduate* soundtrack or left over from the *Parsley* sessions. Themes related to youth, disillusionment, adulthood, relationships and mortality. The lyricism is excellent, while the instrumentation is a bit ordinary.

The "Bookends Theme", an instrumental acoustic guitar composition that is both contemplative and innocent both opens and closes Side 1. The thirty second opener gives way to a loud, bracing distortion noise and then a snare crash, leading into the song, "Save the Life of My Child." It's quite startling after the soft, acoustic intro. The lyrical imagery is quaint and somewhat self-reflective, but also ubiquitous. Interestingly, the song is layered with reverb and distorted backing vocals. The production seems intentionally muddy. The texture suggests the chaos and freedom of childhood, somewhat reckless, but equally naïve.

The next track, "America", is easily the best track on *Bookends*. "America" represents the time period between adolescence and early-20s. Emanating from the distorted cross fade of "Save the Life of My Child", the intro to "America" is soothing – a calm acoustic guitar leads to Simon's familiar, more Folk-oriented vocal delivery. Once Simon sings, "So we bought a pack of cigarettes", the listener is immediately attentive. And then, the line "and walked off to look for America" – the listener goes from attentive to hooked.

Simon illustrates a visual of two young lovers boarding a Greyhound bus in Pittsburgh, riding for four days and hitch-hiking from Saginaw (Michigan), stating "I've come to look for America." The image is crystal clear. Almost reminiscent of the last scene of *The Graduate*, when Dustin Hoffman and Katharine Ross boarded a bus to somewhere – innocent and unknown. While Bob Dylan and many other songwriters utilized prose in the construction of a song, Simon displays an uncanny knack for incorporating simple, basic dialogue in the fabric of the instrumentation. Conveying a conversation and adhering to the thematic allure of the message – a message that echoed the state of America in 1968, but also tracks the aging trajectory important to the album's concept.

> *"Toss me a cigarette,*
> *I think there's one in my raincoat."*
> *We smoked the last one*
> *An hour ago.*

Notice how Simon utilizes the quotation marks in his official lyrics and accentuates the significance in his vocal delivery. The first line is a quote, a statement by one character to the other. The second line is Simon commenting – we smoked the last one an hour ago – conveying a sense of innocence, almost aloofness – and joy. Also, the use of "raincoat" subtly conveys a hint of dreariness, balancing freedom with reality.

> *So I looked at the scenery,*
> *She read her magazine;*
> *And the moon rose over an open field.*
> *"Kathy, I'm lost", I said,*
> *Though I knew she was sleeping.*
> *"I'm empty and aching and*
> *I don't know why."*

Not sure there's a verse in 1968 that more efficiently captures the mood and feeling of young people. Two teenagers propelled to leave home as a result of political instability, a search for identity, a search to be included, to find like minds – finally getting on the road, feeling that freedom, then experiencing the vastness of America – and suddenly, the feeling of being lost. Simon frames the thought by first commenting on relationships – he's looking out the window at the scenery, while she reads a magazine. Together, but apart. He confides in her about his feelings, but he does so when he knows she's sleeping and cannot hear him. He knows he's "empty and aching", but he doesn't "know why." Self-aware, yet unaware. Classic.

Counting the cars
On the New Jersey Turnpike
They've all come
To look for America,
All come to look for America,
All come to look for America

The last verse hammers the hook – *everyone* is looking for America. If considered quickly, one might conclude that the song is about looking *at* America. Two young people, traveling across a marvelous country. However, Simon alertly uses the word *for*. The young couple is looking *for* America. Because, America is lost, too. Where did America go? What happened to America? While the concept arc of *Bookends* falls a bit short, "America" is one of the most important statements about 1968.

Citing the New Jersey Turnpike, Simon conjures an image of congestion, of typical suburban America, traffic, millions of people that have all "come to look for America." Simon uses the pronoun "they" instead of he or she as in prior verses. Simon is stressing that it's not just the two young teens in the story that are looking for America – it's everyone – everyone is looking for America. With a dramatic musical peak, Simon one last time implores the listener to go and look for America, insinuating that if you're looking for America, you care deeply about America, and its state of disrepair.

The first two tracks on Side 2, "Fakin' It" and "Punky's Dilemma", were tracks that Simon initially wrote for *The Graduate*, but were rejected by Mike Nichols. Both tracks are highly listenable and provide an upbeat template, departing from the solemnness of Side 1. The third track on Side 2 would end up becoming Simon & Garfunkel's biggest hit – "Mrs. Robinson." The track hit #1 on the *Billboard* Hot 100 and finished the year at #9 on the *Billboard* Hot 100. The version of "Mrs. Robinson" that appears on *Bookends* was completed on February 2, 1968 and now serves as the definitive version of the song, as opposed to the more raw version on *The Graduate* soundtrack.

The penultimate track on *Bookends* deserves attention as well. "Hazy Shade of Winter" was recorded in 1966 during the sessions for *Parsley, Sage, Rosemary and Thyme*. Simon & Garfunkel decided not to use the track for the *Parsley* record, but were compelled to include the track on *Bookends*. The substance of the song follows an uncertain, somewhat hopeless unknown, struggling poet. A topic common in Folk and Folk Rock songs of 1965 and 1966, but not so much in 1967 and 1968. Why then did Simon & Garfunkel come back to the song and release it on *Bookends*?

Not surprisingly, given the events of 1968, Simon & Garfunkel perhaps gravitated towards darkness a bit, making the lyrics about winter relevant. The lyrics and, particularly, the refrain, just fit the tone and mood of the United States in early-1968.

> *I look around,*
> *leaves are brown*
> *And the sky*
> *is a hazy shade of winter*
> *Look around,*
> *leaves are brown*

Artists are cognizant of their lyrical choices. In the Spring of 1968, the leaves were actually not brown – they were green. Trees were budding, daffodils and tulips were blooming. Yet, Simon tells us that, in fact, the leaves are brown and the sky is a hazy shade of winter. A metaphor for the condition of America.

Sly & the Family Stone – *Dance to the Music*

Sly & the Family Stone formed in 1967 in San Francisco. Led by Sly Stone, the band included Sly's brother, Freddie Stone, on guitar and their sister, Rose Stone, on keyboards. The band also included Cynthia Robinson on trumpet, Gregg Errico on drums, Jerry Martini on saxophone and Larry Graham on bass. While Booker T. & the M.G.s, an instrumental Blues band from Memphis, is widely considered the first racially integrated "band", Sly & the Family

Stone was the first racially integrated band in the genre of Pop and Rock. Sly & the Family Stone was also the first, or one of the first, gender integrated bands in Pop and Rock.

The creation of a new genre of music is quite rare. As time passes, the feat becomes even more increasingly rare. Ray Charles is credited with the creation of Soul. James Brown is credited with the invention of Funk. Several lay claim to the origin of Rock & Roll, but let's give it to Chuck Berry. Rap is credited to DJ Kool Herc. What about The Byrds and Folk Rock? What about Nirvana or Pearl Jam and Grunge? The latter are examples of sub-genres. A fusion of two established genres. Fusing genres became a tactic in the late-1960s – a creative way to innovate. Still a feat, and historically significant, but a step removed from outright genre creation.

Raised on R&B and Blues, then a DJ in the Bay Area where he played Rock, Blues and Psychedelic Pop, when Sly Stone began to create his own music, he gravitated towards the Soul music of Ray Charles. But, Sly existed in a more turbulent time. A time when passion infiltrated the creative process in a violent manner. Sly was criticized for "over-singing." His passion seemed misplaced in the tender Soul ballads and R&B standards he coveted. Then, in 1965, Sly Stone heard James Brown. After the release of "Papa's Got a Brand New Bag", Sly knew immediately that he, too – had a brand new bag.

San Francisco in 1967 was the epicenter of Psychedelic Rock. While The Grateful Dead, Jefferson Airplane and Quicksilver Messenger Service were not yet household names, nationally, in San Francisco – these bands were as popular and influential as The Beatles. Not surprisingly, Sly Stone was enamored with the Psychedelic sound, as well as the freedom of experience and culture of psychedelic drugs. Accordingly, Sly's first band was named Sly & the Stoners.

The intersection of Soul, Funk, Psychedelic Rock and drugs resulted in Sly's creation of a sub-genre: Psychedelic Soul. While the genre has undergone name changes since 1968, the musical style still very much exists today, embraced over the years by artists such as: Kool & The Gang, Earth, Wind and Fire, Erykah Badu, War, Stevie Wonder, Shuggie Otis and Frank Ocean. Even acts such as The Temptations, The Four Tops, Marvin Gaye and Curtis Mayfield embraced Psychedelic Soul in late-1968 through the mid-1970s. Music critic Joel Selvin famously stated that "there are two types of black music: black music before Sly Stone, and black music after Sly Stone." Marc Coleman of *Rolling Stone* described the music of Sly & the Family Stone as the "bridge between James Brown's bedrock grooves and George Clinton's cosmic slop" (I believe the use of the word "slop" was meant to be endearing).

Sly & the Family Stone's first record, *A Whole New Thing*, received critical acclaim, but sales were miserable. Then, Clive Davis entered the picture. An entire book could be written about how Clive Davis transformed the careers of struggling musicians – it is nothing short of incredible how Davis managed to realize the merit of an artist and understand how best to market and sell the artist. Clive Davis, an executive at the time for CBS Records, caught a Sly & the Family Stone performance in late-1967 and immediately approached Sly Stone. It is unclear exactly what advice Clive Davis provided to Sly Stone, but the general message was to preserve the musical template, but create songs that are "commercially viable."

Davis instructed Sly to submit a Single to him as quickly as possible. Sly Stone reluctantly (according to Sly) sent Davis a rough cut of "Dance to the Music." Floored, Davis and CBS released the track as a Single in February 1968 and the track reached #8 on the *Billboard* Hot 100.

"Dance to the Music" was certainly original. The track featured four lead vocalists, exchanging lead vocals and backing vocals. The core of the song is a funky, Motown-esque bass line from Graham that provided an accessible template. Equally as dominant was a psychedelic, fuzzy Rock guitar riff from Freddie Stone, combined with Gospel-tinged organ playing by Sly Stone. Mix that with

Martini and Robinson on horns and a simple drum back beat from Errico. The result? Well, a new sound.

The music of Sly & the Family Stone has been described as "democratic." Sophisticated music aficionados appreciated the complexity of the rhythms and varied style, while novice music fans were drawn to the energy and appeal of an addictive Pop sensibility.

The remainder of *Dance to the Music* is a bit uneven, but the quality of the album as a whole was less significant than the establishment of a new sound. Sly & the Family Stone will again be featured later in The 1968 Project, with the release of *Life*. As the historical events of 1968 unfolded, Sly Stone will retreat from corporate desired commercialism, and project his views on unity, integration and peace.

The Zombies – *Odessey and Oracle*

Two classic pieces of artistry were released in April 1968 that used the word "odyssey." Well, not exactly. Due to a misspelling by the artist that designed the album cover for The Zombies, the title of the Zombies' album is *Odessey*, not Odyssey. Either way, was it just a coincidence that two renowned pieces of art gravitated to the word "odyssey?" Not sure we'll be able to answer that question but it is interesting that each of The Zombies and, as will be detailed below, Stanley Kubrick, utilized the word "odyssey" in April 1968 to name the foremost creation of their career.

To continue the riff, the story of The Zombies and *Odessey and Oracle* is in fact – an odyssey. In late-1964 and 1965, The Zombies experienced early success after the release of "She's Not There." The track hit #2 on the *Billboard* Hot 100, while the album, *Begin Here*, that featured the hit single climbed to #39 on the *Billboard* Top 200 Albums chart. Very much a "British Invasion" band, The Zombies fused Blues and Rock, much like The Rolling Stones, The Yardbirds, The Kinks, The Hollies, The Animals and, to some extent, The Who. While many of the aforementioned evolved, either embracing

Psychedelic Rock or steadfastly rejecting it, The Zombies seemed to stay caught in the middle.

After the success of *Begin Here* and capitalizing on the popularity of the British Invasion, The Zombies toured extensively. The Zombies, led mainly by Rod Argent on organ and vocals and Colin Blunstone on lead vocals, wrote and released multiple tracks in 1966. The tracks were released as Singles and each failed miserably. In 1967, despite the lack of success, attempting to capitalize on the waning moments of the British Invasion, CBS Records funded the recording of a full length album by The Zombies. Recorded during the Summer of Love, between June and August 1967, the music embraced the psychedelic creativity of 1967, with distinct British attributes. The album was recorded at Abbey Road studios and utilized the very same four track tape machine used on *Sgt Pepper's Lonely Hearts Club Band*. The Zombies insisted that the album be recorded in Mono, rather than the more modern, two channel Stereo.

While The Zombies believed they had created a significant work, CBS Records disagreed. First, CBS required that the record be remixed in Stereo. The Zombies preferred the texture and fullness of the Mono recording, but reluctantly acquiesced. Then, CBS was unable to designate a Single worthy of release ahead of the full album. The Zombies lobbied for "Care of Cell 44." CBS finally agreed and released "Care of Cell 44" in November 1967. The track failed to gain traction, not charting in the US or the UK. Gasping, CBS released "Friends of Mine" as a Single in December 1967 – same result, nothing.

To make matters worse, demand for live performances of The Zombies declined precipitously throughout 1967. Morale was shattered within the band. In late-December 1967, after the failure of "Friends of Mine", The Zombies disbanded. Not surprisingly, CBS decided not to release *Odessey and Oracle*. This is where the story of *Odessey and Oracle* becomes an odyssey. Going from shelved in late-1967 to released in April 1968 to a hit Single in 1969 and, eventually, a ranking of the 100th best album ever recorded (according to a 2003 *Rolling Stone* poll).

Credit for the release of *Odessey and Oracle* is attributed to none other than Al Kooper. The significance of Al Kooper is discussed in The 1965 Project, but in short – Kooper was a session musician for Bob Dylan's landmark *Highway 61 Revisited*. Kooper was hired to play guitar at the recording session, but once Mike Bloomfield, the other session guitarist, plugged in and started running through scales – Kooper quietly packed up his guitar and slid over to the organ. Bloomfield was that good. We'll hear more from both Kooper and Bloomfield later in The 1968 Project, as the two collaborated for one of the most underrated records of 1968.

So, how did Al Kooper influence the release of *Odessey and Oracle*? In early-1968, on a trip to London, Kooper came across an album cover that he found intriguing. He asked whether he could borrow the record and take a listen. The response from CBS was essentially, "you can have it, there's nothing there." Kooper played the album incessantly and became convinced of its merit. In addition to performing, Kooper had recently been hired by Columbia Records as an A&R Representative, charged with finding talent. Kooper met with Clive Davis at CBS and negotiated a deal whereby CBS and Columbia would jointly release the album on a small record label owned by Columbia, Date Records.

Under the direction of Kooper, Date Records released a Single in March 1968, "Time of the Season." The track sold well in 1968, but in March 1969, "Time of the Season" reached #3 on the *Billboard* Hot 100. The song has come to be regarded as a classic – a song that invokes an indelible moment in music and culture. With an almost primal, percussive intro, the track features an odd exhale, or breath, in between each drum line, giving way to Blunstone's high register vocal. Argent sprinkles piano fills, leading to a full band vocal on the chorus. The track takes off during an organ solo by Argent that dictates mood, referencing The Doors and leans Jazz. When the solo ends and the percussion returns, the listener is committed.

Unfortunately, the success of "Time of the Season" didn't come quickly enough for The Zombies. Rod Argent had already formed another band, aptly named Argent, and was experiencing considerable success. In 1972, Argent had a significant hit with the album *All Together Now*, featuring the Single "Hold Your Head Up" (yes, Phish fans – that "Hold Your Head Up"). Blunstone attempted to continue a career in music after the break-up of The Zombies, but experienced little success, eventually obtaining a job as an insurance clerk. Blunstone resurfaced as a solo artist in 1971 and experienced modest success, with several tracks charting in the UK.

As for *Odessey and Oracle*, the album sold well in 1968, but without a touring band to support the record, attention waned. However, beginning in the late-1970s and continuing through the 1990s, a renewed spirit returned to *Odessey and Oracle*. The record became a prime example of a sub-genre known as Baroque Pop, fusing elements of Classical music with Rock and Pop.

Despite decades of critical acclaim and a significant cult following, The Zombies did not reunite until 1997. The five original members of The Zombies performed live for the first time in thirty years in support of a box set, *Zombie Heaven*. In 2001, Argent and Blunstone resurrected The Zombies, booking live shows and recording new material for *As Far As I Can See*, released in 2004. In 2008, to honor the 40th anniversary of the release of *Odessey and Oracle*, The Zombies performed the record live, in its entirety.

The live recording was released in conjunction with a remastered recording of *Odessey and Oracle*. The remastered version possessed one interesting difference from the original version. The Zombies finally got some revenge, as the remastered version was released in Mono.

2001: A Space Odyssey

Directed and produced by Stanley Kubrick, *2001: A Space Odyssey* was released on April 3. Written by Kubrick and Arthur C. Clarke, the film "follows a voyage to Jupiter with the sentient computer, Hal, after the discovery of a mysterious black monolith affecting human evolution" (Wikipedia). Themes of "existentialism, human evolution, technology, artificial intelligence and extraterrestrial life" dominate the narrative, but cinematically – the use of sounds and music instead of dialogue is perhaps the lasting accomplishment of the movie (Wikipedia).

Neil Armstrong would not step foot on the moon until July 20, 1969. In April 1968, there had not yet even been a manned American spaceflight. After three astronauts were killed on board Apollo 1 on January 27, 1967, NASA halted manned missions, favoring test flights and research. Despite the chaotic divide in American politics, the country was very much unified in the pursuit of, and fascination with, space exploration. In 1968, Americans monitored the performance of each test flight and were eager to understand NASA's strategy.

Ultimately, on October 11, 1968, aboard Apollo 7, the first successful manned spaceflight occurred, fueling the societal fascination and energizing the effort to beat the Russians to the moon (commonly referred to as, The Space Race). However, in April 1968, humans in space, the substance of Kubrick's movie – was still a dream, an aspiration. A fiction.

2001: A Space Odyssey finished 1968 as the highest grossing film in North America and was nominated for four Academy Awards, winning one for Visual Effects. While purely fiction in terms of the narrative, Kubrick insisted on utilizing exact replicas of actual space crafts, satellites and planets. Kubrick's depiction of space is considered "scientifically accurate" and his use of special effects in rendering the images has been called "pioneering" (Wikipedia). In addition to the accuracy, the images and scenery created by Kubrick are stunningly beautiful.

That said, of course, the legacy of *2001: A Space Odyssey* might just be the music.

Initially, Kubrick struggled with the notion of sound in the film. Given the extreme care to ensure the scientific accuracy of space and space exploration – the notion of a Simon & Garfunkel song playing in the background while astronauts flew towards Jupiter? Just wasn't going to work. Kubrick determined that only one form of music could match the drama, intensity and intellectualism inherent in the film's script: Classical.

Movies had incorporated Classical music in the past, namely *The Sound of Music* in 1965, but the exclusive use of Classical music as a soundtrack was uncommon. As Kubrick began to film *2001: A Space Odyssey*, he brilliantly realized that several of the scenes should be devoid of dialogue, urging the viewer to focus on the docking of a space ship or the landing of a lunar module or scores of apes dancing on a beach. Yes, weird movie. These scenes were long and, in each case, were accompanied by a distinct Classical piece.

The primary Classical works used by Kubrick were *On the Beautiful Blue Danube* by Johann Strauss and *Also Sprach Zarathustra* by Richard Strauss (Johann and Richard were unrelated). In the final scene of the movie, the protagonist finds himself not in space, but in his bedroom, accompanied by older versions of himself, some dressed in a spacesuit, some in leisure attire, some eating dinner. Then, a black monolith appears at the foot of his bed and as the protagonist reaches for it, he is transformed into a fetus enclosed in a transparent orb of light.

The film ends with the fetus in the transparent orb of light floating beside Earth, with the fetus gazing back at Earth. As the screen turns to black, Kubrick brilliantly employs *Also Sprach Zarathustra* to accompany the closing credits, leaving viewers generally speechless (and likely, confused). Again, weird movie.

The Classical music became inextricably linked to the film and was separately released as a soundtrack later in 1968. The soundtrack reached #21 on the *Billboard* Top 200 Albums chart.

May

May

HISTORY

Little Tet
Paris Peace Talks
The Paris Spring

MUSIC

Creation of Apple Records by The Beatles
The Rolling Stones – "Jumping Jack Flash"
Johnny Cash – *At Folsom Prison*
Quicksilver Messenger Service – *Quicksilver Messenger Service*
Small Faces – *Ogden's Nut*

HISTORY

After the historical morbidity of April, and prior to the heartbreak and fury on the horizon in June, the focus in May returns to the lighter subjects of war, political instability and cultural revolution. Brutal year.

If a silver lining exists, it must be the music. While the music released in May includes a classic Single by The Rolling Stones and the most famous album of Johnny Cash's career, May marks the turning point, the calm before the storm, the last gasp of 1967. After May, we'll focus on classic releases by Pink Floyd, The Doors, The Band, The Grateful Dead, Cream, Jimi Hendrix – and then, Van Morrison, The Beatles, The Kinks, The Rolling Stones.

The cauldron is nearing the brim. And, while the typical analogy might include an image of the cauldron tipping over as a result of each iteration of chaos – a more appropriate visual might be the spontaneous combustion of the cauldron. Not able to absorb any further pain, as the events of May led into June, the cauldron would explode and the toxic, boiling liquid in the cauldron – the product of death and darkness – would spill throughout American culture. Each horrific event from January to June combined to form a toxic plague of tragedy. The product of such horror would materialize in rage, but the initial consequence was a much different liquid – tears. The events of May are a small gasp of air prior to suffocation.

Little Tet

During the earliest hours of May 1, North Vietnamese forces commenced a series of attacks that are commonly referred to as either "Little Tet", the "May Offensive" or "Mini-Tet." Considered "Phase 2" of the Tet Offensive, the North Vietnamese simultaneously targeted 119 sites controlled by the South Vietnamese and American forces. While the South Vietnamese and Americans were surprised by Phase 1 of the Tet Offensive in January, such would not be the case in May.

After the Tet Offensive, President Johnson demanded that intelligence efforts be improved and data be analyzed on a regular basis, including enemy troop movement. Beginning in mid-April, intelligence reports suggested that the North Vietnamese forces were mobilizing. However, the mobilization depicted small, isolated troop movements, rather than full battalion relocation. General Abrams was briefed on the intelligence data and ordered all American forces to prepare for a widespread, fractured attack and instructed each of his commanding officers to develop an intercept strategy, with the goal of attacking the advancing North Vietnamese units, rather than simply defending territories by waiting for an insurgency.

As North Vietnam attacked on May 1, all but 13 of the North Vietnamese units were intercepted and either captured, killed or forced to retreat. Each of the 13 units that eluded detection converged on Saigon. In 1968, Saigon was the most populated city in Vietnam and was also the primary location of senior American governmental officials. Perhaps more important, Saigon was the home of the one group of individuals that most dramatically influenced the course of the Vietnam War – the media.

As North Vietnamese forces attacked Saigon with grenades and gunfire, American soldiers responded in defense, while journalists and photographers sent media reports and images of the bloodshed back to the United States.

Strategically, the North Vietnamese forces occupied the Y-Bridge, a critical access point for commercial and military supply. The North Vietnamese also overtook American forces at the Tan Son Nhur Air Force Base. The logistical strategy of the North Vietnamese obstructed the ability of the American forces to react to the insurgency. General Abrams ordered additional troop deployments to assist. By May 12, all of the North Vietnamese units were forced out of Saigon. However, the combined death total – including American soldiers, South Vietnamese soldiers, North Vietnamese soldiers and South Vietnamese civilians – was in excess of 3,000, with an additional 7,500 injured. Several of the American soldiers killed at the Tan Son Nhur Air Force Base were at the base preparing for a trip home to their families, having completed their deployment.

The loss of life was paramount, but the consequence of Little Tet in terms of American perception was dramatic. After a slight reprieve from the tragedy of the Vietnam War in March and April, including President Johnson's (too late) plea for peace, after Little Tet, the American people again demanded peace. Demonstrations spiked in early-May and media outlets covered the conflict on a nightly basis. The notion that the American forces defeated the Tet Offensive and had forced the North Vietnamese toward diplomacy and peace – such a notion was no longer credible and no longer rhetoric that the American people could (or would) embrace.

In some respects, from my research, it seems as though Little Tet provided the perfect recipe for America to transition from grief to passion after the assassination of MLK. Newspaper headlines almost universally changed from three weeks of racial tension and mourning to anti-war demonstrations and politics. The emotional roller coaster of 1968 was unstoppable. Each event, each touchstone of controversy possessed an exponential amount of energy and vitriol.

Students reacted. Liberal politicians reacted. The anti-war movement coalesced from a divided minority to a unified majority. Demonstrations were coordinated and impactful. The anti-war movement transformed from a political nuisance to the most coveted political demographic.

Paris Peace Talks

Success or failure in Vietnam had become President Johnson's legacy. A negotiated, productive, peaceful withdrawal from Vietnam prior to the end of his Presidency would certainly have resulted in historical gain.

Despite the coordination displayed by the North Vietnamese during the Tet Offensive and Little Tet, the North Vietnamese government

134

was highly decentralized, both militaristically and politically. The political leadership of North Vietnam desired a peaceful resolution, motivated by gaining territories and maintaining a governmental regime. The North Vietnamese military leaders sensed that the United States was reeling and were confident in the ability to defeat the Americans on the battlefield.

North Vietnamese soldiers were instructed to fight until all South Vietnamese territories were under the control of the North Vietnamese, at the same time the political leaders were discussing a peace treaty, with the first meeting set for May 10 in Paris.

Not surprisingly, as the events of Little Tet unfolded on May 1, just 9 days before the Paris Peace Talks, President Johnson was incensed. The American people skewered President Johnson for attempting to negotiate with such an untrustworthy foe. The American people demanded an immediate withdrawal, rather than a negotiation. Nonetheless, President Johnson continued with his goal of negotiating his way out of Vietnam.

As American forces completed their defense of Little Tet by ridding Saigon of the remaining North Vietnamese soldiers, on May 10, President Johnson dispatched U.S. ambassador at-large W. Averell Harriman to meet the North Vietnamese representative, Xuan Thuy, in Paris. Coincidentally or not, the meeting would juxtapose with the most turbulent and culturally relevant week in French history.

The Paris Spring

Political and cultural unrest was not isolated to the United States. The revolution percolating in the United States was the consequence, and confluence, of several factors – many of which existed in other countries. In the early-1960s, the United States and the dominant countries of Western Europe remained affected by the aftermath of World War II. Democracy prevailed due in large part to the enormous sacrifice of the "Greatest Generation" – the children of the

135

Great Depression that in early adulthood defended the United States and its allies.

Culturally, the United States cherished the veterans of World War II. American society immortalized middle and lower class veterans just the same as the celebrities that served – Ted Williams, Joe DiMaggio, Joe Louis, Mel Brooks, Henry Fonda and, to some extent, Elvis Presley. The American people even elected Dwight D. Eisenhower as President of the United States, a decorated General of the United States Army in World War II. American culture was drenched in post-World War II prosperity.

The sentiment in Western Europe was quite different. The defeated countries of Germany and Italy were understandably reeling – militaristically, but more damaging – ideologically. The United Kingdom, France and Spain, were crushed, physically, but a moral and psychological will to rebuild was pervasive, requiring a collaborative effort of the lower, middle and upper classes. Such a nationalistic spirit unified Western Europe, and to some extent homogenized a once wonderfully diverse cross-section of cultures.

This sentiment and effort continued throughout the late-1940s, 1950s and early-1960s. By 1965, Western Europe had sufficiently returned to economic dominance, with political stability and a reinforced military. A 20-year old young adult in 1968, born in 1948, did not exist in a time plagued by World War II, and barely had a recollection of the post-World War II rebuild. The parents of that 20-year old, however, lived through the horrors of World War II and sacrificed their adult life to return Western Europe to its former glory. Understandably, the generational gap facilitated a tremendous divide. The motivations and desires of young adults diverged, rather dramatically, from the aspirations of their parents.

Today in Paris, "1968" is symbolic – cherished in a way. The cultural revolution that began in May was cause agnostic. Students fought for political freedom. Factory workers fought for economic equality. Minorities fought for equality. Different causes, same fundamental right. Each fought for a voice. The students, as they so often do, initiated the uprising.

Similar in many respects to the "Occupy" movement of 2011 in the United States, students at the University of Paris at Nanterre organized peaceful protests against capitalism, consumerism and traditional conservative institutions, including the government of France. The University of Paris was a government-controlled institution (similar in the United States to a "State School"). Fearing a more widespread movement, the French government ordered administrators at Nanterre to close the University until the students agreed to return to class and cease the demonstration. The administrators also suspended the students leading the demonstration and threatened expulsion.

While the student demonstration may have eventually evolved into a movement, the government's reaction was the action that eventually "brought the entire economy of France to a virtual halt." On May 3, after news of the government's attempt to suppress speech at Nanterre, students at the University of the Sorbonne commenced another demonstration. The Sorbonne demonstration, albeit peaceful, included an occupation of the campus administration building. Police were instructed to "retake" the administration building, and did so – with force.

On May 6, close to 20,000 students and teachers organized a march from the center of Paris to the Sorbonne, in protest of the police brutality and arrest of students. As the demonstration reached the administration building at the Sorbonne, without warning, the police charged, attacking the marchers with batons. The students and teachers responded by throwing rocks at the police and fighting back with their hands and feet. After an hour of chaos, the police fired tear gas into the crowd, neutralizing the demonstration. Thousands were injured and hundreds were arrested.

The next day, over 50,000 people gathered in the Latin Quarter in Paris to protest the French government's treatment of the students and the alarming lack of respect for free speech and non-violent demonstration. In hindsight, the French government might have been able to quell the spread of revolution – but, the government again reacted with force (echoing the theme of 1968). Police and military personnel were instructed to attack and arrest the demonstrators. This time, though, the demonstrators were more prepared. As the police attacked, the demonstrators fought back – with sticks and clubs. When the police turned to tear gas, the demonstrators turned to Molotov cocktails. The Latin Quarter was a war zone.

The news articles and historical accounts of the Paris riots are interesting in that the accounts are ominously devoid of a central theme, or a demand. What did the students and youth in Paris actually desire, what did they want from the government? Posters included the phrases "Be Realistic, Demand the Impossible" and "All Power to the Imagination." One critic of the movement described the student leaders as "irresponsible utopianists who wanted to destroy the consumer society." While not entirely crystallized in May, the youth uprising signaled an importation of the liberal, counterculture movement that swept the United States in 1967. No specific motive, rather a general anti-authoritative disposition. Beginning in May, the youth of Paris officially had a voice, directly as a result of revolt and directly as a result of the tenor of 1968.

Just as the French government compromised with the students and youth, agreeing to drop all charges against the arrested students and provide for greater youth independence, another mistreated group of French citizens took action. The large middle, or working, class in the United Kingdom and France desired similar freedom and independence. In the two decades immediately after World War II, the upper, middle and lower classes of the United Kingdom and France unified to physically rebuild infrastructure and community. Setting aside the divisions of wealth. The effort was historically successful, as the decimated region regained strength.

By 1965, the United Kingdom, France and much of Western Europe had returned to economic stability and growth. Unfortunately, the once economically unified countries of the United Kingdom and France reverted to a divisive class system. The middle class was again relegated to a position of inferiority, lacking a political voice, and experiencing economic stagnation. After several years of decline, the middle class would no longer remain idle – specifically in France, the middle class would embrace a fundamental tenet and strategy of 1968 – revolt. Public protest and demonstration. The spirit of 1968 was infectious, possibly an infection.

On May 14, factory workers at the Sud Aviation Company initiated a strike, locking management inside their offices and shutting down the plant. The workers demanded higher pay and safer working conditions. The following day, workers at the Renault Company initiated a strike. As word of the working class uprising spread throughout France, a half dozen additional strikes were initiated. By May 16, fifty factories were occupied by factory workers, amounting to 200,000 workers on strike.

On May 17, students from the Sorbonne gathered at various factories to support the striking workers. The spirit of rebellion had coalesced. Workers refused to negotiate with factory owners and government officials. The strike became a movement. An estimated ten million workers were on strike by May 18, representing two-thirds of the French workforce. What was once a relatively small workforce strike, suddenly seemed like a civil war.

The workers then seized the National Theatre in Paris and set fire to the Paris Stock Exchange. While the students may not have had formal demands, the workers certainly did. The workers demanded the resignation of President Charles de Gaulle and aggressive wage and hour improvements. de Gaulle refused to resign and rejected the wage increases. Rather than negotiate, de Gaulle mobilized the French military to control the insurgency. Finally, de Gaulle announced that an interim Presidential election would be held on June 23 to determine whether de Gaulle should remain in power. The workers returned to work.

Ironically, or maybe – not surprisingly, the political consequence of the Paris uprising was immaterial. President de Gaulle prevailed in the June election and maintained power. The violent nature of the demonstrations, the images of chaos and the lack of a consistent, clear desire of the revolution cut against the movement. French citizens may have identified with the movement, but at the ballot box – voted for stability, tradition and, ultimately, peace.

Through protest and congregation, the workers obtained higher wages, safer working conditions and announced their presence as a voting class. Similarly, the students and the younger generation in Paris established themselves as culturally relevant, both artistically and expressively.

According to Alain Geismar, one of the leaders of the movement, "the movement succeeded as a social revolution, not a political one." The protests and demonstrations facilitated songs, art in the form of graffiti, paintings and movies, along with slogans that would be embraced for decades. "May 68" is considered to be the "moral turning point in the history" of France and served notice to the world that cultural revolutions were not isolated to the United States.

MUSIC

Creation of Apple Records by The Beatles

Let's start with John Lennon's description of Apple Records, or at least the motivation behind the creation of Apple Records: "It's a business concerning records, films and electronics. We want to set up a system whereby people who just want to make a film about anything don't have to go on their knees in somebody's office." Lennon advertised that "anybody with a good idea could get funding" to make a record. An example of The Beatles espousing socially conscious business practices?

Well, not really. Based on research, interviews and investigation, music journalist Douglas Wolk determined that "the idea behind

Apple was a tax dodge. The top tax rate in England at that time was enormous." Lennon would later admit, "we talked to our accountants [and] we realized we could either give the money to the government or we could put it into a business." So, the band decided to create a record label, including a recording studio – to record new material for The Beatles, but also to produce records by other artists.

Initially, Apple Records was a massive success – not financially, though. Apple Records became a mecca – a destination. Musicians (and fans) flocked to the studio and attempted to gain entry. Despite the hysteria, records got made. After opening its doors in May, Apple released its first Single in September: "Hey Jude" by The Beatles. Next, the debut release from James Taylor was recorded and released in December 1968 and Apple also signed the incredibly popular Modern Jazz Quartet.

Then, The Beatles broke up in 1970. The solo projects of each of John, Paul, George and Ringo were recorded at Apple – but, largely, Apple Records existed to bring lawsuits against distributors and record companies, regarding royalty disputes and distribution rights. Apple Records famously sued Apple Computer over trademark infringement.

Fast forward to the present. Apple Records is far less litigious and not only has continued to release music, but Apple Records has provided a template. Apple Records created the model of musicians recording and releasing their own music, as well as spotting talent and recording the music of other musicians. This template is rampant in today's music industry. Perhaps the best illustrations are Jack White's Third Man Records and Jay-Z's Roc Nation.

We will get back to "Hey Jude" in September, then cover the landmark *The White Album* in November.

The Rolling Stones – "Jumping Jack Flash"

Before diving into the Single, "Jumping Jack Flash", it is important to contextualize The Rolling Stones in May 1968. Debuting in 1964 with cover renditions of Blues standards, The Rolling Stones catapulted into the public's conscious in 1965 with the hit, "(I Can't Get No) Satisfaction", then "The Last Time" and "Get Off Of My Cloud." In 1966, The Rolling Stones released *Aftermath*, featuring "Mother's Little Helper" and "Under My Thumb." Then, in early-1967 the band released *Between the Buttons*, featuring "Let's Spend the Night Together" and "Ruby Tuesday." *Between the Buttons* reached #3 on the *Billboard* Top 200 Albums chart, with "Ruby Tuesday" reaching #1 on the *Billboard* Hot 100.

Certainly, a nice string of hits – but, over the same period, the chief rival to The Rolling Stones, The Beatles, released *Help!*, *Rubber Soul*, *Revolver* and *Sgt. Pepper's Lonely Hearts Club Band*. The Beatles were ahead of The Rolling Stones in album sales, but possibly of greater importance, The Beatles were ahead of The Rolling Stones in popularity and social importance. The Beatles teased Psychedelic Rock on *Rubber Soul*, then embraced Psychedelic Rock on *Revolver*, finally, perfecting (and exploiting) the genre on *Sgt. Pepper's*. In 1967, it was time for The Rolling Stones to dip a toe into the colorful, magical psychedelic river.

On December 8, 1967, The Rolling Stones released *Their Satanic Majesties Request*. The album received "mixed reviews", which is a nice way of saying that nobody liked it. Utilizing studio effects, drug references and majestic imagery, The Rolling Stones abandoned the Blues in an attempt to contend with *Sgt. Pepper's*. In short, they failed quite famously.

Let us not fault The Rolling Stones, though. The entire world was swept up in the brilliance of psychedelics. Even the coolest, baddest, hippest band in the land – The Rolling Stones – succumbed to the excesses of 1967. But, as we have seen with many of the greats – The Rolling Stones would realize the error of their way, shed the

142

psychedelic impulses and cut through the haze with a return to Rock and Blues in 1968.

According to Keith Richards, he and Mick Jagger wrote the lyrics to "Jumping Jack Flash" while staying at Richards' country house in early-1968. As Richards recalls, he and Mick were awoken by the sound of a gardener mowing the lawn. Mick asked Keith about the noise and Keith explained, "oh, that's Jack – Jumping Jack." Apparently, that nugget led to the pair writing the lyrics.

Frankly, the lyrics are quite secondary – as the star of "Jumping Jack Flash" is definitely the guitar. The track opens with guitar chords that certainly signal Rock, but after 16 seconds, Mick calls out "1-2" and the band drops into a driving, swampy Blues groove, leading to the first verse and then the backup vocals join on the chorus. The guitar lick is simply addictive.

In describing how he obtained the guitar sound on "Jumping Jack Flash", Keith recounted, "I used a Gibson Hummingbird acoustic tuned to open D. Open D or open E, which is the same thing – same intervals – but it would be slackened down some for D. Then there was a capo on it, to get that really tight sound. And there was another guitar over the top of that, but tuned to Nashville tuning. I learned that from somebody in George Jones' band in San Antonio in 1964. The high strung guitar was an acoustic, too. Both acoustics were put through a Philips cassette recorder. Just jam the mic right in the guitar and play it back through an extension speaker." Keith is a real gem.

After its release, Brian Jones viewed "Jumping Jack Flash" as "getting back to the funky, essential essence" of The Rolling Stones. Jagger stated in 1995 that "Jumping Jack Flash" was a reaction to "all of the acid of *Satanic Majesties*. It's about having a hard time and getting out. Just a metaphor for getting out of all the acid things." Continuing the theme of The 1968 Project, The Rolling Stones were revolting – revolting even against themselves – rejecting 1967 and taking action, returning to the Blues, but incorporating the fury and rage of 1968.

Amid the political chaos, war and death, the public embraced the harder Rock sound. "Jumping Jack Flash" hit #1 in the UK and reached #3 on the *Billboard* Hot 100. "Jumping Jack Flash" remains the only song that The Rolling Stones have played on every single tour since its release in 1968, making it the most played song in the band's catalog.

"Jumping Jack Flash" revived the band's devotion to Rock and provided the template for a sound and an attitude that would materialize in one of the greatest four album stretches in the history of Rock: *Beggar's Banquet* in 1968, *Let It Bleed* in 1969, *Sticky Fingers* in 1971 and *Exile on Main Street* in 1972. The pinnacle of the band's recording career began in May 1968, thanks to an English gardener. Chaos and Evil would become images that The Rolling Stones would graciously adorn for the next five decades.

Johnny Cash – *At Folsom Prison*

Prior to 1968, Johnny Cash was a Country music superstar, releasing 26 albums. However, Cash experienced little success among Pop and Rock audiences. Cash's 1965 release, *Orange Blossom Special*, received acclaim from mass media critics, largely as a result of Cash covering three Bob Dylan tunes, but the record only received modest consumer attention. In 1968, though, Johnny Cash would become a household name.

Johnny Cash's life story is captured brilliantly in the movie, *I Walk the Line*, so we are not going to dive into the details of Cash's life (go watch the movie). But in short, after traveling to Memphis in search of the record producer Sam Phillips, Cash released several Country hits in the late-1950s, including "I Walk the Line" in 1957. After a decade of touring, drug abuse and divorce, Johnny Cash was searching, musically.

Ironically, as Cash searched for career success, his personal life was stable in 1968. Recently married to June Carter, Cash was also clean – not using drugs, avoiding arrest and, by all accounts, attending Church and remaining faithful to his wife. Cash approached Columbia Records about performing live at a prison and recording the show for a live release. Columbia Records had rejected the idea several times in years past, but due to management changes – and a desire to capitalize on Johnny Cash and June Carter's publicity – Columbia Records agreed to the performance. The result would be the highest selling release of Cash's career, reaching #15 on the *Billboard* Top 200 Albums chart.

Joined by June Carter and Carl Perkins, Johnny Cash took the stage at Folsom State Prison in California, famously opening the show with the words "Hello, I'm Johnny Cash", then rolling into "Folsom Prison Blues", a song Cash wrote and released in 1957. Columbia Records released the live version "Folsom Prison Blues" as a Single and the track reached #32 on the *Billboard* Hot 100, Cash's first Top 40 hit since 1964.

Cash performed two separate sets at Folsom State Prison. Different audiences, but consisting mainly of the same tracks (the only material difference was the inclusion of "I Got Stripes" in the second performance). The album has countless precious attributes. First and foremost, Cash's voice is exceptionally strong, not simply in tone and volume, but in conviction and purpose. The carefully crafted set is not entirely raucous and upbeat. Cash crushes several ballads, including "I Still Miss Someone", "Long Black Veil" and "Send a Picture of Mother."

The beauty of *At Folsom Prison*, though, is the feeling of being present. Cash's set featured several prison-related songs, such as "Folsom Prison Blues", "Dark as a Dungeon", "25 Minutes to Go" and "The Wall." Cash doesn't necessarily glorify prison life, but he most certainly identifies with it. Equally as important to the success of *At Folsom Prison* is the recording.

In 1968, releasing live records was a strategy for artists and labels to capitalize on a musician's popularity without the need for (or cost of) a new album. Most live records, however, were recorded at a theatre or small club…not a prison. The artist would play a track, the audience would applaud in between tracks. The artist might address the crowd with some form of short banter, but the listener could envision the scene – a band on a stage, probably a curtain backdrop, possibly velvet, low lit with overhead stage lighting, a seated crowd of everyday Americans. That was the visual for almost every live record.

At Folsom Prison is quite different – the recording has an uncanny ability to convey the image of Johnny Cash standing on a makeshift stage at a maximum security prison. The banter in between songs is priceless. One announcement asked that a certain prisoner report to "reception." Another announcement by a lieutenant (that received a series of boos) asked that a prisoner report to "custody" and then directed the prisoners on how to exit the room (which again was met with boos).

Cash himself commented on the quality of the prison's drinking water, noting that it was brown and probably ran off of "Luther's boots." Cash queried whether everything was served in "tin cups?" Equally as impactful, the recording captures the audience's whistles, chatter, applause and energy, painting a razor sharp illustration of the prison setting. The listener can see the inmates, their uniforms, their faces.

Columbia Records promoted the lead Single, "Folsom Prison Blues" quite vigorously. However, just as the Single started to trend on the *Billboard* Hot 100, history in 1968 once again intervened. We'll cover this in greater detail in the next chapter, but on June 5, Robert F. Kennedy was assassinated in California. Radio stations, almost unanimously, decided to not play "Folsom Prison Blues" due to the lyric "I shot a man in Reno/Just to watch him die."

Columbia Records asked Cash to edit the track and remove the line. Cash rejected the request, until he realized that it wasn't a "request", it was an order, a directive. While Cash maintained creative control, Columbia Records maintained the promotion budget and the funds to support Cash's concert tour and his future studio work. Cash relented and edited the song. The edited version hit #1 on the *Billboard* Country Singles chart and, as mentioned, trended to #32 on the *Billboard* Hot 100.

The success of "Folsom Prison Blues" Single fueled *At Folsom Prison* to reach #1 on the *Billboard* Top Country Albums chart and #13 on the *Billboard* Top 200 Albums chart. Al Aroniwitz of *Life* stated that Cash sang like "someone who has grown up believing he is one of the people that these songs are about." Fredrick Danker of *Sing Out!* noted that the album is "structured as an aural experience." So many of the critic reviews praise the music as well as the setting/prison experience.

The success of *At Folsom Prison* launched the second chapter of Cash's career, or according to Cash, "that's where things really got started for me again." ABC signed Cash to a television contract, broadcasting several seasons of *The Johnny Cash Show* – an interview and musical performance evening program. Cash returned to a prison in 1969, recording a performance at the San Quentin State Prison. The album, *At San Quentin*, became Cash's first album to hit #1 on the *Billboard* Top 200 Albums chart, featuring the #2 hit "A Boy Named Sue."

At Folsom Prison is an artifact that doesn't age. A distinct energy and rawness exists in the recording that possesses an eternal characteristic. *Rolling Stone* ranked *At Folsom Prison* at #83 on its Greatest Albums list, while *Blender* listed the album at #63 and *Time* listed the album in the Top 100. The accolades are universal.

Quicksilver Messenger Service – *Quicksilver Messenger Service*

In 1966, The Beatles introduced the masses to Psychedelic Rock with "Tomorrow Never Knows", the final track on the incredibly popular *Revolver*. Truth is, Psychedelic Rock had been germinating in San Francisco in 1965. Music genres seem to be either the (1) product of circumstance or (2) synthesis of existing genres. An example of circumstance was the early iterations of the Blues, reflecting the persecution and discrimination against African Americans. Similarly, Folk was created by a class of Americans that lacked a political voice, during a time of great economic turmoil. Genres borne from circumstance.

As discussed previously, an example of the synthesis of genres, Hip Hop fused R&B and Funk. More prevalent is the synthesis of genres to create sub-genres. Examples include Folk Rock, Alt-Country (fusing Rock and Country), Jazz Fusion (fusing Jazz and Rock).

So, what genre did Rock combine with to create Psychedelic Rock? Folk? Nope. Country? Definitely not. Jazz? Not really, but a little bit. Blues? Nah. Then, what? Psychedelic Rock was the product of circumstance, not the combination of genres. The circumstance was Drugs.

Endeavoring to cover the history of LSD and its impact on music in the late-1960s is not the motive of this book. That said, drugs and in particular, LSD, had such a profound impact on music in 1967 and 1968 that the topic must be touched. So, in the general context of Quicksilver Messenger Service, let's briefly cover LSD.

Lysergic acid diethylamide (or LSD) was first created by Albert Hoffman in Switzerland in 1936. Hoffman was a chemist, aiming to isolate a blood stimulant. In 1943, Hoffman accidentally consumed the compound and immediately discovered psychedelic attributes. In 1947, LSD was introduced as a medication for certain psychiatric disorders, including schizophrenia, depression and alcoholism. The drug was produced by Sandoz Pharmaceutical under the trade name

Delysid. Patients experienced relief from their psychiatric condition, but often became intolerant to the prescribed low dosage. As patients (and doctors) increased the dosage, the psychedelic and mind altering properties became well known.

In the early-1950s, as the United States and the Soviet Union were embroiled in the early stages of the Cold War, the Central Intelligence Agency (CIA) began experimenting with LSD, hoping to utilize the drug to solicit information from captured enemy soldiers, essentially – chemical warfare. To understand the capability of LSD, the CIA conducted a series of studies that tested the effect of LSD on young adults, including students. The CIA's testing program was called MKULTRA.

While the CIA became more and more convinced that LSD would not be helpful in soliciting confidential information from an unwilling discloser, the young people that were testing the LSD became more and more convinced that LSD would be helpful in having fun. The more testing the CIA conducted, the more young people were exposed to LSD and the more the drug spread into recreational use. Remember, at this point in time LSD was legal.

By 1960, certain scientists, professors and intellectual leaders advocated the use of LSD, including Timothy Leary, a Harvard psychologist, and Aldous Huxley, a noted author. Famously, Leary urged young folks to "turn on, tune in and drop out." The verb "drop" is a reference to dropping acid. In 1963 and 1964, the use of LSD was still an underground phenomenon, used in hip, art communities and academia. By 1965, the use of LSD was widespread in urban environments, culminating in communal gatherings, known in San Francisco and Los Angeles as The Acid Tests.

The Acid Tests were fantastically idyllic. Well intentioned. Endorsed and organized by Ken Kesey, the author of *One Flew Over the Cuckoo's Nest* and *Sometimes a Great Notion*, an Acid Test was a traveling experience that featured a house band, typically The Grateful Dead, and a large batch of LSD, sometimes referred to as

Kool Aid. Admission was free and young people came from far and wide to experience the effects of LSD and the counterculture scene. Everyone, including Kesey and The Grateful Dead, were under the influence of LSD. All of this was legal.

Given the circumstances, the bands involved in the scene adopted a stretched out experimental form of Rock, which allowed for noise, illusion and most of all, weirdness. Given the manner in which LSD was entwined with the creation of Psychedelic Rock, the bands of San Francisco received immediate national attention. The initial focus was on The Grateful Dead and Jefferson Airplane. However, several other bands existed that were equally as influential to the counterculture scene – mainly, Quicksilver Messenger Service and Big Brother and the Holding Company (featuring Janis Joplin).

Stemming from the popularity and promotion of the "Summer of Love" in 1967, many bands adopted Psychedelic Rock as a commercial endeavor. However, for the genre's inventors, Psychedelic Rock was not a fad or a fleeting ploy, it was a style of music, bordering on a way of life. Initially, Quicksilver Messenger Service was as popular in the Bay Area as The Grateful Dead and Jefferson Airplane, but drugs, jail and death prevented Quicksilver Messenger Service from achieving national stardom. Released in May, Quicksilver Messenger Service's debut self-titled record remains an essential listen and represents the core of Psychedelic Rock.

In 1965, Dino Valenti had a distinct vision of the band he wanted to create. Needing an ace lead guitarist, Valenti went straight to John Cipolina. Cipolina was the most hip, creative and musically talented guitarist on the scene. According to Cipolina, Valenti described a band that would "have wireless guitars [and] leather jackets. We were going to have leather jackets made with hooks that we could hook these wireless instruments right into. And we were gonna have these chicks, backing rhythm sections that were gonna dress like American Indians with real short little dresses on and they were gonna have tambourines and the clappers in the tambourines were going to be silver coins."

While that might sound a bit absurd, in San Francisco in 1965, Cipolina immediately thought, "this guy is gonna happen and…set the world on its ear." The very next day, Valenti was arrested for possession of marijuana and spent the next two years in jail. Fortunately, just prior to Valenti's abrupt departure, he had organized a high quality group of musicians. Along with Cipolina, Valenti had recruited Gary Duncan on guitar and vocals, David Freiberg on bass and Greg Elmore on drums.

The hallmark of Psychedelic Rock was creativity. The hallmark of creativity was diversity. A confluence of musical influences was the seed. Drugs may well have been the water or the sunlight, but the origin of Psychedelic Rock was the fusion of various unrelated music genres. Most purveyors of Psychedelic Rock previously studied either Folk, Bluegrass, Classical or Jazz.

Quicksilver Messenger Service had resisted signing with a record label, opting to play shows (a business model that is relevant today). As a result, when Quicksilver Messenger Service finally went into the studio in late-1967 to record their debut record, they brought a "live" sound. The lyrics are not substantive, but the instrumentation is quite progressive. The opening track, "Pride of Man", is basic Psychedelic Rock, but consistent with most tracks, a longer than typical guitar solo is placed in the middle of the track. While Hendrix and Clapton would have taken the opportunity to rage, Cipolina displayed his lean towards melody and Jazz. Such a style would define the sound of Quicksilver Messenger Service and influence the likes of The Grateful Dead. Melody over power. Full band interaction and communication over a soloist. The beginnings of the "Jam Band."

If you are unable to hear the melodic tone of the guitar solo on "Pride of Man", you will certainly be able to detect the style on "Gold and Silver." The intro is played by Duncan and sets forth a Jazz canvas that Elmore (drums) and Cipolina utilize to craft a defining piece of music. Elmore rides the hi-hat in true Jazz form, but Cipolina tweaks out a lead guitar solo that is drenched in Rock, but somehow retains the melodic qualities of the canvas. The middle of the "jam" (the track is a seven minute instrumental) features Duncan on guitar layering Spanish licks over the Jazz chords. Quite a guitar extravaganza. Check it out.

The closing track, "The Fool", is a 12 minute Psychedelic Rock journey that includes periods of vocals and noise. It's not entirely pleasant, frankly, as the vocals (by Duncan) are off key and seem highly unnecessary. While I cannot recommend "Gold and Silver" enough, I can recommend skipping "The Fool."

So what happened to Quicksilver Messenger Service? They suffered the fate of most bands of the late-1960s. The culture of drugs and experimentation led to Duncan being hospitalized for drug abuse in 1969. Coincidentally, Dino Valenti was released from jail in late-1969 and (re)joined the band on guitar and lead vocals. The band experienced some success, but Valenti began to express himself as the leader of the band, which prompted Cipolina's departure. Freiberg was jailed for possession of marijuana in 1971.

After a brief full-band reunion in 1975, along with Nicky Hopkins (the ace session pianist that played with The Rolling Stones, The Kinks and The Beatles), the band released *Solid Silver*. While the record is actually a decent listen, it experienced very little commercial success. The band officially dissolved in 1979.

Lack of success notwithstanding, *Quicksilver Messenger Service* represents an essential example of Psychedelic Rock in 1968.

As for LSD, as the recreational popularity of the drug grew, so did the attention paid to it by the government. In 1967, the Federal government of the United States banned the use and production of LSD and deemed the substance an illegal narcotic. We'll revisit the influence and effect of LSD in the context of the 1968 release of Tom Wolfe's masterpiece, The Electric Kool-Aid Acid Test.

Small Faces – *Ogden's Nut*

You always hear, "no, not Faces, the *Small* Faces." What's the difference? Kind of the same members, right? Both are British bands? Well, the difference is quite significant. The following will briefly lay out the background on Faces and the Small Faces, and discuss one of the most heralded releases of 1968, *Ogden's Nut Gone Flake.*

The Small Faces were formed in East London in 1965 (yet another band that formed in 1965) by Steve Marriott, Ronnie Lane, Kenney Jones and Jimmy Winston. In 1966, Ian McLagan replaced Winston on keyboards. Initially, the Small Faces were members of the Mod Scene, an underground music scene in London that centered on art, style and modern tendencies, as opposed to the more traditional, grungy Blues and Rock scene championed by The Yardbirds, The Kinks and The Rolling Stones. Mod groups wore tailored suits and rode Italian motor scooters. The Mod Scene was also publicly against drugs. The Who were the most dominant Mod band in London in 1965 and 1966.

As Rock gave way to Psychedelic Pop in 1967, both in the United States and the UK, bands were forced to make a choice: embrace Psychedelic Pop or stay true to musical roots? The Rolling Stones jumped into Psychedelic Pop, chasing The Beatles, then reverted to Rock. The Who stuck to Rock. Cream and Jimi Hendrix incorporated elements of psychedelia into Rock, but largely avoided the temptation of Psychedelic Pop. The Small Faces dove head first into the pool of Psychedelic Pop.

After two years of unsuccessfully covering James Brown and other traditional R&B artists, the Small Faces, like many others in 1967, turned to drugs. Mainly using marijuana, the Small Faces began writing their own material and experimented in the studio. The band released a self-titled album in 1967 that featured several veiled references to drugs and drug dealers, which somehow eluded a fairly rigid censorship impediment in the UK. The album was critically acclaimed, but achieved little commercial success.

In August 1967, on the heels of the "Summer of Love", the Small Faces had a hit, as "Itchycoo Park" reached #16 on the *Billboard* Hot 100 and #3 in the UK. The track begins with a strummed acoustic guitar and organ fills, leading into a catchy chorus of "It's all too beautiful", then a psychedelic interlude using a flanger (guitar effect), a lyric of "get high" and then, repeat, repeat. Classic example of Psychedelic Pop in 1967. Everything is beautiful, everyone is getting high, having fun – while the world is slowly crumbling. Yeah, that was 1967.

After experiencing commercial success, the Small Faces were not about to abandon the template in 1968 and return to Rock. The Small Faces doubled down and started work on *Ogden's Nut Gone Flake*, a concept album (of course). The decision paid off, as *Ogden's Nut* is considered a classic studio album, reaching #1 in the UK and remaining at #1 for six consecutive weeks in 1968 (among stiff competition). In the United States, however, perhaps as a result of the darkness and depression engulfing American citizens as a result of the Vietnam War and the assassination of MLK, *Ogden's Nut* only reached #159 on the *Billboard* Top 200 Albums chart.

Ogden's Nut features six original songs on Side 1 and a narrated psychedelic fairy tale on Side 2. The tracks on Side 1 are solid, if a bit overproduced, using strings and horn accents – but, several of the tracks are quite good ("Song of a Baker" is a prime example). Then, on Side 2, it seems as though the drugs took over.

Side 2 recounts the story of Happiness Stan. Now, my tolerance for nonsense is notably low, but I do have the ability to recognize creativity and, even if my distaste is evident, I am able to praise accomplishment. That said, Side 2 of *Ogden's Nut* is a real challenge.

The tracks on Side 2, along with interspersed narration, tell the story of Happiness Stan's "quest to find the missing half of the moon, after seeing a half-moon in the sky one night. Along the way, Stan saves a fly from starvation and in gratitude, the insect tells him of someone who can answer his question about the moon and also tell him the philosophy of life." The fly then grows to a gigantic size and Happiness Stan climbs on the fly and "takes a psychedelic journey to the cave of Mad John the Hermit", who explains to Stan that the moon's disappearance is only temporary. Mad John the Hermit then sings Stan a cheerful song about the meaning of life.

I am sure this tale was novel in 1968, and it certainly is not any more ridiculous than the adventures of The Beatles in *Yellow Submarine*, but the problem is that the music accompanying the story about Happiness Stan is less than stellar. Nonetheless, *Ogden's Nut* was a massive success in the UK and remains a cult favorite. Famously, the original packaging to *Ogden's Nut* was a round case, mimicking a tobacco canister. Eventually, the merits of that genius idea were determined economically impractical and *Ogden's Nut* was re-released in a standard record sleeve. Crazy times.

In light of the incredible success of *Ogden's Nut*, the Small Faces were booked all over Europe and the United States. However, one small issue arose: the Small Faces were unable to reproduce *Ogden's Nut* live in concert. Not only did the record include complicated overdubs and creative splicing techniques, the voices and, in some cases, the instruments of the Small Faces were manipulated. Not to mention, the narration didn't seem to work in a noisy music hall.

Steve Marriott quit the Small Faces at the end of 1968, walking off the stage during a show on New Year's Eve. Marriott cited the frustration of not being able to reproduce the material from *Ogden's Nut*. Shortly thereafter, in 1969, Marriott formed a new band, Humble Pie, featuring a young Peter Frampton.

The remaining members of the Small Faces merged with two musicians that had recently departed from The Jeff Beck Group: Rod Stewart and Ronnie Wood. The band, wanting to trade on the success and notoriety of the Small Faces, decided to just drop the "Small" from the band's name – creating decades of confusion.

The music of Faces is unlike that of the Small Faces. Centered around the Blues guitar of Ronnie Wood and the raw, barroom vocal of Rod Stewart, along with the keyboard playing of McLaglan (which was more at home in Faces), Faces became highly successful and influential, if short-lived. Faces disbanded in 1975, with Rod Stewart embarking on a successful solo career and McLaglan and Wood landing with The Rolling Stones.

June

June

HISTORY

Assassination of Robert Kennedy

MUSIC

Pink Floyd – *A Saucerful of Secrets*
The Doors – *Waiting for the Sun*
Buffalo Springfield – *Last Time Around*

Five months of death and destruction. Senseless loss of life in Vietnam. Senseless loss of life in American streets. The unconscionable murder of Martin Luther King, Jr. Yet, somehow – Americans still cherished a morsel of hope. A hope that the United States would emerge from darkness, guided by righteousness, peace and stability. For many in 1968, that morsel of hope resided within the candidacy of Robert F. Kennedy. Young voters, old voters. Liberals and conservatives. Optimism somehow briefly existed among the chaos.

In charting the course of 1968, the murder of Robert F. Kennedy is the vertex. Hope ceased to exist. Suddenly, nobody cared about progress. People simply wanted to fight. Aggression had prevailed. The assassination of John F. Kennedy in 1963 left the American people numb. Sad beyond contemplation. The assassination of Robert F. Kennedy in 1968 left the American people incensed. Many say the Sixties died on May 4, 1970 at Kent State, but I offer that the Sixties died on June 5, 1968.

HISTORY

Assassination of Robert F. Kennedy

It is unclear whether Robert F. Kennedy had planned on running for President at the outset of 1968. Kennedy would have had to challenge the incumbent President Johnson, assuredly creating a divide in his own political party – an action seen by many as unpatriotic. However, given the well-publicized animosity between President Johnson and Bobby Kennedy, stemming from Kennedy's elevated role during John Kennedy's tenure as President that often relegated then Vice President Johnson powerless. After John Kennedy's assassination, Robert Kennedy refused to work in President Johnson's cabinet, opting to run for the Senate in New York.

Whether Robert Kennedy intended to run, or not, the political landscape underwent a sea change in March 1968 after the New

Hampshire Democratic primary. As discussed in the March chapter, amid extreme opposition to the Vietnam War, the Democratic voting base revolted. Rallying behind Eugene McCarthy, a Senator from Minnesota that campaigned on a single issue – the immediate withdrawal from Vietnam, the people of New Hampshire influenced the political pulse of the United States.

Possibly the greatest trait of a Kennedy is/was the ability to sense weakness, and then exploit it. Just four days after the showing of Johnson's weakness in New Hampshire, Robert Kennedy announced his candidacy for President. President Johnson had not yet announced his decision not to seek reelection, but Kennedy exploited. Without a campaign strategy or formal organization, Kennedy was immediately embraced. Reeling from New Hampshire and the insurgency of Kennedy's popularity, President Johnson announced he would not seek reelection, opening a chasm for Kennedy.

After mobilizing a campaign team, streamlining his message and employing the Kennedy charm, Kennedy was officially the frontrunner for the Democratic nomination for President heading into the California Primary on June 4. Robert Kennedy did not publicly endorse an immediate withdrawal from Vietnam, but he certainly was critical of United States involvement in foreign conflict. As an insider throughout his brother's term as President, Robert Kennedy was notoriously aggressive in terms of engaging foreign nations in conflict, and achieving economic and political goals through the use of force, but Kennedy knew he must conform.

Ultimately, Robert Kennedy was a Kennedy – and Kennedys knew how to win elections. An ability to sense the direction of an electorate. An ability to project optimism. After examining McCarthy's success in New Hampshire, Robert Kennedy calculated that if he adopted an "immediate withdrawal from Vietnam" campaign platform, he would neutralize McCarthy and (somewhat easily) secure the Democratic nomination for President of the United States. Thus, Kennedy pivoted to "immediate withdrawal."

Kennedy's calculation was correct. Leading up to the primary elections in California and South Dakota on Tuesday, June 4, Kennedy was the frontrunner. A win in California would all but seal the nomination. After a relentless day of campaigning throughout several counties in Southern California, Kennedy claimed victory four hours after the polls closed, defeating McCarthy 46% to 42%. At 12:10 am on June 5, Kennedy addressed a packed room of supporters at the Ambassador Hotel in Los Angeles.

After a rather plain victory speech in the Ambassador Hotel's main ballroom, Kennedy was scheduled to address another, smaller group of supporters in a separate conference room. However, because the election took longer to call than expected, the horde of reporters following the Kennedy campaign lobbied for a press conference before Kennedy addressed the smaller group of supporters. Notoriously media friendly, the Kennedy campaign staff agreed that Kennedy would address the press in the Ambassador Hotel's designated area directly after Kennedy's main victory speech in the ballroom.

As Kennedy completed his victory speech, he began to exit the platform en route to the smaller conference room, but William Barry, an ex-FBI agent and chief security officer, told Kennedy, "No, it's been changed. We're going this way." Barry and the Hotel's maître d'hotel Karl Uecker, led Kennedy through the crowd, en route to a back exit where Kennedy could cut through the Hotel's kitchen leading to the press conference area. Note that in 1968 candidates for President were not protected by the Secret Service. Only incumbent Presidents received Secret Service protection. After June 5, 1968, all candidates for President would receive Secret Service protection.

As Kennedy turned down a narrow hallway towards the back of the kitchen, passing an ice machine and a steam table, Kennedy was greeted by Juan Romero, a busboy that worked at the Hotel. Kennedy stopped momentarily to shake Romero's hand when Sirhan Sirhan emerged from behind a stack of trays and fired at Kennedy with a .22 caliber revolver. Kennedy fell immediately, blood pouring from his

161

head. Romero famously knelt beside Kennedy and held Kennedy's head in his hands, trying helplessly to stop the bleeding. The photograph of Romero kneeling next to Kennedy would appear in *Life* magazine and become the lasting visual of the assassination.

While Kennedy laid on the kitchen floor, a swarm of men attacked Sirhan, attempting to wrestle the revolver from the assassin. The swarm included Barry and Uecker, but it wasn't until writer George Plimpton, Olympic gold medalist Rafer Johnson and former NFL player Rosie Grier joined the effort that Sirhan Sirhan was forced against the steam table and disarmed.

Before leaving Kennedy's side, Kennedy asked Romero, the busboy, "Is everybody OK?" Romero responded, "Yes, everybody's OK." Kennedy then uttered, "Everything's going to be OK." These, however, were not Kennedy's final words. Kennedy's wife Ethel was hurried to the side of her wounded husband, as campaign staffers searched for a doctor. As emergency medical personnel arrived they attempted to slide Kennedy onto a stretcher and lift the injured Kennedy to wheel him to an ambulance. Not wanting people to see him wounded, Kennedy instructed the medical staff, "Don't lift me." He didn't want people to see weakness. Those, in fact, would be Kennedy's last words.

Kennedy was initially taken to Central Receiving Hospital, located a mile from the Hotel. Kennedy arrived without a heartbeat, but doctors immediately massaged Kennedy's heart and provided oxygen, ultimately obtaining a strong enough heartbeat to transfer Kennedy several blocks to the Hospital of the Good Samaritan for surgery. Kennedy had been shot three times. One bullet entered behind Kennedy's right ear, dispersing fragments throughout his brain. The second bullet entered the rear of his right armpit and exited cleanly through the front of his chest. The third bullet also entered through the rear of his right armpit but lodged in the back of his neck.

After ten hours of surgery, doctors were able to remove the bullet from Kennedy's neck, but were not able to remove all of the bullet fragments in Kennedy's brain. Desperate for information, the country remained glued to the radio and television. At 5:30 pm (PCT) on June 5, Frank Mankiewicz announced to a room full of reporters at a local gymnasium serving as a temporary headquarters for the Kennedy campaign – that Kennedy was out of surgery, but the doctors were "concerned over his continuing failure to show improvement." Mankiewicz reported that Kennedy's condition was "extremely critical as to life."

Because Kennedy was shot at such a close range, the bullet that entered his head shattered upon reaching his skull. In order to survive a gunshot wound of this sort, doctors must be able to remove all of the bullet fragments, to prevent internal bleeding, swelling and infection. Such was not possible. Robert Kennedy died at 1:44 am on June 6, almost 26 hours after the shooting. At 2:00 am, Mankiewicz reluctantly approached the podium in the local gymnasium, delivering an unthinkable message:

"I have, uh, a short…I have a short announcement to read, which I will read, uh…at this time. Senator Robert Francis Kennedy died at 1:44 am today, June 6, 1968. With Senator Kennedy at the time of his death were his wife, Ethel, his sisters, Mrs. Stephen Smith, Mrs. Patricia Lawford, his brother-in-law, Mr. Stephen Smith, and his sister-in-law, Mrs. John F. Kennedy. He was 42 years old. Thank you."

Shattered. The country was shattered. The resounding question after the assassination of John F. Kennedy in 1963 seemed to be: "How did this happen?" The resounding question after the assassination of Robert F. Kennedy seemed to be: "Why did this happen?"

Sirhan Sirhan was a citizen of Jordan, born in Jerusalem, with Palestinian Arab affiliation. Sirhan Sirhan was vehemently opposed to an independent Israel and was petrified of United States economic and military support of Israel. In a diary found at Sirhan's home in a search conducted after the assassination, Sirhan wrote, "My determination to eliminate RFK is becoming more and more an

163

unshakable obsession. RFK must die. RFK must be killed. Robert F. Kennedy must be assassinated." When police booked Sirhan, a newspaper article was found in his pocket detailing Kennedy's support for Israel.

After a two-month trial, Sirhan Sirhan was convicted of the murder of Robert F. Kennedy and sentenced to death. In 1972, as Sirhan awaited execution, the Supreme Court of California decided *California v. Anderson*, outlawing the death penalty in the State of California and invalidating all pending death sentences. As of this printing, Sirhan Sirhan is alive and imprisoned at the Richard J. Donovan Correctional Facility in San Diego County. He has been denied parole 15 times.

The impact of the assassination was abrasive, propelling an already chaotic generation towards unthinkable evil. Optimism was trampled by negativity and violence. Every shred of culture – whether literature or music or film – every morsel of creativity was affected, or infected. No longer would citizens of the United States blindly embrace hope – citizens of the United States were immediately conditioned, and remain conditioned, to embrace optimism with caution. Skepticism had been learned. Ingrained.

Political scientist, Ross Baker, stated "I trace the most violent phase of this turbulent period (the late-1960s) in our history to [Robert] Kennedy's assassination. The hopefulness of the early 1960s was replaced by a pervasive cynicism and a conviction that change was impossible within the bounds of normal politics." In the wake of morbidity, musicians would react, digest, rage and ultimately permit tragedy to influence and infiltrate their craft.

The only way to end this horrific section is with a Robert Kennedy quote from a speech given exactly two months prior to his death. His words convey the violence existing in American culture in 1968 and illustrate the manner in which he believed Americans should react.

"What has violence ever accomplished? What has it ever created? No martyr's cause has ever been stilted by an assassin's bullet. No wrongs have ever been righted by riots and civil disorders. A sniper is only a coward, not a hero; and an uncontrolled, uncontrollable mob is only the voice of madness, not the voice of reason. Whenever any American's life is taken by another American unnecessarily — whether it is done in the name of the law or in the defiance of the law, by one man or a gang, in cold blood or in passion, in an attack of violence or in response to violence — whenever we tear at the fabric of the life which another man has painfully and clumsily woven for himself and his children, the whole nation is degraded."

MUSIC

Coincidence? Hardly. For six months in 1968, amid exponential tragedy, political instability and the horrors of war, the musical consequence of such evil was mounting. The music released in June was born from the darkness of the prior six months. A palpable venom resonated – at times through percusive, psychedelic rhythms, at other times, through desperate lyrical phrases. The fateful historical events of 1968 have finally intersected with the music of 1968 – and while the quality of political and cultural existence was futile, the quality of music borne from such tragedy is nothing short of exceptional.

Pink Floyd – *A Saucerful of Secrets*

A Saucerful of Secrets is the second studio release by Pink Floyd, released on June 29. The band's debut release, *The Piper at the Gates of Dawn*, established Pink Floyd in 1967 as a formidable addition to England's thriving Psychedelic Rock scene. Originally, Pink Floyd consisted of Roger Waters on bass and vocals, Richard Wright on piano, Nick Mason on drums and Syd Barrett on guitar and vocals. As Barrett spiraled into drug abuse and increasingly episodic psychotic spells, Waters enlisted David Gilmour to join the band on guitar and vocals, not replacing Barrett, but rather in support of Barrett and the band's effort to complete *A Saucerful of Secrets*. The album remains the only work that features all five members of Pink Floyd, with "Set the Controls for the Heart of the Sun" being the only track on which all five members contribute.

Waters loved Barrett's spirit and creative mind, but Waters and his bandmates were also highly engaged and focused on making music and achieving success. Maybe not commercial success, but success as they defined success. During the sessions for *A Saucerful of Secrets* and coinciding live performances, Barrett's behavior became peculiar, challenging and ultimately untenable and destructive. Barrett would detune his guitar on stage, string by string, in the middle of a song in which he was supposed to be playing lead guitar.

Barrett's unraveling is covered in detail in many biographies about Pink Floyd, and later Pink Floyd lyrics speak to the ordeal, including the Waters classics, "Wish You Were Here" and "Shine On You Crazy Diamond." For purposes of this passage, though, we'll explore the content and texture of *A Saucerful of Secrets*, rather than Barrett's demise (however, I'd offer that the historical events of 1968 strongly influenced Barrett's mental imbalance).

As we've discussed in prior chapters, the musical landscape in 1968 began to shift from Psychedelic Pop back to Rock, tracking the shift from delusional cultural obliviousness to unfathomable death and political despair. Prime examples are The Beatles and The Rolling Stones, each of which dramatically pivoted, abruptly abandoning the Psychedelic Pop genre and returning to a more traditional, charged version of Rock. However, not all bands changed so abruptly. Some, like Pink Floyd (and The Doors), preserved elements of psychedelia that fueled passion and creativity, combining perfectly with a heavy Rock spine.

While *Piper* contained mostly Barrett originals, *Saucerful* contains only one Barrett track ("Jugband Blues"), as Waters officially asserted himself as the lead songwriter and composer. Consequently,

Saucerful marks the beginning of a sound that Pink Floyd would develop and master. *AllMusic* describes the sound on *Saucerful* as "dark and repetitive pulses." The seeds of Pink Floyd are sowed on *Saucerful*.

The opening track, "Let There Be More Light", begins with a cool lead bass riff by Waters and then Wright on organ, completing a one minute instrumental intro that fades to a Space Rock vocal verse, eventually winding into a harmonized, energetic, rather spooky chorus. Gilmour emerges on lead guitar around 3:30, with a solo that is both uniquely Spanish and overwhelmingly "David Gilmour." Gilmour's tone has become legendary and the roots can be traced to the song-ending solo on "Let There Be More Light." Gilmour relies a bit more on distortion, rather than the super clean Fender tone used on subsequent records, but you can hear it, you can hear the phrasing. You can hear David Gilmour.

The next track, "Remember a Day", along with "See-Saw", is reminiscent of the songs on *Piper* and neither are remarkable. The third track on *Saucerful*, though, was a monumental leap forward. "Set the Controls for the Heart of the Sun" is just over five minutes, but seems like it could, and should, last forever. The backdrop is a meditative, percussive rhythm from Mason, which – as the song unfolds – becomes the lead. The vocals by Wright and Waters are sparse, and quiet, and haunting. Gilmour seems to run through scales on the guitar, rather than contribute a traditional lead guitar part. Wright alternates between a vibraphone and an eerie organ, both of which fit perfectly. As you listen, think about the word "pulsing", that's really the heart of the track. Soon to be replicated by The Grateful Dead, Pink Floyd was one of the first Rock bands to include experimental improvisational tracks on a studio release. The result is a masterpiece that will forever be played in every opium den, college dorm room and hippie living room.

"Corporal Clegg" is highly significant for different, non-instrumentation reasons, as the track represents the first political expression by Roger Waters – beginning a more than fifty year tradition of progressive, liberal and dynamically poignant and polarizing political expression. Waters took direct aim at the political issue of the moment – opposition to the Vietnam War. Fusing elements of humor, Psychedelic Pop and the prevailing Hard Rock trend in early-1968, including Gilmour using a wah pedal – Waters crafts a song that remains catchy, even if a bit dated.

Other than an annoying kazoo section that is reminiscent of the immaturity of 1967, "Corporal Clegg" is an essential statement on the uselessness of war and the existence of governmental deception. The opening lyric conveys that Corporal Clegg had a wooden leg that he "won" in the war. Waters states that Clegg "had a medal too" that he "found in the zoo." Waters goes on to undermine the significance of service by stating that Clegg "received his medal in a dream/from Her Majesty the Queen" but Clegg's "boots were clean." Waters concludes with "Mrs. Clegg, you must be proud of him/Mrs. Clegg, another drop of gin."

The attack is not completely formed, but the basic, underlying motivation is present. In subsequent years, Waters would refine his craft and lead the way in musical expression of government and corporate persecution. The genesis of Waters fusing substance with instrumentation was conceived in the unlikely confines of "Corporal Clegg", and I offer that the motivation for the marriage was the historical and political climate in 1968.

Arguably, the centerpiece of *Saucerful* is the title track. Nestled in the middle of the album's seven tracks, "A Saucerful of Secrets" is a 12 minute instrumental. Beginning with four minutes of space that feels theatrical, Mason starts in with a tribal drum segment, with sound effects bouncing in stereo behind the rhythm. The segment is akin to the Jazz Fusion that would become popular several years after this release. "Saucerful" concludes with a four minute passage, led by Wright on organ that overwhelmingly conjures the image of a funeral. Whether intentional or not, it is hard to view the close of the title track in any other way than a goodbye, or eulogy, to Syd Barrett.

Saucerful reached #9 on the UK chart, but failed to chart in the United States, likely due to the decision not to release a Single (the only Pink Floyd album not to chart in the United States). Recently, though, critics have adored *Saucerful* and consider it one of Pink Floyd's most important records.

A slight digression, but I wrote in The 1965 Project, I consider Pink Floyd to have the best four consecutive album stretch of any band: *Dark Side of the Moon* in 1973, *Wish you Were Here* in 1975, *Animals* in 1977 and *The Wall* in 1979. All due respect to The Beatles, with *Revolver* in 1966, *Sgt. Pepper's* in 1967, *The White Album* in 1968 and *Abby Road* in 1969, however *Magical Mystery Tour* breaks up that stretch as it was released in 1967. The Rolling Stones' streak is perhaps the closest (for me), with *Beggar's Banquet* in 1968, *Let It Bleed* in 1969, *Sticky Fingers* in 1971 and *Exile On Main Street* in 1972).

As for Syd Barrett, surprisingly, he did not suffer the fate of many contemporaries. Despite heavy drug use, and undiagnosed psychiatric conditions, Barrett lived until age 60, dying in 2006 of complications from diabetes. Barrett spent several decades in seclusion, focusing on painting and gardening. Reflecting on Barrett's condition in 1968, experts suspect that Barrett suffered from Asperger's syndrome that was not only untreated, but exacerbated due to heavy use of LSD.

Pink Floyd would go on to become one of the most commercially successful bands in the history of music, while somehow preserving a brand of non-commercialism. The events of 1968 dictated the trajectory of the band's musical texture and lyrical comment. In 2014, Nick Mason declared *Saucerful* his favorite Pink Floyd album, noting that, "I think there are ideas contained there that we have continued to use all the way through our career. I think it was a quite good way of marking Syd's departure and Dave's arrival. It's rather nice to have it on one record, where you get both things. It's a cross fade rather than a cut."

If you are a fan of Pink Floyd's prime career material, please check out or revisit "Let There Be More Light" and "Set the Controls for the Heart of the Sun", if not the whole record.

The Doors – *Waiting for the Sun*

Recorded between February and May 1968, *Waiting for the Sun* is the third studio release by The Doors. The record featured the #1 hit "Hello, I Love You", propelling *Waiting for the Sun* to #1 on the *Billboard* Top 200 Albums chart, the only #1 album by The Doors. *Waiting for the Sun* also experienced success in the UK, reaching #16. Where, though, does *Waiting for the Sun* fit into the catalog and career of The Doors and how were The Doors influenced by the events of 1968?

The story of The Doors is so well told by Oliver Stone in the 1991 feature film, *The Doors* that recounting even a snapshot seems like a crime. But, here's some brief context. The Doors formed in Los Angeles in 1965 (yep, another 1965 band formation). The four piece consisted of Jim Morrison (vocals, songwriter), Robby Krieger (guitar), Ray Manzarek (organ) and John Densmore (drums). Morrison named the band after a book by Aldous Huxley, *The Doors of Perception*. After becoming somewhat of an underground sensation in Los Angeles, graduating to performing regularly at The Whiskey A-Go-Go in opening slots for bands such as Them (featuring Van Morrison) and Love, The Doors were eventually signed to Elektra and cut their self-titled debut in January 1967.

The debut record featured the 12-minute epic, "The End", as well as "Break On Through" and "Light My Fire." The first Single pushed by Elektra was "Break On Through", but the track failed to obtain radio play. A bit desperate, Elektra turned to the Kreiger original, "Light My Fire." However, the track was seven minutes long. Despite Bob Dylan paving the way for longer Singles after the release of "Like A Rolling Stone" in 1965, The Doors were not exactly Bob Dylan. So, Elektra edited "Light My Fire" to remove most of the

Manzarek organ solo and gutted one of Krieger's guitar solos. Famously, that's not all that would get edited…or, asked to be edited.

On September 17, 1967, The Doors appeared on *The Ed Sullivan Show* and were to play "Light My Fire", by that time a #1 hit on the *Billboard* Hot 100 (reaching #1 on July 29, 1967). The producers of *The Ed Sullivan Show* demanded that the word "higher" be removed and replaced with another word. The Doors, and Morrison specifically, agreed and took the stage in front of a primetime, national television audience. When it came time for Morrison to replace the lyric, he instead stayed with the word "higher", to the outrage of Sullivan and the "network." Livid, the producers cancelled six scheduled appearances by The Doors over the next several months.

Morrison's erratic behavior dominated the headlines, and to some extent, obscured the music of The Doors. Morrison was notorious for weaving lengthy stories throughout live performances, detailing instances of death and gore, backed by Manzarek's thematic organ, Krieger's distorted guitar and a rolling snare from Densmore. Crowds devoured the improvisation, but unfortunately – Morrison's behavior grew increasingly "inappropriate", escalating to Morrison yelling at the audience, offending security and police and eventually indecent exposure. Free speech is one thing, but indecent exposure? Morrison found himself in trouble with the law, banned from performing in several states.

Needing a reprieve from the road, The Doors went into the studio to record *Strange Days*, completed in August 1967. In addition to the title track, the record featured "Love Me Two Times", "People Are Strange" and "When the Music's Over." With *The Doors* still in the Top 10 on the *Billboard* Top 200 Albums chart, The Doors released *Strange Days* in late-September 1967 and the album reached #3. The Doors were incredibly popular commercially, but critics universally felt that *Strange Days* was lacking in quality compared to the debut release. Nonetheless, renowned critic Robert Christgau proclaimed The Doors to be "America's heaviest group." That's high praise in

1967. Unfortunately, The Doors remained a risky live booking. Drugs had initially functioned as a portal for The Doors to access musical creativity to accompany Morrison's poetry. Problematically, Morrison excelled in excess.

In addition to psychedelic drugs, mainly peyote and LSD, Morrison was an alcoholic. While the band seemed to tolerate the drugs, the alcohol became a burden – as it inhibited creativity, rather than promoting it. Unable to book shows outside of liberal, urban cities, The Doors went back into the studio in February 1968, in an effort to force Morrison to write new material and regain focus in a controlled environment.

Amazingly, the lyrical material comprising the first two albums by The Doors originated from a single journal, or notebook, written by Morrison over the course of 1964 to 1966. Morrison abstractly weaved phrases and themes to construct songs. The results are legendary, especially when emboldened by improvisation. Unfortunately, the well was dry as the band had exhausted Morrison's previous writings/musings, with one exception.

In 1965, The Doors cut a demo of "Hello, I Love You", using lyrics from Morrison's notebook – however, the instrumentation didn't quite work – and the track was left off *The Doors* and *Strange Days*. Grasping for material, the band revisited "Hello, I Love You" and included "new" guitar chords developed by Krieger. The band rearranged "Hello, I Love You" into a #1 hit.

Of course, not everyone loved the track – as The Kinks, or – actually, their label, brought a lawsuit against The Doors for copyright infringement – alleging that Krieger ripped off the chord progression of "Hello, I Love You" from The Kinks hit song, "All Day and All of the Night." Krieger denied the allegation and the lawsuit was dropped. Krieger later admitted that he ripped off the chord progression, but not from The Kinks, as he copied it (or, got inspiration) from Cream's "Sunshine of Your Love."

Other than "Hello, I Love You", the session for *Waiting for the Sun* was initially a struggle. Morrison was intent on recording "The Celebration of the Lizard", a lengthy multi-part composition that, according to the producer of the recording session, Paul Rothschild, was "not that great" and definitely not commercially viable. Rothschild forced Morrison to write new material. Morrison's writing, and general disposition, was dramatically affected and most certainly influenced by the historical events of 1968.

Morrison wrote two songs that focused entirely (and explicitly) on the political infrastructure supporting the Vietnam War. Morrison also echoed fellow Los Angeles musician, Frank Zappa, by indicting the oblivious, care-free hippie culture existing within the youth of America. Of course, Morrison's version of substantive comment was direct, poignant and dark.

"Unknown Soldier" is abrasive and complicated. The track is the centerpiece of *Waiting for the Sun*. The Doors were notorious for recording several takes in the studio, due in large part to Morrison's mental and physical condition, but also due to the perfectionist culture of Manzarek and Krieger. For example, "Hello, I Love You", which is a relatively simple song, took 39 takes to arrive at the version on the album. That, though, pales in comparison to the 130 takes it took the band to finalize "Unknown Soldier."

The song has few lyrics, but Morrison expertly depicts a family sitting at breakfast, with children present, watching coverage of the Vietnam War on television. Overtly, the song was an anti-war statement by The Doors, but the underlying message focused more on the normalization of war, promulgated by a corrupt government, a capitalist media and the passivity of American citizens.

At the time "Unknown Soldier" was released in 1968, Morrison's father was serving in the United States Navy as an Admiral, commanding an air craft carrier outside of Vietnam. Morrison respected the service of American soldiers and tried hard to direct his ire and commentary towards the manner in which Americans consumed information about the war. Possibly, Morrison abhorred that Americans digested horrific details of war while eating breakfast, then going to work and living a routine, normal life, while young men and women were dying in pursuit of an unjust, unsupported cause? I have gleaned this mostly from interviews with Morrison, but with that context, the lyrics that open the track (and are also refrained to close the track) suggest the notion: "Breakfast where the news is read/Television children fed/Unborn living, living, dead/Bullet strikes the helmet's head." Despite the charged lyrics, the track charted at #39 on the *Billboard* Hot 100.

In addition to the lyrics, the band incorporated a middle section that included sound effects of soldiers marching, an officer barking orders and eventually a military gun salute with shots fired. It is not a musical interlude, just sound effects. After the military sound effects, the melody resurfaces, with Morrison embracing a much more somber tone with the line, "Make a grave for the unknown soldier." Manzarek layers in a funereal sounding organ and Krieger and Densmore generally lay out (don't play). The mood is depressing and sorrowful, but slowly builds to joy as Morrison yells, "It's all over/The war is over/It's all over/The war is over."

In live performances, during the middle section, Krieger would point his guitar at Morrison and Densmore would lay on the snare drum to mimic gunfire – Morrison would act as if he was shot and then fall to his death. Theatrics, sure – but accompanied by the spirit of 1968 – the message was strong.

"Five to One" not only was the subject of an infamous live performance in Miami, but also contained poignant and topical lyrical statements. Whereas Dylan and many other songwriters utilized abstract imagery to convey substance, Morrison opted for a more direct approach. With lines such as "No one here gets out alive" and "The old get old/The young get stronger...They got the guns/We got the numbers." In addition to descriptive thoughts, Morrison was also instructional, urging the hippies to wake from their 1967 haze. Morrison sings, "Your ballroom days are over/Night is drawing near/Shadows of the evening crawl across the years/You walk across the floor with a flower in your hand/Trying to tell me no one understands/Trade in your hours for a handful of dimes/Gonna make it, baby, in our prime." Classic prose and classic delivery and cadence.

Morrison's intolerance of inaction was evident. Not only did the lyrics activate the audience, Morrison's renditions of "Five to One" were…interesting. At a 1969 performance in Miami, Morrison, reportedly very drunk, called the audience "idiots" and "slaves." The crowd reacted "negatively" and Morrison was ultimately arrested for "inciting a riot" and indecent exposure. An audio recording of the incident was released on *The Doors Box Set* and a wonderful performance by Val Kilmer reenacts the scene in Oliver Stone's movie.

Waiting for the Sun also featured "Love Street", which was the B side to "Hello, I Love You." The ballad is quite underrated, including a wonderful piano solo from Manzarek (refreshing to hear him abandon the organ). "Love Street" also features a spoken word bridge, possibly replicating the manner in which Morrison spoke to audiences during live performances.

"Not to Touch the Earth" was originally part of "The Celebration of the Lizard" composition, and while not remarkable, the track features a noteworthy Morrison lyric that would spawn Morrison's nickname – Morrison closes the song with the line, "I am the Lizard King/I can do anything." The final track of significance is "Spanish Caravan", which features Krieger playing a flamenco style guitar, paired with a crooning vocal from Morrison. "Spanish Caravan" illustrates a late-1960s Psychedelic Rock fascination with Spanish music elements (The Grateful Dead were known to include a "Spanish Jam" in their live sets during 1968 and 1969 and David Gilmour and Eric Clapton both flirted with the style).

In many respects, I am not a devout fan of The Doors. The music of The Doors had been an entry point for me. Easily accessible in high school, especially paired with the Oliver Stone film. The catalog of The Doors is relatively small, due to Morrison's untimely death at age 27. The music is quite easy to devour. After a couple years of listening to The Doors, I guess I moved on – to more complicated music? The Doors, and Morrison in particular, had become a caricature. A symbol for a time period. Upon re-listening to the first two records from The Doors, then *Waiting for the Sun*, and the follow-up, *Soft Parade*, I have located a heightened appreciation for the band.

The Doors could write hits – and they not only wrote a lot of hits, they wrote hits that sounded different than almost every other band during the era. The hits sound a bit dated, sure, but when compared to other bands from the same period – The Doors in retrospect were ahead. The Doors were neither guitar-based, Rock nor organ-driven Rock (i.e., The Animals). The Doors were masters at crafting musical templates to surround, supplement and, eventually, propel the lyrics and stage presence of Jim Morrison. Having now digested (almost all of) the Rock music created between 1963 and 1972. I encourage you to revisit the first three albums by The Doors, then skip to *L.A. Woman* (1971).

Buffalo Springfield – *Last Time Around*

I wish I could include cover art in this book, as sometimes – the album cover art demonstrates salient aspects of the intersection of history and music. But, such are copyright laws and licensing arrangements. The cover photo for *Last Time Around* by Buffalo Springfield is a statement. Not so much a statement about history, although just seeing the clothing, hair and facial hair of the band members is relevant, but rather a statement about the condition of Buffalo Springfield, as a band. Stephen Stills and his other bandmates facing one direction, Neil Young facing in the opposite direction. Aptly titled, *Last Time Around* was the final Buffalo Springfield record.

Formed in Los Angeles in 1966, the band consisted of Neil Young (guitar, piano, vocals), Stephen Stills (guitar, piano, vocals), Richie Furay (guitar), Bruce Palmer (bass) and Dewey Martin (drums). Originally signed to Atlantic Records by famed record label executive Ahmet Ertegun, Buffalo Springfield adopted the Folk Rock sound invented and promoted by The Byrds in 1965 (with "Mr. Tambourine Man"). Seeking commercial success, Ertegun signed Buffalo Springfield for four records, in exchange for a $12,000 advance.

Buffalo Springfield entered the studio in early 1966 and completed a record that, in retrospect, is quite good, but failed to achieve consumer traction. Then, in December 1966, Stephen Stills wrote "For What It's Worth" (you know it, "Something's happening here/What it is ain't exactly clear"). Given the undercurrent of political instability, the track was immediately released as a Single and subsequently added to later pressings of Buffalo Springfield's self-titled debut. "For What It's Worth" peaked at #7 on the *Billboard* Hot 100 in March 1967.

A hit song. The talent of Stills and Young. So, what happened to Buffalo Springfield? You know by now. Drugs, alcohol and arrests. Same formula, different band. Bruce Palmer was arrested for drug possession and summarily deported (back to Canada). Jim Messina took over on bass. Then, Young was arrested for drug possession (in a bust that also involved Eric Clapton). Unable to travel, due to legal restrictions, the band became highly unfocused and fractured.

Perhaps most significant, Neil Young was developing a characteristic that would become the hallmark of his music career: independence. Neil Young has always followed his desired musical path, at the expense of everything around him – both a plague and a gift. This characteristic manifested itself somewhat unprofessionally in 1968, affecting the band.

Neil missed a few gigs in California and appeared only episodically in the recording studio. Fueled by drugs and alcohol, Young and Stills argued about every detail. After a lazy intervention aimed at curbing

Young's drug habit, the band decided to separate in April 1968. Buffalo Springfield played its last show on May 5, 1968 at the Long Beach Arena in California.

One small item remained, though – a contract with Atlantic Records. Buffalo Springfield had agreed to release four records. With Young absent and Stills unwilling to put any effort towards the project, Furay and Messina sorted through unreleased studio material, some old, some new. The effort resulted in the posthumous release of *Last Time Around*.

The record opens with Young's "On the Way Home", incorporating a string section, and harmonized vocals from Stills. The song is bouncy and remained in Young's live performance for decades (as did "Mr. Soul" from *Again*, a prior Buffalo Springfield release). Young's other main contribution was "I Am a Child", which directly echoes Young's solo material on *Neil Young* (December 1968), as well as *After the Gold Rush* (1970) and *Harvest* (1972). Acoustic, major key fingerpicking, harmonica – and that voice.

The best track by Stills is "Four Days Gone", a song about being on the road, hitchhiking, feeling lost, but pressing forward. Stills, speaking to one of the kind souls that agreed to pick him up on the highway, "And my baby is waiting, I hope, sir/After fifteen trucks and an old Ford/And the government madness…I ran away." He closes the verse with "I can't tell you my name/Cause I'm four days gone into running." The track is my favorite on *Last Time Around* and illustrates Stills' talent as a singer.

Furay actually does a heck of a job singing on "Kind Woman", which provides a soulful context to juxtapose with the Folk Rock. "Kind Woman" also includes beautiful interaction between piano (Young) and slide guitar (Stills), reminding the listener that this band had a ton of unfulfilled potential. For a record that was patched together from various demos and featured musicians recording new material separately in piecemeal fashion, *Last Time Around* is quite an accomplishment.

Despite the quality of the sons, *Last Time Around* sold terribly, due in large part to the break-up of the band, and Atlantic failing to promote the record. The unfulfilled potential of Buffalo Springfield turned out to be positive – at least for us, the listeners. The breakup resulted in Young and Stills pursuing separate paths – that, oddly, crossed against when Young joined Crosby, Stills and Nash. The original Buffalo Springfield would not play live together until the band reunited in 2011, for six shows in Los Angeles and Santa Barbara, then a festival headlining slot at Bonnaroo.

Ultimately, *Last Time Around* is a unique glimpse at the evolution of Folk Rock and is an integral puzzle piece in the undying quest to understand the roots and foundation of Neil Young. Without question, one of the great musicians of the 20th Century. We'll hear from both Young and Stills later in The 1968 Project, with Stills featured on one of the most underrated records of 1968 (in the following chapter) and Young's brilliant debut solo released in December.

July

July

HISTORY

The Youth International Party

MUSIC

The Band – *Music From Big Pink*
Creedence Clearwater Revival – S/T
The Grateful Dead – *Anthem of the Sun*
Cream – *Wheels of Fire*
Mike Bloomfield/Al Kooper/Stephen Stills – *Super Session*

HISTORY

The Democratic primary election was tumultuous, wide open and yet very much closed as of July. With Lyndon Johnson not pursuing reelection, Eugene McCarthy falling to Robert Kennedy, then Kennedy's assassination – the Democratic Party craved stability. Fearing four years of Richard Nixon, Democratic Party strategists determined that the most viable path for competing with Nixon was in fact the current Vice President of the United States, the overwhelmingly plain Hubert Humphrey.

The ascension of Humphrey remains a historical footnote. Rather than summarize Humphrey's campaign, I prefer to provide you with a reprieve – analogous to the reprieve that existed in July 1968. In researching this book, the dominant historical event of each month was immediately apparent. News coverage focused exclusively on each such event. Nothing else mattered. A scan of newspaper headlines, magazine covers – a review of timelines and important events – the narrative was consistent. Each month in 1968 possessed a historical event that overwhelmed and dominated the American conscious. Except for July.

Fortunately, the music released in July is unparalleled. July is when the music of 1968 went from great to classic. From influential to historically relevant. The Band released *Music From Big Pink*. The Grateful Dead released *Anthem of the Sun*. Cream released *Wheels of Fire*. Creedence Clearwater Revival released their self-titled debut. And, Stephen Stills, Mike Bloomfield and Al Kooper released the most underrated album of the year, *Super Session*. But, real quick – prior to detailing those records, an introduction to some radical folks that will play a leading role in August.

The Youth International Party

Founded by Abbie Hoffman and Jerry Rubin on December 31, 1967, The Youth International Party was equally serious, progressive, disruptive, theatrical, intelligent, comedic, well-intentioned, downright immature and most certainly, radically idealistic. Combining the fundamental tenets of free speech and opposition to the Vietnam War, The Youth International Party professed peaceful anarchy. However, The Youth International Party sought attention at the expense of its cause. Favoring pranks as opposed to marches, the Youth International Party received a plethora of media attention.

For example, striving to demonstrate the commercialism of society and culture, Abbie Hoffman, Jerry Rubin and a few others applied for a tour of the New York Stock Exchange (NYSE). Seemingly young, energetic future bankers, the NYSE granted the tour. When Hoffman and his cohorts reached a platform overlooking the trading floor, Hoffman and crew began throwing money down onto the floor. Stacks of bills floating through the air – one and five dollar bills, along with some tens and twenties.

Now, reportedly, some of the bills were real, but most were really good counterfeits. The traders scrambled to collect the cash, diving across the floor and wrestling each other for the bills. Hoffman and The Youth International Party used the embarrassing scene to describe corporate greed and the moral inferiority of Wall Street. Ultimately, though, while the prank received considerable press – only the prank resonated, not the underlying message. The NYSE immediately installed thick glass protecting the stock exchange floor – and the glass remains today.

After a Federal investigation of Hoffman and Rubin led to no filed charges, Rubin was asked to appear before the House Un-American Activities Committee, a remnant of McCarthyism and a tactic for Congress to investigate, and understand, civilian activity contrary to the "prevailing spirit of America." Rubin's testimony is largely uninteresting, however, he famously testified while dressed as a Revolutionary War soldier and upon entering, he passed out copies of the Declaration of Independence to members of Congress. These folks had terrific wit. Like, real high-end situational humor. Generally, nobody got hurt – just a bunch of idealistic kids, having fun, caring about issues and doing the best they could to make a difference.

The stakes, though, would intensify quickly.

Hoffman and Rubin targeted the most high-profile upcoming political event – The Democratic National Convention in Chicago. At covert, rather expertly planned meetings throughout July, Hoffman and Rubin met with key operatives in The Youth International Party, to outline the arrangements for a six-day festival in Chicago that would coincide with the Democratic National Convention. Hoffman named his festival the Festival of Life. In the weeks before the Convention, the Yippies (nickname of The Youth International Party) finally made a demand. Hoffman demanded the "immediate withdrawal from Vietnam." Not a surprising demand, but the threat that accompanied the demand was in fact, well…different.

In addition to the demand of immediate withdrawal, Hoffman pledged that the Yippies would put LSD in the Chicago water supply. Hoffman also famously declared that his large cohort of young people would "fuck on your beaches." Hoffman predicted chaos and used sensationalized statements such as "we demand the politics of ecstasy." Typically, sarcastic – Hoffman and The Youth International Party would find themselves at the center of a situation that would, in August, veer out of their control and became a classic American scene of unrest.

MUSIC

Imagine being a kid, or a young adult, in July 1968. Maybe you sensed a change. Maybe you considered that what you were hearing was different. But, likely not – it's hard to recognize or articulate musical greatness when it is contemporaneous. The art form is incredibly subjective. Sports is the opposite, as it is relatively easy to determine greatness through statistics. A running back setting the NFL single season rushing record. An NBA player averaging a triple double over the course of a single season.

Point is, was it possible in July 1968 to comprehend the greatness of the records released? Frankly, I suspect that most Americans, even young Americans, were focused more on whether or not they, or their friends or children, might be forced to fight in Vietnam. Maybe young African Americans were focused more on Civil Rights? Maybe young women were focused on equal rights and status in the workplace?

Whether or not people recognized greatness at the time, people were certainly influenced by it. Influence in 1968 was cyclical. The cycle of influence began with anti-Vietnam War demonstrations, leading to political pressure, tension and, unfortunately, death. This tone, or tenor, influenced the trajectory of music, pushing music from a creative, exploratory state, with a colorful palate – to a darker, violent disposition. Louder, heavier Rock. More distortion. More noise.

The harder, darker Rock, in turn, amplified the very political uprising from which it was born – serving as the soundtrack to riots and chaotic demonstrations. The music propelled the movement, attracting more attention, more demonstrators, more voices. The music affected and propelled the trajectory of history. The cycle continued, until the minority became the majority. The smallest voice became the loudest voice.

The Band – *Music From Big Pink*

"This is IT." Or, perhaps he said, "THIS is it." Either way, that is what he said, exactly what he thought. After just one listen to *Music From Big Pink*. The foremost guitarist of his generation, the leader of the most popular Rock band in the world in July 1968. A legendary musician's life changed after just one listen to the debut record by Bob Dylan's backing band. Really?

True story. Eric Clapton stated in an interview with *Biography* that, in the midst of Cream's unparalleled success, in July 1968, he listened to *Music From Big Pink* and became immediately "discontent."

185

Clapton stated that the music "stimulated me, moved me and it upset me." Shocking, but understandable.

Clapton's conscious had been rooted in the Blues, specifically traditional Blues, or Delta Blues. Clapton exercised his passion by starring in The Yardbirds and then John Mayall and the Bluesbreakers, eventually joining forces with Ginger Baker and Jack Bruce to form the supergroup, Cream.

Seemingly awash in money, fame and attention as a result of Cream's success, Clapton trended towards anti-commercialism. Uncomfortable with the direction of Cream in early-1968, Clapton referenced a vague sense of searching – knowing that the music he was making with Cream was not genuine – but, Clapton was unable to isolate what genuine actually sounded like.

That's the context for Clapton's comment of "This is IT." Clapton heard the genuineness he sought. An amalgamation of Folk, Blues, Gospel, Country – accompanied by a timeless original songwriting aesthetic and expert musicianship. Clapton abruptly left Cream, citing a desire to make more "genuine" music – a reference many music historians trace directly to *Music From Big Pink*. So, the real question is: How did a group of backing musicians make a debut record that, at a minimum, affected and changed the career path of Eric Clapton, if not the course of music, generally?

The story of The Band is essentially a fairy tale. Four Canadian session musicians, one American from the deep South, nomadically coming together in 1958 to support a relatively unsuccessful Rockabilly singer, Ronnie Hawkins. Between 1958 and 1963, Robbie Robertson (guitar, songwriting), Levon Helm (drums, vocals), Rick Danko (bass, vocals), Richard Manuel (piano, vocals and songwriting) and Garth Hudson (organ) traveled the United States with Hawkins, perfecting the art of supporting a lead musician. Referencing Malcolm Gladwell's thesis in *Outliers*, that the "greats" typically spend 10,000 hours on their craft prior to becoming "great"

– The Band obtained about half of their 10,000 hours on tour with Ronnie Hawkins.

The other half – well, those were obtained under the tutelage and presence of Bob Dylan. But, how did that happen? Loosely, in 1964, The Band informed Ronnie Hawkins that they wanted to start their own band. Robertson stated, "Eventually, [Hawkins] built us up to the point where we outgrew his music and had to leave. He shot himself in the foot, really, bless his heart, but sharpening us into such a crackerjack band that we had to go out into the world."

After releasing two unsuccessful Singles, Robbie Robertson drove up to New York in a rented Buick in early-1965, in search of "something." Robbie navigated the conglomerate of club owners, agents and musicians, seeking a meeting with John Hammond, an experienced and well known Blues singer. Hammond had hired Robbie, Levon and Garth Hudson the year prior, as session musicians on his record, *So Many Roads*. Hammond was renowned for identifying the premier session and backing band musicians.

In mid-1965, Bob Dylan was undergoing the most influential music change in Rock. Primarily a Folk musician, Dylan had been trending towards electric amplification, veering overtly towards Rock. In March 1965, Dylan released *Bringing It All Back Home*, featuring both electric and acoustic songs. However, at live shows, Dylan mainly played only the acoustic songs, lacking a supporting cast that could replicate the electric Rock that Dylan derived in the studio.

Dylan was convinced of his new direction. Songwriting sessions later in 1965 produced tracks such as "Like A Rolling Stone", "Desolation Row", "Queen Jane Approximately", "Ballad of a Thin Man" and "Just Like Tom Thumb's Blues." Dylan was moving forward, and was desperate to take his "new sound" on the road. Needing a backing band, Dylan turned to John Hammond for a suggestion. Immediately, Hammond suggested Robbie and Levon.

After a meeting between Robbie and Dylan, Dylan offered a spot to Robbie and Levon. Admirably, Robbie replied that he couldn't part from his mates – that his band, formerly The Hawks, were a package deal. Dylan, ever the negotiator, didn't bite. He urged Robbie and Levon to play one gig with him in New York, so Dylan could get a sense for the sound, then he would consider hiring the rest of the band. Robbie and Levon agreed. Immediately after the gig, Dylan indicated that Robbie and Levon could bring in Manuel, Danko and Hudson. Starting in September 1965, through May 1966, the musicians toured the world as Bob Dylan and the Band.

What came next has been covered repeatedly – books, documentaries, video footage, legendary audio recordings, fictional cinematography and thousands of magazine references. In short, the audiences revolted. Desiring the Folk music that Bob Dylan had adorned, the audience was blasted by a raging, loud wall of electric Rock. The audience booed, screamed in displeasure. Sure, the audience knew it was coming, but it became sort of a badge of honor, in the Folk community, to revolt against Dylan's new path. And, unfortunately, The Band symbolized Dylan's new path. Accordingly, The Band assumed much of the hatred, and much of the criticism.

A few months into the late-1965 tour, Levon quit – not willing to play the music he loved in front of a heckling, disapproving crowd. Levon spent the better part of a year and a half working on an oil rig in the Gulf of Mexico. The remaining members of The Band soldiered on in support of Dylan, soaking in the ethos of a master songwriter, refining a sound that blended original songwriting with Rock, steeped in the Blues, but with elements of Pop, Country and Folk. This experience provided the completion of The Band's musical education.

On July 29, 1966, on a break from touring with The Band, Dylan was injured in a motorcycle accident outside of Woodstock, NY. Dylan suffered a neck injury, but oddly was not treated in a hospital. Most historians believe that Dylan wasn't so much injured – but, rather – Dylan was exhausted. Tired of the road and tired of the scene.

Dylan had always been a year or two ahead of the scene, ahead of society as a whole. Dylan seemed to astutely sense the forthcoming commercialism of the anti-Vietnam War movement and the capitalism of Free Speech. Dylan retreated, skipping the psychedelic period of late-1966 and 1967.

In August 1967, still in a reclusive period, at least publicly, Dylan invited The Band to Woodstock, NY. No agenda. No producers, no record label pushing for an album release. No tour dates scheduled. Dylan and The Band just hung out, jammed and eventually recorded a slew of songs, both originals and traditional American songs. However, uniquely, the originals sounded just like the traditional American cover songs. The music recorded by Dylan and The Band in 1967 would be released in 1975 as *The Basement Tapes*, but in 1967, the recordings were only legend.

The Basement Tapes were recorded at several houses in and around Woodstock, NY, including the basement of a house rented by Danko and Manuel in West Saugerties, NY. When the members of The Band were not hanging with Dylan, they congregated regularly at Danko and Manuel's house, affectionately referred to as "Big Pink."

Today, musicians routinely rent houses in distinct places – to write and even record – but, in 1968 – the concept was foreign. In 1968, if a band wanted to record a new album, it amassed just enough material to warrant the cost of studio time, then went into a recording studio along with a producer, and the band cut a record – usually in a matter of days or weeks. The Band, however, found themselves in a much different environment, with a much different pace.

Having spent almost 18 months on the road with Dylan, Robbie started to assert himself as a songwriter, or – a storyteller. In the confines of a home, perhaps feeling more comfortable, Danko and Manuel began to find each of their singing voices. Danko's voice was incredibly versatile and generally pleasing, both as lead and backing. Manuel, however, exhibited a stunning falsetto that remains a thing of unmatched beauty. These elements, along with Levon's voice and

189

rhythm and Garth's virtuosity, resulted in a remarkable turning point in American music, *Music From Big Pink*.

Critics immediately praised the record, but sales were insignificant. The world had devolved into rage and hatred, revolt and anger. The music of The Band, while certainly substantive, was subtle. Young folks were angry – and craved powerful guitar solos and overt comments about government and free expression. *Music From Big Pink* didn't appeal commercially, but musicians understood.

Writing a review for *Rolling Stone*, Al Kooper stated "There are people who will work their lives away in vain and not touch [*Music From Big Pink"*]." We heard earlier about Clapton's reaction to *Music From Big Pink*, but other musicians were equally floored. Roger Waters deemed *Music From Big Pink* the "second most influential record in the history of Rock and Roll" (Waters cited *Sgt. Pepper's* as first). A bold statement, sure, but Waters further stated that *Music From Big Pink* "affected Pink Floyd deeply, deeply, deeply."

Dylan, Clapton and Waters – each seem to reference the word "affected." Why did *Music From Big Pink* affect musicians? Dylan was a Folk enthusiast, leaning towards Rock. Clapton was an electric guitarist steeped in the Blues. Waters was the bassist in a Psychedelic Rock band. Where is the thread?

"Tears of Rage" opens with the following lyric: "We carried you in our arms/On Independence Day." The instrumentation is ancient – not in clarity or simplicity, but it just sounds old. It sounds traditional. Old songs from the American songbook reference Independence Day, the Civil War, prison life, the railroad – so, you might think – "Tears of Rage" could be a cover. Then, the chorus hits – and Dylan announces his presence. Dylan does not appear on the record (although he did paint the cover album art), but Dylan and Manuel co-wrote "Tears of Rage", with Dylan apparently penning the chorus:

Tears of rage, tears of grief
Why am I the one who must be the thief?
Come to me now, you know
We're so alone
And life is brief

There's so much there, as it relates to Dylan's life and critics, but we are focusing on The Band. The post-chorus instrumentation features Robbie's lead guitar fills, in between organ and piano accompaniment. But, the overwhelming element of the song is the pace. Manuel and the various backing vocalists ride a patient melody that is both soulful and pained. After a refrain of the chorus, the track closes with the haunting line, "life is brief."

The second track, "To Kingdom Comes", kicks off with a rhythm groove that is more familiar – rhythm guitar, piano, bass and drums. After a pre-chorus, The Band pauses ever so briefly, accentuating an infectious chorus that screams authenticity and is one of my favorite passages on *Music From Big Pink*.

The lyrics are meaningless, but that's kind of the point – the music and tone and passion are overwhelming and, most definitely, affecting. The lyrics are "Tarred and feathered, yeah/Thistled and thorned/One or the other/He kindly warned." But, please, listen to the delivery. It is vaguely essential.

After "In A Station", another mid-tempo track from Manuel, Rick Danko emerges on lead vocals for "Caledonia Mission", a song written by Robbie. The arrangement is relatively standard, but Danko's vocal is so entirely different than Manuel that the listener is forced to realize – "this band has two lead vocalists?" Other than The Beatles, most bands relied on a single lead vocalist. "Caledonia Mission" also announces the songwriting ability and style of Robbie Robertson. After the impossible task of rhyming "garden gate" with "magistrate", Robbie magically pairs the following lines: "You know how I do believe in your hexagram/But can you tell me how they all knew the plan?" Danko just kills on the delivery.

191

Music From Big Pink is an album that conveys a sound. In total, the blend of Folk, Country, Rock, Blues, R&B and Gospel established the lasting effect and influence of the album, rather than any individual track. With one exception, though. Nestled in the middle of *Music From Big Pink* is a hit. One of the greatest songs ever recorded. "The Weight" reached #63 on the *Billboard* Hot 100, reaching #21 in the UK. The song remains nostalgic and current. After hearing from Manuel and Danko on lead vocals, the first verse of "The Weight" ("Pulled into Nazareth") is sung by Levon. A third lead vocalist?

On the second verse ("Picked up my bags"), Levon again takes the lead vocal and accentuates a couple classic lines: "Picked up my bag/Went looking for a place to hide" and "When I saw Carmen and the devil walking side by side/I said 'Hey Carmen, come on let's go downtown'/She said 'I gotta go, but my friend can stick around'." The image of the vocalist, in first person, heading downtown with Carmen's friend, the devil – it just screams of Dylan's influence on Robbie. Levon again leads on the third verse ("Go down Ms. Moses") and announces his vocal prowess on the line "Well Luke my friend, what about young Anna Lee." The passion in Levon's voice would become the hallmark of The Band. Raspy and primal, yet sweet and warm. Levon was a rare, really rare, vocal talent.

Danko takes over lead vocals on the fourth verse ("Crazy Chester followed me"). Why the lead vocal switch? The verse is in the same key, exact same chords. Just an example of The Band being authentic, genuine and original. The song closes with a final verse ("Catch a cannonball"), with Levon taking the lead, but Manuel and Danko harmonizing.

The beauty of "The Weight" is incredibly hard to describe. Yes, the harmonized vocals are wonderful, but other bands sang better than The Band. The instrumentation is excellent, but other tracks – even on *Music From Big Pink* – are better, musically. The lyrics are interesting, but not compelling. Yet, the song seems like a reluctant anthem. Why? My thought is that more than any other song in The Band's catalog, "The Weight" exemplifies that The Band is a democracy, a sum of various parts, with the mathematical result larger than the various components. "The Weight" is the essential amalgamation of lyrics, voices, instruments, arrangement and production. And, one other element – passion.

After an upbeat run through "We Can Talk" to open Side 2, Danko resumes lead vocals on a cover version of "Long Black Veil." The Band's arrangement is slow and haunting, yet Danko's vocal exudes youth. "Long Black Veil" was written by Danny Dill and originally recorded by Lefty Frizzell, as a Country ballad. Johnny Cash covered "Long Black Veil" at the Folsom Prison concert. "Long Black Veil" seems like a natural outgrowth of *The Basement Tapes*.

"Long Black Veil" tells the story of a man that is accused of a murder he did not commit, but when he is asked to testify about his alibi, essentially proving his innocence, the man remains silent. The man remains silent because at the time of the murder, he was sleeping with his best friend's wife. To protect the woman, he decides to not present his alibi, resulting in the man's death by hanging. I have always been fascinated at how this song carries the plot of a novel in just a few lines.

After a run through "Chest Fever", an R&B-driven track sung by Manuel and featuring a classic pump organ intro by Garth, and "Lonesome Suzie", a ballad also sung by Manuel (which highlights Manuel's tremendous voice), the album closes with two tracks written by Dylan. "This Wheel's On Fire" was written by Dylan and Danko, with Danko on lead vocals. The track has a messy, almost garage rock vibe propelled by Robbie on lead guitar. Danko's voice settles into a cadence that would become his hallmark (see "Stage Fright" from 1970) and each of Levon and Manuel support Danko's vocals during the chorus – creating the closest comparison to the music created by Bob Dylan and The Band on their controversial tour in 1966. The track fades out with a guitar solo by Robbie.

And, as the guitar solo fades into a few solemn yet hopeful piano notes, followed by a slightly haunting, swirling organ effect from

Garth – the swirling organ drops into the background just as Richard Manuel begins a cherished vocal performance. Utilizing a high register, falsetto-esque tone, Manuel delivers a beautiful, yet simultaneously pained performance. Recognizing the talent of Manuel, The Band expertly play in back of the vocals, limiting fills, providing context, but demanding focus on Manuel. However, while Manuel's vocal is the lasting memory, Dylan's lyrics are essential. "I Shall Be Released" has since become a classic track in the canon of American music.

Dylan alternates, rather randomly, between first person and third person. The substance of the song references prison life –"a man who swears he's not to blame", "crying out that he's been framed", "Yet I swear I see my reflection/Somewhere so high above this wall." However, Dylan never tells the story – never includes the listener in the facts that resulted in the imprisonment, or why the man feels he is wrongly incarcerated. The storyline – the prison life – is simply misdirection.

The message that Dylan is conveying is redemption. He uses the cover of prison to illustrate that redemption, is possible – and advisable. Dylan suggests the importance of forgiveness – the importance of being "released" – perhaps providing a template for society – an alternative to action and passion and an alternative to the violence sweeping across America. Perhaps, Dylan is suggesting that forgiveness, rather than aggressiveness, is in order?

"I Shall Be Released" has been covered by dozens of artists, including Jeff Buckley, The Byrds (of course), The Hollies, The Jerry Garcia Band, Nina Simone, and more recently, Wilco, Kesha and Jack Johnson. Famously, at The Band's final concert in 1976, *The Last Waltz*, "I Shall Be Released" was the final song sung by the ensemble cast of musicians that included Neil Young, Eric Clapton, Stephen Stills, Van Morrison, Joni Mitchell, Muddy Waters, Ringo Star and, of course, Bob Dylan. While many have covered the song admirably, even Dylan himself, Manuel's version on *Music From Big Pink* remains the essential version.

After debuting relatively flat on the *Billboard* Top 200 Albums chart, *Music From Big Pink* slowly attracted attention in late-1968. Critic after critic lauded the record and musician after musician cited *Music From Big Pink* as hip and influential. Eventually, the masses joined the cavalry and *Music From Big Pink* peaked at #30 on the *Billboard* Pop Album chart. Yes, the "Pop" album chart, not the *Billboard* Top 200 Albums chart.

Music From Big Pink represented a very quiet minority – a group of young folks that, while they may have cared about the issues of 1968, decided to check out. Fly away. Vacate the premises. Bunker down in a rural community. Selfish? Apathetic? Cowardly? Not really.

The foundation of America is freedom. The Band, and *Music From Big Pink*, is an example of freedom. The subconscious behind, or within, *Music From Big Pink* quietly started a revolution. No longer did musicians have to progress, push forward, innovate and comment – The Band announced that looking backwards, to a simpler time was just as important, just as cool and just as influential. By avoiding a message of action and revolt, The Band pleaded for peace – The Bank established "genuineness" as essential.

Creedence Clearwater Revival – S/T

Creedence Clearwater Revival features only eight tracks, three covers and five original songs written by John Fogerty. With two tracks charting on the *Billboard* Hot 100, "Suzie Q" peaked at #11 and "I Put a Spell on You" at #58, *Creedence Clearwater Revival* was no doubt a commercial success, but such success would pale in comparison to the popularity of CCR between 1969 and 1972.

In just four years, CCR had five #2 hits on the *Billboard* Hot 100. Only Elvis Presley and Madonna accumulated more (each had six). Surprisingly, CCR never scored a #1 hit, thus possessing the dubious distinction of having the most #2 hits without a #1 song. Nonetheless, CCR has sold over 26 million records in the United States alone. This album marks the beginning.

Meeting at Portola Junior High School in El Cerrito, California, John Fogerty, Doug Clifford and Stu Cook formed a band called The Blue Velvets. In 1964, the trio was joined by Tom Fogerty, John's older brother. The band changed its name to The Golliwogs in 1965 and found steady work, playing gigs in and around San Francisco in early-1966. In late-1966, after receiving draft cards, Tom Fogerty and Stu Cook enlisted in the military. John Fogerty and Doug Clifford continued to promote The Golliwogs and secured a recording contract with Fantasy Records. There was one condition, though.

Fantasy Records despised the band name, The Golliwogs, and recommended (or demanded) that the band conjure a new moniker. Now, CCR wrote some amazing songs, accessible, catchy and eternal – but, their talent for naming a band seems a bit challenged. The band kicked around Muddy Rabbit, Gossamer Wump and Creedence Nuball and the Ruby. Finally, riffing a bit off of Buffalo Springfield and Jefferson Airplane, John Fogerty strung together Creedence Clearwater Revival. With the new band name etched, once Tom and Stu returned from service in early-1968, CCR entered the recording studio.

Despite possessing pieces of a few original songs written by John Fogerty, CCR opted to first record a cover. On their debut studio recording, CCR arranged the definitive version of a popular Dale Hawkins tune, "Suzie Q." CCR's version is like a freight train. The arrangement is thick and dark, but paced and ominously accessible. Perhaps that is the most lasting quality of CCR's music – it is accessible, yet raw. Easy to digest, easy to understand and easy to love. "Suzie Q" begins with a fade in of drums and the lead guitar lick from John Fogerty. Equally as important is Tom Fogerty's rhythm guitar – as the tight, swampy rhythm allows John Fogerty to rip off a killer lead guitar solo after the first verse. Such an early (and long) guitar solo alerts the listener to the notion that the track will not be a standard, three minute Single.

After two more verses (the second verse featuring John Fogerty singing through a megaphone) and two more guitar solos, most bands would have naturally ended the track. But, such was not the intention of CCR. CCR were a group of working class kids from a dusty California town, lacking economic support from family and friends. Each member of the band decided to quit their day jobs and focus on CCR, but this left the band with very little resources. John Fogerty stated in a 1993 interview with *Rolling Stone* that the intent behind the studio version of "Suzie Q" was to get the track played on the hip, progressive, underground radio station, KMPX in San Francisco.

KMPX avoided traditional Pop tracks, in favor of Psychedelic Rock and improvisation. CCR devised a plan to record an eight and half minute version of "Suzie Q", but release the first part of the track on Side A and the jam section on Side B. Thus, the Side A Single would be a four minute track, but the album version was eight and half minutes. KMPX latched onto the full album version, propelling CCR into the Bay Area consciousness.

While later CCR classics such as "Down on the Corner", "Bad Moon Rising", "Green River" and, of course, "Proud Mary" illustrate the band's gravitation towards Country and Southern Rock, each track on *Creedence Clearwater Revival* displays the Blues foundation of CCR. John Fogerty's vocals and guitar lead the way, but CCR is a tight Rock band, very much on display during the album's final cut, "Walking on the Water", as well as the coda and jam sections in "Suzie Q."

While the eccentrics and progressives may have leaned towards The Grateful Dead and Jefferson Airplane, CCR was embraced by the masses, the young folks flooding to the counterculture movement, yet unconditioned to deep exploration. Psychedelic, yet grounded in Hard Rock. Raging, yet unknowingly contained. Wild and creative, but again – accessible due to basic time signatures, simple production and intelligently common lyrics.

For an illustration, check out "Working Man." The first original recorded by John Fogerty at Fantasy Records, the track conveys a characteristic of CCR's music that would resonate with millions.

197

Backed by a Chuck Berry-esque guitar riff, Fogerty sings about a concept foreign to many young people in the Bay Area in 1968. John Fogerty wrote a song about working – having a job and earning money. Preaching responsibility and maturity, rather than idealism and using drugs. "Working Man", and Fogerty's other classic original on this album, "Porterville", foreshadowed Fogerty's later assault on wealth and the inequity of certain kids being sent to Vietnam and other, more "fortunate" kids, dodging military service ("Fortunate Son").

After the success of *Creedence Clearwater Revival*, CCR earned a slot at the Woodstock Festival in 1969. The exposure at Woodstock led to sold out world tours, but one thing made CCR an international success – songs. Fogerty crafted quick, catchy choruses, accompanied by equally quick and catchy guitar licks. Many of CCR's most famous songs, commercially, are upbeat – the aforementioned "Proud Mary" and "Down on the Corner", for example – but, critics and hardcore fans gravitate towards equally stunning ballads such as "Who'll Stop the Rain", "Lodi", "Have You Ever Seen the Rain" and, my favorite, "Long As I Can See the Light."

In late-1970, the original lineup of CCR parted ways. Maybe at one time compelling, the story of the break up is quite boring. Two brothers fighting over money. Problems with a record label. Maybe even some drug abuse. CCR continued as a trio after Tom Fogerty quit, but released its final album, *Mardi Gras*, in 1972. The album sold a bit, but critics ripped the effort. Famously, Jon Landau from *Rolling Stone* declared the album "the worst album I have ever heard from a major rock band." So, yeah – that pretty much was it for CCR.

CCR rarely reunited after 1972. The original four member lineup jammed at Tom Fogerty's wedding in 1980, then John, Stu and Doug played a few songs at the El Cerrito High School 20 year reunion in 1983. After that, though, as the music industry shifted towards royalty payments accruing to the songwriter, rather than the band – John Fogerty became incredibly wealthy, while Stu, Doug and Tom – well, they didn't. Tom died from AIDS in 1990. Shortly thereafter,

Stu and Doug brought a series of lawsuits against John and Fantasy Records.

In 1993, CCR was to be inducted into the Rock & Roll Hall of Fame. Each of the three surviving members attended the ceremony, however, John refused to play or take the stage with Stu and Doug. The details are unclear, but Stu and Doug were barred from the stage as John jammed on two CCR songs with Bruce Springsteen and Robbie Robertson. Assuredly, a tough night for Stu and Doug.

CCR was an integral force in 1968, and through 1972, providing an access point for listeners to embark on a further, perhaps more complicated, musical journey. Similar to the role played by The Doors. A gateway band – drawing you in with songs and before you know it – you're going out of your mind at a Grateful Dead concert.

The Grateful Dead – *Anthem of the Sun*

If you would like to know what The Grateful Dead sounded like in 1968, please don't listen to *Anthem of the Sun*. *Anthem of the Sun* was the second studio record by The Grateful Dead, and the first with second drummer, Mickey Hart. The album is a patchwork of live performances, along with studio embellishments by each band member. Jerry Garcia refers to *Anthem of the Sun* as a "collage." Joe Smith, a Warner Bros. executive refers to *Anthem of the Sun* as "the most unreasonable project with which we have ever involved ourselves." Ultimately, *Anthem of the Sun* is okay – it has a few "moments of blinding brilliance" – but, the record is so incredibly inferior to the tremendously well recorded live performances by The Grateful Dead that unfolded on a nightly basis during this period in 1968.

The sound of The Grateful Dead was the amalgamation, or result, of diverse musical backgrounds. Jerry Garcia was initially a banjo player, then a guitarist focused on Chuck Berry and Elvis Presley. Ron "Pigpen" McKernan was a semi-accomplished Blues singer and organist. Phil Lesh was a Classically trained bassist that focused on

Jazz. Likewise, Bill Kreutzman was a drummer that almost exclusively played Jazz. Lastly, Bob Weir was a young kid just looking to be in a band, with an affinity for Cowboy songs. Only in the Bay Area in 1965 could these musicians have connected and felt that it was a productive idea to form a band.

After a short stint as a Jug Band in 1965, The Grateful Dead embraced the psychedelic revolution incubated by Ken Kesey and the Merry Pranksters. The Grateful Dead served as the "House Band" for drug-fueled gatherings ("Acid Tests") in and around San Francisco (and Los Angeles). Influenced by an environment of creativity, improvisation and spontaneity, The Grateful Dead logged countless hours playing as a unit, learning each other's tendencies and allowing for synchronized unknowing.

Meaning, each member of the band had a license to innovate. Similar to Jazz, each member of The Grateful Dead essentially soloed throughout a composition, returning to a song's melody, occasionally. The product was at times cluttered and disorganized, and at times the foremost example of Rock improvisation, then and now. The music was intense and blissful – two extremes The Grateful Dead would harness, and master.

The Grateful Dead were notably and historically apolitical. And, not like Dylan. Dylan claimed to be apolitical, but his lyrics were loosely political and often, outright political commentary. The Grateful Dead rarely incorporated political speech into their lyrics, and usually did not cover songs that alluded to politics. Yet, I contend that the political events of 1968 did in fact shape the *music* of The Grateful Dead in 1968.

Early recordings from 1966 depict a band immersed in traditional Rock and Blues covers ("Pain in My Heart", "Spoonful" and "Sitting On Top of the World"). In 1967, like many (or most) Rock musicians, The Grateful Dead sunk deeper into the Psychedelic Rock chasm. However, while mainstream Rock and Pop artists utilized elaborate studio effects to create a kaleidoscope of expression, The Grateful Dead drifted in a different direction.

On December 13, 1967, The Grateful Dead debuted "Dark Star", a meandering, yet simple, mid-tempo track that leaned towards Jazz, but possessed a haunting template that at times was cinematic and at times without boundary. Renditions of "Dark Star" increased in length nearly every time the band played the song live, some versions lasting over 20 minutes. "Dark Star" became an anthem, but not in the traditional sense, as "Dark Star" did not peak or possess a sing-along chorus – "Dark Star" became an anthem for exploratory action. "Dark Star" was patient and flowing, as opposed to raging and intense.

In mid-1968, though – the music of The Grateful Dead noticeably changed. Coincidence? Jerry's lead guitar solos became more poignant, almost piercing at times and most definitely, louder. Jerry was experimenting with different guitars during this period, going back and forth between a Fender Stratocaster and a Gibson SG. Jerry's approach was aggressive, attacking and relentless. The music of The Grateful Dead suddenly coalesced around a primitive rage, with focus on energy and speed. This period of Grateful Dead in 1968 is referred to as "Primal Dead." A consequence, I believe, of the tension, rage and violence of the time.

The rhythm section pounded in unison, resulting in a collaborative, primitive manifestation of rhythm. The band expertly crafted chaos. The texture was dissonant, utilizing guitar and bass feedback to create an undying tension, which built to an unimaginable peak, eventually releasing into a cathartic breath. A sense of relief. The Grateful Dead specialized in creating chaos, then offering a respite. The Grateful Dead did not comment on the political and social turmoil of the moment, The Grateful Dead created the moment.

Despite preferring live performances, in 1968, The Grateful Dead wanted to make a studio album. After a relatively straight-forward debut release, The Grateful Dead desired to capture their "live sound" in the studio. Most bands operated in the studio by recording each instrument separately, then overdubbing harmony and fills, along with a multitude of sound effects. Some bands, though, actually recorded live in the studio, meaning – the band would set up and run through each track together, as if they were on stage. Clearly, The Grateful Dead would prefer the latter approach, but the problem was – it was quite impossible to replicate a Grateful Dead concert in a studio.

Sure, the musicians were the same, instruments were the same – but, there's a heck of a lot that went on at a Grateful Dead concert that could not possibly be replicated in the studio. The audience, the drugs, the lights, the smell, the various characters. Thus, The Grateful Dead opted to mesh various live recordings together in the Studio with certain new overdubs and accents. Warner Bros. dispatched David Hassinger to produce *Anthem of the Sun*. A veteran of more than 20 years. Hassinger quit the project after just two weeks, reportedly after Bob Weir asked Hassinger to create – on tape – the illusion of "thick air" by trekking out to the desert and recording silence. Hassinger also famously noted that "nobody [in the band] could sing."

After getting rid of Hassinger, The Grateful Dead asked their in-house sound engineer, Dan Healy, to produce and mix the record. Healy accepted and worked tirelessly with Garcia and Lesh to locate the best sounding live concert recordings in The Grateful Dead's burgeoning tape vault, hoping to extract bits and pieces of songs in order to assemble a composition.

Once Healy, Garcia and Lesh arranged the patchwork of song sections, the band engaged in a process that they called "interlacing" – a process of layering studio takes over and in between the live show recorded material. Garcia described the process as "mix[ing] it for the hallucinations." Not sure what That means. Kreutzman described the process (just a little bit) better: "Phil and Jerry were the ones who figured out that we could exploit studio technology to demonstrate how these songs were mirrors of infinity, even when they adhered to their established arrangements. It's the old paradox of 'improvisational compositions.' Jazz artists knew all about the balance between freedom and structure."

Despite only five tracks, the album clocks in at just under 40 minutes (and one track, "Born Cross-Eyed", is only 2 minutes). The album opens with a four part suite entitled, "That's It For the Other One (Parts I-IV)." On the first vinyl pressing, each "Part" was separated into a separate track (for songwriting royalty purposes...nothing got past those hippie businessmen). "That's It For the Other One" is a prime example of The Grateful Dead's sound in early 1968 – alternating between high energy and hauntingly quiet – but, at all times – dominated by expert musicianship. I'd love to tell you that the mixing, or weaving, of various live versions ended up sounding pretty cool, but it just doesn't. It is quite easy to identify the different live versions, based mainly on Garcia's vocals, but also due to the sound quality disparity. I suppose, though, it was easier than replicating a Grateful Dead concert in the studio.

The best track on the record is "Alligator", an 11 minute Blues-based Rock song with Ron "Pigpen" McKernan on lead vocals. The track begins with a terribly annoying kazoo (one of the studio embellishments), but otherwise, "Alligator" actually has some melody and in fact does achieve the stated goal of "sounding live" or "sounding like a Grateful Dead show." And, yes – of course, "Alligator" contains a drum solo, starting at 3:13 and lasting until 5:30. Not so bad, right? If you make it through the drum solo, you are rewarded with an incredible guitar solo by Garcia, followed by a full band onslaught of energy and orchestrated chaos. The instrumental jam carries on (awesomely) until the band arrives back at the original "Alligator" melody (kind of). The energy and chaos, and sheer violence of the instrumentation certainly mirrors the cultural condition of 1968.

That said, if you thought "Alligator" sounded like crap, don't listen to the next track, "Caution (Don't Step on the Tracks)." The first five minutes of "Caution" are relatively benign. Then, at 5:25 the track abruptly cuts to massive guitar and bass feedback. Such noise was not atypical at a Grateful Dead show – and this version of "Feedback" was taken from a show in Los Angeles (early-1968). The feedback quiets a bit at around 7:02, but things get weird again – real weird – for the remaining 2:35. And then – that's it. That's how the album ends.

This is the part of the chapter that I normally comment on the chart success of the record and then segue into what transpired with the band after the album release. Well, that's pretty simple in the case of *Anthem of the Sun*. The album was a commercial failure, and critics didn't care much for it either. I know, you're shocked. Look, The Grateful Dead took a shot. While most bands were using the studio to create bizarre, inorganic sounds – The Grateful Dead attempted to innovate in the studio by trying to recreate their live sound through a unique layering process.

So, it didn't work – but, they learned from the mistake. In 1969, The Grateful Dead released a classic record – cherished by fans and critics alike. The album was *Live/Dead*. This time, the band took an easier approach. They simply released full tracks from a live performance. No studio manipulation. Not surprisingly, The Grateful Dead used a breathtaking version of "Dark Star" to open *Live/Dead*.

With the popularity of counterculture sweeping the United States in 1968 and 1969, The Grateful Dead became a national sensation. Yet, the band had no hit song, no album of significance. The Grateful Dead had a culture. More importantly, The Grateful Dead had virtuous musicianship. The Grateful Dead were never about songs. Songs were just vehicles for improvisation. And, the improvisation of The Grateful Dead is a pure reflection of mood, moment, feeling and expression. After the song structure broke down and the musicians prepared to innovate and drift away – it's hardly surprising that the output of expression in 1968 was violent, powerful and aggressive. The Grateful Dead were affected by historical events in 1968, but they don't tell you with their lyrics, they show you with their instruments.

Cream – *Wheels of Fire*

I am well aware that this chapter is getting a bit long, but it's not my fault. Sure, I ramble a bit and head off on some tangents. But, am I supposed to glaze over albums by The Band, CCR, The Grateful Dead and Cream? I could trim some information. Like, I could gloss over how a band was formed and the context that led to the band's music in 1968? Just focus on the album released in 1968? Maybe, but not likely.

In early-1966, Eric Clapton quit The Yardbirds after arguments over the musical direction of the band. Clapton favored a traditional Blues approach, while the rest of the band craved a Pop presence (see The 1965 Project for a discussion of "For Your Love" by the Yardbirds). Clapton ceded power in The Yardbirds to Jeff Beck, then Jimmy Page. Soon after departing The Yardbirds, Clapton joined John Mayall and The Bluesbreakers. Mayall was an accomplished and well known organist and songwriter, preferring the traditional Blues approach that Clapton coveted. Clapton's tenure with Mayall was productive, but ultimately – Clapton was destined to form his own band.

After leaving Mayall in mid-1966, Clapton contacted Ginger Baker (drums) and Jack Bruce (bass). Both Baker and Bruce played in a somewhat well-known UK band called The Graham Bond Organization. Baker was an accomplished Jazz and Rock drummer and Bruce was a technical master on bass and had a great voice. The only minor issue was that Baker and Bruce hated each other. Or, maybe that's harsh – but, they certainly didn't get along. However, when the foremost electric guitar player in London asks you to form a band, you say, "yes."

The band chose the name "Cream" as a nod to each musician being the "cream of the crop." The band released *Fresh Cream* in late-1966, featuring the lead Single, "I Feel Free." The album charted at #6 in the UK and #39 on the *Billboard* Top 200 Albums chart. The attention was sufficient enough for promoters to book a tour in the United States.

Cream "landed" in March 1967, playing a string of dates in Brooklyn, NY. The shows were wildly successful. Cream returned to New York City in May to play additional live gigs, but also to record their second album, *Disraeli Gears*. Featuring hit Singles "Sunshine of Your Love", "Strange Brew" and "Tales of Brave Ulysses", *Disraeli Gears* peaked at #4 on the *Billboard* Top 200 Albums chart. "Sunshine of Your Love" reached #5 on the *Billboard* Hot 100. Cream was instantly an international sensation, offering a brand of Rock that was Blues-based, but heavier and harder. Cream was respected by musicians, praised by critics and beloved by fans. A rare feat.

After a successful string of shows in California in early-1968, Cream entered the studio to record *Wheels of Fire*. Being citizens of the UK, the members of Cream may not have been as influenced by American politics as musicians in the United States, but the members of Cream were quite adept at creating their own political chaos.

Tensions between Baker and Bruce became overwhelming. Clapton was essentially the peacekeeper – and, he was getting quite tired of the role. While the tension and arguments were wreaking havoc on the "business" of Cream, the "music" of Cream was benefiting. The tension manifested itself in the music by each of Baker, Bruce and Clapton pushing each other, forcefully. Each of Baker and Bruce created highly technical musical compositions, to test the other musicians. Songs consisted of odd time signatures, irregular changes. The product of this "competition" resulted in a slightly different sound – a sound now referred to as Progressive Rock or "prog."

As for Clapton, he was still addicted to the Blues. Clapton suggested cover versions of "Sitting On Top of the World", a classic by Howlin' Wolf, and "Born Under a Bad Sign", an Albert King standard. Clapton also advocated for "Crossroads" (a Robert Johnson song, rearranged by Clapton). "Crossroads" featured a Clapton guitar solo after the second verse that remains one of the best recorded guitar solos in Rock. Clapton's more traditional contributions worked well with Baker and Bruce's new direction, balancing an album that – was becoming quite long.

In fact, *Wheels of Fire* became a "double album." Double albums were quite rare in 1968, in fact, *Wheels of Fire* was the first platinum selling double album. In addition to three Baker originals, four Bruce originals, the two covers suggested by Clapton and the rearranged "Crossroads", *Wheels of Fire* included two sides of live material, recorded at the Fillmore West in San Francisco and the Winterland Ballroom, also in San Francisco. The live material is excellent, but *Wheels of Fire* didn't hit #1 on the *Billboard* Top 200 Albums chart and #3 in the UK due to the live material. The chart success of *Wheels of Fire* was a result of the album's lead Single, "White Room."

Written by Jack Bruce, "White Room" begins with an anthemic chord progression, followed by a snare drum crack and then Bruce's lead vocal. The rhythm is pulsing. Driving towards a falsetto chorus by Bruce. A slight pause allows Baker to rip a drum fill that leads into the second verse, which features Clapton on the wah pedal in the background (which kind of sounds like the foreground).

After a refrain of the opening chord progression, Bruce leads the band through a third verse, with Baker pounding on the drums and Clapton raging on guitar. Then, then – after settling down into the chorus and another refrain of the opening chord progression, Clapton unleashes (another) classic guitar solo. Cream has never sounded more like Cream than during Clapton's guitar solo on "White Room."

The lyrics of "White Room" convey darkness and certainly portray a dirty underworld, but it is the chorus that resonates. Not in a "making a statement" sort of way, but in a "fans can latch onto it" sort of way. Bruce sings in the softer voice, "I'll wait in this place/Where the sun never shines/Wait in this place/Where the shadows run from themselves." Just a wonderfully dark, dire image – the shadows running from themselves.

Despite the success of *Wheels of Fire*, Clapton no longer could tolerate the feuding between Baker and Bruce. Clapton recalled one show where he just stopped playing his guitar in the middle of a song and neither Baker nor Bruce even noticed. Clapton was also losing faith in the harder, Blues/Rock genre. Remember, it was right about this time that Clapton heard that little album from Bob Dylan's backing band, *Music From Big Pink*.

Cream would play a string of sold out shows billed as a "Farewell Tour" in late-1968, then Clapton, Baker and Bruce parted ways. Clapton formed Blind Faith, which included Steve Winwood (a young ace vocalist and underrated guitar and organ player with the band, Traffic) and Baker. Blind Faith recorded one album and toured successfully, eventually splitting up in 1970. Clapton then formed Derek & The Dominos, initially featuring Duane Allman on slide guitar. Under the Derek & The Dominos moniker, Clapton wrote several of his most revered songs, including "Layla." After Derek & The Dominos, Clapton embarked on an incredibly successful solo career.

Baker and Bruce bounced around, playing in several successful bands and several unsuccessful bands. In 1993, Cream was inducted into the Rock & Roll Hall of Fame and each of Clapton, Baker and Bruce set aside their differences and played together for the first time in 25 years. The trio played "Sunshine of Your Love", "Crossroads" and "Born Under a Bad Sign." In the years since, Cream has played a few "reunion" shows, and despite the shows being complete "money grabs", the story of Cream seems to have ended well. Cream was supremely influential, wildly popular and a critical element of music in 1968.

Mike Bloomfield/Al Kooper/Stephen Stills – *Super Session*

Somehow, this record has been lost in the shuffle a bit. It is understandable, as this group of musicians only made one record together – and the band doesn't even really have a name. The record is credited to each of Mike Bloomfield, Al Kooper and Stephen Stills and titled *Super Session*. The album has a back story, which I'll provide below, but it is critical to note that *Super Session* was quite popular in 1968, reaching #12 on the *Billboard* Top 200 Albums chart. Maybe more importantly, though – the album has held up, as three of the tracks are essential and worth as much of your time as anything covered above, sans *Music From Big Pink.*

Super Session was conceived by a couple of musicians that, for lack of a better explanation, had some time on their hands. Al Kooper and Mike Bloomfield were session players on Dylan's classic recording, *Highway 61 Revisited* in 1965. Kooper famously attempted to play lead guitar, but once Mike Bloomfield unpacked his Fender and started working through some scales, Kooper quietly slid his guitar case back under his chair and jumped on the organ. The rest is history, right – Kooper was an amateur organ player and therefore was routinely a quarter note behind on each change. The result can be heard on the greatest song ever recorded, "Like A Rolling Stone."

Kooper continued to collaborate with Dylan until Dylan's motorcycle accident and subsequent seclusion in 1966. Kooper then formed Blood, Sweat and Tears in 1967. Blood, Sweat and Tears experienced some success, incorporating elements of Jazz, but the band entered dormancy in early-1968. Likewise, after the *Highway 61* session, Bloomfield initially continued as the lead guitarist in the Paul Butterfield Blues Band, but after pushing the Butterfield Band towards exploratory compositions, as opposed to traditional Blues (See "East-West" as an example), Bloomfield quit. Bloomfield formed The Electric Flag in 1967, debuting at the Monterey Pop Festival. After the release of one, somewhat forgettable album, in April 1968, The Electric Flag broke up.

Kooper and Bloomfield remained friends, and according to Kooper, he suggested to Bloomfield that he (Kooper) could secure some studio time (Kooper worked for Columbia Records at the time). Kooper had witnessed several Jazz recording sessions and desired to replicate the format. Essentially, grab a few session players (on bass, drums and horns), hit record and jam for a while. Kooper pitched the vision to Bloomfield and they entered the studio.

On the record's opening track, "Albert's Shuffle", the freedom afforded Bloomfield is apparent. Patience quickly gives way to the classic Bloomfield tone and pace. When the horns enter at around 1:54, you begin to get the sense that the track will be an instrumental. Then, when Bloomfield's solo gives way to a Kooper organ solo at 3:09, it's clear that "Albert's Shuffle" is a Blues jam – similar to a track from Booker T. & The MG's circa 1965 or 1966.

After a run through "Stop" and "Man's Temptation", the band launches into "His Holy Modal Majesty", a nine minute exploration into various forms and styles of music. The track opens with an almost tribal, Indian raga percussive feel, then an organ solo from Kooper that is both bizarre and incredible. The organ is distorted in some fashion, not sure how, but the result is psychedelic. At 2:02, Bloomfield enters with Jazz chords that perfectly back Kooper's organ solo (yes, another organ solo). Using a typical Jazz progression, Bloomfield assumes the lead at 2:58 while Kooper retreats to modal Jazz chords. Bloomfield's guitar solo is more contained and less piercing, but no less impressive.

Kooper and Bloomfield bounce back and forth on lead a few times over the nine minute composition, and while Kooper's organ playing is surprisingly interesting and impressive, Bloomfield playing Jazz guitar is a wonder. His solo at 7:05 is so well crafted, so well conveyed and so well spirited, leading to a guitar passage that borrows from Joe Pass or Kenny Burrell to close the song. If you're a fan of Jazz fusion, experimental music, improvised Grateful Dead – definitely check out "His Holy Modal Majesty."

After recording "His Holy Modal Majesty", reportedly dedicated to John Coltrane, the band shut it down for the night, aiming to complete the session the following evening. Unfortunately, not everyone showed up the following evening. Bloomfield had battled drug and alcohol abuse, among other issues, which resulted in a well-deserved reputation of being irresponsible. With all of the session players ready to go (and ready to be paid), Kooper frantically called around for a lead guitarist that could fill in for Bloomfield. Kooper connected with Stephen Stills. Coincidentally, Stills was looking for some work after the demise of Buffalo Springfield (and before CSN).

Stills plays lead guitar on Side 2 of *Super Session*, also contributing backing vocals. If "His Holy Modal Majesty" is the best track on *Super Session*, the next two best tracks are on Side 2. The first track with Stills, "It Takes a Lot to Laugh, It Takes a Train to Cry", a Dylan cover that appeared on *Highway 61*, was likely intended as a warm-up for Stills. Kooper handles lead vocals and arranges the song in a Country or Folk-Rock style, possibly in light of Stills' stylistic leaning. Fortunately, the arrangement prompted Stills to take a sweet guitar solo at 1:40 (Kooper audibly says, "play it Stephen").

The solo from Stills is totally different than Bloomfield's playing on Side 1. Stills immediately grabs a Country lick and just settles into a twangy mood, foreshadowing his playing on CSN's debut release. The song actually concludes with Kooper using the same organ effect that he used on "His Holy Modal Majesty" (an odd choice to fit into the Country vibe, but evidence of experimentation). Not the definitive cover version of "Train to Cry", but a fun arrangement and a groovy track to add to a sunny day playlist.

The next track is a must listen. At eleven minutes, Kooper and Stills sound awesome on a cover version of "Season of the Witch." Originally written and performed by Donovan, Kooper and Stills stretch the track out and Stills impressively lays down a funky rhythm guitar. Kooper's vocals again are better than passable, but early on – the key is the rhythm set by Stills, and of course the horn section.

The patience within, or between, each verse conveys looseness and spontaneity. When musicians of this caliber are not confined by the parameters of time, meaning – squeezing the track into a four minute box – true talent shines. That said, some would argue, me included, that true talent is when a musician is able to shine within the confines of the four minute box. Two paths, but on "Season of the Witch", Kooper and Stills display a keen awareness of energy and skill. If you are only familiar with the guitar playing of Stephen Stills in Buffalo Springfield and CSN, I think you will be quite impressed by his work on this track.

Ultimately, *Super Session* is a "one-off", a successful session featuring a few classic musicians. Kooper, Bloomfield and Stills created an atmosphere that enabled exploration and openness. Did it work? I'd say that it worked on most of the tracks. Specifically, "Albert's Shuffle", "His Holy Modal Majesty", "Train to Cry" and "Season of the Witch." Listen to those tracks.

August

August

HISTORY

Democratic National Convention

MUSIC

James Brown – "Say It Loud – I'm Black and I'm Proud"
Big Brother & The Holding Company – *Cheap Thrills*
The Byrds – *Sweetheart of the Rodeo*
Jeff Beck – *Truth*

HISTORY

In 1968, August was the consequence. August became the reality of the irrational, unrealistic pre-existing condition. Dissension, violence, hatred, tragedy, action, heat – unfolding in the streets of Chicago. Omnipresent evil. The government of the United States chose force to achieve strategic political goals in Vietnam. Likewise, the people of the United States chose force to achieve strategic political goals in the United States. The government of the United States then, unconscionably, chose force against the American people. The definition of a dictatorship. A disastrous cycle of alarming, mutually assured destruction. January through June set the course. July toppled the cauldron. August was the consequence.

Democratic National Convention

Haynes Johnson, a Pulitzer Prize winning reporter wrote in *Smithsonian Magazine* that the Democratic National Convention in Chicago was a "lacerating event, a distillation of a year of heartbreak, assassinations, riots and a breakdown in law and order that made it seem as if the country were coming apart." Johnson continued, "In its psychic impact, and its long-term political consequences, it eclipsed any other such convention in American history, destroying faith in politicians, in the political system, in the country and in its institutions. No one…could escape the memory of what took place before their eyes."

The following will recount the facts, the events that transpired during and leading up to "Chicago." Reflecting upon Chicago, it strikes me as the point in which the war – not just the Vietnam War, but the economic war, the class war, the racial war, the generational war, the ideological war, the war against speech and expression – Chicago marks the point upon which people chose sides. You were either *For* or *Against*. For the War or Against the War. For the institution of the United States, or Against.

215

As discussed in the previous chapter, a movement was underway that targeted Chicago as the battleground, the locale for a high profile presence and the proliferation of a (loud) message. Led by Abbie Hoffman, the Yippies applied for demonstration and camping permits. The Yippies intended on camping in Lincoln Park and convening a rally outside of Soldier Field, on Lake Michigan. Despite making outrageous claims prior to arriving in Chicago, documentation suggests that the Yippies planned only to gather and march, peacefully. On July 29, Chicago Mayor Richard Daley denied almost all of the demonstration and camping permits, including all of the permits sought by the Yippies.

The permit denials did not dissuade "the movement" from flocking to Chicago. If anything, the lack of permits fueled the chaos, as demonstrations were not organized and orderly, not confined or scheduled. Mayor Daley requested and was granted Federal support from the National Guard. Over 6,000 members of the National Guard arrived in Chicago on August 23, practicing riot-control drills in public view, presumably as a deterrent. Additionally, 3,000 soldiers from the Army, stationed at Fort Hood, were ordered to report to Chicago. Notably, 100 of the soldiers held an all-night protest, refusing to report, citing political views and free expression. The following morning, 43 of the soldiers were arrested – all of whom were African American. The United States was regressing.

August 23 also marked the day that the Yippies landed in Chicago. In typical fashion, the Yippies organized a rally at the plaza in front of the Chicago Civic Center. Abbie Hoffman addressed a large crowd and announced that the Yippies were officially nominating a Presidential candidate. As the crowd roared, Hoffman introduced Pigasus – an actual pig. Chicago Police quickly moved in and interrupted the rally, arresting Hoffman and six other Yippies. According to the Yippies, the pig was also arrested.

Despite not obtaining a permit, the youth movement, which included the Yippies, congregated in Lincoln Park, for the Festival of Life. A concert was held on the evening of August 25, featuring MC-5 and various local bands from Chicago. Police were instructed to contain the crowd, allowing the concert to continue. At around 10:00 pm, the concert organizers drove a flatbed truck into Lincoln Park, intended as a second stage. Police blocked the path of the flatbed truck, refusing to allow the second stage. As tensions escalated, the police, dressed in full riot gear, enforced a Mayor Daley-initiated curfew by initiating a sweep of Lincoln Park.

When protestors refused to vacate, police engaged. Several people were arrested and police officers used clubs to beat innocent, passive demonstrators. This was the spark. Police reinforcements were summoned and over 1,000 people were arrested. However, most of the demonstrators fled the scene, congregating between Stockton Drive and Clark Street. The crowd of roughly 2,000 decided to march to the police precinct where their friends and fellow demonstrators were being held. The protestors reached the police precinct just after midnight. The precinct was surrounded by a barricade of police officers. Instead of simply protecting the precinct, the police engaged, beating several people and arresting hundreds. Fearing for their safety, the demonstrators dispersed.

Later on August 26, Mayor Daley officially opened the Democratic National Convention. Having been informed of the uprisings, Mayor Daley famously stated in his opening remark, "As long as I am Mayor of this city, there's going to be law and order in Chicago." In 1968, "law and order" became a tag line of sorts – a symbol of strong government, a statement in support of the institution of the United States. But, "law and order" also symbolized violence. Violence as a means of exerting governmental control. The psychology of "law and order" stems from the conduct of the United States in Vietnam, embracing force as a tool for political control.

After an evening of increased violence, which included the use of tear gas, on August 27 the Chairman of the Black Panther Party, Bobby Seale, spoke to a massive audience of young people. Seale urged people to "defend themselves by any means necessary if attacked by the police." Shortly after Seale's remarks, the Yippies convened an event at the Chicago Coliseum titled, the "Unbirthday Party for LBJ." Speakers included William Burroughs, Allen Ginsberg, Phil Ochs and, of course, Abbie Hoffman. The event unfolded without incident.

On August 28, a group of approximately 4,000 people gathered for a rally and demonstration in Grant Park, featuring Hoffman, Ginsberg and Norman Mailer. The Chicago Police Department dispatched over 600 officers, ordering the officers to surround the demonstration. Members of the National Guard were posted on the roof of nearby buildings, including the Field Museum. The rally had no violent motivations, but the ominous police presence perpetuated fear and promoted anxiety.

Attempting to leave, after the conclusion of the speeches, the crowd was met with force. Police officers refused mobility and tempers flared. Several hundred people leaked out of Grant Park, towards the Balbo and Congress bridges, but were met by National Guardsman armed with machine guns and grenade launchers. This is Chicago, remember – not Vietnam. Fearing a clash, the crowd migrated north, towards the Jackson Street bridge. Finding the Jackson Street bridge unguarded, thousands of people surged onto Michigan Avenue.

Coincidentally, as the crowd moved along Michigan Avenue, towards Balbo Street, a march led by Ralph Abernathy, a leading African American civic leader and former confidant of Martin Luther King, Jr., was passing by, intersecting with the throng of young folks. Abernathy had successfully obtained a demonstration permit for his march, and therefore was escorted by police officers. According to Mayor Daley, police officers engaged the large non-Abernathy crowd – attempting to clear a path for the permitted Abernathy march. However, by "engaging" the crowd, the police officers beat the young people with clubs. Not exactly normal police behavior. Witnesses insist that the young people were not inciting the violence, nor were they retaliating. The police officers actually beat innocent people in the streets of Chicago.

Now, that may sound like "the other side of the story", but in this case – there really was only one side of the story. The entire scene was caught on film. The intersection of the Grant Park crowd of young folks and the Abernathy march happened right in front of the Hilton Hotel, the exact hotel that most reporters and television crews were staying, covering the Democratic National Convention. As the brutality escalated, television crews turned on their cameras and captured some of the most raw and disturbing footage in the history of the United States.

Millions of viewers witnessed police officers beating civilians that were already lying on the ground, in the street, bloodied and defenseless. Tear gas and smoke filled the television screen, along with police officers in riot gear and brandishing machine guns. The violence and chaos was unimaginable and indelible. Chicago looked like Vietnam.

Never has there been a scene quite like Chicago in August 1968. Never before has America seemed so unstable. Never before have the people of the United States feared their own government with such reality. Defending his conduct, and the conduct of his police officers, Mayor Daley uttered a now famous statement: "The policeman isn't there to create disorder, the policeman is there to preserve disorder." Of course, he meant to say "preserve order." The mistake remains perfectly relevant.

In total, 668 people were arrested in Chicago during the week of the Democratic National Convention. Approximately, 111 people were treated at Chicago hospitals. Mobile medical units estimated that they treated over 1,000 people for wounds stemming from police brutality. And, for what? To make a statement? To influence the government of the United States? To influence the Americans that remained undecided about the Vietnam War?

I'm not intimating that the demonstrations were worthless. I'm not suggesting that the events of Chicago were not tragic. They were, absolutely. People sustained physical injuries – and the scene penetrated the hearts and minds of millions of Americans. However, the real damage – the real tragedy was the loss of life in Vietnam. Chicago may have *looked like* Vietnam, but it most certainly was not. While protestors were beaten in the streets of Chicago, during the week of the Democratic National Convention, 308 soldiers were killed in Vietnam, with 1,144 sustaining serious injuries. Somehow, the focus became Chicago, while the tragedy was still very much Vietnam.

"Chicago changed minds, Chicago changed politics, Chicago changed the Left, Chicago changed the media. What happened in Chicago in August of 1968 changed our political and cultural institutions, and so it shaped our current political and cultural life" (*Chicago Tribune*). The television images are so vivid, so blatant – and yet, so foreign. For those that had yet to "choose a side", the events of Chicago were decisive. Millions of Americans flocked to the movement of immediate withdrawal from Vietnam.

What happened to Hoffman, Rubin and the Yippies? What began as a thoughtful, well-intentioned, often comedic, organized mission resulted in a Federal indictment. Hoffman, Rubin, David Dellinger, John Froiner, Rennie Davis, Bobby Seale, Tom Hayden and Lee Weiner were indicted on March 20, 1969 on charges of "conspiring to cross state lines with the intent to incite, organize, promote, encourage, participate in, and carry out a riot." The charge carried a ten year prison sentence. The defendants became known as "The Chicago Seven" (charges were dropped against Bobby Seale, thus leaving only seven defendants).

On February 18, 1970, a jury reached a verdict in the case, convicting each of Davis, Dellinger, Hayden, Hoffman and Rubin. The defendants were sentenced to five years in Federal prison. After months of appeal, on November 21, 1972, the United States Court of Appeals for the Seventh Circuit reversed the conviction. The Justice Department decided not to retry the case, dropping all charges against The Chicago Seven.

As for Abbie Hoffman, he remained active as an agent of protest, but continuously lamented throughout the 1980s about the lack of passion from young people in America. Hoffman became dismayed with the conservatism of the United States under President Ronald Reagan. Hoffman demonized a relatively peaceful time in American society by praising the activism of the Sixties, a demonstratively turbulent period. Hoffman was a remnant of a more complicated time. On April 12, 1980, Hoffman swallowed 150 phenobarbital tablets, drank a bunch of liquor and never woke up. He was 52 years old.

MUSIC

As discussed, with respect to timing and chronology, now in August – we are at a point where the events of March, April and May took place prior to the recording of most of the music released in August. While the aesthetic of 1968 threads through most of the music released in 1968, the music in August and thereafter carries a more overt and direct volume – not only in terms of instrumentation, but lyrically.

James Brown – "Say It Loud – I'm Black and I'm Proud"

Perhaps, James Brown had the most remarkable career in music? Prior to 1964, with tracks such as "Please, Please, Please", "Night Train" and "Try Me", James Brown was the premier singer in Soul. In 1965, with the release of "Papa's Got a Brand New Bag" and "Cold Sweat", James Brown invented an early incarnation of Funk by shifting from 6/8 time to a rhythmic, driving 4/4 structure. While innovative and influential, musically – the instrumentation was not expressive in terms of substance. The music was intentionally devoid of political message.

As described in The 1965 Project, African American musicians were largely reticent to "speak out" on race and discrimination (through song). Notoriously, labels such as Motown prohibited African American artists from including social commentary in lyrics. Berry Gordy, founder of Motown, required African American artists to wear

221

sharply tailored suits, mandated smiles and favored bright arrangements. Gordy was an incredibly successful capitalist, but to some extent, prioritized revenue over utilizing music as an instigator for social change.

James Brown was not controlled by Gordy and Motown, but Brown largely followed the path – focusing on rhythm, showmanship and accessibility. Brown, like Louis Armstrong before him, was a devout capitalist and business-minded artist. In 1968, though, something changed. Despite Brown initially functioning as a calming influence in April – advocating for self-restraint and responsibility – Brown assumed the prevailing posture of action and revolt in August. Brown became enraged.

"Say It Loud – I'm Black and I'm Proud" was recorded in Los Angeles at Vox Studios on August 7. The track was released just weeks after the recording, as Brown insisted the track be immediately mixed and pressed. Rather than traditional lyrics in a verse/chorus structure, the words on "Say It Loud" are basically declarations. Only one chord is used throughout the song, with a bridge that focuses on a single note. According to *A.V. Club*, "the very idea of rap music is laid out in this Single; it just took the rest of the world ten years to catch on" (referencing "Rapper's Delight", the first mainstream rap song).

After a classic James Brown "grunt" to start the track, Brown and a chorus of young children from the Watts and Compton neighborhoods of Los Angeles engaged in "call and response." Brown yells, "Say it loud" and the young voices yell "I'm black and I'm proud." Very cool, if not "cute", but then Brown made the most serious statements of his career:

> *Some people say we got a lot of malice*
> *Some say it's a lot of nerve*
> *But I say we won't quit movin'*
> *Until we get what we deserve*

Brown had steadfastly believed in civil disobedience, rather than revolution and action, but the historical events of 1968 changed Brown's psychology. The assassinations of MLK and RFK changed Brown's disposition. The lyrics to "Say It Loud" illustrate the shift. Brown emphasizes:

> *Now we demand a chance to do things for ourselves*
> *We tired of beatin' our heads against the wall*
> *And workin' for someone else*
> *There's one thing more I got to say right here*
> *Now, we're people – we're like the birds and the bees*
> *We rather die on our feet than keep livin' on our knees*

"Say It Loud" was embraced by the Black Panthers as their unofficial anthem. More broadly, though, the "chorus" or refrain of "Say it loud/I'm black and I'm proud" was a rallying cry for millions. Musically, "Say It Loud" was downright Funk. The popularity of "Say It Loud" was the product of society's support of the song's message. "Say It Loud" reached #10 on the *Billboard* Hot 100. The message is strong and the groove is thick.

"Say It Loud" was a call for black empowerment and self-reliance. Notably, with respect to semantics, or word choice, in 1968 – African Americans were still called, or referred to publicly as "negroes." Calling someone "black" was more pejorative than "negro" or "colored." "Say It Loud – I'm Black and I'm Proud" was Brown's way of reclaiming the word "black." Brown forced the narrative and thereafter, "black" became a more widely used term.

For Brown, "Say It Loud" was yet another step toward a darker, more hostile version of Funk. "Say It Loud" features Maceo Parker on tenor saxophone, as usual, but the track also includes the legendary Fred Wesley on trombone and Jimmy Nolen on electric guitar. Bob Marley covered "Say It Loud" in a medley that also included "Black Progress" and Miles Davis used the bassline from "Say It Loud" on "Yesternow", the best track on Davis' classic *A Tribute to Jack Johnson*. The Temptations "sampled" or "borrowed" parts of "Say It

Loud" on several recordings. Perhaps most influential, the drum track on "Say It Loud", by Clyde Stubblefield, is widely considered the most sampled drum track in Hip Hop and Rap.

Big Brother & The Holding Company – *Cheap Thrills*

Big Brother and the Holding Company formed in San Francisco in 1965 (yet another). Big Brother was among the family of bands borne from the psychedelic, counterculture movement in the Bay Area, which included The Grateful Dead, Jefferson Airplane and Quicksilver Messenger Service. While The Grateful Dead, and even Jefferson Airplane, eventually amassed a larger following, and obtained more fame as a band, during 1968 – no band from the Bay Area was more popular, nationally, than Big Brother. Understandably, though – no other band had a lead singer anything like Janis Joplin.

Similar to the roots of The Grateful Dead, the foundation of Big Brother was a plethora of diverse musical backgrounds. Peter Albin was a Country and Blues guitarist that played in and around San Francisco. Albin gravitated towards a fellow, local guitarist named Sam Andrew. Andrew was a professional guitarist, meaning he was already a studio session musician and played frequently around the Bay Area and in Los Angeles. Andrew focused mostly on Rock, but was trained as a Jazz and Classical guitarist. After a few jam sessions, the pair decided to form a band.

Chet Helms, the owner of the Avalon Ballroom and an influential agent and promoter in San Francisco, asked Big Brother to serve as the house band at the Avalon Ballroom. While Big Brother drew decent crowds, Helms felt as though the band could achieve greater success if they had a more capable lead vocalist. Having heard a demo of a young, Blues singer from Austin, Texas named Janis Joplin, Helms invited Joplin to San Francisco for an audition with Big Brother. Big Brother and Janis were not exactly a perfect match, though, as Big Brother preferred extended compositions that favored a blend of Jazz and Rock, with emphasis on improvisation, rather than vocals, arrangements and melody.

Helms, though, was infatuated with Janis and urged Big Brother to play a few gigs with Janis on lead vocals. Big Brother instantly became the hottest act in San Francisco. Audiences lined-up to see Janis perform with Big Brother and critics flocked to San Francisco to catch a glimpse of the sensation. Setting aside their initial creative vision, Big Brother adapted, pursuing a more conventional structure that highlighted the band's strength – Janis Joplin. Big Brother expertly crafted a brand of Psychedelic Rock that possessed an energetic, youthful Blues foundation. Big Brother was able to afford Janis space, yet not relegate the instrumentation to a secondary facet.

Big Brother released their debut album in 1967, in advance of their appearance at the Monterey Pop Festival. The album sold reasonably well in the Bay Area, but did not attract interest, nationally (and did not chart on *Billboard*). However, things changed dramatically after the Monterey Pop Festival.

As national media and a national audience converged at the Monterey Pop Festival, seeking an understanding and first-hand view of the San Francisco scene, Janis became a star. Audiences obsessed over Joplin's soulful presence and gravitated to the sheer emotion and power of her vocals. Michelle Phillips, co-founder of the Mama's and the Papa's, recalls being in the audience at the Monterey Pop Festival and hearing Janis for the first time, "I remember being amazed that this white woman was singing like Bessie Smith. I was astounded."

After the Monterey Pop Festival, national magazines featured Big Brother (mainly, Janis) in lead stories and cover photos. The media attention led to concert bookings across the country, including the headline slot for the opening night performance at the Fillmore East in New York. Capitalizing on the attention, Big Brother released a second Single from their debut record, "Down on Me." The track became incredibly popular and energized album sales, resulting in Big

Brother's debut record charting at #60 on the *Billboard* Top 200 Albums chart, remaining on the chart for 30 weeks. "Down on Me" peaked at #43 on the *Billboard* Hot 100.

In late-1967, Big Brother was approached by Albert Grossman, the long-time manager of Bob Dylan. Grossman desired to represent the band and suggested that he pitch Columbia Records, seeking a deal for Columbia to produce, and finance, Big Brother's next/second album. Columbia Records agreed and Big Brother entered the studio. Despite having new material, Big Brother was a sensation due to its live performances – and therefore, the band concluded that the next album should be a live record, recorded at the Grande Ballroom in Detroit. Preferring a studio recording, Columbia Records reluctantly agreed. Big Brother's performance in Detroit was exquisite, but the recording just wasn't clean, as the mix was inconsistent, volume levels were erratic and the crowd noise uneven. Columbia Records rejected the release.

Without a suitable live recording, Big Brother entered the recording studio in early-1968, but progress was quite slow. Similar to the initial experience of The Grateful Dead, Big Brother was having trouble recreating the energy and soul of the band's live performance (in the studio). The frustration was compounded by pressure from Columbia Records, and even Grossman. Studio time was incredibly expensive, not to mention the opportunity cost associated with committing resources to a relatively unproven group.

As usual, though – talent prevailed. Relying primarily on a core of three cover songs – "Summertime", "Piece of My Heart" and "Ball and Chain" – Big Brother tightened up the rhythm behind Joplin's vocals and the result is considered a masterpiece. *Cheap Thrills* debuted on August 12 and by October the album hit #1 on the *Billboard* Top 200 Albums chart, maintaining the top slot for eight non-consecutive weeks. *Cheap Thrills* was the most popular record of 1968, selling just shy of one million copies, more than any other artist.

The record begins not with the opening chords of
"Combination of the Two", but rather with the far
Graham, introducing Big Brother to a live audier
Columbia Records won the war in rejecting Big
recording from Detroit, but Big Brother won a
recording process. Big Brother strategically u
certain places to convey the illusion of a live
worked magically. Fans and critics alike we
assumed the record was a live recording. L
"Combination of the Two" – I think you, tou
one track on *Cheap Thrills*, "Ball and Chain",
recording.

Cheap Thrills goes from great to classic on the thir
"Summertime." Joplin's vocals are chilling on "Sum
perhaps, Joplin's greatest vocal performance. The trac
Albin and Andrew expertly crafting a delicate guitar intr
slow Blues palate, but an atypical tone. The guitar intro w
a vocal from Janis that is immediately captivating. Both
heartbreaking and heart-warming. After Albin takes a wander
guitar solo that is more textured than poignant, overtly leaning
towards Jazz, Andrew initiates a lead at 2:15 using a crunchy,
distorted guitar effect that echoed the tone promoted by Clapton,
Townsend and Jeff Beck. An example of how Big Brother blended
traditional Blues with contemporary Rock. Janis finished the track
with a highly compelling vocal flourish, demonstrating her ability to
convey emotion and soul in the context of a studio recording.

"Piece of My Heart" is next and begins with an upbeat Rock guitar
intro/riff that leads into the famous Janis vocal intro: "Now, come on,
come on, come on, come on." After the energetic intro, the band
drops, shifting the spotlight to Janis, as she slowly delivers the first
verse. The pace is sultry, highlighting melody and rhythm. "Piece of
My Heart", originally written by Jerry Ragovoy and Bert Berns and
originally performed by Erma Franklin in 1967, has an ascending pre-
chorus that unfolds into a seriously catchy, upbeat and wonderfully
bright chorus.

I (just) said that "Summertime" may be Joplin's greatest
mance, but scratch that – it is without question, "Piece of
Joplin's passion and energy are overwhelming, turning a
n, but otherwise non-descript song, into an anthem.
bility to build the volume and force of her vocal delivery is
ing hallmark.

of My Heart" is also the best example of Big Brother
ming to Joplin's strengths. Big Brother was notoriously loud
ften competed with Janis on stage, and in the studio, but on
ce of My Heart", Big Brother settles for arrangement over
me/power. For example, after the first verse and chorus, Albin
Andrew's tendency would have been to include a guitar solo prior
the second verse. On "Piece of My Heart", the band simmers into
e second verse, shining the spotlight on Joplin's voice. The pause,
r lack of a solo, essentially pulls the listener in – urging the listener
to not only listen to Janis, but to hear Janis (yes, loosely referencing
White Men Can't Jump). And, Janis delivers. She kills on the second
verse, with the highlight being the cadence of: "You're out on the
streets/Looking good", with just the perfect emphasis and screeching
tone on the word "Looking."

After the second verse and chorus, well....Andrew couldn't wait
much longer, as he launches into a now well-known guitar solo at
2:30. His tone again exudes Psychedelic Rock and Blues, but this
guitar solo exemplifies the growth of Big Brother. Andrew's solo is
wonderfully contained. Bands that embrace an improvisational
objective typically wander for a bit – sometimes ten or twenty
minutes – but, the wandering often winds into a peak, typically a
terrific guitar solo or lead riff.

The beauty of Andrew's solo on "Piece of My Heart" is that every
note is thoughtful – almost like Big Brother jammed the song out for
twenty minutes in the studio and condensed the jam, arriving at this
very guitar solo. Perfectly placed, perfectly executed. The guitar solo
leads into a refrain of the pre-chorus and chorus, then just prior to
another refrain, at 3:30 – the band pauses for a second as Janis

screams. You know the scream. Janis often screamed like this in Big Brother's live performances, but the inclusion on the studio take of "Piece of My Heart" was a stroke of brilliance, continuing the faux live motif.

"Piece of My Heart" was an immediate hit, peaking at #12 on the *Billboard* Hot 100. The popularity of "Piece of My Heart" propelled the commercial success of *Cheap Thrills*, but the success of *Cheap Thrills* was squarely attributable to one person: Janis Joplin. Janis was at the height of her power on *Cheap Thrills*. After the energetic Pop of "Piece of My Heart", Janis delivers an essential slow Blues on "Turtle Blues", backed by piano and a Delta Blues-style finger picked guitar. Again, sound effects are used to provide a "lounge" feel, sounding almost like a live Ella Fitzgerald or Billie Holiday recording, including crowd chatter and even some glasses clanking together. The song is simple, easy to like, but when Janis sings "If you just want to go out drinking, honey/Won't you invite me along, please", "Turtle Blues" becomes hard not to love.

I know I made this claim previously (twice), but Joplin's vocal performance on "Ball and Chain" is the best of her career. "Ball and Chain" remains the lasting jewel of *Cheap Thrills*. Recorded live, the track is eight and a half minutes, but feels like twenty (that's a compliment). After a few notes on the guitar by Albin, the band pauses for about six seconds, then propels into a distortion-laden guitar solo, backed by a steady drum beat and a heavy bass. After a minute of rather pleasant chaos, Janis enters and declares "Ball and Chain" a slow Blues. Admittedly, the slow Blues lane was Joplin's specialty, and she leaned on the style heavily, but "Ball and Chain" redefined the genre – borrowing traditional aspects of a slow Blues, but incorporating contemporary elements of Rock and even psychedelic attributes.

"Ball and Chain" was typically used as a set closer for Big Brother, and therefore, the track marked a logical conclusion for *Cheap Thrills* (complete with applause and then a fade-out with house music faint in the background). Please take a listen to "Ball and Chain", as it is the closest audio-only opportunity to hear Janis and Big Brother at their intoxicating best. I say "audio-only", because the best way to *experience* the power of Janis and Big Brother is to head over to YouTube and watch a few videos from the Monterey Pop Festival or the shows Janis performed while on the Festival Express (a tour of Canada where Janis was joined by The Grateful Dead and The Band). Seeing, or watching, Janis do her thing on stage is an unparalleled experience.

Now, I rarely do this in <u>The 1968 Project</u>, but I feel compelled to note the demo version of "Flower in the Sun" that appeared on a reissue of *Cheap Thrills*. No idea why "Flower in the Sun" didn't make the cut on *Cheap Thrills*, but the track is a terrific representation of how Big Brother could morph into a seriously competent Rock, Pop and even R&B band. "Flower in the Sun" has a terrific bounce, just a unique brand of Psychedelic Rock/Pop. Not on the official, original release of *Cheap Thrills*, but if you get in a "Janis" mood, don't forget "Flower in the Sun."

Like so many iterations of greatness from the "Sixties", the story of Big Brother and the life of Janis Joplin ended tragically. After the commercial and critical success of *Cheap Thrills*, Janis announced that she was leaving Big Brother to pursue a solo career. The members of Big Brother were devastated, but not surprised. Likewise, the media. In fact, I couldn't locate a single news or magazine article where an author or critic expressed shock that Janis was leaving Big Brother to pursue a solo career. Her talent was so apparent and while Big Brother was a more than capable outfit for Janis to convey her gift, Janis seemed confined. In hindsight, such confinement was critical to Joplin's success, and essential to her existence.

Janis toured relentlessly throughout late-1968 and 1969. Along with economic success, though, came a new crowd. Everyone wanted a piece of Janis, and without the protective cover of Big Brother, Janis was exposed. By early-1969, Janis was allegedly shooting over $200 of heroin each day ($1,300 in 2018 dollars). Janis was invited to perform at Woodstock in 1969, and several notable musicians reported that Janis was drifting, seemingly in terrible shape, mentally and physically.

Pete Townsend stated in his 2012 memoir, "She had been amazing at Monterey, but tonight [at Woodstock] she wasn't at her best, due probably, to the long delay, and probably, too, to the amount of booze and heroin she'd consumed while she waited. But even Janis on an off night was incredible." Janis took the Woodstock stage at 2:00 am, following Creedence Clearwater Revival. I've listened to the Woodstock set – it's okay, nothing awful, but clearly lacking the energy and spirit of her earlier performances.

Later in 1969, on Thanksgiving Day, Janis played a concert at Madison Square Garden in New York along with The Rolling Stones and Tina Turner. The concert was eagerly anticipated and attended by a slew of critics and celebrities. Janis sang a duet with Tina Turner during a set by The Rolling Stones. Biographer Myra Freidman wrote that Janis was "so drunk, so stoned, so out of control, that she could have been an institutionalized psychotic." Friends and management, along with Columbia Records, encouraged Janis to head into the studio. Not the safest, cleanest environment, but certainly better than "the road."

Accompanied by members of her touring band, Janis recorded several tracks that would appear on *Pearl*. *Pearl* would become Joplin's biggest selling record, featuring the hit "Me & Bobby McGee", a song written by Kris Kristofferson, and "Mercedes Benz", an a capella track written by Janis, Bob Neuwirth and beat poet, Michael McClure. Unfortunately, *Pearl* was released posthumously.

On August 24, 1970, Janis checked into the Landmark Motor Hotel in Hollywood. Janis was recording *Pearl* at Sunset Sound Recorders, a short car ride from the Landmark Motor Hotel. The Landmark Motor Hotel was a known haven for drug dealers and drug users, but Janis was reportedly showing up on time at the studio and her performances were excellent, rather than alarming. On September 26, Janis was asked by Yoko Ono to record a song for John Lennon, which would appear on a 30th birthday record that Yoko was compiling for John. Janis obliged, of course, and, ironically, recorded a version of "Happy Trails."

On October 1, Janis recorded "Mercedes Benz." The track is jovial, simple, if not cute – however, the recording would be her last. On October 4, after Janis failed to arrive at Sunset Sound Recorders, producer Paul Rothchild asked Joplin's road manager, John Cooke, to check on Janis. Cooke arrived at the Landmark Motor Hotel and noticed Joplin's tie-dye painted Porsche 356C in the parking lot. Cooke entered Joplin's room and found her dead on the floor beside the bed.

The official cause of death was a heroin overdose, compounded by the simultaneous use of alcohol. Janis was an experienced drug user, and surely understood the dangers of mixing alcohol with heroin, so what happened? Police concluded that the heroin Janis was shooting on October 3, the night prior to her death, was either tainted or, more likely, much stronger than the heroin she normally used. Police reported several other heroin overdoses in and around Los Angeles the same week as Joplin's death, concluding that most of the victims, including Janis, purchased heroin from the same dealer.

Janis Joplin died at the age of 27. Too early is an understatement. Janis was a flash of light. She exploded into public consciousness, then disappeared. Her personality equaled her voice and her flaws equaled her grace. Joplin's musical legacy is concrete – the audio and video remnants are as stunning today as they must have been in 1968.

The Byrds – *Sweetheart of the Rodeo*

Throughout the course of researching, listening and writing The 1965 Project and The 1968 Project, the music of The Byrds continues to be difficult to contextualize. Difficult to analyze, not in form – and not really in substance – but, rather – in magnitude, importance and legacy. While the music released by The Byrds in 1965 and 1966 was pleasant, accessible, even excellent at times, and certainly commercially successful – I continue to be troubled by the band's reliance on covers, rather than original material.

The Byrds had hits, though. "Mr. Tambourine Man" was an international #1 hit, as well as "Turn! Turn! Turn!" Other hits by The Byrds throughout their career were "Eight Miles High", "So You Want to be a Rock 'n' Roll Star", "Ballad of Easy Rider" and "Chestnut Mare." Yeah, I know – you've certainly heard of "Mr. Tambourine Man" and "Turn! Turn! Turn!", but you're not so sure you know the others. That's kind of the point – the two songs you know are covers, of Bob Dylan and Pete Seeger, respectively. The others are originals, penned by The Byrds. The "others" are good, they were commercially successful, but not classics.

Sweetheart of the Rodeo is the exception. Yes, the record contains covers – and yes, the album even begins with (yet another) Dylan cover, and then ends with another Dylan cover, but *Sweetheart of the Rodeo* is an original statement. The songs themselves don't really matter. I mean, of course they matter – but, the album is the statement, not each song. In the midst of the most violent and chaotic period in American social history, while most musicians gravitated towards Psychedelic Pop and Hard Rock, The Byrds forged a new musical path, inciting generations to embrace and incorporate....Country music?

Formed in 1965, The Byrds were led by Jim (Roger) McGuinn (lead guitar, vocals), Chris Hillman (bass), David Crosby (rhythm guitar, vocals) and Michael Clarke (drums). With the immediate commercial success of "Mr. Tambourine Man" and "Turn! Turn! Turn!", The Byrds developed a formula. The Byrds not only covered Dylan and Seeger (and others), The Byrds invented a sub-genre, Folk Rock.

By fusing distinct elements of Rock and Pop with Folk, mainly McGuinn's bright and jangly guitar playing (usually, a 12-string Rickenbacker) and Crosby's wonderfully harmonized backing vocals, The Byrds discovered a template for expressing Dylan's complex songwriting to a massive, younger, mainstream audience. Dylan "went electric" at the Newport Folk Festival on July 25, 1965, but Dylan's electrified versions of his songs were rough, raw, loud and uneven. Dylan focused on electric amplification, intentionally obscuring his words. The Byrds, however, created electric arrangements for Dylan's music that allowed listeners to access Dylan's words. Eventually, in maybe the ultimate show of respect, Dylan actually embraced and copied many of the arrangements crafted by The Byrds (Dylan even hired McGuinn to lead his touring band in the mid-1970s).

Like many artists – The Byrds were affected, and influenced, by the psychedelic and counterculture revolution that unfolded in late-1966 and 1967. The Byrds released *The Notorious Byrd Brothers* in 1967, which implemented studio experimentation and effects (a phaser on several tracks) and lyrical references to "magic carpet rides", "natural harmony" and "a dolphin's smile." Other bands certainly dove into the Psychedelic Pop ocean more than The Byrds, but similar to maybe The Rolling Stones, The Byrds dove into the ocean, and for a brief period of time, remained underwater – struggling to breath. Audiences didn't care much for *Notorious Byrd Brothers*, or the band's shift away from Folk Rock. As expected, band turmoil unfolded.

In late-1967, due in large part to a nasty drug problem that resulted in erratic behavior and long on-stage rants about topics ranging from the JFK assassination to LSD, David Crosby was fired from The Byrds. Commenting on his firing in a 1980 interview, Crosby stated, "They came over and said that they wanted to throw me out. They came zooming up in their Porsches and said that I was impossible to work with and I wasn't very good anyway and they'd do better without me. And, frankly, I've been laughing ever since. Fuck 'em. But it hurt like hell. I didn't try to reason with them. I just said, "it's a shameful waste...goodbye."

Somehow, I don't feel like it went down exactly like that – but, regardless, Crosby was out and The Byrds were lost. The band lacked a rhythm guitarist and lost the best backing vocalist in the scene, but more importantly, the band lacked direction. Touring in support of *Notorious Byrd Brothers* as a three-piece (McGuinn, Hillman and Clarke), it quickly became apparent that the three-piece could not recreate the studio material from *Notorious Byrd Brothers* in a live performance, due to the effects and layers of instrumentation. Desperate for a solution, based on a referral from their manager, Larry Spektor, McGuinn and Hillman turned to a little known, 21-year old guitar player from Los Angeles named Gram Parsons. Parsons would last only five months with The Byrds, but his impact results in yet another new sub-genre: Country Rock.

Upon joining The Byrds, Parsons was reliably collaborative. However, *Notorious Byrd Brothers* was not selling well and the inability to perform it live left McGuinn and Hillman exposed. Parsons not only was an adept rhythm guitarist, he played piano and organ and also could sing lead. But, his primary talent was songwriting. Parsons began writing original material and McGuinn and Hillman utilized their primary skill – arranging the songs.

Parsons surprisingly found himself in a position of influence within The Byrds, facilitating a confidence to pursue Country. Parsons believed that Country was the "purest form of musical expression." In advance of the *Sweetheart of the Rodeo* recording session, Parsons wrote "Hickory Wind" and "One Hundred Years from Now." The songs were excellent, especially "One Hundred Years from Now", but an additional factor led McGuinn and Hillman to accept Country as their new direction.

Columbia Records was addicted to the economic success of The Byrds, relying on a formulaic rearrangement of Dylan songs. Nervous after the failure of *Notorious Byrd Brothers*, the departure of Crosby and the hiring of an unknown replacement, Columbia Records contacted McGuinn and provided him with an unreleased recording, labeled "The Basement Tapes." Yes, those Basement Tapes – Dylan's session with The Band in Saugerties, NY. It is still unclear how Columbia Records obtained a copy of the recording session, or how the recording actually came into McGuinn's possession, but it happened.

McGuinn was floored. Dylan had hinted at a more rustic, traditional style of Rock and Folk on *John Wesley Harding* in 1967, but *John Wesley Harding* was certainly not a Country record (the record included "All Along the Watchtower" and "The Wicked Messenger", both classic Rock songs). Having the utmost respect for Dylan, McGuinn became convinced, along with Hillman, that Country music – and traditional Folk and Bluegrass – was the path forward. Such a decision was critical. Not only did the decision influence generations after the release of *Sweetheart of the Rodeo*, but the decision emphasizes a critical element of <u>The 1968 Project</u>.

After the tragic historical events in the beginning of 1968, there was a palpable shift towards Hard Rock. Musicians digested the political and social events, experienced rage and revolted, both in the streets and in the recording studio. However, not all musicians, let alone people, react in such a manner. Some people intuitively retreat. Dylan retreated. The Band retreated. And, now – The Byrds retreated. And, please – the use of the word "retreat" is not meant to be negative – these folks did not "give up", they simply revolted in a different, more passive manner – possibly, yearning for a simpler time in the face of an increasingly complex society.

Are you thinking, "didn't *Music From Big Pink* come out before *Sweetheart of the Rodeo*?" Yes, of course, but remember – *Music From Big Pink* was released in July and *Sweetheart of the Rodeo* was recorded in March and May. So, The Byrds had yet to hear *Music From Big Pink* prior to recording *Sweetheart of the Rodeo*. And, while *Music From Big Pink* is certainly the aggregate of Folk, Rock, Blues, Country and Gospel, *Music From Big Pink* is certainly not a Country record. *Music From Big Pink* and *Sweetheart of the Rodeo* may both be outliers in 1968, but the records are quite different. Ultimately, the common strand between the two records was a quest for a new and different musical path, maybe a retreat – but, also a quest for something solid, something genuine and something sacred.

Parsons insisted that The Byrds record in Nashville, in order to utilize expert session musicians – mandolin, banjo, pedal steel. In addition to the original tracks written by Parsons, The Byrds chose to cover three traditional Country tracks: "I Am a Pilgrim" (Merle Travis), "Blue Canadian Rockies" (popularized by Gene Autry) and "The Christian Life" (The Louvin Brothers). In pursuit of tradition, The Byrds did not change the original arrangements, instead they accentuated the acoustic, Country twang characteristics of each song. These covers certainly don't dominate *Sweetheart of the Rodeo*, but the tracks ground the album in Country and because "I Am a Pilgrim" and "The Christian Life" are placed as the second and third tracks on the record, respectively, the songs form the basis of the listening experience.

The record, however, opens with a Dylan cover. Why not, right? That's what fans, and Columbia Records, wanted – and on *Sweetheart of the Rodeo*, the selection fit perfectly. This Dylan cover, though, was a bit different than the dozen previous Dylan covers arranged and released by The Byrds. McGuinn was enamored with the music he heard on The Basement Tapes. Dylan's unique voice paired with a traditional, stripped-down arrangement was a revelation. Plowing through the hours of recorded material on The Basement Tapes, McGuinn selected two tracks that he thought best echoed the context of *Sweetheart of the Rodeo*.

"You Ain't Goin' Nowhere" was written by Dylan during The Basement Tapes sessions with The Band. The song exemplifies the intersection between Folk and Country, but I suspect that the song's catchy chorus is what led McGuinn to select "You Ain't Goin' Nowhere" as the album's lead track ("Ooh wee, ride me high/Tomorrow's the day my bride's gonna come/Oh oh we gonna fly/Down in the easy chair"). McGuinn sings the lead vocal, but Hillman and Parsons harmonize on the chorus, providing a wistful, almost back-porch feeling.

Columbia Records utilized "You Ain't Goin' Nowhere" as the lead Single for the promotion of *Sweetheart of the Rodeo* and the track reached #74 on the *Billboard* Hot 100. The public didn't recognize the track as a Dylan cover, as Dylan had yet to release his version, but writing credit was attributed to Bob Dylan. Dylan released his own version of "You Ain't Goin' Nowhere" three years later, in 1971, on his *Greatest Hits Vol. 2* compilation.

After "You Ain't Goin' Nowhere", The Byrds launched into the aforementioned strategically placed traditional Country covers, "I Am a Pilgrim" and "The Christian Life." McGuinn took lead vocals on "I Am a Pilgrim" and Parsons took lead vocals on "The Christian Life." The instrumentation of "I Am a Pilgrim" is notable. As stated, The Byrds could have covered the track in a Folk Rock style, but The Byrds instead embellish the Country attributes. The track opens with a fiddle and includes a banjo, not to mention the accent placed on the acoustic guitar turn around after each verse – a hallmark of traditional Country.

The song is written and sung in the first person, with the opening verse setting a tone and theme that threads the record – nostalgia and purity. McGuinn sings, "I am a pilgrim and a stranger/Traveling through this wearisome land/I've got a home in that yonder city, good Lord/And it's not, not made by hand." In a later verse, McGuinn declares, "I'm goin' down to the river of Jordan/Just to bathe my wearisome soul." No mention of the Vietnam War, no mention of political turmoil, but two references to religion ("good Lord" and "river of Jordan"). A message from The Byrds? Perhaps, but subtle and most definitely, indirect. That said, if the listener missed the religious references in "I Am a Pilgrim", The Byrds made sure the listener didn't miss the point on the next track.

"The Christian Life" is so overtly religious, making the selection an odd choice, but Parsons insisted on the cover. Parsons adored The Louvin Brothers and the selection was more of a tribute to The Louvin Brothers rather than a religious statement. The track features slide guitar licks between each verse, with the lead vocal of Parsons up front in the mix. McGuinn and Hillman harmonized with Parsons during the chorus, but not in the typical Byrds fashion, as the lead

238

vocal of Parsons remained louder in the mix, above the harmony. A characteristic of Country, and a departure from Folk Rock.

"The Christian Life" advocates for the foundation of religion, but in my view, the choice of "The Christian Life" by Parsons and The Byrds was a choice to convey purity rather than religion. The Byrds stay true to the lyrics, with references to "Jesus" and a Christian way of life, but a certain skepticism exists, right? This certainly isn't conveyed by The Byrds – but, as a listener – we know these guys, The Byrds, were not good Christian men. I mean, maybe they were, but they also had shoulder-length hair, wore ratty jeans, smoked cigarettes, drank constantly, abused drugs, were popular among the ladies and drove Porsches. So, I'm sure they were good people, but they were not exactly living "The Christian Life." Either way, The Byrds went to great lengths to preserve the traditionalism and integrity of "The Christian Life."

If you're listening to "The Christian Life" – and, seriously – I really hope you are listening to the music discussed and associated with The 1968 Project – it is an essential piece of the narrative – but, anyway – if you're listening to "The Christian Life" and think the lead vocal sounds like McGuinn and not Parsons, well – you've got a great ear. After the recording session, McGuinn went back into the studio and recorded his own lead vocal on "The Christian Life", replacing Parsons. While this maneuver was one of two contributing factors in Parsons quitting The Byrds (we'll get to the other shortly), in my view, from a musical perspective, McGuinn got it right. The Parsons version is ragged and weary, somber and low – which is what we love about Parsons – but, such was not the right fit for "The Christian Life." McGuinn's voice is brighter, rounder and cleaner. It just fits better. You can hear the Parsons version on a recent deluxe reissue of *Sweetheart of the Rodeo*.

McGuinn also re-recorded the lead vocals on the next track, "You Don't Miss Your Water", again replacing Parsons. I genuinely love both versions. If I had to choose, I might side with Parsons, but it is really close (again, you can hear the Parsons version on the deluxe reissue). Finally, we get to hear Parsons on "You're Still on My Mind." If fans of The Byrds were still hanging on to hope that *Sweetheart of the Rodeo* would be a cross-over record – a tinge of Country added to the expected Folk Rock – well, "You're Still on My Mind" crushed such hope. After the textbook Country swing intro, Parsons sings, "A jukebox is playing/A honky tonk song." This is straight Country.

The tempo and arrangement of "You're Still on My Mind" are upbeat and bright, yet the lyrics depict a guy in a bar, "alone and forsaken", with a girl on his mind. Upbeat, yet sad – classic Country. Parsons sings, "The people are dancin' and havin' their fun/And I sit here thinkin' about what you have done/To try and forget you, I've turned to the wine/An empty bottle, a broken heart and you're still on my mind." Great song and Parsons nails the vocal.

Next up – and, sorry – but, by now you know that I don't typically go through each album, track by track – I tend to jump around and highlight the key tracks, however – this record is an exception. *Sweetheart of the Rodeo* is incredibly important in the canon of Country Rock, alt-Country and Americana and I find it imperative to highlight (almost) every track. Note that if you go and listen to *Sweetheart of the Rodeo,* and you feel as though it sounds pretty standard, similar to Willie Nelson or the Country output from The Grateful Dead in the early 1970s, or perhaps Wilco or The Avett Brothers or Mumford & Sons? Well, you're right – but, all of it was derived from *Sweetheart of the Rodeo*.

A student of Bob Dylan, and therefore a student of Dylan's mentor, Woody Guthrie, McGuinn chose "Pretty Boy Floyd" with intent and purpose. Pretty Boy Floyd was a notorious bank robber in the United States during the Great Depression (early-1930s). Floyd was responsible for many deaths and the subject of a nation-wide police and FBI manhunt. Floyd was eventually apprehended and killed in 1934. Five years later, Guthrie, a native of Oklahoma, wrote "Pretty Boy Floyd."

240

Guthrie, along with Pete Seeger and many others, were overtly political – both through song and through actions. Guthrie protested government policies that favored the wealthy. Guthrie was an activist that represented poor and working class Americans. Despite assertions that Guthrie was a Marxist/communist enthusiast, Guthrie unequivocally loved America and wrote several songs about freedom, the wonders of a democratic society and the sheer beauty of America, including "This Land is Your Land." With "Pretty Boy Floyd", though. Guthrie used the story of an outlaw as a vehicle for political speech.

Guthrie brilliantly analogized Floyd's actions to that of the government of the United States by turning the following phrase: "As through this world you travel, you'll meet some funny men/Some will rob you with a six-gun, and some with a fountain pen." Not stopping there, referencing the manner in which banks foreclosed on homes during the Great Depression, Guthrie wrote, "And as through your life you travel, yes, as through your life you roam/You won't never see an outlaw drive a family from their home." Incredible songwriting. Sure, Guthrie romanticized a criminal, a thief and a murderer, but such is the expense for which Guthrie is able to poignantly attack.

McGuinn stayed true to Guthrie's lyrics and the arrangement is basic, including fiddle, upright bass, banjo and acoustic guitar. No drums, no electric guitar accents, no piano – basically, Bluegrass. Is McGuinn drawing a line between the abuses of government in the 1930s to the abuses of government in 1968? Perhaps, shining a light on Woody Guthrie was akin to a direct, negative comment about the government of the United States in 1968. Perhaps an ode to the recently departed Guthrie.

"Hickory Wind" was written by Parsons and he also sings lead on the track. A ballad, the track is quite neutral from a substantive perspective, again highlighting a somber, lightly depressive ambience. "Hickory Wind" is essentially a showcase for the voice of Gram Parsons. Possessing, but also conveying, emotion – Parsons had an uncanny ability to communicate a story, yet the listener believes there is more untold. Parsons would write better songs later in his (short) career, but "Hickory Wind" is an early example of the depth of Parsons' voice.

"One Hundred Years" is the third track where McGuinn re-recorded the lead vocals, replacing Parsons. Comparing the McGuinn version to the Parsons version is pointless. The original version, by Parsons, is slow and stripped-down, with focus on the lead vocal by Parsons. The original arrangement includes a few drum fills and electric lead guitar licks, but Parsons never lets the track veer hard towards Folk Rock. The Parsons version is very much Country.

On the re-recording, McGuinn and Hillman included harmonized vocals, a more driving rhythm and a bright, likely 12-string, Rickenbacker lead guitar. "One Hundred Years" instantly became the closest iteration of Folk Rock on *Sweetheart of the Rodeo*. The change is dramatic, and meaningful, as the entire objective of the song shifted from poignancy to accessibility. For example, the Parsons version highlights culturally relevant lyrics such as "Nobody knows what kind of trouble we're in." Parsons is somber, reflective and steadfast. McGuinn and Hillman's recitation of the line "Nobody knows what kind of trouble we're in" is airy, upbeat and weirdly positive. Parsons understood the track, the inner soul of the song and Parsons understood the cultural relevance, but McGuinn and Hillman understood exactly how to commercialize music.

The final two tracks of note are "Life in Prison" and "Nothing Was Delivered." The second to last track on *Sweetheart of the Rodeo*, "Life in Prison" was originally written by Merle Haggard. In 1968, Haggard was a Country star, yet viewed as an outlaw, having served actual jail time. Not surprisingly, Haggard was a character that Parsons gravitated towards and desired to emulate. Parsons chose "Life in Prison" – a song about death, sadness and, of course, prison. However, the tempo is upbeat and the rhythm swings. Parsons shines on vocals (and piano). McGuinn and Hillman support well and the walking bass line alarmingly urges you to dance to a song titled, "Life in Prison." Such is the beauty of Country music.

Finally, the closing track – another Dylan cover. "Nothing Was Delivered" was also a track that McGuinn "borrowed" from The Basement Tapes. Perhaps no two tracks better illustrate the (slight) difference between Parsons and McGuinn/Hillman than "Life in Prison" and "Nothing Was Delivered." "Life in Prison" is simple, easy and dominated by rhythm and a lead vocal. "Nothing Was Delivered" is dominated by melody and a chorus.

Bookending the record with Dylan covers was likely not a coincidence. Dylan's music has a certain consistency, and while I've certainly been critical of McGuinn's reliance on Dylan's songwriting, McGuinn genuinely understands the sentiment and wit in Dylan's songwriting. McGuinn selects certain elements within Dylan's songs to embellish. The only way to fully appreciate the wonders of McGuinn's ability to rearrange Dylan's music is to compare the version of "Nothing Was Delivered" on The Basement Tapes to the version by The Byrds on *Sweetheart of the Rodeo*. It is night compared to a bright, sunny, warm and breezy day. Listen to each version back to back.

Just a couple notes on Parsons and the legacy of *Sweetheart of the Rodeo*. Parsons, as noted, lasted only five months with The Byrds and had left the band prior to the release of *Sweetheart of the Rodeo*. Parsons was furious with McGuinn for replacing his vocals. Of course, Parsons preferred his vocals, but Parsons also disagreed with the manner in which the re-recorded vocals changed the style of the tracks, incorporating Folk Rock elements rather than Country. However, Parsons never cited McGuinn's re-recordings as the impetus for his departure.

In May 1968, prior to the release of *Sweetheart of the Rodeo*, The Byrds booked several tour dates in Europe and Africa. The Byrds were previewing the material from *Sweetheart of the Rodeo*, which attracted the attention of The Rolling Stones. After a show in England, The Byrds hung out with Mick Jagger and Keith Richards. After a long night, Jagger and Richards expressed concern, or disappointment, to The Byrds about their upcoming travel to South

Africa. Jagger and Richards talked to The Byrds about South Africa's apartheid policies and the need for opposition.

A few days later, after a show at The Royal Albert Hall in London, The Byrds readied to fly to South Africa. Parsons, though, informed The Byrds that he would not accompany them on the trip, citing the apartheid policies. McGuinn and Hillman reluctantly hired a few session players and played the shows in South Africa. Parsons stayed in London and forged an important friendship with Jagger and Richards (Parsons would become an influential force in pushing The Rolling Stones towards Country).

As for Parsons, after leaving The Byrds, he kicked around Los Angeles for a bit, then formed the Flying Burrito Brothers with Hillman (no hard feelings between Parsons and Hillman, but McGuinn was a different story). The Flying Burrito Brothers were popular, mainly in California, but not commercially successful, nationally. Do check out *The Gilded Palace of Sin*, the debut release by the Flying Burrito Brothers, as the record, like *Sweetheart of the Rodeo*, has aged incredibly well. Hillman noted in a recent interview that, while *Sweetheart of the Rodeo* was seminal in terms of Country, and Country Rock, the Flying Burrito Brothers were essentially the first "alternative country band...[as] we couldn't get on Country radio and we couldn't get on Rock radio."

In 1970, Parsons was signed to A&M Records and asked to release a solo record. Unfortunately, an addiction to heroin and a fascination with The Rolling Stones prevented the debut solo release. In 1971, Parsons moved in with Keith Richards at Villa Nellcote, during the recording sessions for *Exile on Main Street*. Several sources have stated that Parsons was in a state of constant incapacitation during his stay at Villa Nellcote. Ultimately, Keith Richards' girlfriend, Anita Pallenberg, asked (or demanded) that Parsons leave. However, in Richards' autobiography, *Life*, Richards queries whether Jagger was actually the person that asked Parsons to leave Villa Nellcote, as Richards suspected Jagger was upset that he (Richards) was spending so much time with Parsons, doing drugs – but, also working on songs

244

and playing music. Rumors do exist speculating that Parsons can be heard singing back-up vocals on the *Exile on Main Street* classic, "Sweet Virginia."

In 1972, Parsons was signed by Mo Ostin to Reprise Records. Featuring Emmylou Harris in his band, Parsons recorded *GP*, his debut solo record, released in 1973. The album received almost universal critical acclaim, and sold relatively well. Parsons immediately began recording a follow-up to *GP*. Again, with Harris on supporting vocals, Parsons recorded original material and completed *Grievous Angel*. *Grievous Angel* was universally lauded, even more so than *GP*, and remains a classic recording. Unfortunately, and this seems to be a recurring theme throughout The 1968 Project, the record was released posthumously.

On September 19, 1973, Parsons was found dead at the Joshua Tree Inn (Room #8) in the heart of Joshua Tree National Park. The official cause of death was an overdose of morphine and alcohol. Despite the recent success, Parsons was reportedly depressed and suffering from a recent divorce and the complete destruction of his house outside of Los Angeles (by fire). Speculating that Parsons' death may have been a suicide, Keith Richards stated in a 2004 documentary (*Fallen Angel*) that Parsons understood the danger of combining opiates and alcohol and, thus, "should have known better." Parsons was 26 years old, just 56 days shy of joining the "27 Club."

It is quite difficult to emphasize the importance and influence of *Sweetheart of the Rodeo*. Again, the music you hear on *Sweetheart of the Rodeo* is so familiar. Americana is entrenched as a mainstay genre in American culture. The roots of Americana trace back directly to *Sweetheart of the Rodeo*, a trajectory that includes the likes of Neil Young, Bob Dylan, The Band, The Rolling Stones, George Harrison's solo work, The Eagles, Creedence Clearwater Revival and The Grateful Dead. Each of these artists gravitated towards Country music after *Sweetheart of the Rodeo*.

Sweetheart of the Rodeo is timeless. Not just because the music is traditional, but the presentation of the songs by The Byrds (and Parsons) is brilliant. Tension existed, clearly – but, the product is both accessible and yes, genuine. McGuinn and Hillman expertly infused the Country songs with just enough Rock and Pop to fuse the genres, but Parsons provided just enough of a wall, just enough resistance – maintaining the Country spine.

Rather than existing as a product of influence, The Byrds had finally influenced others.

Jeff Beck – *Truth*

As the opening percussion of "Shapes of Things" descends into a familiar voice, it's natural for you to think to yourself, "Is this Rod Stewart?" Yes, it is Rod Stewart – and at 1:17, when the guitar enters the arrangement – you should also most certainly say, "that must be Jeff Beck." *Truth* tightropes a balance between Stewart's amazing vocals and Beck's legendary guitar. Ultimately, though, as he should, Beck triumphs and *Truth* prevails as a seminal record, marking a critical point in the emergence of Hard Rock and Heavy Metal.

In 1965, chasing the commercial success of The Beatles and The Rolling Stones, the core members of The Yardbirds (not including Eric Clapton) favored a Pop approach, rather than traditional Blues. The battleground was the track "For Your Love", the title track of The Yardbirds highly successful second release in 1965. Clapton played lead guitar on "For Your Love", but hated the song, refused to promote the track and eventually resigned from The Yardbirds (opting to join the more traditionally focused, John Mayall and the Bluesbreakers).

Needing an ace to replace Clapton, The Yardbirds turned to session musician extraordinaire, Jimmy Page. Page preferred his steady studio gig, but strongly recommended Jeff Beck. After one audition, or possibly the first five minutes of the audition, Beck was hired. Beck took over on lead guitar and contributed four tracks to *For Your*

Love, with Clapton appearing on the others. The album cover photo for *For Your Love* featured Beck, rather than Clapton.

For Your Love was a massive success, in both the United States and the United Kingdom. Given the economic success, Jimmy Page decided to join The Yardbirds in June 1966, on bass. In September 1966, Page started playing lead guitar, sharing duties with Beck, both on stage and in the studio. The reason for Page sharing lead guitar was not driven by instrumentation, arrangement or skill – it was due to Beck's unreliability and irresponsibility.

After missing a series of live shows, and a studio session, Beck was fired by The Yardbirds in late-1966. Beck's tenure with The Yardbirds lasted roughly 20 months, recording two records (really, a record and a half). However, the music Beck created with The Yardbirds is generally viewed as the peak period for The Yardbirds, both critically and commercially. Jimmy Page continued with The Yardbirds for a few years, eventually leaving to form Led Zeppelin in late-1968, releasing their debut record in 1969.

As for Beck, he bounced around for most of 1967, immersed in the psychedelic scene in London, but only habitually, not musically. The creativity and experimentation cultivated by the counterculture movement affected Beck differently than most guitarists. Beck didn't experiment with pedals or studio effects. Nor did Beck gravitate towards long-improvised spiritual guitar journeys. Rather, Beck experimented with compositional songwriting, borrowing from Jazz and Classical.

In early-1968, Beck was signed to Columbia Records. Despite lacking enough original material for a full record, Columbia Records urged Beck to enter the recording studio. Beck did not have a proper "band", having not yet formed The Jeff Beck Group, so *Truth* is attributed simply to Jeff Beck. Needing a vocalist, Beck turned to Rod Stewart, still a young, relatively unknown talent in London (this was prior to Stewart joining Faces). Beck reportedly was enamored with Stewart's rustic, empathetic voice.

Beck's next hire was a rhythm guitarist. Playing rhythm guitar behind Jeff Beck is no easy task. Beck is a dynamic lead guitarist, but also exacting with respect to timing, tone and skill. Beck convinced his first choice to play on the recording – Ronnie Wood (again, prior to Wood joining Faces). Both Stewart and Wood would eventually form the core of The Jeff Beck Group, before pursuing a legendary solo career (Stewart) and joining The Rolling Stones (Wood).

Truth features ten tracks, with three originals attributed to "Jeffrey Rod" (Beck and Stewart) and seven covers. The originals are really just rearrangements of classic Blues tracks, but given Beck's guitar approach – the connotation of "original" is justified. Critics and historians firmly hold that Beck's playing on *Truth* represents the original voice of Heavy Metal. That said, I believe *Truth* leans much more towards Hard Rock, with the exception of the middle section of "Beck's Bolero", which I'll concede may indeed have been the birth of Heavy Metal.

Truth opens with a cover of "Shapes of Things", a track written by Paul Stamwell-Smith of The Yardbirds. You might be thinking, "that's an interesting choice by Beck to choose as the opening track for his solo debut, after being fired from The Yardbirds?" Well, I thought the same thing. Despite being fired, maybe Beck showcased his respect by covering one of their hit songs?

Well, that's not really how Rock & Roll works. Beck's version of "Shapes of Things" is essentially an assault on The Yardbirds. While the basic structure is similar, Beck replaces the Pop elements, namely the bridge, with a searing and cacophonous lead guitar solo. The driving percussion and Stewart's vocals render Beck's reworking of "Shapes of Things" the definitive version of the track. Beck wasn't showing respect to The Yardbirds, he was demanding respect from The Yardbirds.

"Let Me Love You", the second track, is my favorite song on *Truth*. The track opens with a nasty guitar lick from Beck. Just no other way to describe it. Possibly, a microcosm of 1968. Fine, that's an overstatement, but whatever. Stewart's vocal starts with the song's title and Beck continues lead guitar licks over the verse vocals, while the rhythmic backbone thunders. Throughout *Truth*, Beck exhibits an uncanny ability to frame Stewart's vocals, accentuating certain elements. On most tracks, Beck plays in between the vocals, turnarounds after verse lines or riffs around the chorus. But, on "Let Me Love You", Beck plays over the vocals, a strategy that rarely works, but most certainly does on this track. Beck's guitar solo steps up an octave, maybe two, and exemplifies Beck's rendition of the Blues, which (again) many describe as Hard Rock.

Beck had always been enamored with the Blues guitarists from Chicago, and in some respects, he pays homage to his heroes on *Truth*. "You Shook Me" is a track written by Willie Dixon and originally featuring Muddy Waters on lead guitar. Beck slows the track down considerably, highlighting Stewart's vocal (and Nicky Hopkins on piano). Despite the traditional arrangement, Beck experiments – mainly in the background – with a wah pedal and possibly the tremolo bar, or a phaser.

After a series of energetic opening songs, Side 1 of *Truth* seems to purposefully descend in pace, winding down to the final track on Side 1, "Ol' Man River." Originally written by Jerome Kern, "Ol' Man River" has been covered by many, including Otis Redding, Sam Cooke and Ray Charles. Quite the company. But, if you think a young, white kid from London would be scared to give "Ol' Man River" a shot – you'd be mistaken.

Astutely, Beck arranges "Ol' Man River" in a way that highlights Stewart's strengths as a vocalist. Beck drops the key and incorporates a haunting, ominous texture – rather than accentuating the typical Soul and R&B attributes of prior versions. The instrumentation is sparse. The song takes off around 2:35, as Beck enters on guitar and Stewart's voice reacts accordingly. After a quick guitar flourish, the track fades out. Remember, albums were built around a Side 1 and a Side 2. The fade-out on "Ol' Man River" is how your listening experience would have ended on Side 1 in 1968.

249

When the listener flipped the record to Side 2 and placed the needle down, the first sound to emanate from the speaker was not Beck's crunchy electric guitar. Quite the opposite: a finger-picked acoustic guitar. After a few bars, Ronnie Wood joins Beck on acoustic guitar for a rendition of "Greensleeves", a traditional Folk instrumental. The track certainly projects diversity, and while an interesting choice to open Side 2 of *Truth*, I really love the decision. In some ways, the acoustic and calming "Greensleeves" emphasized the electric, raging Blues/Hard Rock that followed.

The next track, "Rock My Plimsoul" is credited to "Jeffrey Rod", indicating a rearrangement by Beck and Stewart – but, I suspect B.B. King might have taken issue with the writing credit. "Rock My Plimsoul" is essentially a cover of King's "Rock Me Baby." Whereas on "You Shook Me", Beck steered clear of refraining Muddy's licks, on "Rock My Plimsoul", Beck inches a bit closer to King's tone and style. Beck's tone is not as piercing as King's, but the phrasing is similar – less deferential, more confident. "Rock My Plimsoul" is a highly accessible, excellent representation of Beck's take on traditional Blues.

"Beck's Bolero" remains the most meaningful, or influential, track on *Truth* – however, the song was not recorded in May 1968 along with the other tracks on *Truth*. "Beck's Bolero" was recorded in late-1966, just prior to Beck's departure from The Yardbirds. Beck stated recently that he recorded "Beck's Bolero" after "it was decided that it would be a good idea for me to record some of my own stuff...partly to stop me from moaning about The Yardbirds."

Disagreement continues as to who actually composed "Beck's Bolero" – Beck or Jimmy Page, but Beck conceded that the session began with Jimmy Page strumming chords on a 12-string guitar, referencing *Bolero*, a one movement orchestral piece by Maurice Ravel in 1928. Beck and Page incorporated a persistent rhythm, featuring a middle section that increases in pace. Such a technique, commonly referred to as a "rave up", had been utilized successfully by The Yardbirds on "For Your Love" and "Shapes of Things",

250

among others. That said, the "rave up" in "Beck's Bolero" was a bit….well, different.

First, though – the musicians. Joining Beck and Jimmy Page on "Beck's Bolero" were John Paul Jones (a founding member of Led Zeppelin) on bass, Nicky Hopkins (The Rolling Stones, The Kinks and many, many more) on piano and Keith Moon (The Who) on drums. Not having played much together prior to the recording session, the notion of a composed piece of music was helpful. The lineup featured on "Beck's Bolero" would record only this one track.

Completed in late-1966, "Beck's Bolero" was released as a Single on March 10, 1967. "Beck's Bolero" was actually the B-Side, with "Hi Ho Silver Lining" as the A-Side. "Beck's Bolero" reached #14 on the UK chart and #123 on the *Billboard* Hot 100. The track was publicly embraced and lauded by each of Jimi Hendrix, Pete Townsend and Keith Richards. The song conveys a certain cinematic element. Beck demonstrates a passionate independence.

"Beck's Bolero" consists of three distinct sections. The first section begins with Page on the 12-string guitar. Beck introduces the melody via the use of a distorted, fuzz effect. Beck's sound on this track has been described as both "piercing" and "sinister." At 0:37, Beck layers in a slide guitar that transitions back to the melody.

The first section of "Beck's Bolero" is like a threatening sky. Dark, clouds are hanging low, moving fast. After you notice the sky, you notice the winds picking up. Trees swaying. The trees know the storm is coming. Then, you hear the first faint rumble. You know it's coming. That's when the thunder, Keith Moon, enters. Picking up the tempo on the bass drum, riding the snare a bit, Moon creates pace and enables tension. Similarly, Hopkins pounds on the piano.

Each musician locked into the driving rhythm, raging on their respective instruments, the thunder is consistent, omnipresent. Then, an ominous silence exists for a split second, just before the monstrous flash of lighting. After the brief pause, Moon screams from behind his kit and the band launches into the heaviest, hardest Rock ever recorded. If you are looking for the birth of Heavy Metal, try 1:32 of "Beck's Bolero." Unquestionably, the eye of the storm.

Moon's drumming is incredible. Beck's guitar tone is downright evil. As Hopkins pounds the piano, Beck segues back into the melody at 2:03. "Beck's Bolero" returns to the phrasing of the song's first section, but with dramatically enhanced intensity. The storm passed, but the question surfaces: "what kind of damage has been done?" "Beck's Bolero" certainly pushed Rock forward and remains an essential piece of music history.

Astonishingly, "Beck's Bolero" was not chosen as the album's closer. *Truth* concludes with two relatively standard Blues tracks, an original ("Blues Deluxe") and another Willie Dixon cover ("I Ain't Superstitious"). Both feature stellar vocals by Stewart and perfectly phrased guitar playing from Beck. Particularly, hearing Beck play on "Blues Deluxe", just one track after his playing on "Beck's Bolero", underscores how magnificently Beck adapts his style and playing to accommodate a vocalist.

Truth reached #15 on the *Billboard* Top 200 Albums chart, but despite the success, *Truth* is regarded mainly as an influence. I did not come across many reviews of *Truth* that praised the music, other than "Beck's Bolero." Rather, almost every review focuses on the impact of *Truth*, the influence. Most reviews cite that Beck launched a revolution.

Beck's playing on the standard, Blues tracks is phenomenal, delicately incorporating contemporary elements with tradition. Additionally, the musical diversity on *Truth* is refreshing. Not only incorporating slower tempo Blues tracks such as "Ol' Man River", but the inclusion of an acoustic instrumental ("Greensleeves") and the accessible Rock/Pop of "Let Me Love You", not to mention the wild, primal passion of "Beck's Bolero." *Truth* is listenable and most definitely, current.

After the success of *Truth*, Beck officially formed The Jeff Beck Group in 1969, featuring Stewart and Wood. The band released the highly successful *Beck-Ola* in 1969. Unfortunately, the success of *Truth* and *Beck-Ola* led to Stewart's departure from The Jeff Beck Group, in pursuit of a solo career. Ronnie Wood would leave shortly thereafter. Nonetheless, Beck continued to conquer new territory.

In late-1969, after the death of Brian Jones, Mick Jagger and Keith Richards asked Beck to join The Rolling Stones. Beck was flattered, but declined. Such a decision was not entirely surprising, as Beck was asked by Roger Waters in 1967 to replace Syd Barrett in Pink Floyd. As stated, Beck was, and remains, fiercely independent. The Rolling Stones would turn to Mick Taylor and the aforementioned Ronnie Wood, and Pink Floyd of course turned to David Gilmour. All seems to have worked out fine.

In 1971, influenced by the Jazz Fusion of Miles Davis (think, *Bitches Brew*), Beck fully embraced a highly experimental form of improvisational Jazz-Rock. Beck released *Blow By Blow* in 1975, another seminal record. *Blow by Blow* reached #4 on the *Billboard* Top 200 Albums chart and remains Beck's highest grossing record. *Blow by Blow* is a tough listen, but Beck's exacting brilliance is easily identifiable, despite the dated genre.

On the success of *Blow by Blow*, Beck toured with the Mahavishnu Orchestra, which featured one of Beck's guitar heroes, John McLaughlin. Now, that must have really been something – McLaughlin and Beck on the same stage in 1975? Beck continued to make music, eventually uniting with Roger Waters on the critically acclaimed *Amused to Death* in 1992, perhaps the most highly regarded solo effort from Waters.

Without a hit song to his credit, without a lead guitar role in one of Rock's legendary bands, without an instantly recognizable guitar solo – Jeff Beck is one of the most highly regarded electric guitarists in Rock. According to *Rolling Stone*, Beck is the fifth greatest guitarist in history – behind only Hendrix, Clapton, Page and Richards. Who knows? Lists are subjective. Music is subjective. But, listen to *Truth*. Listen to *Beck-Ola* and listen to *Blow By Blow*. Technique and tone. Versatility and personality. Beck was an influencer and *Truth* influenced a generation and encouraged a genre.

September

September

HISTORY

Feminism and the Miss America Pageant
The Electric Kool-Aid Acid Test by Tom Wolfe

MUSIC

The Beatles – "Hey Jude"
The Who – "Magic Bus"
Steppenwolf – "Magic Carpet Ride"
Jefferson Airplane – *Crown of Creation*
Sly and the Family Stone – *Life*

HISTORY

Do you, the reader, feel as though you need to catch your breath? Escalation of the war in January and February, political turmoil in March, the assassination of Martin Luther King, Jr. in April, then Robert Kennedy in June, riots in August. Month after month after month. Need a break? Such seemed to be the sentiment of the United States in September 1968. Increasing violence, aggression, anger and action matriculated the hearts, minds and streets of the United States. The spirit of the nation was falling further and further into a depression unseen since the assassination of John F. Kennedy in 1963. After the violence in August 1968, the spirit of the nation could fall no further, the spirit of the nation was broken.

The newspaper, television and magazine headlines in September 1968 were ominously passive, surprisingly benign. Perhaps a sensation of acceptance? The public was resigned to the notion that Nixon would become President of the United States. The country was unquestionably at war. Socially, the chasm between young America and older America had widened to such a degree that both sides agreed to disagree – neither accepting of the other, but each accepting of the divide.

Accordingly, in this chapter – we will take a collective breath. Before focusing on a critically important novel by Tom Wolfe, <u>The Electric Kool-Aid Acid Test</u>, it is essential to discuss an immeasurably poignant protest in September 1968 by a group of women in Atlantic City, New Jersey. A protest that reinvigorated the Feminist movement and sparked a cultural and legal revolution in furtherance of the rights of women.

Feminism and the Miss America Pageant

The plight of African American equality was unfinished in 1968 (and remains unfinished even today), however, in 1968 the African American community was united and active in the pursuit of equality. A movement existed that was organized and respected. Likewise, citizens seeking peace in Vietnam were organized and active. Jews in America were united and active in eradicating anti-Semitism. Feminism, though, was relatively dormant. Women had obtained rights, yet were not treated fairly or equally.

In the 1920s and 1930s, mainly with respect to voting rights, the feminist movement was active and effective. In the ensuing decades, specifically the 1950s, women were relegated to the home – a symbol of stability and love, but lesser in stature than men. Lesser in terms of economics and power. Then, it got worse.

In the 1960s, as the television revolution promulgated the eruption of commercialism, women became symbols. Advertisers, movie and television producers, and corporations portrayed women as sex symbols, requiring beauty and fostering a view of women based on physical features and appeal, rather than intellect, strength and security. Women were not organized to contest such portrayal and prevent further discrimination. Then, in late-1967, Robin Morgan, Shulamith Firestone and Pam Allen organized The New York Radical Women. The New York Radical Women demanded that women "reclaim ourselves for ourselves."

After a few small gatherings that featured speakers, The New York Radical Women organized their first full scale protest – a public demonstration at the famous (or infamous) Miss America Pageant in Atlantic City, New Jersey. The stated purposes of the demonstration included the following ten items:

1. The degrading mindless-boob-girlie symbol.
2. Racism with roses.
3. Miss America as military death mascot.
4. The consumer con-game.
5. Competition rigged and unrigged.
6. The woman as pop culture obsolescent theme.
7. The unbeatable Madonna-whore combination.
8. The irrelevant crown on the throne of mediocrity.

9. Miss America as Dream Equivalent to --?
10. Miss America as Big Sister watching you.

On September 7, 1968, 400 women gathered on the Atlantic City boardwalk, outside the hall that hosted the Miss America Pageant. After marching, chanting and singing, the protestors held a ceremony to crown a sheep as Miss America. The demonstration was relatively peaceful and therefore, not many members of the press stopped to cover the event (they were, of course, there to cover the Miss America Pageant). However, when the protestors positioned a large trashcan in the middle of their protest and lit the trashcan on fire, press (and the police) began to take notice.

The protestors had no intention of destroying property or harming anyone, rather – the protestors proceeded to throw symbolic objects into the trashcan. Bras, mops, high heels, copies of Cosmopolitan and Playboy, false eyelashes, makeup, girdles, corsets and, of course, pots and pans. Such items were described as "instruments of female torture."

In addition to the amped-up protest outside the venue, four protestors were able to gain entry to the actual Miss America Pageant. As the prior year's winner was making a speech, the four women – seated way up in the balcony – rolled out a large sign that read "Women's Liberation" and shouted, "No more Miss America, no more Miss America." While the television cameras were unable to catch the sign and the chanting before security guards escorted the women out of the venue, newspaper reporters covered the outburst and the story hit every major publication in the morning.

"Women's Liberation" became a ubiquitous term, as did "Bra Burner", both signifying the strength of women and the need for progress and equality. The protest in Atlantic City "marked the end of the movement's obscurity and made both women's liberation and beauty standards topics for national discussion." (Wikipedia)

One last point. As stated, the Civil Rights Movement achieved a modicum of progress by 1968, mainly through the Civil Rights Act of 1964 and the Voting Rights Act of 1965, but how did the Civil Rights Movement intersect with and affect the Women's Liberation movement? Well, it didn't. In 1968, the Miss America Pageant only included white women. African American women participated in a separate contest titled, "Miss Black America." More than a decade after *Brown v. Board of Education* (1956), the heroic actions of Rosa Parks, the events in Selma and Watts and progressive government legislation – the United States still had separate beauty pageants for white women and African American women. This is both surprising and disgusting.

Beginning in 1970, the Miss America Pageant was integrated – certainly a fine development, but unfortunately women still are fighting for equal pay, equal opportunities, and equal respect, while also battling the very stereotypes that existed fifty years ago. We must do better.

The Electric Kool-Aid Acid Test by Tom Wolfe

The Electric Kool-Aid Acid Test is an acclaimed piece of non-fiction, researched and written by Tom Wolfe. The story reads like a novel, as Wolfe embraced Ken Kesey as the protagonist by weaving a colorful, sometimes disturbing, often hilarious – but, ultimately accurate – account of the birth of Psychedelic America. Wolfe brilliantly incorporated music, drugs and sex – but, Wolfe never commented on the morality of the scene. Wolfe operated as a journalist, reporting on the facts and events. Wolfe utilized the technique that he, Hunter S. Thompson and Norman Mailer would eventually master – "New Journalism" or "Gonzo Journalism." The author inserted himself into the story as a character. The technique works brilliantly as Wolfe is neither inside nor outside, hardly omniscient – yet, the reader adopts Wolfe as the narrator.

From the outset, Ken Kesey is the leader, having already published the critically acclaimed novel, *One Flew Over the Cuckoo's Nest* in

1962 and *Sometimes a Great Notion* in 1964. Originally from Oregon, Kesey was living in Palo Alto, California and in 1960 had enrolled in a government study sponsored by the CIA, where the CIA administered controlled doses of LSD to each participant. Obsessed with the effects of the drug, Kesey encouraged friends and strangers to try LSD. Many of these friends and strangers became Kesey's closest comrades, adopting the name, "The Merry Pranksters."

Kesey and the Merry Pranksters began to hold "experiments" that included large gatherings of people in the woods, initially at Kesey's home in La Honda, then in music clubs throughout California. Kesey and his cohorts would prepare a batch of LSD-spiked liquid (later called, "Electric Kool-Aid") and provided the juice to the attendees. The "experiment" was to see what happened – to enlighten the minds of young people, whether for creative purposes, political purposes or no purpose at all. These "experiments" became known as "Acid Tests."

Wolfe documented the Acid Tests with incredible clarity and deference capturing the spirit and shortcomings of the concept. In addition to the drugs, Wolfe chronicled the elements of arts and music – interlacing the scene. Wolfe described in intimate detail the vibrant colors that were used to decorate each Acid Test. Called Day-Glo, the color and style was an early incarnation of "tie-dye", with splatters and swirls of red, orange, purple, yellow, blue, green and every combination thereof. Often, lights pulsated with these colors, usually projected on a large screen or white sheet.

Typically though, the music was the center of each Acid Test. Once the attendees were sufficiently intoxicated, a live band would take the stage and (try to) play. After a few performances by each of The Grateful Dead and Jefferson Airplane, The Grateful Dead were officially deemed the primary entertainment for the Acid Tests. By this time, The Grateful Dead had written songs, but their repertoire for the Acid Tests was quite different – pure improvisation. Jefferson Airplane was a better band in 1966 and 1967, in terms of crafting songs, but The Grateful Dead excelled at improvisation and spontaneity. Recordings exist of The Grateful Dead playing various Acid Tests – and while the music is confusing and unhinged, as opposed to progressive and interesting, the experience of long, improvised playing formed the basis for the Dead's musicianship, style and excellence.

If this scene sounds insane and unbelievable, well – it likely was, but the most unbelievable aspect was – it was perfectly legal. LSD was still being researched by the FDA and the FBI, as well as the aforementioned CIA. Many scientists believed the drug, or formulation, had benefits that could prevent addiction and psychosis. The government believed the drug could be helpful in gaining information from hostages and enemy soldiers.

Free of the fear of law enforcement, Kesey was determined to spread the movement across the United States. In short, Kesey purchased a bus, named "Furthur", and along with the Merry Pranksters set out on a cross-country journey to enlighten the youth of America. Kesey intended to "turn them on" to the movement. Ultimately, he pretty much freaked everybody out.

Wolfe captured the essential moments of Kesey's mission. Many of the book's premier moments involve the reaction of America, the reaction of regular people and law enforcement as Kesey and the Pranksters drove the bus down Main Street. The bus was equipped with a speaker on the roof, sometimes blaring Psychedelic Rock and other times featuring Kesey or one of the other Pranksters reciting a poem or speaking to the ordinary folks in a cadence that sounded like a preacher.

Upon the release of Electric Kool-Aid Acid Test in 1968, with the nation reeling and young people looking for an alternative – an alternative to society, an alternative to family and an alternative to the norm, The Electric Kool-Aid Acid Test provided a road map. The freedom exposed by Wolfe became incendiary. Addictive, young people flocked to San Francisco, in search not of Ken Kesey and the Merry Pranksters necessarily, but in search of freedom. Young people flocked to The Grateful Dead and young people flocked to LSD. A culture was born, a counter-culture.

The legacy and influence of <u>Electric Kool-Aid Acid Test</u> is undeniably significant from a substantive perspective, but the book is also wonderfully written. Wolfe's language is stellar and remains undated. However, Wolfe was dealt a wonderful hand. Kesey was a star. The lunacy of Kesey and his friends formed the plot and the wild and often comical events of the book are indelible and literary.

As the story goes, when the police couldn't bust Kesey for possession of LSD, local and Federal law enforcement declared Kesey a "menace" and monitored his every move. In 1967, Kesey was busted for possession of marijuana, and instead of standing trial, he fled to Mexico. Wolfe followed Kesey and the Pranksters to Mexico, but the hiatus didn't last – as Kesey engineered a plan to sneak back into the United States. The plan failed and Kesey was apprehended.

Every great book needs a court scene, so Wolfe covered Kesey's trial. As the judge lectured Kesey, not only for the possession of marijuana but for his creation of a culture surrounding LSD, Kesey surprisingly embraced a new strategy. Kesey explained to the judge that he envisioned a society that could "move beyond acid." Kesey declared that the culture he created didn't need LSD to achieve an expansion of the mind.

The judge released Kesey under the condition that Kesey influence the youth to move away from LSD. Accordingly, upon his release, Wolfe covered each move of Kesey as he organized the famous "Acid Test Graduation." The premise was that the Pranksters would attempt to "transcend time and space" without the assistance of LSD. The Graduation was covered by local and national press.

Predictably, the Graduation was a massive failure. The event was poorly attended and those who did attend were reportedly tripping on LSD. Kesey's image was tarnished and worse, he was forced to serve jail time for the marijuana possession (not having fulfilled his pledge to the judge).

The book concludes with Kesey returning to his family farm in Oregon (which would host a truly amazing Grateful Dead concert in 1972). The Merry Pranksters scattered, with some continuing the movement and others settling into normal existence. Wolfe concludes with a sympathetic illustration of the bus, Further. Parked beside Kesey's small house on his Oregon farm, Further sat, surrounded by tall grass, seemingly passive, but still colorful, passionate and idealistic. Retired, but unwillingly. A metaphor for Kesey.

The overwhelming cultural significance of <u>Electric Kool-Aid Acid Test</u> is the glorification of the hippie culture and the music associated therewith. The hippie movement exploded after the release of the book, inciting a generation. From a literacy standpoint, Wolfe's insertion of himself into the story is one of the essential examples of "New Journalism." The manner in which Wolfe pivots between reporting and experiencing is the crux of the reading experience. Sure, the subject matter is gold – but, Wolfe's writing is the legacy.

MUSIC

The Beatles – "Hey Jude"

"Hey Jude" was a Single released by The Beatles in August, but "Hey Jude" dominated September 1968, reaching #1 in the United States and the United Kingdom. "Hey Jude" spent a record nine consecutive weeks at #1 on the *Billboard* Hot 100.

The Beatles epitomize the shift in music during 1968. With the release of *Sgt. Pepper's Lonely Hearts Club Band* and *Magical Mystery Tour*, both in 1967, The Beatles facilitated, encouraged and led the exploration and commercialization of Psychedelic Pop. The Beatles rarely included direct, or overt social and political comments in their lyrics. While fans and young adults most definitely looked to The Beatles for instruction and influence, The Beatles were more a driver of style and genre-shaping sounds, rather than message. That said, it would be a mistake to conclude that the music of The Beatles was not influenced and affected by the historical events of 1968.

The Beatles released only one full length album in 1968 and that record, *The White Album*, was not released until November. So, The Beatles had ample time to watch and listen. They absorbed the shift away from Psychedelic Pop and towards a heavier Rock sound. No longer was it cool to dress up, act goofy and write catchy, whimsical Pop songs. It was cool to be angry, it was cool to take action. Colors were replaced by black, or *white*. Complicated studio effects were replaced by distortion pedals and amps were turned to 10.

The Beatles most definitely adapted and shifted along with the music scene in 1968. Whether such a shift was the result of the Vietnam War and Civil Rights – or, rather, just a reaction to the shift of other musicians – either way, the difference in sound of The Beatles between *Magical Mystery Tour* and *The White Album* is massive.

And then, in the middle of those two…there's "Hey Jude." The track was composed by McCartney while on a drive from London to Lennon's home in Weybridge. John and his then wife, Cynthia, were going through a divorce, and Paul decided to head out to check on them and spend some time with John's son, Julian. McCartney recalls penning the lyrics, "'Hey Jules, don't make it bad, take a sad song and make it better." In 1997, McCartney stated that he was trying to say to Julian, "'Hey, try and deal with this terrible thing.' I knew it was not going to be easy for him."

Despite the factual motivation, McCartney notoriously writes in a vague style – circling an event or theme, but never directly stating his intention. Given such misdirection, Lennon was okay with the substance of the track, as the lyrics didn't overtly reference his divorce. McCartney recalled that after playing the demo of "Hey Jude" for Lennon the first time, McCartney, trying to preempt John's criticism, assured John that he would fix the line "the movement you need is on your shoulder", with Paul admitting to John that the phrase is "a stupid expression." Lennon immediately replied, "you won't…that's the best line in the song."

The Beatles entered Abbey Road Studios in July to record "Hey Jude", the first track to be recorded on the Apple Music label. The recording of "Hey Jude" was surprisingly pleasant. Author Peter Doggett described "Hey Jude" as a song that "glowed with optimism after a summer that had burned with anxiety and rage." Of course, every Beatles recording session had some drama and "Hey Jude" is no exception. Apparently, George Harrison wanted to insert guitar phrases in between each line, but McCartney objected, eventually vetoing the idea (as was his right according to "band policy", due to it being McCartney's composition).

Typical of McCartney's compositions, "Hey Jude" is a ballad, beginning with McCartney on piano and lead vocals. The second verse includes acoustic guitar and tambourine. However, what is in between the verses is most interesting. "Hey Jude" is structured as a verse-bridge (four verses and four bridges), then a coda leading to a fadeout/refrain. The verse-bridge section of the song is approximately three minutes, while the coda is over four minutes. McCartney also changes the key for the coda, from C to E – brightening the tone.

Released on August 26 (Happy Birthday, Michael) in the United States and August 30 (Happy Birthday, Mom) in the United Kingdom, with "Revolution" on the B Side, "Hey Jude" reached #1 on the *Billboard* Hot 100 on September 28 (Happy Birthday, Drew). By November 30, "Hey Jude" had sold six million copies and was ranked by multiple reader polls, including *NME*, as the best song of 1968.

The legacy of "Hey Jude" is the coda. I actually find that the beginning of the track borders on boring. It's not until 2:18 that McCartney inflects his voice in a way to suggest energy – only to return to the verse at 2:30, but the inflection was a dose of foreshadowing, as the band builds the bridge to a frenzy at 3:06, complete with a yell from McCartney. From there, the coda emanates in a transcendental fashion – built around a driving acoustic guitar strum, clapping in unison (by the orchestra hired for the session) and a droning bass. But, the focus of the coda is the backing vocal on "na-na-na-na-na-na-na" and McCartney improvising a scat sort of vocal delivery, with the repeat phrase "Hey Jude." The tone is upbeat and optimistic, but the rhythm is oddly meditative.

"Hey Jude" represents the initial shift in sound by The Beatles – away from Psychedelic Pop but not yet entirely towards Rock. "Hey Jude" is a bridge, or perhaps a deep breath, perhaps the very same deep breath the world was taking after a brutal summer.

The Who – "Magic Bus"

The Who may not have been the *most* popular band in the world in 1968, but they likely claimed the distinction in 1969 (through 1973). Actually, writing in *Esquire* in early-1968, noted music critic Robert Christgau stated that The Who were the "third best [band] not just in Britain but the world" (presumably, behind The Beatles and The Rolling Stones, or maybe Cream). After The Who's highly anticipated performance at The Monterey Pop Festival in 1967, The Who became a sensation both in the United States and abroad.

The Who formed in London in 1965 and, like The Rolling Stones, relied mainly on covers (Blues and, occasionally, Soul/R&B). However, once lead guitarist Pete Townsend asserted himself as a songwriter, The Who ascended.

Possibly, the crux of analyzing music in 1968 is "How did the band deal with, or react, to the Psychedelic Pop/Rock trend existing in 1967." As discussed, some bands fully embraced the trend, such as The Beatles, The Rolling Stones, Cream and The SmallFaces, while other bands fled – opting for a decidedly non-Psychedelic style, leaning heavily on Country, Folk and traditional Rock, such as Bob Dylan, The Band and Johnny Cash. How about The Who? How did The Who navigate the Psychedelic excess of 1967?

Well, The Who, not surprisingly, took a completely different route. The Who embraced the creative spirit of 1967, but the consequence was in form, rather than substance. In 1967, The Who experimented with a format that would define the band's later output: the concept album. The Who released *The Who Sells Out* in December 1967. The songs on *The Who Sells Out* are relatively straight-forward, relying heavily on the Blues and focusing on rhythm and power as opposed to melody, but the "concept" is not within the songs, but rather – around the songs.

The Who Sells Out included faux commercials, written and recorded by The Who, interspersed between seemingly unrelated tracks. The faux commercials purported to sell products and services, with some of the commercials referencing actual products (which, yes of course, led to lawsuits). *The Who Sells Out* was an early example, perhaps the earliest, of the band pairing theatrics with music. *The Who Sells Out* reached #13 in the United Kingdom and #26 in the United States. The success of *The Who Sells Out* led directly to the creation of *Tommy* in 1969 and *Quadrophenia* in 1973.

Townsend spent all of 1968 writing (and struggling with) *Tommy*, while The Who toured Europe and the United States. Keenly aware of the business of music, with no record release slated for 1968, The Who decided to stay in the forefront of minds by releasing a Single, "Magic Bus."

If "Magic Bus" sounds a bit older or out of place with the direction of music in 1967 and 1968, it is not because The Who decided to convey a vintage or traditional Rock intention. "Magic Bus" sounds like 1965 because it was written in 1965. Townsend wrote "Magic Bus" during the *My Generation* sessions. The Who never actually recorded the track in 1965, but the band rehearsed the song a bit, eventually deciding to scrap the composition.

Released on September 18, "Magic Bus" reached #25 on the *Billboard* Hot 100 and #26 in the United Kingdom. "Magic Bus" has since become one of The Who's most popular songs and is typically used by the band as a set closer or encore. The studio version of "Magic Bus" did not appear on an LP until the inclusion of the track on the compilation/soundtrack for *The Kids Are Alright* in 1979. Perhaps, though, the most well-known recording of "Magic Bus" is from the live album, *Live At Leeds* (recorded on February 14, 1970 and released on May 16, 1970).

The *Live At Leeds* version is extended, reaching almost eight minutes, and featuring Roger Daltry on harmonica. The *Live At Leeds* recording was utilized by Martin Scorsese as the music for one of the closing montages in the 1991 classic, *Goodfellas*. Illustrating the wide appeal of "Magic Bus", Cameron Crowe used the track during the opening sequence of *Jerry Maguire* in 1996.

"Magic Bus" is not progressive. "Magic Bus" is not Psychedelic. The track embraces the hallmarks of Rock: major chords, choppy rhythm, call and response vocals (Daltry singing "too much" and the rest of the band singing "magic bus"), a healthy distorted guitar solo by Townsend, pounding drums by Keith Moon, Blues harmonica and lots of changes in pace and feedback. The song itself – the melody and lyrics – are quite basic, but such simplicity afforded The Who an opportunity to rage. Townsend's most intriguing guitar leads are within "Magic Bus."

"Magic Bus" is an important reminder of the power of The Who – the sheer force and volume at which the band communicated. While bands such as The Beatles and The Rolling Stones experienced rather immediate commercial success, The Who were late bloomers. Sure, the band scored a hit ("*My Generation*") in 1965, but it wasn't until Townsend improved dramatically as a songwriter on *Tommy, Who's Next* and *Quadrophenia* – that The Who became internationally compelling.

Listen to the Single version of "Magic Bus." You'll hear a band on the precipice of domination. Then listen to the version on *Live At Leeds*. Once The Who aggregated and incorporated elements of force, aggression, melody, lyricism and poignancy, The Who became legendary.

Steppenwolf – "Magic Carpet Ride"

Released by Steppenwolf in September 1968, "Magic Carpet Ride" peaked at #3 on the *Billboard* Hot 100 chart. "Magic Carpet Ride" appeared on Steppenwolf's second album, creatively titled *The Second* (released in October 1968). "Magic Carpet Ride" was released as a Single, with "Sookie Sookie" on the flip side. The track remains Steppenwolf's highest grossing and most well-known song.

Quite unusually, though – the Single version of "Magic Carpet Ride" is a different version than the track appearing on the album. Even more unusual, the Single version is arguably less accessible and traditional. The Single version includes a guitar feedback intro – not exactly perfect for radio disc jockeys. Additionally, the Single version is actually longer than the album version, as the Single clocks at 4:27 while the album version is only 2:55.

The time difference is due to an extended jam after the last verse/chorus. The jam is steady and upbeat, but also quite mellow. The backbone is a repeating acoustic guitar strum, embellished by psychedelic electric guitar fills and a basic snare drum. Then, somewhat out of nowhere, the vocals enter with a refrain of the chorus, which actually begins to fade out in the middle. Interesting.

Unquestionably, though – the most memorable part of "Magic Carpet Ride" is the feedback intro giving way to the line, "I like to dream/Right between my sound machine/On a cloud of sound I drift in the night/Any place it goes is right/Goes far, flies near, to the stars away from here." The verse is (wonderfully) both abstract and physical. Now, I wouldn't deem "Magic Carpet Ride" a lyrical masterpiece, but these lyrics flow well and are sung perfectly, with a memorable cadence.

Young folks had endured several months of turmoil and pain...and young folks needed an escape. Some fled to San Francisco – others fled to Upstate New York. Some, though, simply escaped through the music. Steppenwolf advocated the latter: "Close your eyes girl/Look inside girl/Let the sound take you away." Not to mention the chorus, "Well, you don't know what we can find/Why don't you come with me little girl/On a magic carpet ride."

While lyrics containing images of magic carpets, Aladdin and fantasy may harken back to the aesthetic of 1967, it is critical to note the musical texture of "Magic Carpet Ride." The track is harder and edgier, with rough and raspy vocals. A backing of distorted and feedback-heavy electric guitar along with a highly improvised B-3 organ – the instrumentation leans heavily towards 1968 (not to mention the inclusion of the extended jam), even if the words trend back to 1967.

Does the track sound dated? Maybe a bit, but give it a listen. I suspect you'll immediately think of youth, maybe high school – then, you'll be thinking of something else, drifting a bit. When the chorus refrains after the jam, you return briefly, then leave happily energized

Jefferson Airplane – *Crown of Creation*

Crown of Creation is the fourth album by Jefferson Airplane. Jefferson Airplane, along with The Grateful Dead and Quicksilver Messenger Service, created a sub-genre. Coming of age in 1965 in San Francisco, each band experimented with LSD and experimented with musical composition, or rather – the lack thereof. LSD enabled users to set aside anxieties, embrace change and explore without reservation. Eviscerate boundaries and dilute form. The creative youth of America utilized LSD to escape military and political information.

While LSD would eventually become illegal, due in large part to the drug's causal link to schizophrenia and other negative mood and mind disorders, the lasting remnant of LSD may actually be psychedelic

271

music. Jefferson Airplane, The Grateful Dead and Quicksilver Messenger Service used LSD as a portal to experiment and explore/destroy musical form. While several bands exhibited creativity by exploring studio effects and production techniques, the bands from San Francisco experimented on stage. Each of Jefferson Airplane and The Grateful Dead played hundreds of shows between 1965 and 1967 – creating, evolving, devolving and ultimately, honing a craft that at times sounded chaotic and amateur and at other times utopian and virtuoso.

Only one band played at each of the Monterey Pop Festival (1967), Woodstock (1969) and Altamont (1969). That band is Jefferson Airplane. Note that The Grateful Dead played Monterey and Woodstock, and were scheduled to play Altamont, but due to the violence that ensued during Jefferson Airplane's set, which included the stabbing death of a fan by the Hell's Angels, The Grateful Dead canceled their performance. The Grateful Dead certainly ascended to incredible commercial heights, particularly in the 1980s – but in the late-1960s, Jefferson Airplane was the main attraction.

Jefferson Airplane was formed in 1965 (seriously) by Marty Balin (vocals), Paul Kantner (guitar and vocals), Signe Anderson (vocals), Jorma Kaukonen (lead guitar), Jack Casady (bass) and Spencer Dryden (drums). The band released their debut record, *Jefferson Airplane Takes Off*, in September 1966. The record was basic in form and style, focusing largely on Folk and Folk-Rock interpretations of traditional American songs. *Jefferson Airplane Takes Off* sold well locally in San Francisco, but the band failed to gain national attention.

After giving birth in 1966, Signe Anderson quit the band and was replaced by Grace Slick. Slick had been the lead singer of The Great Society, a band that focused more heavily on Psychedelic Rock (and named after LBJ's attempted social and political reform). Slick's voice was stronger and less melodic than Anderson's. Slick was also a former model. Most importantly, when Slick joined Jefferson Airplane, she brought two songs with her: "White Rabbit" and "Somebody to Love." Both tracks were written by Slick's brother,

Darby, and The Great Society actually recorded a version of "Somebody to Love" (coincidentally, the studio producer of the "Somebody to Love" session was Sylvester Stewart, later known as "Sly", see below).

As the San Francisco counterculture movement began to sweep across the United States, including a feature on Jefferson Airplane in the December 1966 issue of *Newsweek*, Jefferson Airplane readied the release of their second album, *Surrealistic Pillow*. Released in February 1967, the album peaked at #3 on the *Billboard* Top 200 Albums chart. "White Rabbit" reached #8 on the *Billboard* Hot 100, while "Somebody to Love" reached #5. These two tracks dominated the soundtrack of the Summer of Love.

The music of Jefferson Airplane was raw. Loud and raw. Barbara Rowes, author of a biography on Grace Slick, described the music in 1967 as "a declaration of independence from the establishment" and noted that "[Jefferson] Airplane never strived for a synthesis of its divergent sensibilities...There remain strains of the individual styles of the musicians [creating] unusual breadth and original interplay within each structure." The ideology of the counterculture scene facilitated and influenced musical freedom, experimentation and expression. Symbiotically, the music in turn influenced the scene. This cyclical relationship exponentially raised the quality and uniqueness of both the music and the scene. But then – the consequence was commercialized.

In June 1967, Jefferson Airplane took the stage at the Monterey Pop Festival, after a short introduction by Jerry Garcia. The Monterey Pop Festival also featured Jimi Hendrix, The Who, The Grateful Dead, The Byrds, Simon & Garfunkel, Otis Redding, Buffalo Springfield and many others. Thanks to television and film coverage, millions of young Americans witnessed the beauty and energy of the music and the expression and openness of the scene. Perhaps, behind Elvis first appearing on television and The Beatles playing *The Ed Sullivan Show*, The Monterey Pop Festival might just be the most important and influential moment in televised music history.

273

Jefferson Airplane became an immediate international sensation in 1967 – and being an international sensation in 1967 meant one thing: a new album.

Jefferson Airplane released *After Bathing at Baxter's* in November 1967. *Baxter's* is loaded with the hallmarks of 1967 – creativity and excessive studio production. Sound effects, musical suites, long compositions and, of course, lyrical obscurity. The album possessed no track that could function as a commercially viable Single. *Baxter's* did okay, peaking at #17 on the *Billboard* Top 200 Albums chart, but on the heels of *Surrealistic Pillow*, "White Rabbit" and "Somebody to Love", *Baxter's* was labeled a disappointment. As a result, Jefferson Airplane quickly entered the studio in February 1968. This timing is critical, as Jefferson Airplane would write and record most of the tracks released on *Crown of Creation* **before** the tragic and violent historical events of 1968.

Accordingly, *Crown of Creation* is more reminiscent of late-1967, rather than encompassing the macro shift towards Hard Rock in 1968. After recording the tracks on *Crown of Creation*, Jefferson Airplane embarked on an extended tour of Europe and Australia. Incomplete, *Crown of Creation* sat, awaiting a final mix, tracking and artwork. The intervening months included assassinations, riots, political instability and the escalation of the Vietnam War – topics Jefferson Airplane most certainly would have incorporated had they recorded *Crown of Creation* a few months later.

Instead, *Crown of Creation*'s most notable two tracks are about Slick's affair with Dryden ("Lather") and a "threesome" ("Triad", written by David Crosby). Other tracks portray the hippie culture in a positive light and endorse libertarian politics – whereas, the music recorded later in 1968 criticized the commercialism of hippie culture and endorsed action and reaction, as opposed to diplomacy and abstention.

Frankly, the timing of *Crown of Creation* underscores the premise of The 1968 Project – the effect of historical events on the music created in 1968. In the case of *Crown of Creation*, the evidence is the absence of consequence. As expected, Jefferson Airplane's next release, *Volunteers*, focused on Hard Rock and advanced explicit messages regarding the Vietnam War and the need to prevent the commercialism of society. A little late, but they got there.

Despite the music on *Crown of Creation* being a bit misaligned with the tenor of American society in September 1968, *Crown of Creation* remains an intriguing relic – an indelible example of Psychedelic Rock. While "Lather" and "Triad" are acoustic, yet atypical, Folk arrangements, *Crown of Creation* sounds best during the energized electric Rock of "In Time" and "Star Track." To emphasize the misalignment, listen to the instrumental jam in "Star Track." Kaukonen unleashes a guitar solo at 1:15 that includes use of a wah pedal, and while the solo is great, the overall rhythmic template is short of Hard Rock. Similarly, the title track is experimental and certainly Psychedelic, but not Hard Rock.

Crown of Creation should not be skipped. The music of Jefferson Airplane is the essence of counterculture in 1967. *Crown of Creation* is surprisingly listenable and compelling. No single track stands out, but straight-through, the album still possesses an uncanny ability to transport the listener to the condition of Psychedelic Rock.

After *Volunteers* in 1969, and the tragedy witnessed by the band at Altamont, Jefferson Airplane began to unravel. Dryden was fired in 1970 and Balin left shortly thereafter. Slick and Kantner, who were romantically involved, emerged as the lead songwriters and vocalists, ostracizing Kaukonen and Casady. Kaukonen and Casady remained members of Jefferson Airplane through 1972, but the two formed Hot Tuna in 1971 and devoted significant time to the (side) project. After Jefferson Airplane's final performance at the Winterland Ballroom in San Francisco on September 22, 1972, the band would not play together until a reunion show in 1989. Of course, drama ensued between 1972 and 1989 – most notably stemming from Slick and Kantner forming Jefferson Starship (yes, "We Built This City"). And

275

yes, then a lawsuit, then a settlement and ultimately a rebranding as just "Starship."

As you've noticed throughout this book, there is only one thing that brings an end to musician acrimony: the Rock & Roll Hall of Fame Induction Ceremony. In 1996, after an introduction by Phil Lesh and Mickey Hart of The Grateful Dead, Balin, Kantner, Kaukonen, Casady and Dryden reunited to accept enshrinement (Slick was scheduled to attend, but suffered a medical emergency). Dryden died in 2005 and Kantner in 2016, but Balin, Kaukonen, Casady and Slick are alive and well at the time of this writing and in the case of Kaukonen and Casady, still performing as Hot Tuna.

Jefferson Airplane are a microcosm of the purity of the San Francisco scene. Fleeting, meaningful, true, genuine and (sometimes) accessible. Sure, hippie culture lasted past 1972, and to some extent survives today, but between 1966 and 1968, hippie culture was at its most pure – simple and engaging. Jefferson Airplane dominated this short period and provides the context for the counterculture revolution. And, while *Volunteers* aligns more with the trajectory of The 1968 Project, *Crown of Creation* is a glimpse of the recent past.

Sly and the Family Stone – *Life*

We have already covered Sly and the Family Stone, so no need to dive into a career retrospective, but a few data points. As mentioned, Sly Stone was a highly regarded record producer in the Bay Area in the late-1960s. Sly was a musician, but his passion was writing, producing, arranging and, later, expressing. Sly's experience in the studio afforded a perspective that resulted in the awareness to blend four distinct genres, creating a unique and influential sound.

The core of Sly and the Family Stone's sound was Funk, driven by a punchy rhythm and a horn section accentuating the melody. The band then incorporated elements of Rock – mainly electric guitar, but the band also relied on power chords and most tracks are in 4/4 time. The vocals leaned on Soul, both in substance and spirit. And, finally – Sly was keenly aware of, and quite good at, incorporating elements of Pop – a catchy chorus, repetition, guitar riffs and a familiar verse/chorus/verse/chorus song structure. Combining genres is commonplace in 2018, but in 1968 – it was unusual to blend four genres. The Byrds trail blazed by blending Folk and Rock, then Country and Rock. Miles Davis blended Jazz and Rock. It had been done, but no band amalgamated more styles than Sly and the Family Stone.

Achieving national attention and commercial success after the release of *Dance to the Music*, Sly and the Family Stone quickly entered the studio to record a follow-up. Notoriously prepared, with songs written and arranged prior to entering the studio, Sly Stone had yet to compose the material on *Life*. The sessions were scattered and plagued by the lack of a Single. Without lyrical hooks, Sly focused on compositions.

Life was not a commercial success. However, in the late-1980s and 1990s, critics and musicians revisited the music of Sly and the Family Stone. Critics flocked to praise *Life* as Sly and the Family Stone's most consistent and compelling record. Musicians, mainly Hip Hop artists, began to sample drum tracks from "Love City" and guitar licks from "Dynamite."

From my (overly critical) perspective, *Life* is a better listen than *Dance to the Music*. *Life* does not sound dated. The record remains an excellent Funk/Soul/Rock/Pop album. On subsequent releases, Sly and the Family Stone would announce race and peace as central themes, but on *Life* – the band is locked into the rhythm and the groove. Sure, it has a vintage vibe, but *Life* has aged extremely well and is absolutely suitable, if not recommended, for Summer days and Summer nights.

October

October

HISTORY

Black Power and the Summer Olympics

MUSIC

The Chambers Brothers – "Time Has Come Today"
Jim Hendrix – *Electric Ladyland*
Traffic – S/T
Merle Haggard – *Mama Tried*

HISTORY

In the midst of racial inequality and police brutality, highly visible athletes decided that a public display of dissatisfaction, or protest, was required. The athletes chose to demonstrate in a manner viewed by many as antithetical to the sanctity of patriotism. The athletes chose to protest during the "Star Spangled Banner", the great anthem of the United States. Outrage ensued.

People chose sides, the media fanned the flames. Images of the demonstration were plastered on newspaper and magazine covers. News anchors, not sportscasters, covered the story. Politicians intervened, consequences were levied. Some likened the conduct of the athletes to treason. Others supported the athletes. Many Americans struggled to articulate exactly what the athletes were protesting.

This is not the story of Colin Kaepernick. This is the story of Tommie Smith and John Carlos. The forum was not the domestic confines of an NFL sideline. Smith and Carlos protested on an infinitely larger, more sacred global stage – the Olympic podium. Did it matter? Does it matter? Why are we still having the exact same discussion?

Black Power and the Summer Olympics

In 1968, amid chaos and divisiveness at home, death and instability abroad, the United States sent athletes to Mexico City for the Summer Olympics. Not a diversion, simply tradition. While social and political leaders targeted the Olympics as a forum for activism, the International Olympic Committee (IOC), the (notoriously crooked) organization that governs the Olympics, reminded that the Olympics must remain apolitical, devoid of policy and without protest. Unfortunately, the Olympics were long ago politicized.

In 1936, two years after Adolf Hitler rose to power in Germany, Berlin hosted the Summer Olympics. Many nations, including the

United Kingdom, France, Spain and the Soviet Union (not the United States), threatened to boycott, citing opposition to Hitler and the Nazi regime. Ultimately, only two countries boycotted the Olympics in 1936 – Spain and the Soviet Union, marking the first time in history a country boycotted the Olympics.

In 1956, Spain and the Soviet Union were again at the center of an Olympic protest – however, this time on opposite sides. In response to the Soviet Union's invasion of Hungary, the Netherlands, Spain, Switzerland and Cambodia each boycotted the Summer Olympics (held in Melbourne, Australia).

In 1964, the IOC banned South Africa from competing in the Olympics due to South Africa's refusal to end apartheid policies. By 1976, most countries of the developed world had imposed sanctions on South Africa, which included prohibition of travel to South Africa. Notwithstanding such prohibition, the national rugby team from New Zealand decided to tour South Africa in early-1976, playing mostly exhibition games against local South African clubs. In response, several African nations demanded that the IOC ban New Zealand from participating in the 1976 Olympics in Montreal. The IOC refused. Led by the Congolese government, twenty-nine African countries boycotted the Olympics.

Just four years later, the Summer Olympics were held in Moscow, Soviet Union. At the height of the Cold War, the Olympic Games – not military conflict – took center stage. The Olympic Games in Moscow marked the first Olympic Games to be held in Eastern Europe. The Soviet Union became the first Socialist country to host the Olympic Games (Beijing became the second in 2008). Led by President Jimmy Carter and the United States, sixty-five countries boycotted the Summer Olympics in 1980, including Canada, Japan, Argentina, Chile, Israel, Norway, Saudi Arabia, Turkey and West Germany (each citing the Soviet Union's invasion of Afghanistan, but in substance – a protest of Communism).

Coincidentally, or maybe not, the next Summer Olympics, in 1984, were held in Los Angeles. In response to the United States-led boycott in 1980, the Soviet Union, Cuba and East Germany led a 14 country boycott.

So, are the Olympics apolitical? Devoid of protest? Quite definitively, "No." In fact, the Olympics have been a forum for political discourse and dissent for a half century. Yet, in 1968, the IOC condemned protest regarding social issues (racism)? Perhaps domestic issues were treated differently than international conflict? Perhaps a protest during the Olympics was different than a boycott of the Olympics? Or, perhaps a protest engineered by two African Americans just wouldn't be tolerated.

On October 16, 1968, at the Summer Olympics in Mexico City, two American sprinters, Tommie Smith and John Carlos, competed in the 200 meter track and field event. Smith won gold, setting a world record (19.83 seconds), and Carlos won bronze. Peter Norman, an Australian, won silver. After a brief cool down, the three athletes headed to the podium to accept their medals, to the tune of the "Star Spangled Banner."

Smith and Carlos were not radicalized, never participated in a protest or a march and certainly were not members of the Black Panther Party. Smith and Carlos had been sympathetic to the message of the Black Panther Party, but each athlete put athletic competition above activism.

The Black Panther Party was a group of African Americans that favored a socialist revolution to unite America, both racially and economically, rather than peaceful demonstration. The Black Panther Party endorsed militancy and functioned as a militia to protect African Americans from police brutality (however, the result was not always peaceful). The Black Panther Party was endorsed by many academics, including the renowned Sociologist, Harry Edwards.

Edwards received his Ph.D. from Cornell University and taught Sociology at the University of California, Berkeley. In 1968, Edwards created the Olympic Project for Human Rights (OPHR), an organization focused on the eradication of racial segregation and racism in sports (both in the United States and South Africa). Edwards took aim at the Summer Olympics in 1968. He tried diligently to convince African American athletes to boycott the Summer Olympics. Unfortunately for Edwards, he underestimated each athlete's commitment to competition and career. Edwards was not able to convince a single African American athlete to boycott.

Unbeknownst to Edwards, though – he had made quite an impression on both Smith and Carlos. Smith and Carlos were both expected to medal in the 200 meter event, so prior to the race, Smith and Carlos decided to stage a protest on the podium (the exact story remains unclear and Smith and Carlos are still today in dispute over the facts). Smith and Carlos decided they would each wear a black glove on their right hand and raise a closed fist, head bowed – the universal salute of the Black Panther Party. The protest would continue for the duration of the National Anthem.

As Smith and Carlos went to put on their gloves, Carlos realized he had left his gloves at the Olympic Village. Peter Norman, the silver medalist from Australia, suggested that Carlos use Smith's left-handed glove and just raise his left hand. Smith and Carlos agreed and each took the podium wearing black socks, no shoes, Smith wore a black scarf around his neck while Carlos wore a beaded necklace, Smith wore the right black glove and Carlos wore the left black glove. Each of Smith, Carlos and Norman wore OPHR badges. As the National Anthem began, each of Smith and Carlos bowed their heads and raised their black glove fisted hand. The image is iconic, the reaction was abhorrent.

The hypocritical IOC deemed the protest a domestic political statement unfit for the apolitical Olympic institution. Avery Brundage, Chairman of the IOC, demanded that Smith and Carlos be immediately suspended and expelled from the Olympic Village. The

United States refused. Brundage, citing IOC jurisdiction over the Olympic Village, threatened to ban the entire United States track and field team. Fearing further negative attention, the United States conceded. Smith and Carlos were suspended and ordered to return home to the United States. A jubilant official from the IOC lauded the expulsion of Smith and Carlos, characterizing the protest as "a deliberate and violent breach of the fundamental principles of the Olympic spirit." Really? In the wake of the Vietnam War, Smith and Carlos were characterized as *violent*?

Smith and Carlos returned to the United States as heroes to an unfortunate minority. Smith and Carlos were ostracized. The media vilified Smith and Carlos for showcasing America's racial divide. Smith and Carlos suffered physical abuse and each of their families received death threats. Not unlike the treatment American soldiers received when they returned from Vietnam. Such was how the United States treated heroes in 1968.

Smith and Carlos were forbidden from subsequent Olympic competition (by the United States authorities, not the IOC). Smith took his talents to the NFL, playing for the Cincinnati Bengals. After retiring from the NFL, Smith became a physical education teacher at Oberlin College. Similarly, Carlos turned his attention to football, but was cut by the Philadelphia Eagles after suffering a knee injury. Carlos became a track and field coach at Palm Springs High School. In 1984, Carlos was asked by the Organizing Committee for the 1984 Summer Olympics in Los Angeles to serve as a liaison to the African American community.

What about Peter Norman? Upon his return to Australia, Norman was met with criticism. The conservative media chastised Norman for sympathizing with the African American athletes. The Australian government did not recognize Norman's accomplishment at the Summer Olympics (silver medal). Most significant, after qualifying (13 times) for the Summer Olympics in 1972 (Munich, Germany), Norman was not selected to participate. Norman died in 2006, with Smith and Carlos pallbearers at his funeral.

Smith commented after the protest: "A lot of people knew…something was needed but didn't want to put up the collateral. There are those who are willing to say…that what we did needed doing. Those were the times of the beginning. Now is the time of the ending of the beginning."

The image of Smith and Carlos with their fists in the air has become a symbol. A symbol of what, though? Not racial equality. We still have yet to achieve racial equality. Does the image represent the pursuit of racial equality? Did Smith and Carlos put racism above patriotism? Did Smith and Carlos raise awareness, achieve progress? While the image may be iconic, impactful and indelible, the image is also an unimaginable failure – not a failure of Smith and Carlos, but rather – a failure by us, by every citizen of the United States.

Smith hoped that 1968 was "the ending of the beginning", but unfortunately, the protest by Smith and Carlos was not the end of the beginning. Is there no end of the beginning? It is unthinkable, but fifty years after the Smith and Carlos protest, we are still engaged in the exact same disgusting, maddening and sad discussion. We must continue the pursuit of eradicating racism. Tell the story of Smith and Carlos. Use the spirit of action inherent in 1968. Make a difference.

MUSIC

In 1968, songwriters expressed through words, musicians expressed through volume. No longer whimsical, music became serious. Less entertainment and more discourse. The music of October 1968 is critically important. A landmark album by Jimi Hendrix, the influential self-titled release by Traffic and a hit record by Merle Haggard. However, perhaps the most important song of October 1968 was a track recorded in…1966? The track was not influenced by 1968 – rather it became popular because of 1968. The time had come.

The Chambers Brothers – "Time Has Come Today"

The Chambers Brothers were raised in Carthage, Mississippi, moving to Los Angeles in 1952. Consisting of four brothers (George, Lester, Willie and Joe), the Chambers Brothers initially favored Gospel and Folk, having gained experience singing in the family's all-African American church (Southern Baptist). After opening for Ramblin' Jack Elliot and Reverend Gary Davis, Barbara Dane, a well-known Folk singer, booked the Chambers Brothers as her opening band on a cross-country tour.

Dane introduced the Chambers Brothers to Pete Seeger and Seeger orchestrated the addition of the Chambers Brothers to the lineup of the Newport Folk Festival in 1965. Of course, Bob Dylan changed the course of music by "going electric" at Newport Folk in 1965, but Newport Folk also changed the path of the Chambers Brothers.

A track by the Chambers Brothers, "I Got It", was included on a 1965 Newport Folk Festival compilation record. Instantly, the Chambers Brothers were headlining shows. The band worked throughout the early and mid-1960s, but without a hit record or hit Single. Nothing even close, actually. Unfortunately, the Chambers Brothers were a bit ahead of their time, as the band fused Gospel, Folk, Soul and Rock. In 1966, the band recorded "Time Has Come Today." Originally, the track was 11 minutes long. The Chambers Brothers released the track in November 1967 on the record, *The Time Has Come*. Needing a Single, at the demand of studio executives, the Chambers Brothers cut "Time Has Come Today" down to 4:51.

The track failed to chart. The album failed to chart. The spirit of the Chambers Brothers was damaged, but not broken. Having come up in the Gospel and Folk circuit, the band was happy to just be working and making a living on the road. Then, 1968 happened. And, suddenly, the words and message of "Time Has Come Today" were bracingly relevant. The darkness and despair resuscitated an unknown, unsuccessful track. The events of 1968 did not influence "Time Has Come Today", the events of 1968 rendered "Time Has

Come Today" influential. Further evidence of the cycle of influence existing through 1968.

Traditionally, the Chambers Brothers harmonized in the context of Gospel and Folk with multiple vocalists and a round texture. As the band evolved to Rock in 1965 and 1966 (or Psychedelic Soul), the Chambers Brothers employed a lead vocal, instead of the multi-part harmony. Unfortunately, the shortcoming of the designated lead vocalist, Lester Chambers, was exposed. While the lead vocal on "Time Has Come Today" is more spoken than sung, the tone and pitch of Lester's vocal seem off and Lester included odd vocal inflections (on the word "psychedelicized", for example).

The song famously opens with alternating strikes of a cow bell, warped together by a studio effect. You know the sound – it's the "tick-tock" – simulating the second hand of a clock (while also symbolizing that time is ticking away and that action is required). Despite the tick-tock gimmick, "Time Has Come Today" is both musically experimental and lyrically poignant.

After the tick-tock opening, the track begins with a distorted, fuzz-driven yet bright guitar lick that is equally recognizable and instantly addicting. Endorsing the experimental movement of late-1966, the Chambers Brothers recorded the guitar riff by stacking two guitars (recording two guitars playing the same part at the same time), with one guitar playing the riff clean and one utilizing a fuzz pedal.

Ultimately, the lyrics were the driving force. The first verse introduces the underlying message of the song: "Time has come today." The phrase is immediately bracing and impactful, but also basic and accessible. Plain and simple. But, the Chambers Brothers show depth with subsequent lines, which are sung in an audible, clear manner:

> *Young hearts can go their way*
> *Can't put it off another day*
> *I don't care what others say*

They say we don't listen anyway
Time has come today

The lines speak directly to the young people engaged in action. The second verse introduces politics and sadness, while also echoing the social liberalism then sweeping the youth of America. The verse in its entirety:

The rules have changed today
I have no place to stay
I'm thinking about the subway
My love has flown away
My tears have come and gone
Oh my Lord, I have to roam
I have no home
I have no home

Interestingly, the second verse leads right into the third verse, stacked verses – no chorus or refrain of the song title – a technique borrowed from Folk. However, the backing vocal repeats the word "time" after each line (with the tick-tock still in the background). The third verse:

Now the time has come
There's no place to run
I might get burned up by the sun
But I had my fun
I've been loved and put aside
I've been crushed by the tumbling tide
And my soul has been psychedelicized

More than a few dynamic phrases. The first two lines pair "come" and "run", somewhat of an obvious rhyme, but sometimes the obvious path is the most cogent and appropriate. Pairing "aside" and "tide", though – that gets me each time, brilliant craft. It isn't clear what the Chambers Brothers contemplated when they used the term "tumbling tide" in 1966, but in 1968, people had a menu of interpretations: the Vietnam War, racial inequality, police brutality, Nixon? Maybe the

Chambers Brothers were prescient in 1966, able to visualize the ensuing chaos and darkness, or maybe the Chambers Brothers were fortunate to have written a track that became instantly relevant? Doesn't so much matter, and most likely, listeners didn't even realize the track was released two years prior.

After the third verse and a refrain of the chorus, the track devolves into a psychedelic interlude that is dark and sparse, replete with warping effects that are downright spooky and a bit weird, even for 1966 and 1967. The interlude begins at the 2:30 mark and continues for just over a minute. As the psychedelic mischief gives way to a rolling and increasingly energetic snare and rhythm, the tempo boils into a climatic passionate refrain of "Now, the time has come today."

After the climax, the first two verses are repeated (which I'm not sure was necessary) and then the track winds down, literally. Beginning at 4:20, the track gradually slows down – using an obvious warping effect – slowing down until only the tick-tock remains, just as the track began.

"Time Has Come Today" peaked at #11 on the *Billboard* Hot 100 in October 1968. It was the only song by the Chambers Brothers to chart. The song remains one of the most unlikely, yet deserving, anthems in music history and is indelibly part of the soundtrack of 1968.

Jimi Hendrix – *Electric Ladyland*

Electric Ladyland was the third and final record released by The Jimi Hendrix Experience, a band that included Hendrix on guitar and lead vocals, Noel Redding on bass and Mitch Mitchell on drums. *Electric Ladyland* was released as a double record (four sides of vinyl). Parts of the record were recorded in London in early-1968, with the majority of the session recorded in June at the Record Plant in New York. Released on October 16, *Electric Ladyland* became Hendrix's highest charting release, reaching #1 on the *Billboard* Top 200 Albums chart and #6 in the UK.

Jimi Hendrix was the centerpiece of 1968. The following is a glimpse of how Jimi arrived, followed by a deep dive into *Electric* Ladyland. Jimi was born in Seattle in 1942 and lived in Seattle until joining the Army in 1961 (stationed at Fort Ord in Carmel, California – the same exact base that welcomed Steve Seltzer seven years later). Hendrix wasn't much of a soldier, as he received an Honorable Discharge in 1962, his Platoon Commander stating, "Private Hendrix has no interest whatsoever in the Army and it is my opinion that Private Hendrix will never come up to the standard required of a soldier. I feel that the military will benefit if he is discharged as soon as possible."

Hendrix notoriously practiced guitar every waking moment. After his discharge, and stints with Jr. Walker and Little Richard, Hendrix moved to New York City in 1965 and joined Curtis Knight and The Squires, an R&B band. Jimi was committed to Knight, but once Hendrix experienced Greenwich Village – his style, outlook and path changed dramatically. Influenced by Dylan and other Folk artists writing their own music and using imagery and poetry to express concepts, Jimi began writing his own songs and playing solo gigs. Jimi crafted a style that blended Blues, R&B, Rock, Folk, noise and dissonance.

His break came in early 1966 when he was noticed by Linda Keith, girlfriend of Keith Richards. Linda recommended that Richards see Jimi in New York. After two songs, Richards decided that he had to recommend Hendrix to Andrew Loog Oldham, manager of The Rolling Stones. Oldham checked it out and passed – he felt it was too challenging to market an African American artist playing Rock/Pop to white fans, especially in the United States. Linda and Keith then recommended Hendrix to Chas Chandler, former guitarist of The Animals, who at the time was embarking on a management career. Chandler loved Hendrix immediately and insisted Hendrix fly to London, where the grungier Blues he was leaning towards was way more in style – and "nobody cared about race in London."

Once in London, Hendrix's ascension to stardom was instantaneous. On September 30, 1966, Chandler was promoting a show for Cream in London and Chandler asked Clapton if Hendrix could join Cream for a couple songs. Clapton agreed and Hendrix joined Cream for three songs. On a rendition of Howlin' Wolf's "Killing Floor", Hendrix took a solo that set the entire room into a frenzy. Clapton later stated that Hendrix utilized every style and technique imaginable and synthesized the notes together in a way that Clapton had never heard. In 1989, Clapton stated that after that gig, "my life was never the same."

The next three years were a flash. Hendrix released his first record, *Are You Experienced*, in early 1967 – which spent 33 weeks on the *Billboard* Top 200 Albums chart, peaking at #2 (blocked by *Sgt. Pepper's*). Despite the chart success of *Are You Experienced*, Hendrix would become a sensation only after his performance at the Monterey Pop Festival in June 1967.

It was the "Summer of Love" and the buzz in Northern California was about two bands, both playing the Monterey Pop Festival: The Jimi Hendrix Experience and The Who. Famously, the two artists argued backstage about which act would go on stage first, as neither act wanted to follow the other. The Who were known to smash their equipment and send the crowd into an unmatched hysteria. Hendrix didn't want to follow that spectacle. Pete Townsend, one of the leading electric guitarists on the scene, had never witnessed Hendrix's guitar playing, but he heard that it wasn't advisable to go on after Jimi. Ultimately, Hendrix relented and let The Who go on first. As expected, The Who smashed their equipment and achieved a loud and energetic response from the California audience.

After the crowd settled down a bit, and a short intro by Brian Jones (of The Rolling Stones), Hendrix walked slowly out onto the stage – and proceeded to give the performance of a lifetime. Hendrix opened with "Killing Floor" (the tune he tore up with Clapton in London) and then launched into "Foxy Lady", "Hey Joe", "Wind Cries Mary", "Purple Haze" and closed with "Wild Thing." Unbelievable.

The crowd was stunned – nobody had ever seen anything quite like it…and then – amid a wave of distortion and dissonant feedback, Jimi walked to the front of the stage, gently laid his guitar on the ground, knelt on both knees and set the guitar on fire – "sacrificing something he loved" (according to Hendrix), upstaging The Who (backstage, Townsend admitted to being "motionless and speechless"). Hendrix left the audience mesmerized and left the music world forever changed.

After Monterey, Hendrix immediately went back into the studio (in London) to record *Axis: Bold As Love*. *Axis* was released in December 1967. *Axis* solidified Hendrix as a sensation, reaching #3 on the *Billboard* Top 200 Albums chart and #5 in the UK. Hendrix embarked on a massive string of tour dates, but record executives pleaded with Hendrix to return to the studio to cut another record, wishing to (financially) capitalize on Jimi's popularity.

After recording some material in London, Jimi moved to New York and booked large blocks of studio time at the Record Plant (a renowned studio in Manhattan). The sessions became legendary, not only for the music produced, but the scene. Jimi invited friends to hang at the studio during the recording session. Friends invited friends. Each day was a party, with drugs, alcohol, songwriting, jamming and, of course, some recording. Noel Redding recalled, "There were a ton of people in the studio, you couldn't move. It was a party, not a session."

Not everyone, though, was interested in the party. Chas Chandler, still Hendrix's manager, quit – citing the atmosphere and Hendrix's intolerable perfectionism. The juxtaposition of Jimi's attention to detail and his insatiable appetite for a loose, party environment is fascinating. One would surmise the atmosphere plagued the product, however, with Chandler removed from the scene, Hendrix asserted complete creative control. The consequence? Nothing short of the best, most powerful and gorgeous album of Jimi's career (and, some argue, anyone's career).

The double album opens with "...And the Gods Made Love", a one minute and 22 second instrumental, featuring a gong (or bass drum), strange voices and tons of warping and phaser effects. The introductory track is dark and deep, but segues into one of the sweetest vocal performances of Hendrix's career – on the pseudo-title track, "Have You Ever Been To (Electric Ladyland)." Listeners craving a ripping guitar solo from Hendrix would have to wait (although the wait would only be about 2 minutes). "Have You Ever Been To (Electric Ladyland)" showcases Jimi's roots in R&B, exhibiting endless range, rhythmically. Jimi's lead vocals typically leaned towards the Blues, and often were simply spoken word, but his vocals on "Have You Ever Been To (Electric Ladyland)" signaled confidence and foreshadowed experimentation.

For those craving Jimi's guitar prowess, the wait ended with the third track "Crosstown Traffic", a quintessential Rock song, reminiscent of Hendrix's work on *Are You Experienced*. The song is catchy, both with the guitar lick and the chorus. "Crosstown Traffic" is also said to symbolize Jimi's triumphant return to the United States. Then, finally, on the fourth track, the consequence of Jimi's environment in the studio, and the consequence of 1968, unfolded. "Voodoo Chile" is a 15 minute slow Blues jam, and no minute is wasted. "Voodoo Chile" is exquisite – traditional, yet simultaneously experimental. Hendrix dominates, mainly with an incredibly dark and sinister guitar tone. But, Jimi had some help on "Voodoo Chile."

Prior to recording "Voodoo Chile", Noel Redding abruptly quit. Redding, like Chandler, became incensed with the environment in the studio. Filling in for Redding on bass was Jack Casady, bassist of Jefferson Airplane. Casady was a skilled Blues player, but excelled in highly experimental environments (a product of growing up in the San Francisco scene). Desiring a "haunting" vibe for "Voodoo Chile", Hendrix enlisted his friend, Steve Winwood, to play organ (at the time, Winwood was a member of Traffic, coincidentally at the Record Plant recording the album discussed below).

"Voodoo Chile" follows the pattern of verse/chorus/solo. Each solo raves up, sometimes to a frenetic pace, only to drop back into the slow Blues. After a particularly ripping Hendrix solo – cheers and clapping are audible. Most listeners assumed the track was recorded live, but no – the cheers and clapping are the dozens of people hanging out in the studio and in the control room. No doubt, the live energy fueled the track. Pay particularly close attention to Winwood's organ on "Voodoo Chile." It's hard to upstage Hendrix, but Winwood really shines on "Voodoo Chile", even exchanging mimicked leads with Hendrix, no small feat.

After a short, somewhat out of place, tune sung by Redding ("Little Miss Strange") and another Rock song ("Long Hot Summer") that would be the centerpiece of anyone else's record (yet just *another Rock song* on *Electric Ladyland*), Jimi lays down a lighting fast guitar run and jumps right into a loose version of "Let the Good Times Roll", which he calls "Come On (Let the Good Times Roll)." The pace is quick and the guitar solo after the first verse and chorus is insane. Hendrix utilized effects throughout the *Electric Ladyland* session, but on "Come On", Jimi relies on just his Fender Stratocaster and Marshall amp. The guitar playing on this track is stunning. A must listen.

"Gypsy Eyes", "Burning of the Midnight Lamp" and "Rainy Day, Dream Away" are solid, with "Gypsy Eyes" leaning towards excellence thanks to a killer/cool/inventive guitar strum/rhythm, but the tracks seem pedestrian compared to the epic that followed: "1983...(A Merman I Should Turn to Be)." "1983" is the clearest illustration of Hendrix's intention in 1968. The clearest illustration of 1968's effect on Hendrix. Given every freedom – economic (Hendrix was the highest paid performer in music in 1968), control (Jimi always had control, but with Chandler gone, Jimi had no manager present), studio, sophistication, autonomy (Jimi produced the album), label (unlimited studio time and budget) and choice of personnel – "1983" is the cleanest product of Jimi's imagination and musical abilities. "1983" might not be the best track on *Electric Ladyland*, but I'd argue it's the purest.

"1983" is expansive. At 13:40, the track unfolds in segments – focus is on the instrumentation – but, also includes meaningful and substantive lyrics. "1983" is interesting because the track progresses from tangible to abstract, both lyrically and musically. The first two verses of the song are accompanied by a musical arrangement rooted in melody and form. The second part of the song is a wild excursion, unhinged in form and tone. Likewise, the lyrics are bold, solid and formed in the beginning, then rather unknowing and abstract, in the second part.

The song begins with ten seconds of noise, followed by clear, clean finger picked electric guitar in a minor key, reminiscent of "Wind Cries Mary" or even "House of the Rising Sun." Hendrix then launches into a guitar solo that is both beautifully melodic and anthemic. Hendrix sounds tired and dreary on the first verse:

> *I awake from yesterday*
> *Alive but the war is here to stay*

Direct, plain, observant and desperate. If "1983" is the clearest expression of Hendrix's consciousness in 1968, it is evident what is foremost on his mind (war). Hendrix openly adored Dylan and tirelessly worked on the craft of songwriting. Ultimately, Jimi's lyrics evolved to decent, but his guitar playing is so overwhelmingly amazing that his lyrics are often overlooked. That said, "1983" has some terrific lines. After a refrain of the melodic guitar lead, the second verse emerges:

> *Oh say can you see it's really such a mess*
> *Every inch of Earth is a fighting nest*
> *Giant pencil and lip-stick tube shaped things*
> *Continue to rain and cause screaming pain*

The first line cleverly references the "Star Spangled Banner", while the third line describes, in a somewhat odd and/or psychedelic manner, bombs falling. Hendrix's use of the word "rain" in the fourth line must be a nod to Dylan (a reference to "A Hard Rain is Gonna

295

Fall", Dylan's classic 1963 description of a nuclear apocalypse). After another short guitar phrase, the third verse is delivered with noticeably more energy, angst and ferocity:

> *Well it's too bad*
> *That our friends*
> *Can't be with us today*
> *Well that's too bad*
> *"The machine that we built,*
> *Would never save us"*
> *That's what they say*
> *And they also said*
> *"It's impossible for a man*
> *To live and breathe underwater...forever"*

The abstract final two lines of the verse mark the shift in the track's form. The song shifts to a narrative about Jimi and a female friend fleeing – presumably, fleeing a terrible place (Earth) – perhaps in a machine – en route to a fictional land that is underwater. Now, after the nonsensical opulence of 1967, Jimi's "story" is really not that bizarre – likely a comment on the tragedy of existence, citing an escapism mentality common in 1968. Ultimately, the path of the music that accompanies the lyrics is the resounding intrigue.

After a run of descending notes leading to a tempo break at 3:10, Hendrix quietly sings a verse, heavily distorted by reverb – and then leads a fiery guitar jam that again breaks tempo at 4:20. The next seven minutes are either bliss or bullshit, depending on your tolerance for indulgence. This section of "1983" relies on Jazz concepts, highly experimental, loose, improvised and abstract. Hendrix and Redding generally lay out (don't play) between 4:20 and 6:00, as Mitchell employs a snare and brush texture while bells clamor and clang and swirling effects linger in the background.

At 6:12, Jimi returns with a series of gentle notes – a pure tone reminiscent of Jerry Garcia in 1968 and 1969 (sounding similar to when The Grateful Dead emerged from a chaotic space). The next few minutes are wistful, easy and while still abstract, not spooky (a flute even peaks through the collage). As expected, the tempo builds (at around 8:00), led again by Mitchell (if you're a drummer, definitely check out Mitchell on this track).

Before Redding embarks on a rather stunning bass solo, Hendrix plays a few Blues licks that are just amazing (pick it up at 9:24 and check out the tone at 9:35). The brief diversion into the Blues by Hendrix is aborted, as Redding emerges at 9:42 and unleashes a bass solo that is melodic, inventive and moving. At 10:27, after another touch of flute, Mitchell again ramps up the tempo and at 10:44, Jimi reminds us that we're listening to Jimi Hendrix. Jimi unleashes thirty seconds of Hard Rock. The flurry, or fury, is a bit of a tease to be honest – as the tempo (again) breaks/slows at 11:08.

Lyrics return, but again with heavy effects and distortion – the words are both unintelligible and barely audible. At 11:53, Jimi steps in front and shreds a guitar solo, backed by chaos. The solo gives way to noise. Cymbals and a weird chirping sound close the track at 13:40. Certainly, a wild ride and an epic composition.

If you're thinking: there's no way a straight Rock song could follow "1983", you're absolutely right. After "1983", Hendrix included a one minute and two second instrumental consisting of ambient noise, most closely resembling a swirling wind. Not exactly peaceful, but certainly a moment to catch your breath.

Electric Ladyland closes with two monumental tracks – instantly turning a great album into a classic album. While unanimity does not exist as to how Hendrix decided to cover a Bob Dylan track from *John Wesley Harding*, an album released by Dylan in 1967, unanimity does seem to suggest that "All Along the Watchtower" is the best cover in music history.

Several people claim to have first played "All Along the Watchtower" for Hendrix, but I'm going to go with the least interesting and most realistic version. Hendrix's girlfriend at the time, Kathy Etchington, stated that upon the release of *John Wesley Harding*, just before Jimi left the United States en route back to London, Jimi – like every other Dylan fan – went to a record store and bought a copy. Etchington distinctly recalls that Jimi arrived at her apartment in London holding a brand new copy of *John Wesley Harding* and a bottle of American whiskey. She stated, "we played it over and over again. He just loved it."

Supporting the notion that Jimi was an enormous fan of Dylan, several sources report that Hendrix carried a Dylan songbook in his travel bag (a book listing the chords and lyrics to every Dylan song). Hendrix also once approached Dylan's guitarist, Robbie Robertson, in 1967 to ask not about Robbie's guitar tone, but rather "how does Bob write his lyrics?" Never lacking wit, Robbie replied, "usually on a typewriter."

The recording session for "Watchtower" is legendary and requires a moment. Recording began in London, with Hendrix obsessing over the intro guitar chords – insisting on an acoustic strum. As usual, the studio was littered with friends and musicians. Dave Mason, a member of Traffic, suggested that Jimi pair a 12-string acoustic guitar with Hendrix's standard 6-string acoustic strum – and run both guitars through a Marshall amp (adds natural distortion). Jimi obliged, Mason grabbed a 12-string acoustic guitar and after two takes, Hendrix was in love with the result.

On take 14, a frequent guest, Brian Jones (The Rolling Stones), suggested that he join on piano. The recording engineer, Eddie Kramer, described Jones as "completely out of his brain." At this point in 1968, Brian Jones was in the midst of a massive drug and alcohol spell, leading to his demise and death in 1969. Hendrix and Jones were close friends and Jimi again obliged. Unfortunately, it was a mess. Kramer recalled, "Brian's playing was all bloody horrible and out of time" and "Brian was gone after two takes....(he) practically fell on the floor in the control room." However, Jones resurfaced hours later, having sobered up (just) a bit, and is actually credited with percussion on the final recording of "Watchtower", playing an instrument called a vibraslap (heard at the end of each bar in the intro – sounds like a rattlesnake or shaker whip).

Recording stopped after take 27, with only the intro complete, along with a rough cut of the drums. No lyrics, no guitar solos, no bass. After Hendrix completed a series of tour dates, Jimi rented an apartment in New York and endeavored to complete *Electric Ladyland* at the Record Plant. First order of business was to record the bass. Redding had already quit the band, so Jimi recorded the bass himself. With the intro, drums and bass intact, Hendrix turned his attention to the guitar solo. While many of Hendrix's greatest guitar solos were improvised in the studio, Jimi spent hours mapping out every note for the lead solo in "Watchtower."

The solo has four distinct parts. Beginning at 1:43 and lasting until 2:00, the first section is traditional and classic (for Hendrix, anyway). A rare combination of speed and tone, the notes are more Rock than Blues and the pace is quick. At 2:00, the tempo drops and Jimi incorporates a slide guitar solo. According to Velvert Turner (a friend that was in the studio for the session), Jimi was "running around, trying to get a sound out that he had in his head…he grabbed beer bottles, soda bottles, knives and everything trying to get the middle section." Eventually, Hendrix decided on a cigarette lighter. Jimi's slide solo doesn't possess the traditional twang of a slide guitar, rather a deep, almost patient, passage. Eddie Van Halen has called the slide section of the "Watchtower" solo his "favorite guitar solo ever."

After a yell of "Hey" at 2:15, Jimi kicks the wah pedal and extends the calm template of the slide solo, infusing psychedelic elements, but never veering from the song's structure, perhaps in deference to Dylan. At 2:31, Jimi ends the 30 seconds of calm by unleashing a torrent of notes, led by a fierce rhythm solo quoting the intro, but with fire. The scratching sound he makes at 2:41, likely by playing rhythm over muted strings, is wonderfully nasty.

At 2:51, Jimi emphatically sings the first line of the last verse "All along the watchtower", then settles for the middle lines of the verse, only to open up on the last line, "And the wind begins to howl." Jimi ends the vocal with another emphatic "Hey" at 3:22. From there, the outro is a short guitar solo, featuring a frenzy of piercing notes starting at 3:41 until the fade out.

All packed into 4:01. Surprisingly, "Watchtower" is Hendrix's only Top 40 single, reaching #20 on the *Billboard* Hot 100 (#5 in the UK). Perhaps, more impressive than chart position, Dylan has not only commented favorably on Hendrix's version, but Dylan immediately adopted the Hendrix version and still today plays Hendrix's version in concert, rather than the *John Wesley Harding* version. If you're looking for a statement or comment from Dylan, well – that's a bit more difficult, as Dylan isn't exactly direct. Dylan commented in 1988, "It's not a wonder to me that [Jimi] recorded my songs...but that he recorded so few of them because they were all his." Dylan is the best, really. The best.

Electric Ladyland closes with "Voodoo Chile (Slight Return)." At only five minutes, "Slight Return" reprises the third track. "Slight Return" is quite simply – evil. If someone wants to make the case that "Slight Return" is the best track on *Electric Ladyland*, there would be no argument from me.

The track begins with thirty seconds of Jimi showcasing his mastery of the wah pedal. The intro is funky, but it becomes evident that Funk would not be the way *Electric Ladyland* closes. At 0:33, Hendrix slams into a Hard Rock power chord, then alternates between rhythm and lead – filling the space between power chords with searing guitar runs. The sound is heavy and dark, a classic projection of late-1968. The vocals are sung by Hendrix with noticeably more passion.

"Slight Return" rocks really hard, no doubt about that – but, the legacy of the track is Jimi's guitar solos. For example, Jimi's solo between 1:55 and 2:30 is one of those where you just laugh, and say out loud, "that is just ridiculous, like – really comical." Hendrix was also a master of bringing down the pace after a solo, or between solos,

300

resulting in the solos having even more impact when they hit. The section after 2:30 is a prime example.

A two minute guitar solo closes "Slight Return", but the closing solo is looser, less piercing and backed by a cacophonous rhythm section, rather than a tight pocket. The final solo serves a purpose, as it brings *Electric Ladyland* to a thoughtful goodbye, with focus on Hard Rock, a symbol of the musical shift in 1968.

Biographer Michael Heatley stated that "most critics agree" that *Electric Ladyland* was "the fullest realization of Jimi's far-reaching ambitions." Author Tom Larson deemed the record "essential" in his compendium on Hard Rock. Robert Christgau described the record as "an aural utopia that accommodates both ingrained conflict and sweet, vague spiritual yearnings, held together by a master musician."

Praise for *Electric Ladyland* is boundless. Praise for Jimi Hendrix is undying. Please consider, though, not only the magnitude and power and quality of *Electric Ladyland*, but the manner in which Hendrix was affected by, and incorporated, the culture, political climate and violence of 1968. Jimi synthesized the spectrum of emotions that existed in 1968, harnessing despair, rage and sadness to produce a medium guided by passion – utilizing both conscious and subconscious visions.

Normally, I would end this passage by detailing the demise and/or death of the artist. Really? Again? Not going to do it. You know the story. Hendrix died at age 27 of a drug overdose. Another theme of 1968. Senseless death.

Traffic – S/T

Traffic formed in 1967 after connecting at a club (The Elbow Room) in Aston, Birmingham (UK). The founding members of Traffic were Steve Winwood (guitar, organ, lead vocals), Jim Capaldi (woodwinds, piano, percussion, vocals), Dave Mason (guitar, bass) and Chris Wood (woodwinds, drums). While Capaldi, Mason and Wood were experienced, working musicians in 1967, Winwood was already an international star.

In 1963, at the age of 15, Winwood became the lead singer of the Spencer Davis Group, a successful and popular Rock/R&B band. In 1966, with Winwood on vocals, the Spencer Davis Group released two singles, both charting in the Top Ten on the *Billboard* Hot 100 ("Gimme Some Lovin'" and "I'm a Man"). Despite the success, at age 19, Winwood quit the Spencer Davis Group in 1967, in search of a more experimental and creative version of Rock.

Naturally, Traffic's first album, *Mr. Fantasy*, recorded and released in late-1967, included a healthy dose of Psychedelic Pop. Given Winwood's notoriety, three singles sold well in the UK ("Paper Sun", "Hole In My Shoe" and "Here We Go Round the Mulberry Bush"), but other than the title track, *Mr. Fantasy* is decidedly average.

After a series of successful live shows, Traffic entered the Record Plant Studio in New York to record the follow-up to *Mr. Fantasy*. Immediately, Winwood, Capaldi and Wood expressed an interest in moving away from Psychedelic Pop and towards a more unstructured song template that included aspects of Jazz, woodwind instruments and percussion. Mason was against the change in direction and quit the band.

Now, as a quick aside, it is important to note – yes, we are talking about the same Steve Winwood that you know from the 1980s. The same Steve Winwood that sang "Higher Love", "Finer Things" and "Back in the High Life." Same guy – but, prior to those classics (seriously, I love those songs), Winwood was a highly regarded guitarist, one of the best lead vocalists of the generation and a sought after organ player (as stated above, he played organ on Hendrix's *Electric Ladyland*). Winwood wasn't simply among the greats, he was one of the greats. He just navigated the Eighties differently than most.

In early 1968, after Traffic (without Mason) recorded a handful of tracks that would appear on *Traffic*, Mason returned, regretful of his decision to quit. Traffic welcomed Mason back into the band, but didn't realize they were welcoming Pop back into the band. Mason had written a few songs and offered them to Traffic for use on the record. While Winwood and Capaldi desired a different musical direction, both agreed that the songs were too good to pass. The first Mason track was "Feelin' Alright."

"Feelin' Alright" is not Psychedelic Pop, but it is certainly Pop. With a solid Rock/Soul spine, the tune is anchored by a catchy chorus, a tight groove and a horn section. Winwood and Capaldi wanted to experiment with song structure, and they would do so later on *Traffic*, but "Feelin Alright" is in standard time (4/4). Mason sings lead vocals and plays guitar on the track, with Winwood on backing vocals and organ. Mason also contributed the first track, "You Can All Join In", which was briefly a hit in the UK (but today sounds dated). Mason's other contributions were not as popular – "Don't Be Sad" and "Cryin' to Be Heard", although the latter is a personal favorite.

Ultimately, *Traffic* can be split into the Mason tracks and the non-Mason tracks. The first non-Mason track is "Pearly Queen." Like many Traffic songs, the band enters quietly – usually with a woodwind or organ intro (neither of which are conducive to radio play). After 22 seconds of soft noise, a snare hit (by, I think, Capaldi) launches into the Winwood vocal, sounding Bluesy and full of Soul. After two verses, it is clear the direction of Traffic has changed from their 1967 release, but also from the opening Mason track. At 1:07, after a Hendrix-esque yell of "yeah", Winwood unleashes a blistering electric guitar solo (also reminiscent of Hendrix). Winwood's playing is not virtuoso, like a Hendrix, Clapton or Jimmy Page, but Winwood is incredibly melodic within his solos, choosing each note as if mimicking his vocal delivery. After another solo, the track fades out with heavy percussion. Nothing legendary, or "classic", but "Pearly Queen" was the first sign of a new Traffic.

Perhaps the grooviest and most underrated track on *Traffic*, "Who Knows What Tomorrow May Bring" again relies on a simple Blues/Soul combination, but after two verses, the band's true intention manifests. From the outset, the organ is up in the mix (Winwood), and despite a couple electric guitar runs (Mason), after two verses – at 1:48 – the band drops into a tight jam, led by impressive organ playing by Winwood and Capaldi holding down the rhythm on drums and bass.

I suspect the listener expected a couple instrumental bars, maybe twenty seconds, but the band stays in the pocket for the remainder of the track (about a minute and a half). The studio version ends at 3:14, but live versions of "Who Knows What Tomorrow May Bring" routinely continued for over 10 minutes (a live version was included on the deluxe version of *John Barleycorn Must Die*, featuring a sax solo).

Possibly the most memorable, or unique, track on *Traffic* is "(Roamin' Thro' The Gloamin' With) 40,000 Headman." Opening with a minor key acoustic guitar, along with a flute, the tempo emerges – slow, shaker-driven and haunting. Winwood's vocals are weary and worn, but the track picks up at 1:06. Winwood's vocals are stunning. Then, the track settles back into the original tempo – slow, but not a ballad – just a very unusual pace. "40,000 Headman" closes with an extended fadeout, dominated by the flute, percussion and other woodwinds (you can imagine audiences listening to this live – stoned and swaying). A great live version was released on *Welcome to the Canteen*.

To close the record, not to be outdone by Mason, Winwood and Capaldi crafted a tight Rock/Soul tune of their own that invokes the sound of "Feelin' Alright." Certainly, not as popular as "Feelin' Alright", "Means to an End" has a cult following and really cooks. The track typically either opened or closed Traffic concerts. Winwood again shines on lead guitar and also handles piano and bass on the studio version.

Traffic peaked at #17 on the *Billboard* Top 200 Albums chart and reached #9 in the UK (*Mr. Fantasy* had peaked at #88). Subsequently, Traffic scored four straight Top Ten albums, with *John Barleycorn Must Die* at #5 (1970), *The Low Spark of High Heeled Boys* at #7 (1971), *Shoot Out at the Fantasy Factory* at #6 (1973) and *When the Eagle Flies* at #9 (1974). Traffic also released two high quality live albums – the aforementioned *Welcome to the Canteen* in 1971 and *On the Road* in 1973 (both charted, at #29 and #26, respectively). I tend to view Traffic as underrated, but the above proves that the band was very popular. Traffic excelled at diversity and crafting high quality complete albums, rather than focusing on Singles.

The following quote from Winwood summarizes the essence of Traffic: "We just wanted to make music that had our own freedom and was more natural." Fairly generic, but Winwood contextualized, "If we wanted to do a nine-minute song. If we wanted a two and a half minute intro before the vocal came in, or if the hook didn't come in until five minutes into the song, we didn't care about it." Winwood's attitude is certainly admirable, but I wonder if he would have adopted that attitude if not for his early success with the Spencer Davis Group. Possibly, early Pop success enabled Winwood to move away from Pop?

Merle Haggard – *Mama Tried*

Amid the turbulence and change in 1968, affecting politics, society and music, as well as film, literature and technology, one thing seemed to stay relatively constant – the wonderfully pure genre of music that is and was, Country. Now, Country music certainly evolves – shifting from traditional to progressive and ultimately, back to traditional. However, the shifts are slow, glacially slow.

In 1961, Nashville had become the epicenter of Country music. Not only were musicians flocking to Nashville, so did record labels, producers and writers. An outright "industry" was solidified, coalescing around a particular sound, or brand, of Country music. A sound that was marketable, accessible and repeatable. The Nashville Sound utilized multi-part harmonies, string arrangements, a crooning vocal style and round, smooth production.

In 1965, Merle Haggard (along with Buck Owens) created a new brand of Country music – but, the new brand of Country music was actually what Country music sounded like before the Nashville Sound. Such is the intriguing "evolution" of Country music – sometimes progress is actually regress. The style of Country music favored by Merle Haggard was called, "The Bakersfield Sound", as Haggard, Owens and others had trekked across America and settled in a dusty enclave – Bakersfield, California.

The Bakersfield Sound was defined by twang – a Fender Telecaster, steel guitar, fiddle, banjo, a minimalist vocal delivery and rough – usually live – production. The architecture of the Bakersfield Sound is devoid of string arrangements, choirs and over-production. Also, the Bakersfield Sound, while still focused on love and lost love, possessed a darker, more rebellious attitude.

Many legendary artists portray a rebellious, poor, eccentric and sometimes outright criminal background, while actually experiencing a regular, suburban, privileged upbringing. And then…there's Merle Haggard. Merle Haggard actually was a rebel. He was downright destitute. He was certainly eccentric. And, he absolutely was a criminal. These qualities influenced his life and shaped his music.

Born in 1937, Merle was first arrested at the age of 13 for theft and sent to a juvenile detention center. Upon his release, Haggard and a friend ran away to Texas, riding freight trains and hitchhiking across the country, until Haggard and his friend were arrested for robbery and again sent to a juvenile detention center. After escaping, Haggard fled to California and found work as a laborer, short order cook and oil well shooter. Around this time, at age 16, he also started performing in local bars – getting paid $5.00 per show…but negotiating for free beer to be included in his performance fee.

Although Haggard stabilized his life and was working hard, he was still a minor and therefore arrested for truancy and petty larceny. He was sent to yet another juvenile detention center and after another escape, he was sent to the Preston School of Industry (a high security juvenile center). After 15 months at Preston, he was released but immediately sent back after beating a local kid (almost to death). Haggard served his term and upon his release, dedicated himself to a music career.

Mainly singing and imitating Lefty Frizzell, Haggard found success and even had a cameo on the television show *Chuck Wagon* in 1956. Despite modest success, Haggard was broke and had recently married. Dejected and desiring to support his wife any way possible, he attempted to rob a Bakersfield roadhouse and was again arrested.

Now 18 years old, Haggard was tried and convicted as an adult and sent to San Quentin State Prison. Finding San Quentin a heck of a lot tougher than the juvenile detention centers, Haggard conspired to escape with another inmate named "Rabbit" (who excelled at digging tunnels). Fellow inmates pleaded with Haggard not to risk escape with Rabbit due to the danger of being caught or killed. Haggard decided not to attempt an escape, opting to stay at San Quentin and start an illegal gambling and beer brewing operation. A much better idea.

To the surprise of the inmates, Rabbit successfully escaped San Quentin. However, days after his escape, Rabbit shot and killed a police officer, was arrested and sent back to San Quentin for execution. Haggard has stated repeatedly that Rabbit's execution was the turning point in his life. Grateful to be alive, Haggard earned his high school equivalency diploma, disbanded the gambling and brewing rackets, got a steady job in the prison's textile mill – and, most significantly, joined the prison's country music band.

Haggard was released from San Quentin in 1958 (yes, he turned 21 in prison – the opening line from "Mama Tried"). Focusing on his music career in the evening, Haggard dug ditches and wired houses for a construction company during the day. Haggard's break came in 1964 when he met Liz Anderson, an older woman and unknown songwriter. Haggard had the uncanny ability to marry Anderson's lyrics with classic Country elements to create a sound that seemed derivative, yet original.

Haggard recorded "(My Friends Are Gonna Be) Strangers" – an Anderson written track that echoed the outlaw personality of Haggard's youth. "Strangers" reached #9 on the *Billboard* Country Singles chart and became the title track for the (great) album *Strangers*, released in September 1965.

After *Strangers*, Haggard went on a run of 12 straight years with at least one #1 hit on the *Billboard* Country Singles chart, with the first five years after *Strangers* featuring the following #1 hits: "I'm a Lonesome Fugitive" (1966), "Branded Man" (1967), "Sing Me Back Home" (1968), "Mama Tried" (1968), "The Legend of Bonnie and Clyde" (1968), "Okie From Muskogee" (1969) and "The Fightin' Side of Me" (1970).

Merle Haggard's influence is exponential. Dylan has toured with him. The Grateful Dead covered "Mama Tried" for over 35 years (and also covered "Sing Me Back Home"). Johnny Cash covered Haggard. The Rolling Stones point to Haggard as an influence. More importantly, Merle Haggard's creation and perpetuation of the Bakersfield Sound has been a constant in Country music and a symbol for tradition, roots and the resistance of popular tendencies, fads and commercialization.

Perhaps the truest example of Haggard's brilliance is *Mama Tried*. In the original review published in *Rolling Stone* in 1968, Andy Wickham wrote: "His songs romanticize the hardships and tragedies of America's transient proletarian and his success is resultant of his inherent ability to relate to his audience a commonplace experience with precisely the right emotional pitch...Merle Haggard looks the part and sounds the part because he is the part."

Country musicians notoriously cover the work of other musicians, recycling traditionals. Haggard certainly covered traditional Country tunes, but he also wrote his own material. *Mama Tried* consists of four Haggard originals, along with a song written by Dolly Parton and a cover of Johnny Cash. Ultimately, though – the tracks on *Mama Tried* are held together by a single theme: prison.

The cover of *Mama Tried* depicts Merle Haggard in prison fatigues, including an old-style prisoner hat. But, the photo doesn't show Haggard behind barbed wire – or digging ditches or cleaning up the mess hall, instead Haggard is holding an acoustic guitar, employing a facial expression that is both serious and badass (for lack of a more appropriate term).

The opening track, "Mama Tried", is an autobiographical account of Haggard's path that led to his incarceration. But, "Mama Tried" is not simply a story that focuses on plot, "Mama Tried" is an ode to Haggard's mother, a sentimental plea for forgiveness and an introspective recognition of the pain Haggard caused his mother. Typical of Country music, the lyrics don't require a ton of interpretation. "Mama Tried" reached #1 in 1968 and held the top slot for 5 weeks. Here are the first two verses:

> *The first thing I remember knowing*
> *Was a lonesome whistle blowing*
> *And a young'un's dream of growing up to ride*
> *On a freight train leaving town*
> *Not knowing where I'm bound*
> *And no one could change my mind but Mama tried*
>
> *One and only rebel child*
> *From a family meek and mild*
> *My mama seemed to know what lay in store*
> *Despite all my Sunday learning*
> *Towards the bad I kept on turning*
> *Till Mama couldn't hold me anymore*

Pairing two verses without an intervening chorus was perhaps a storytelling technique, but the beauty of "Mama Tried" is the Pop sensibility of the chorus. At the core, Merle Haggard was a songwriter. His word choices are masterful and his ability to convey an image in the context of storytelling is brilliant. The energetic chorus:

> *And I turned twenty-one in prison doing life without parole*
> *No one could steer me right but Mama tried, Mama tried*
> *Mama tried to raise me better, but her pleading I denied*
> *That leaves only me to blame 'cause Mama tried*

After the chorus, a slide guitar provides some flare, but the music of "Mama Tried" is straight-forward and simple – standard time, acoustic guitar, snare drum and cymbals (possibly no bass drum) and an acoustic bass very low in the mix. The focus is on the verses, then a slight rave up for the chorus. The final verse:

> *Dear old Daddy, rest his soul*
> *Left my mom a heavy load*
> *She tried so very hard to fill his shoes*
> *Working hours without rest*
> *Wanted me to have the best*
> *She tried to raise me right but I refused*

Another refrain of the chorus and that's it – the track is a brisk 2:13. Actually, there are only two tracks on Mama Tried over three minutes (and they are both only 3:15). Certainly, typical of Country music, but another example of how Country music remained insulated, or isolated – resistant to trends in Rock, Pop, Jazz and even Folk.

After "Green Green Grass of Home", a song written by Curly Putnam about a man returning home after his release from prison, Haggard covers a Dolly Parton song, "In the Good Old Days (When Times Were Bad)." Not really a cover, I guess – as Parton had yet to record the track, but wrote the song and gave it to Haggard to record. The instrumentation is again simple, allowing the lyrics to shine.

310

The song leans more towards Folk than Country in terms of Haggard's vocal delivery (and the dual finger-picked acoustic guitars in the background). The verses are decent, but the beauty of "In the Good Old Days" is the parallel, or lack thereof, between the old days being both "good" and "bad." Parton highlights the subtext with the chorus:

> *No amount of money could buy from me*
> *The memories that I have of then*
> *No amount of money could pay me*
> *To go back and live through it again*

Ultimately, Haggard drives the point with his wonderful delivery of the song's title, "in the good old days, when times were bad." After "In the Good Old Days", Haggard covered a Mel Tillis song, "I Could Have Gone Right." Similar in substance to "Mama Tried", the song has a couple great lines, including: "I went to the places where sin just waits for you, and I fell in with the wrong crowd like sinners always do."

Haggard's cover of "Folsom Prison Blues" is surprisingly straight-forward. Meaning, Haggard didn't adjust the time, tempo or instrumentation. Pretty much just Haggard singing instead of Cash. But, *Mama Tried* is an album about prison, and I guess you can't really have an album about prison and not cover "Folsom Prison Blues."

Mama Tried peaked at #4 on the *Billboard* Country Albums chart. *Mama Tried* received attention from some non-Country music radio stations, but neither the album nor any of the Singles charted on the *Billboard* Pop charts. However, in 1969, Haggard's original composition, "Okie from Muskogee", reached # 41 on the *Billboard* Hot 100.

For the remainder of his career, Merle Haggard was a true crossover sensation, adored by Rock audiences, Pop audiences and Folk audiences. Only Johnny Cash and Willie Nelson experienced more attention. Haggard's ability to relate experiences in the confines of traditional Country music remains unmatched. And, the lack of substantive comment in Haggard's work on *Mama Tried* in 1968, despite a penchant for rebellion, illuminates and reinforces the notion of Country music's steadfast isolationism – a characteristic both questionable and admirable.

November

November

HISTORY

Election of Richard M. Nixon

MUSIC

Van Morrison – *Astral Weeks*
The Kinks – *The Kinks Are the Village Green Preservation Society*
The Beatles – *The White Album*

HISTORY

Election of Richard M. Nixon

On November 5, 1968, Richard Nixon won the 37th election of the President of the United States. Naturally, the election was as chaotic as the wrenching experiences that led to its consequence. Not only was the 1968 election incredibly close and unusual, including a third party candidate winning five states in the Electoral College, the political outcome set the United States on a path of conservative ideology that lasted almost 25 years, and arguably, remains today.

After President Johnson announced on March 31, 1968 that he would not "accept the nomination of my party for another term as your President", despite the fleeting optimism around the candidacy of Robert F. Kennedy, it was evident that the people of America had lost confidence in the Democratic Party. Clark Clifford points to the Tet Offensive as the turning point, stating "its sheer size and scope made a mockery of what President Johnson and the American military had told the public about the war, and devastated administration credibility." As the United States spiraled through violence, the message of Richard Nixon resonated with many Americans. Nixon's campaign harped on two themes, or phrases: "law and order" and "the silent majority."

Political and cultural (race and feminism) demonstrations depicted an instability that Nixon detested. The unrest represented a republic in turmoil. Nixon believed that controlling, or stopping, the demonstrations would project stability and a return to the calm experienced during his terms as Vice President (1952-1960), under President Eisenhower. The logic may have seemed rational but any logic that involves infringement of freedom of speech and other fundamental rights must be carefully examined and viewed with extreme skepticism.

The term "law and order" became a divisive phrase in 1968. You either were in favor of protest and rebellion or you were in favor of "law and order." By alienating the liberal community, Nixon energized his base and received unequivocal political support from military veterans, police officers, fire fighters and government employees and their respective unions. Nixon was a career politician, adept at gaining support – and keenly aware of how to win an election. Sound familiar?

Nixon referred to his supporters as the "silent majority", those that rejected the radicalism and liberalization of American culture. The word "silent" refers to those that were not protesting. The Nixon rhetoric appealed to middle class adults that got up every morning and went to work, trying to make a living to support a family, educate children and protect basic American freedoms. These working adults saw a younger generation that embraced drugs, demonstrated in favor of change and although a generalization, lacked the work ethic of prior generations. The word "majority" conveyed a sense of strength. Perhaps, a false sense of strength, though – as Nixon won the election with only 43.4% of popular vote. Nonetheless, the phrase "silent majority" conveyed a coalition mentality.

This book is intended to recount political events, not comment on politics. However, the parallel between Nixon's ascension and strategy – and Donald J. Trump's election must be acknowledged. Whether you agree with Nixon – or whether you detest Trump – the path is linear. The United States was in a tenuous posture in 1968 and 2016 – perilously both open and depressed, impressionable and vulnerable. Nixon strategically took advantage. A divided nation. Likewise, Trump capitalized.

As you consider Nixon in 1968, consider Trump in 2016. The question for the United States is survival and progress. The question in the context of this book – will the Trump Presidency result in a similar effect on arts, culture and music. Apologies for the digression, but the similarity is uncanny. However, the similarity is not between two men, rather the likeness is that of the disposition of the United States of America in 1968 and 2016.

Opposition to Nixon was fractured, benefiting Nixon's political strategy. Eugene McCarthy experienced success in the Democratic primaries, running on a single-issue platform: immediate withdrawal from Vietnam. Despite loud support from young voters, experts suggested that McCarthy's support was smaller than perceived. McCarthy, a Senator from Minnesota, lacked the requisite experience in international political affairs required to assume the Presidency. Polls suggested that McCarthy would lose to Nixon in a landslide. Thus…the candidacy of Hubert Humphrey, the Vice President of the United States, notoriously aligned with the embattled President Johnson.

While we normally think of the South as a Republican stronghold, this was not the case prior to 1968. The South had been a formidable asset of the Democratic Party for 80 years, dating back to the Civil War. Nixon, though, utilized the conservative rhetoric inherent in the South, adeptly appealing to the religious values of Southern families. By analogizing political turmoil and social chaos with liberalism and the Democratic Party, Nixon masterfully positioned Conservatism and the Republican Party as the political ideology of the South. Nixon branded the Republican Party as the advocate for stable values, clear purpose, religion and justice. Ultimately, experts agreed that if Nixon took the South, along with Republican strongholds in the Midwest, he would easily prevail.

However, Nixon's ability to sweep the South was compromised. George Wallace, the four-term Governor of Alabama, announced his candidacy for President. Wallace was a devout segregationist. The dictionary definition of a "segregationist" is a person that "believes that people of different races should be kept apart" (Webster). Basically, an example of a segregationist is a person who believes that white children and black children should go to different schools. Perhaps a more accurate definition of a segregationist is a racist.

As a third-party candidate in a Presidential election, Wallace's candidacy would typically have been irrelevant. But, this was 1968. Several Southern states voted on racial lines, rather than political lines

317

– supporting Wallace. Wallace had incorporated a populist message into his segregationist platform, a message that appealed to "ordinary people" – working class folks, as well as farmers and the agriculture industry. The populist message enabled Southern voters to mask their vote for Wallace, citing populism as opposed to racism. In reality, a vote for Wallace was a vote for white nationalism, white supremacy and hate. Another paradigm connecting 1968 to 2016.

Nevertheless, in 1968, a racist politician from Alabama unconscionably received 13.9% of the national vote and won five states in the general election. No third-party candidate has since won even one state in a general election. Wallace won each of Mississippi, Louisiana, Alabama, Georgia and Arkansas. Wallace received 46 Electoral Votes, 45 from winning the aforementioned states and 1 from an Elector in North Carolina.

Wallace's performance in the South both disrupted Nixon's path to the White House and crushed Humphrey's candidacy. Wallace prevailing in five Southern states rendered North Carolina, Virginia, Tennessee and Florida critical. If Humphrey could win those states, along with the Northeast, the Electoral Vote would be tight. However, Nixon won each of North Carolina, Virginia, Tennessee and Florida. Humphrey did win the Northeast, but Nixon dominated the Midwest, a classic Republican territory, and also swept every state West of the Mississippi, including his home state, California (Humphrey did win Minnesota, his home state, Michigan and Texas, President Johnson's home state).

Richard Nixon tallied 301 electoral votes, easily exceeding the necessary 270, while Hubert Humphrey won 191 and George Wallace earned 46. The popular vote, though, was much closer. Nixon won 43.4% of the popular vote, while Humphrey earned 42.7%, a difference of only 812,415 votes. Wallace earned 13.9% of the popular vote (9,906,473 votes). Essentially, even in states won by Nixon, the vote was very close, but Wallace played a significant role in tipping the election in Nixon's favor by depriving Humphrey of Electoral Votes.

Additionally, two key factors cut against Humphrey – one unforgiveable and the other a motivating factor for change. Voter turnout in 1968 was historically low. How could voter turnout be low? How could apathy exist at such a critical time? Initially, young voters rallied around Eugene McCarthy, then Kennedy. While McCarthy carried the flame of optimism, young Democrats fell victim to omnipresent despair. The young Democrats were programmed to hate President Johnson more than the Republican Party. When President Johnson's surrogate, Humphrey, received the Democratic nomination instead of McCarthy, the young Democrats voiced their opposition by invoking silence, abstaining from the election – not voting. This mistake led to Nixon's election. Exacerbating the divide, McCarthy failed to endorse and campaign in favor of Humphrey. In Humphrey's memoir, he lamented, "had McCarthy campaigned early and hard for me and the Democratic Party, he might have turned it."

So, voter turnout was lower than expected, but what about all those college kids protesting in the streets? Did they also abstain? The college students demonstrated with vigor and protested with great volume – why did these folks not flock to the polls in support of their passion? The answer: many, or most, of the young people were not allowed to vote. Ironically, the loudest voice was silenced by the Constitution of the United States, the very document that provided the freedoms for which the young people fought.

The 1968 election was a massive defeat for the Democratic Party. Not only did the Presidency go to a Republican, but key races in the House of Representatives and the Senate were won by Republicans. The Democratic Party searched for a path forward. Refine the Party's message, policy and/or fundamental ideology? Not exactly. This is the United States and in the United States change manifests through the legal system. Accordingly, the Democratic Party pursued an Amendment to the Constitution of the United States, changing the voting age from 21 to 18. Rooted in political gain, the Democrats espoused a more neutral and sensible argument: if an 18 year old is eligible for the draft to serve in the United States military, then the 18 year old should have the right to vote.

In 1971, Congress approved the 26th Amendment to the Constitution, permitting persons age 18 or older the right to vote. However, nothing is so simple in our great American legal system. The Amendment provides that states may regulate the voting age for purposes of state elections. What does this mean? Practically, the voting age for Presidential, Senate and House of Representative elections is 18, but states may set the voting age for any election of state officials (governors, state senators, mayors, and municipal officers). While some states initially preserved a voting age of 21 for state elections, all states have since lowered the voting age to 18 (and some states allow 17 year olds to vote in primary elections if they will be 18 years of age at the time of the general election).

The 1968 election is not remembered for how close it was, rather the election is remembered for how far apart the country was, the ideological distance between Republicans and Democrats, whites and African Americans, the young and the older. The result was a nation divided. Experts consider the 1968 election to have "realigned" the political landscape, disrupting the "New Deal Coalition that had dominated presidential politics for 36 years" (www.270towin.com). From 1968 to 2008, other than a single term by Jimmy Carter and two terms by a moderate, Bill Clinton, Republicans controlled the White House. The South has voted Republican in almost every Presidential election since 1968.

On January 20, 1969, Richard M. Nixon assumed the Presidency and made the following remarks to the nation: "The greatest honor history can bestow is the title of peacemaker. This honor now beckons America – the chance to help lead the world at last out of the valley of turmoil, and onto that high ground of peace that man has dreamed of since the dawn of civilization." Nixon closed his address by stating, "we have endured a long night of the American spirit. But as our eyes catch the dimness of the first rays of dawn, let us not curse the remaining dark. Let us gather the light."

Unfortunately, Nixon did not honor his commitment to an "honorable withdrawal" from Vietnam, and he never undertook the title of "peacemaker." The Vietnam War continued for an astonishing six years after Nixon took office, with tens of thousands of American casualties and irreparable damage to the credibility and spirit of the United States.

Amid the darkest time in modern American politics, Nixon urged the American people to not "curse the remaining dark." Who knew the "remaining dark" would come to represent Nixon's own political turmoil, impeachment and resignation in 1974. Could the same fate plague Donald Trump? Will the parallel environment extend? Ultimately, the power of the citizens of the United States will emerge.

MUSIC

The music released in November 1968 is unimaginable – both reflective of the increasing tension existent in the global conscious and a thunderous release of tension in the form of musical wonder. The three albums featured in this chapter were created by European musicians: Van Morrison, The Kinks and The Beatles. Please let me know of another month in music history that rivals the following releases: *Astral Weeks* by Van Morrison, *The Kinds Are, Village Green Preservation Society* by the Kinks and *The White Album* by The Beatles. *Astral Weeks* and *The White Album* consistently rank in "All-Time Top Ten Lists" of critics. A thorough analysis of each record follows, but the critical task is for you to listen to each of these albums and contemplate that they were released in the same month, amid chaos and social disturbance. The musicians were unable to avoid the downward trajectory of political discourse, society and policy. The product, or the output from such a revolution, is unequivocally beautiful, dramatic and, at times, incredibly poignant and utterly masterful. Back to Harry Belafonte. "When the movement is strong, the music is strong."

Van Morrison – *Astral Weeks*

Astral Weeks was the second album released by Van Morrison. In 1967, after separating from his first band, Them, Morrison released *Blowin' Your Mind!* on Bang Records. *Blowin' Your Mind!* was unassuming and relatively plain – except for one track. In June 1967, Bang Records released "Brown Eyed Girl" as a Single and the track reached #10 on the *Billboard* Hot 100. Morrison was immediately a star, but unfortunately, *Blowin' Your Mind!* fell flat upon release in September 1967.

Affected by the experimentation and musical freedom of 1967, Morrison desired a more progressive musical path. His record label had a different perspective. Label owner, Bert Berns, demanded an album of material focused on Pop, possessing a catchy chorus and tale of teenage glory, echoing the template (and financial success) of "Brown Eyed Girl." Morrison refused and a stalemate ensued.

Suddenly, in early-1968, Berns died of a heart attack and his wife, Ilene Berns, not only blamed Morrison for her husband's death (due to the stress of the artistic disagreement), but more importantly (from a business perspective), Ilene inherited Bang Records and the contract between Bang Records and Van Morrison. The contract prohibited Morrison from recording and releasing on other labels, essentially sidelining Morrison.

The contract did permit Morrison – then living in New York after a move to the United States from Belfast, Ireland – to perform on stage and retain any monies from the performance. However, Bang Records was influential and most clubs and halls would not book Morrison, aligning themselves with the label, rather than the artist. Still distraught and convinced Morrison's behavior led to her husband's death, Ilene contacted the Immigration and Naturalization Service of the United States and attempted to have Morrison deported to Ireland. With no citizenship and no green card, Morrison decided to marry his then girlfriend, Janet (Planet) Rigsbee Minto. Van and Janet moved to Cambridge, Massachusetts, fleeing to a city where

Van could perform, even though he was still unable to record and release records. Depressed and broke, Morrison played solo acoustic shows in and around Boston, sometimes persuading an upright acoustic bassist to accompany.

Now, while Van Morrison playing acoustic guitar in a singer-songwriter setting may today seem natural, it is important to note that prior to 1968, Van Morrison's music was electric Rock and Pop, hardly acoustic. From 1965 to 1967, as lead singer and guitarist for Them, Van focused on Garage Rock and a loud, distorted heavy guitar-fueled sound (Them's hit Single was "Gloria"). Van's turn to acoustic music was not so much an artistic choice, but rather – a function of Van being broke, depressed and unable to record.

One evening in April 1968, Lewis Merenstein, a producer and executive at Warner Bros. went to see Van perform in Boston. Admittedly, Merenstein expected to see the Van Morrison that authored "Brown Eyed Girl." He wasn't alone. Reportedly, eight or nine label executives just like Merenstein had made the trek to Boston to see and hopefully sign the author of "Brown Eyed Girl." After witnessing an acoustic set by Morrison that included unstructured songs, free verse lyrics and at times, rambling and avant-garde themes, each executive departed, not understanding what they had witnessed and each wondering, "What happened to Van Morrison?" Merenstein, though, had a dramatically different reaction.

As Van played an early version of "Astral Weeks", Merenstein recalled, "I started crying. It just vibrated in my soul, and I knew that I wanted to work with that sound." Merenstein returned to Warner Bros. and insisted that the label somehow negotiate with Bang Records to release Morrison from his contract. Warner Bros. cut a deal with Bang Records, but the deal had certain conditions. First, Van had to write, record and submit three songs per month to Bang Records (for one year). Bang would own the compositions and could release the songs as they deemed appropriate. Second, Bang Records would own and was entitled to half of any proceeds from any track written or recorded by Morrison that was released by Warner Bros. as a Single, between September 12, 1968 and September 12, 1969.

Morrison was ecstatic and proceeded to immediately record 36 original compositions in one studio session, fulfilling the first condition of the settlement. The material has never been released and the content of the songs has been described as "nonsense" and a farce. Similarly, given the new, experimental acoustic direction undertaken by Morrison, Warner Bros. never actually released a Single from *Astral Weeks* (maybe no track warranted release as a Single, but maybe Warner Bros. and Morrison just didn't want to split any proceeds with Bang Records).

Van Morrison entered Century Sound Studios in New York on September 25, 1968. Van had some lyrics and a few melodies, but was still searching for a sound – a certain aesthetic that incorporated elements of Jazz, Folk and Classical. Searching for a sound in the studio can be expensive, but it also can be especially difficult on the session musicians hired to execute the lead artist's compositions. Ordinarily, session players were provided with charts and possibly even a demo. Morrison did not provide charts or a demo to the session musicians, mainly because he didn't have demos – he didn't even have songs crafted. Van urged the musicians to just follow him and "play whatever you feel."

Maybe Jazz musicians could tolerate such a directive, and maybe Jazz musicians would even welcome the freedom, but the Rock musicians working with Morrison were immediately frustrated. One by one, each musician quit, unable to deal with the lack of direction. Merenstein, though, demonstrated patience, intent on assisting Morrison achieve his vision. After countless discussions with Morrison, Merenstein figured out exactly which musicians to surround Morrison with – of course, Jazz musicians.

Merenstein enlisted Richard Davis to lead the session. Davis was a bassist that worked with several of the greatest improvisational Jazz musicians, including Eric Dolphy. Davis recruited Jay Berliner, an acoustic guitarist that had worked extensively with Charles Mingus (perhaps the greatest improvisational Jazz musician of the generation) and Connie Kay, drummer for the legendary Modern Jazz Quartet.

Still lacking complete song structures, Morrison was suddenly surrounded by musicians that excelled at improvisation and tolerated experimentation and innovation in the studio. Not surprisingly, the songs began to take shape quickly, with Van providing a melody and exquisite vocals, while – according to Connie Kay – Kay, Davis and Berliner "more or less sat there and jammed." Berliner similarly recalled that Van would play the song on acoustic guitar and ask that the musicians played over his guitar track in any manner they felt appropriate.

The product sounds wonderfully seamless and consistent. Berliner stated that he played "a lot of Classical guitar, [which was] very unusual...in that context." Lacking the typical Rock structure and timing, Davis essentially soloed on bass throughout the session, not tied to root notes and chord changes. Kay was at home on drums, as he employed several Jazz techniques – often playing with brushes as opposed to sticks, avoiding cymbal crashes and ultimately – allowing melody to prevail (as opposed to rhythm).

The musical context, or instrumentation, of *Astral Weeks* is critical, but brilliance also lies in Morrison's stream of consciousness lyrics. On the title track, "Astral Weeks" opens with the following lines:

> *If I venture into the slipstream*
> *Between the viaducts of your dream*
> *Where immobile steel rims crack*
> *And the ditch in the back roads stop*
> *Could you find me?*

I have sung those lyrics out loud for 20 years while listening to *Astral Weeks* – and I never considered the meaning of the verse (and I generally consider the meaning of almost everything). The unusual words and phrases echo Dylan, but Van's words are more physical –

still abstract, but the actual words used are more concrete, or hard (*i.e.*, viaducts, steel rims crack, ditch). As "Astral Weeks" unfolds, the instruments surrounding Morrison coalesce around his vocals, building not to a climax, but rather to a place – like a plateau – not quite the top of the mountain, instead to a flat meadow – breezy, green, open and expansive – free of edges – just even and long, a clean white canvas – allowing Morrison to lead with his voice.

Each song on *Astral Weeks* arrives at such a place, with most songs just starting and staying in that place. Accordingly, many argue that *Astral Weeks* is a concept album, but I disagree. Sure, *Astral Weeks* is held together by a consistent musical theme – same instruments, same context – and each song is similarly constructed, or really – not constructed. When the musical context is the theme of an album, I'd rather not deem the album a concept – rather, I would refer to *Astral Weeks* as a song cycle.

Song cycles were popular in Jazz (an early example is *A Love Supreme* by John Coltrane in 1965). Song cycles, though, were originally utilized in Classical music. The definition used in the Classical context is a group of individually composed songs that belong together, designed to be performed in a sequence and as one piece (Webster). The unifying element of the song cycle can be thematic (meaning a story) or musical, involving similar chord structures, tones or aesthetic. In the case of *Astral Weeks*, Morrison relies on the latter, the consistent musical aesthetic.

The beauty of *Astral Weeks* is the function of the record as a portal. The songs emerge in slow, unfolding concentric circles that facilitate and encourage the listener to drift. The listening experience is meditative. Each song has an initial premise, but Morrison is not telling stories – he is reciting poetry. Morrison drifts, and soon enough, the listener drifts. Thoughts flow – sometimes about the song, usually not. The music enables creative mental exploration. Each song is a portal to abstract thought. A portal for Morrison and a portal for the listener.

Morrison has never corroborated such a theory, or acknowledged a similar experience, but Morrison has repeatedly insisted that the songs on *Astral Weeks* have no distinct purpose or substance – each song a patchwork of poetic phrases. Morrison acknowledged focusing on sound instead of substance. In 2008, Van stated, "*Astral Weeks* songs…were from another sort of place – not what is at all obvious. They are poetry and mythical musings, channeled from my imagination…[They] are little poetic stories I made up and set to music. The album is about song craft for me – making things up and making them fit to a tune I have arranged."

It is critically important to not search *Astral Weeks* for substance, but rather to search for substance within, or while listening to, *Astral Weeks*. The lyrics provide context, transporting you to a figurative place, but then the remainder of the experience is up to you, the listener. For example, the third track, "Sweet Thing", references a love interest, but a love story is not told. Instead, Van describes the scene, through abstract phrases and vague references.

Commenting on "Sweet Thing", Paul Du Noyer stated, "Sweet Thing" puts the singer "in a hazy, pastoral paradise where he wanders in 'gardens wet with rain', or counts the stars in his lover's eyes, and vows to 'never grow so old again' or 'read between the lines'. He pleads with his mind to keep quiet, so his heart can hear itself think. He yearns to obliterate experience and rediscover innocence." I love Du Noyer's line, "He pleads with his mind to keep quiet, so his heart can think", but I can't help but think that Du Noyer fell directly into Van's spell. Du Noyer was encouraged to drift away from "Sweet Thing", immersed in vision and scenery, propelled by the song's aural graces and compelled to conjure his own vision.

Despite an unusual consistency, the song cycle of *Astral Weeks* has two loosely connected anchors: "Cyprus Avenue" and "Madame George." In "Cyprus Avenue", Morrison utilized the notion of a person driving in a car down Cyprus Avenue, a popular street in Belfast, Ireland. Morrison sings, "I'm caught one more time/Up on Cyprus Avenue/And I'm conquered in a car seat/Not a thing I can do." After establishing the fundamental place or scene for the song, Morrison escapes.

Borrowing from impressionism, Morrison paints through phrases and rhymes. Akin to Monet's use of pointillism (a painting technique using small distinct dots of color in connected groupings), Morrison spins a web of images – using basic words in complex juxtaposition. After the lines above, Morrison continues:

> *I may go crazy*
> *Before that mansion on the hill*
> *I may go crazy*
> *Before that mansion on the hill*
> *But my heart keeps beating faster*
> *And my feet can't keep still*
> *And all the little girls rhyme something*
> *On the way back home from school*
> *And all the little girls rhyme something*
> *On the way back home from school*
> *And the leaves fall one by one by one by one*
> *Call the autumn time a fool*
> *Yeah baby my tongue gets tied*
> *Every every every time I try to speak*
> *My tongue gets tied*
> *Every time I try to speak*
> *And my inside shakes just like a leaf on a tree*
> *I think I'll go on by the river with my cherry cherry wine*
> *I believe I'll go walking by the railroad with my cherry cherry wine*
> *If I pass the rumbling station where the lonesome engine drivers pine*
> *And wait a minute, yonder comes my lady*
> *Rainbow ribbons in her hair*
> *Yonder comes my lady*
> *Rainbow ribbons in her hair*
> *Six white horses and a carriage*
> *She's returning from the fair*

Baby, baby, baby
And if I'm caught one more time
Up on Cyprus Avenue
And if I'm caught one more time
Up on Cyprus Avenue
And I'm conquered in a car seat
And I'm looking straight at you
Way up on, way up on, way up on....
The avenue of trees
Keep walking down
In the wind and the rain, darling
You keep walking down when the sun shone through the trees
Nobody, no, no, no, nobody stops me from loving you baby
So young and bold, fourteen years old
Baby, baby, baby...

No verse, no chorus. No bridge. The track also has no instrumental passage. For seven minutes, the expert Jazz session musicians, along with the addition of violin and flute, craft a space for Van to express and deliver a legendary vocal performance. "Cyprus Avenue" is absolutely part of the song cycle, but rises above the song cycle. Similar in palette, but superior in sheer beauty and tenderness.

After "Cyprus Avenue" and before "Madame George", Morrison increases the tempo just slightly on "The Way Young Lovers Do", which also includes a horn section. "The Way Young Lovers Do" provides physical separation between "Cyprus Avenue" and "Madame George", but the distance is erased after the first line of "Madame George", as Morrison immediately connects the two anchors with the line: "Down on Cyprus Avenue/With a childlike vision leaping into view."

In *Rolling Stone*, Lester Bangs wrote, "Madame George" is as "heartbreaking a reverie as you will find." Bangs interpreted "Madame George" as a "cryptic character study that may or may not be about an aging transvestite." Morrison denies that "Madame George" is about a transvestite. Who to believe? I'm inclined to believe Van, but lines like "clicking, clacking of the high heeled shoe…He's much older with hat on drinking wine/And that smell of sweet perfume comes drifting through…In the corner playing dominos in drag/The one and only Madame George…And as you're about to leave/She jumps up and says, 'Hey love, you forgot your gloves.'"

Morrison also uses the pronouns "he" and "she" interchangeably. Certainly, confusing – but, Morrison already told us – these are just lines of poetry and rambling imagery set to a consistent musical theme. Interestingly, the song's title was originally "Madame Joy." Morrison changed the title to "Madame George", but still sings the word "Joy" throughout the track, instead of "George." Possibly, Morrison changed the title after the song unfolded in a more somber tone? Either way, for almost 10 minutes, "Madame George" flows beautifully and passionately, ambling to a peaceful close – with Morrison's voice functioning as the lead instrument throughout.

Critic reviews of *Astral Weeks* were initially mixed. *Beat Instrumental* called the record "monotonous and unoriginal" and *NME* described the songs as "indistinguishable" and "stuck in the same groove throughout." *Stereo Review* deemed Morrison's vocals as "incoherent" and the lyrics as "nonsensical." *Rolling Stone*, in a review written by Greil Marcus, labeled the lyrics as "thoughtful and deeply intellectual", citing an affinity for "myths and metaphors." Later in 1968, *Rolling Stone* named *Astral Weeks* the "Album of the Year", describing it as "unique and timeless." There may not be two better words to describe *Astral Weeks*: unique and timeless. *Melody Maker* also named *Astral Weeks* one of the best records of 1968.

Given the mixed reviews and the lack of a Single, *Astral Weeks* was not commercially successful. Warner Bros. deemed *Astral Weeks* a "critically acclaimed but obscure album." How then did *Astral Weeks* become a masterpiece? The answer is highly subjective, largely personal and credit must reside in the timelessness of the music, the beauty of Morrison's voice. Paraphrasing Ritchie Yorke, "other

330

albums were reminiscent of *Astral Weeks*, but *Astral Weeks* was not reminiscent of any other albums."

My view is that people were not ready for *Astral Weeks* in 1968. Not that *Astral Weeks* was too progressive. Quite the opposite, actually. The climate of 1968 welcomed raging Hard Rock and favored lyrics that referenced violence, drugs and tragedy. *Astral Weeks* is the polar opposite in every regard. It is hardly surprising that critics and listeners didn't embrace the quiet and passive texture of *Astral Weeks*. Can you imagine seeing images of bombs and death in Vietnam and deadly protests in the streets of American cities – then just sitting back in a chair to listen to *Astral Weeks*? As the flame of 1968 gave way to the ashes of 1969 and the (relative) stability of future decades, *Astral Weeks* emerged.

Interestingly, in 1968 the historian Andrew Ford analogized the commercial performance of *Astral Weeks* to Classical music, the genre that *Astral Weeks* most closely references, "neither instant nor evanescent, *Astral Weeks* will sell as many copies this year as it did in 1968 and has every year in between." Steven Van Zandt (lead guitarist for Bruce Springsteen's E Street Band) offered, "*Astral Weeks* was like a religion to us." Reportedly, Martin Scorsese has said that the first fifteen minutes of *Taxi Driver* were based on *Astral Weeks*.

Of course, Lester Bangs perhaps best summarized *Astral Weeks* as "a record about people stunned by life, completely overwhelmed, stalled in their skins, their ages and selves, paralyzed by the enormity of what in one moment of vision they can comprehend." If Bangs is correct, it is hardly a surprise that *Astral Weeks* still resonates with people today, as we remain completely overwhelmed, stalled and in many respects, paralyzed by life and the time in which we live. The sound of hope, shrouded in darkness.

The Kinks – *The Kinks Are the Village Green Preservation Society*

Coincidentally, like *Astral Weeks*, *The Kinks Are the Village Green Preservation Society* was not a commercial success in 1968, yet today is widely considered a masterpiece. You might have thought that the hard-charging, guitar Rock of the Kinks would have aligned perfectly with the emotional disposition of 1968. Previous hits such as "You Really Got Me" and "All Day and All of the Night" seem very much at home in 1968. Why then did the public reject *Village Green*?

Two reasons: (1) competition and (2) the misalignment of sound and history. First, the competition that existed in late-1968 was legendary. *Village Green* was released immediately after Hendrix's *Electric Ladyland*, simultaneously with *The White Album* by The Beatles and just weeks before *Beggar's Banquet* by The Rolling Stones. Throw in *Music From Big Pink* and popular albums from The Doors, Pink Floyd and Cream. Tough company.

Second, though – and perhaps more relevant, The Kinks departed from Hard Rock at the height of the genre's popularity, opting for a unique Folk-Pop style that was both ahead of its time, and behind the times. Summarized by *Pitchfork*, "During the Summer of 1968, stateside fans were hooked on a high-intensity diet that had them jonesing for aggressive, overstated fare like "Street Fighting Man" (a track by The Rolling Stones)." *Pitchfork* further described the music of 1968 as "an armored vehicle ready for battle", concluding that "the disconnect between The Kinks and the Rock world's rapidly narrowing palette could hardly have been more pronounced." As the mainstream embraced the very Hard Rock style advocated by The Kinks prior to 1968, The Kinks drifted. Maintaining a devotion to anti-establishment rhetoric, The Kinks conveyed substance through less volume and abstract intellect, rather than poignant and direct commentary. Critics loved it, the masses didn't get it.

Lyricists can be overt, often telling a story within the confines of the song – but, some lyricists hide the core meaning of the song, opting to dress the substance in distraction and diversion. *Village Green* begins with "The Village Green Preservation Society" and the following lyrics "We are the Village Green Preservation Society/God save Donald Duck, Vaudeville and Variety/We are the Desperate Dan Appreciation Society/God save strawberry jam and all the different varieties." What?

To further the disguise, *Village Green* possesses a whimsical, odd and often funny musical template, shifting between Pop, Folk and Rock. *Village Green* is light, colorful and bright. In 1968, listeners gravitated away from this motif and towards a darker, more sinister and aggressive sound. On the surface, *Village Green* sounds more like 1967 than 1968. *Village Green* likely seemed stale in late-1968. Over time, the rage of 1968 dissipated and as *Pitchfork* noted, "the weather changed" and *Village Green* is now "touted as a masterpiece."

Truth is, *Village Green* does contain timely social commentary, along with subtle observations, metaphors and irony regarding the liberalization of English culture. In 1968, listeners rewarded immediacy and volume as their companion to turbulence. *Village Green* is not immediate. *Village Green* is a series of upbeat vignettes about idyllic life in the English countryside. The setting, however, is the mask – the diversion. According to *Consequence of Sound*, *Village Green* is "poking fun at the bourgeois obsession with respectability and uniformity" while presenting a "sedate alternative to the tumultuous urban landscape" in 1968.

War had not gripped the UK as it did the United States. Furthermore, racism was far less pronounced in the UK. Liberalism, though, along with experimentation, drugs and a demonstrative anti-establishment sentiment – dramatically affected culture in the UK. *Village Green* illuminated the idiocy and apathy of the conservative English lifestyle by exposing a mentality of normalcy and tradition in the face of uprising and change. Deep and requiring material analysis, but brilliant.

Ray Davies, lead singer and songwriter of The Kinks, is considered, mostly by critics, to be one of the great songwriters. Davies writes lyrics that require contemplation. Not necessarily the words he uses, as the words are simple, but the intent is complex. Like Frank Zappa, Davies employs sarcasm and wit – tactics sometimes difficult to discern in the context of a song, especially when the music is not consistent with the theme of the substance. In a review of *Village Green* for *Rolling Stone* in 1968, renowned critic Paul Williams stated, "I can't sit here and come up with phrases to argue genius, I can only shout, as modestly as possible, about how deeply I'm affected." Williams closed his review with, "I've never had much luck turning people on to The Kinks, I can only hope you're onto them already. If you are, brother, I love you. We've got to stick together."

Despite an appetite for diversion, Davies foreshadows the intent of *Village Green* on the opening track. At the close of "Village Green", after several lines of comical distraction, Davies accentuates the phrase, "Preserving the old ways from being abused/Protecting the new ways, for me and for you." Those lines are the essence of *Village Green*. Throughout the album, Davies uses the physical setting of the English countryside (the village green) to illuminate the need for social progress. Davies criticizes and indicts the prevailing wisdom, but rather than attack, Davies attempts to bridge tradition with change.

Several characters emanate from *Village Green*, but the characters are simply mechanisms for Davies to illustrate aspects of the lifestyle he indicts. On "Johnny Thunder", Davies romanticized the role of Johnny Thunder, an outsider that forged a different path, rather than conform to given ideals. "Unable to relate to his fellow townsfolk...Johnny cruises the highway in search of deeper meaning" (*Consequence of Sound*). With a refrain of "thunder" and "lightning", Johnny represents youth and freedom. Johnny left town, pursuing his vision, rather than the vision of his community. The track closes with "carefree harmonies" and "we know that he's made the right call" (consequence of sound).

On "Last of the Steam-Powered Train", Davies assumes the role of a steam-powered train. Yes, the song is sung from the perspective of the steam-powered train, in the first person. The metaphor is bright, as Davies is driving home the notion that "times have changed." To enhance the traditionalism metaphor, "The Last of the Steam-Powered Train" is arranged in a classic 12-bar Blues structure – with the lead guitar riff completely ripped off from "Smokestack Lightning."

Davies describes himself (the train) as "the last of the blood and sweat brigade...the last of the good old renegades." Davies then says, "I don't know where I'm going, or why I came", and that all of his friends are "middle class and grey." Davies drives home the overall theme of *Village Green* by stating, "all this peaceful living is drivin' me insane."

The next track, "Big Sky", has Davies singing not from the perspective of a train, but rather from the perspective of the sky. The theme is less about traditionalism and change and more about despair – not necessarily escapism, but rather an illustration of loss of hope. Davies is empathetic, but powerless.

> *Big Sky looked down on all the people*
> *Who think they got problems*
> *They get depressed and they hold their head*
> *In their hands and cry*
> *People lift up their hands*
> *And they look up to the Big Sky*
> *But Big Sky is too big to sympathize*

The premise is that the (big) sky is so large (perhaps, a metaphor for government or the institution of conservatism) and the problems existing in society, albeit tragic, are just part of a larger devastation. The big sky cares, but prioritizes self-interest.

> *Big Sky's too occupied*
> *Though he would like to try*

335

And he feels bad inside
Big Sky's too big to cry

The chorus of the track is redeeming, and hopeful, but hardly suggests
a resolution. Davies finds comfort in the ignorance of the big sky –
fashioning people as small kernels in an enormous universe (and such
problems are equally small).

One day we'll be free, we won't care
Just you wait and see
'Til that day can be
Don't let it get you down.
When I feel that the world
Is too much for me
I think of the Big Sky
And nothing matters much to me.

The first Single released from *Village Green* was "Starstruck",
another major chord, bright, upbeat – predominantly Pop track,
focused on a young protagonist, presumably experiencing success.
Yet, Davies cautions that difficult times lie ahead. Davies writes,
"You're a victim of bright city lights/And your mind is not right/You
think the world's at your feet."

"Starstruck" was not successful as a Single, only charting in the
Netherlands. The instrumentation may have conveyed success as a
Single, but the content was antithetical to the mindset of young
listeners in 1968. While many of the songs on *Village Green* attacked
the mainstream, older generation, "Starstruck" is an assault on the
irresponsible tendencies of young people.

Baby, you're running around like you're crazy
You go to a party and dance through the night,
And you'll drink 'till you're tight,
And then you're out on your feet

'Cause you're starstruck, baby, starstruck.
Taken in by the lights,
Think you'll never look back,
You know you're starstruck on me

Baby, watch out or else you'll be ruined,
'Cause once you're addicted to wine and champagne,
It's gonna drive you insane,
Because the world's not so tame

The theme of "Starstruck" is similar to the views or narrative of Frank Zappa that we heard on *We're Only in it For the Money*. Critical of the younger generation, identifying a narrative that remains today – concerning "millennials."

On "Wicked Annabella", Davies returns to the core concept of describing the various characters of a typical English countryside village. Annabella represents the dark and sinister aspect of every community. Several critics insist that Davies turns the narrative, concluding that Annabella is in fact not evil, instead – a misunderstood character, plagued by rumor and stereotype. Not sure there is enough in the lyrics to definitively arrive at such a conclusion, though. Either way, "Wicked Annabella" presents a musical excursion. Davies stated, "I just wanted to get one to sound as horrible as it could. I wanted a rude sound." Also, the song is sung by lead guitarist, Dave Davies, rather than Ray, as Dave's voice provided a haunting, ominous hushed tone.

Village Green is not a perfect concept album. The Kinks never entirely commit to the concept. Rather, Davies used the concept as a backdrop, or a premise, on which to innovate and express. The characters in *Village Green* are fleeting and underdeveloped, likely by design. The music of *Village Green* prevails – the songs are tremendous, not as part of the overall narrative, but as individual vignettes. Davies threads the theme magnificently and The Kinks developed an instrumentation that supported a vision.

337

The format of *Village Green* as a *loose* concept album informed and influenced many artists subsequent to 1968. David Bowie cites *Village Green* as the template for *Ziggy Stardust* and Pink Floyd adopted the format for several records, including *Animals* and *The Wall*. The Kinks continued the *loose* concept album on *Lola Versus Powerman and the Moneygoround Part One*, a record about...well, about a lot of things. The format affords the songwriter a context to both reference and drift.

Patience was thin in 1968 and *Village Green* failed to resonate, but today it is impossible to deny the beauty and importance of *Village Green*. As I pleaded with readers in <u>The 1965 Project</u>, please don't overlook The Kinks. The songwriting is exceptional. The instrumentation and arrangements are perfectly executed. The Kinks never capitalized on a trend, they crafted the trends.

The Beatles (*The White Album*)

Perhaps the most illustrative example of change in 1968 was *visual* rather than *aural*. The Beatles brought color and vibrancy to 1967 with the release of *Sgt. Pepper's Lonely Hearts Club Band*. The record cover exploded with red, yellow, blue, green, orange – more vivid and bright than any predecessor.

Labeling the cover of *The White Album* a *change* would be a drastic understatement. *The White Album*, originally titled *The Beatles*, is nothing but a white cover, with "The Beatles" set forth in a standard black font, positioned unassumingly small on the middle right side of the record cover. The contrast is incredible. The polar opposite. What caused such a massive digression?

Between 1963 and 1970, The Beatles were the pulse of music, and to a greater extent, culture. The Beatles, however, were never the engine of change. Instead, The Beatles functioned as the proliferator of change, meaning – The Beatles embraced already changing elements of the underground and brought the changes to the surface. The Beatles were influential, no doubt, but The Beatles were also

338

highly influenced. Ultimately, the genius of The Beatles was the manner in which the band selected percolating themes, concepts and trends and incorporated the themes, concepts and trends into an accessible musical palette that was fanatically embraced by consumers, overwhelmingly endorsed by critics and constantly replicated by other musicians.

For example, The Beatles began to introduce meaning into their songs in late-1965 on *Rubber Soul*. Shortly thereafter, in 1966, musicians such as The Rolling Stones, The Kinks and The Who incorporated political and cultural content. But, of course – The Beatles were not the first to intertwine content and Pop music. That award, for the most part, goes to Bob Dylan, after he "went electric" at the Newport Folk Festival on July 25, 1965, infusing Rock and Pop with the words of a poet. The Beatles were enamored with Dylan and immediately embarked on a path of introspection, crafting songs from a subjective posture and incorporating the message within Pop. Dylan incited the change, The Beatles commercialized the change.

Just twelve months later, The Beatles introduced the mainstream to Psychedelic Rock with the release of *Revolver*, and particularly, the classic track "Tomorrow Never Knows." The Beatles, however, didn't invent Psychedelic Rock – that award belongs to The Grateful Dead, Jefferson Airplane and Quicksilver Messenger Service (among others). On May 26, 1967, The Beatles went a step further, releasing *Sgt. Pepper's Lonely Hearts Club Band*, the preeminent relic of Psychedelic Rock. The San Francisco bands created Psychedelic Rock and incited the movement. The Beatles commercialized the movement. The Beatles branded the movement. The Beatles became the movement.

The Beatles, though, did not just peddle costumes, colors and creativity, capitalizing on the ingenuity of other musicians – The Beatles were masterful musicians, songwriters and arrangers. The songs on *Sgt. Pepper's* are dynamic, replete with passion and a certain brilliance that combined psychedelic concepts with song structures that allowed for creativity, yet maintained normalcy. *Sgt.*

Pepper's is deserving of every accolade. The Beatles achieved a balance on *Sgt. Pepper's* – a balance of taste and trend, expertise and enthusiasm. The balance is a fine line, though.

After the glory (and success) of *Sgt. Pepper's*, The Beatles released *Magical Mystery Tour* in December 1967. A few of the songs are memorable – "Penny Lane" and "Strawberry Fields Forever" – but, *Magical Mystery Tour* exemplifies imbalance. The record lacks the intensity of *Sgt. Pepper's*, unfortunately allowing the nonsensical, comedic elements to dominate.

Magical Mystery Tour was not well received by critics and although it sold okay, the record is largely considered to be the least successful Beatles album. Whether the authenticity of *Music From Big Pink* or the passion exuded by Jimi Hendrix or the grunge of Cream or the fiery Blues of Janis Joplin – The Beatles, for a brief moment in late-1967, were dated. Little tolerance existed for silly costumes and songs about tangerine trees, marmalade skies and the sentiment of "getting better all the time" – let alone John Lennon singing "I Am the Walrus" and any song titled "Baby You're a Rich Man."

What did The Beatles do after their first dose of criticism? Naturally, they went to India. The trip was precipitated by two extreme forces – (1) tension and (2) George Harrison. Tension had long existed within The Beatles, but in 1967 the desires of each band member eclipsed the desire of the entity. Lennon was distracted, torn by a failing marriage to Cynthia. Paul was constantly writing, yet filtering his own passion. Harrison's songwriting talent was exploding and he wanted more of his tracks released on Beatles records. The Beatles had no center. No leader. This was the beauty of The Beatles, but eventually – the demise of The Beatles. Tension ruined The Beatles, but before the ruin, tension provided us with three amazing records, beginning with *The White Album*.

The second force? Yes, George Harrison. George Harrison had long been influenced by the power of transcendental meditation and Eastern philosophy, but the psychedelic culture of 1967, and his repeated use of LSD in 1966 and 1967, precipitated a passion and relentless pursuit. In an attempt to heal the wounds of tension and perhaps facilitate a bonding experience, George persuaded John, Paul and Ringo to accompany him on a trip to India. George arranged for his mates to stay in a village and study with the Maharishi Mahesh Yogi, creator and leader of the transcendental meditation movement. The Beatles were also accompanied by an entourage that included Mia Farrow and her sister, Prudence, Mike Love from The Beach Boys and Donovan (the acclaimed Folk singer).

George's idea, or experiment, kind of worked. John was an easy sell. Spiritual by nature, he and George embarked on a spiritual mission that stayed with John for the remainder of his life. Ringo committed as well. Paul, however, wasn't so inclined. Paul spent most of his time in India writing songs and playing guitar. The first song he wrote in India was "Back in the U.S.S.R." Interesting, the chorus came first.

Mike Love, an integral member of The Beach Boys, traveled to India in search of spirituality (and reportedly, "a good time"). Maybe he found both, but in Paul – he found a guy that was along for the ride and simply wanted to make music. Paul wrote the chorus of "Back in the U.S.S.R." as a parody of a Beach Boys song (any Beach Boys song – or, all Beach Boys songs), both in melody and lyrics.

> *Well the Ukraine girls really knock me out*
> *They leave the West behind*
> *And Moscow girls make me sing and shout*
> *That Georgia's always on my mind*

Driving a stake through the heart of "California Girls", Paul both parodied the sophomoric embodiment of The Beach Boys and tacitly criticized the insanity dividing Democracy and Communism. Far from home, Paul framed "Back in the U.S.S.R." around the narrative of "Back in the U.S.A.", a popular track written by Chuck Berry. The track, today, seems like a "skip", but the intention of "Back in the

U.S.S.R." is smart, comedic and interesting. "Back in the U.S.S.R." was hardly political substance – yet, controversy resulted.

The Beatles were accused by the John Birch Society of being sympathetic to the Soviet Union due to the line: "I'm back in the U.S.S.R./You don't know how lucky you are boy/Back in the U.S.S.R." Lucky to be back in the Soviet Union? Not really a popular sentiment in 1968. But, The Beatles were not supporters of Communism.

In fact, The Beatles were also condemned by the Soviet Union. The line "Moscow girls make me sing and shout" – yeah, that didn't go over well in Russia. The Soviets hold grudges, too. In 1982, Paul McCartney was planning a solo tour and sought to play the Soviet Union, in an effort to ease tensions and facilitate political discourse. The Soviet Union denied McCartney entry to Moscow – with pundits citing bad blood related to "Back in the U.S.S.R."

The song is memorable, but not musically relevant to the aesthetic of *The White Album*. Fortunately, "Back in the U.S.S.R." segues into a track that defines *The White Album* – "Dear Prudence."

Mia Farrow was an actress and fashion model, having starred in *Rosemary's Baby*, a 1968 film by Roman Polanski. Mia would also appear in *The Great Gatsby* – and was briefly married to Frank Sinatra. But, in 1968, she was hanging with The Beatles in India. Her sister, Prudence, accompanied Mia and The Beatles on the search for enlightenment. Prudence was immediately engulfed by the practice of transcendental meditation. Prudence meditated for hours and when not meditating, Prudence remained in her tent, rarely commiserating with others – completely secluded and detached. The Maharishi was concerned and tasked John and George with talking to Prudence, encouraging her to remain connected to her community. Impressed with Prudence's commitment (and beauty), John wrote "Dear Prudence":

Dear Prudence, won't you come out to play
Dear Prudence, greet the brand new day
The sun is up, the sky is blue
It's beautiful and so are you
Dear Prudence won't you come out and play

Dear Prudence open up your eyes
Dear Prudence see the sunny skies
The wind is low the birds will sing
That you are part of everything
Dear Prudence won't you open up your eyes?

John crafted the melody when the band returned to London. Oh, right – yes, The Beatles returned to London. Turns out, The Beatles soured on the teachings of the Maharishi. George remained marginally committed to Eastern philosophy, but the rest of the band chose skepticism and returned to the materialistic culture of the West. While the trip to India satisfied George's quest for enlightenment, the primary motivation of the trip had not been accomplished – as tension continued to manifest within The Beatles. The byproduct, though – music – was accomplished.

The White Album essentially is three solo albums. Each musician (minus Ringo) brought original songs to the studio (most of which were written in India) and the other band members functioned as session musicians. The dynamic was supposedly intolerable. On the first take of "Back in the U.S.S.R.", Paul criticized Ringo's drum part and Ringo reacted by quitting the band. Walked right out of the session. Yes, Ringo quit The Beatles in 1968. The climate was so poor that nobody chased after him. Paul simply jumped on the drum kit and recorded the drum part himself. John ended up recording the drum part on "Dear Prudence", with assistance from George.

While worthy, a description of each track is not the purpose of this book. So, we're going to skip around a bit, but focus on the tracks that accentuate the shift and evolution of The Beatles. Perhaps the official announcement that The Beatles had left behind the psychedelic excess of 1967 and returned to Rock was the seventh track on *The White Album*, "While My Guitar Gently Weeps."

George Harrison wrote the first verse of "While My Guitar Gently Weeps" while in India, but given the focus on his studies, the track languished. Upon return to London, Harrison immediately completed the song. George's songwriting and composing skills matured a few years later than John and Paul, but in 1968, George embarked on a 24 month period as the premiere songwriter in The Beatles. Yes, that is opinion, but the following supports the notion: "While My Guitar Gently Weeps", "Here Comes the Sun" and "Something" – not to mention George's solo material just after The Beatles disbanded, "All Things Must Pass" and "My Sweet Lord."

The lyrics are abstract, yet clearly stated. Alluring and attractive. Listeners could sing along and extract meaning. According to George, the song is based on the Chinese concept that "everything is relative to everything else...whatever happens is all meant to be, and that there's no such thing as coincidence." Spiritual and quite meaningful politically and socially, but unfortunately for George – the song he crafted, the power of the music – the vocal performance by George, the piano by Paul and that guitar solo – the music (fortunately) obscured the substantive vision.

"While My Guitar Gently Weeps" went through many iterations, over the course of five separate recording sessions (July 25, August 16, September 3, September 5 and September 6). John and Paul were consistently arriving with fully constructed songs, but George's material required collaboration – and George was not receiving the type of effort – and support he needed from Paul and John. This lack of effort led to George doing something no Beatle had done previously – bring in a guest musician to play on a Beatles track. Other than the band's producer, George Martin, few (if any) musicians appeared on Beatles records prior to *The White Album*.

Early recordings of "While My Guitar Gentry Weeps" featured Harrison on acoustic guitar, which still remains in the mix for the

344

intro, and Paul on a Fender Jazz bass instead of his usual Rickenbacker. Ringo was back on drums at this point. Normally, John would have been on piano, but he insisted on playing electric guitar. Unfortunately, the instrumentation just wasn't working. George set the song aside for almost three weeks.

George resurfaced "While My Guitar Gently Weeps" during the September 5 session. Paul nailed the bassline and then jumped on the piano, crafting notes for the intro and accents throughout. Paul and John started to harmonize behind George's voice (on both the verses and chorus). After the session, George felt that the song was close, but felt the arrangement still lacked abrasiveness. That night, George asked his closest friend, Eric Clapton, to come to the studio and play lead guitar on "While My Guitar Gently Weeps." Clapton politely declined, citing accurately the notion that "nobody else plays on a Beatles record."

George pleaded and Clapton finally agreed to visit the studio the following day. Upon his arrival, John and Paul were reportedly a bit unclear as to why Clapton was in the studio, but George simply stated something like, "I'd like Eric to play some lead guitar." The band acquiesced. Paul switched back to bass, John stayed on rhythm guitar (very low in the mix), George played electric rhythm guitar, Ringo on drums – and Eric Clapton on George's black Gibson Les Paul (named "Lucy").

After the first verse, Clapton unleashes a polite run of notes that announces his presence, yet remains understated – maybe even tentative. Clapton was not credited on the album, so most listeners assumed George played lead guitar on "While My Guitar Gently Weeps." Over time, mainly because the fills and solo sounded so overtly like Clapton, the Clapton rumors were corroborated and now, settled music history.

As the chorus hits, the song shifts from a minor key (Am) to a major key (A). George's voice is brighter, yet there's still a yearning or

345

spirituality to his vocal – certainly not upbeat or positive (which is normally the case for a song written in a major key).

> *I don't know why nobody told you*
> *How to unfold your love*
> *I don't know how someone controlled you*
> *They bought and sold you*

If this were truly a Clapton composition, there would likely have been a guitar solo after the chorus, prior to the second verse, but no – the chorus runs right into the second verse, devoid of even a guitar fill.

> *I look at the world and I notice it's turning*
> *While my guitar gently weeps*
> *With every mistake we must surely be learning*
> *Still my guitar gently weeps*

George extends a hint of positivity, noting that despite the hate and tragedy and pain that existed in 1968, the world is still "turning." The optimism continues as George cites mistakes, presumably political, but contends that "we must surely be learning." Perhaps that line was a question, though? Like, "are we learning from our mistakes?"

After the second verse, Clapton couldn't contain his emotion – and talent. Rather than heading into the chorus, Clapton takes a guitar solo that starts at 1:56 and ends at 2:31. The guitar solo is perfection. Tight, passionate and absolute. After a refrain of the first verse, an extended fade out again features a Clapton guitar solo, accompanied by harmonized vocals from George and Paul.

George used every note of Clapton's lead guitar parts from the September 6 session, as well as Paul's vocals from September 6 and Ringo's drums. Finally, the track was complete. George maintained that Clapton's presence not only finished the instrumental vision, but Clapton's presence pushed the rest of the band. For a brief moment, the tension subsided and the five musicians collaborated. The result

346

is nothing short of magnificent. In my opinion, "While My Guitar Gently Weeps" is the best track on *The White Album*.

Paul and George disagree, though. Meaning, they disagree with me – but, shockingly agree with each other. Each have stated that "Happiness Is A Warm Gun", written and sung by Lennon, is the best track on the album. The track consists of four unique segments, or fragments. John borrowed the title from a line on the cover of a popular gun magazine. John explained that "a warm gun means you've just shot something." A pacifist, John thought the phrase was "a fantastic, insane thing to say."

The song begins with a series of impressionist lyrics, psychedelic and bizarre, yet consistent in rhythm and context. Reportedly, John wrote the lyrics with his friend, Derek Taylor, during an acid trip. The instrumentation around the psychedelic lyrics is not laden with psychedelic studio effects – rather, The Beatles adopt a pure Rock format to root the vagueness of the message.

> *She's not a girl who misses much*
> *Do do do do do do, oh yeah*
> *She's well-acquainted with the touch of the velvet hand*
> *Like a lizard on a window pane*
> *The man in the crowd with multicolored mirrors*
> *On his hobnail boots*
> *Lying with his eyes while his hands are busy*
> *Working overtime*
> *A soap impression of his wife which he ate*
> *And donated to the National Trust*

Beatle historians have researched every word of the verse, but each conclusion and interpretation is plagued by subjectivity. The lyrics are essentially a combination of unusual phrases from newspaper clippings and Lennon's drug-fueled musings. The musical arrangement is dominated by Harrison on lead guitar and Ringo on drums. After the abstract first verse, which again is in A minor, Harrison lays down a fuzzed-out guitar riff that leads directly into the second segment of the track. The chords switch to a major key (A), but the tone of the vocal is still minor key – somber and underground. Lennon, sounding weary and worn, sings:

> *I need a fix 'cause I'm goin' down*
> *Down to the bits that I left up town*
> *I need a fix 'cause I'm goin' down*

Originally, given the visibility of the Vietnam War and Lennon's outspokenness in favor of peace, critics and fans assumed the substance was a mixture of drug-induced imagery and a comment on violence, parodying that violence, or a warm gun, can result in happiness. However, as John's newfound relationship with Yoko Ono became public, attention turned towards the lyrics being a metaphor for sex. John denied the lyrics as a reference to sex, but he also denied that the lyrics were related to gun violence – and he denied that the term "fix" insinuated drugs. John's denials were not convincing, at least not for the British government.

"Happiness Is A Warm Gun" was banned by the British government. The government pointed to the "I need a fix 'cause I'm goin' down" line, holding that The Beatles advocated, or at a minimum, condoned the use of drugs. Of course, as a result of the ban, "Happiness Is A Warm Gun" received tremendous attention and support. Having a song banned by the British government, along with a musical shift to a heavier Rock disposition – the image of The Beatles was hardened, allowing the band to reach a more skeptical and anti-commercial audience.

The third segment of "Happiness is a Warm Gun" featured an increase in tempo, as John repeats the following line six times: "Mother Superior jumped the gun." Again, John denied that the reference was sexual in nature, but the prevailing theory is that John was in fact referring to his relationship with Yoko Ono, which reportedly involved a massive amount of sex at the time the band was recording *The White Album*. Referring to this period in 1968, Lennon stated, "that was the beginning of my relationship with Yoko and I was very sexually oriented then. When we weren't in the studio, we were in bed" (Sheff).

For the final segment, the song dropped into a new key (C) and included backing vocals from Paul (along with overdubs by John). The final segment is incredibly triumphant, as Lennon again includes a sexual reference and expands his vocal range considerably (compared to the first three segments). After a refrain of the song title, John unleashes the following lines:

> *When I hold you in my arms*
> *And I feel my finger on your trigger*
> *I know nobody can do me no harm, because:*
> *Happiness is a warm gun, mama*

Make of that what you wish, but the metaphor seems quite clear. Leaving the meaning aside, the beauty of the fourth segment of "Happiness Is A Warm Gun" is undoubtedly the return to R&B and the note that John hits at 2:22 on the word "gun." You know it. If not, go listen. "Happiness Is A Warm Gun" took 95 takes to finalize. An incredible amount of attention and detail for a track lasting only 2:45.

Let's rip through a few wonderful songs – apologies for the minimal attention, but these tracks, while great – are not essential to the purpose of this book. "Martha My Dear" showcases McCartney's bright, rather stunning piano playing – but, the song is about Paul's first pet, a sheep dog. "I'm So Tired" is a sweet, classic expression by Lennon – written while in India and based on his inability to sleep after giving up drugs and drinking. "Blackbird" is another incredibly sweet song with an alluring finger-picked guitar arrangement (by Paul) and "Rocky Raccoon" is a fantastic story and likely the most fun track on the album (again written by Paul). All 30 tracks on *The White Album* are relevant to the narrative of The Beatles, and indicative of a return to simpler, song-focused compositions, but the remainder of this passage must focus on the heaviness of "Yer Blues",

"Helter Skelter" and "Revolution", each appearing on the second LP of the double album.

Reflecting on "Yer Blues", John states, "The funny thing about the Maharishi's camp was that although it was very beautiful and I was meditating about eight hours a day, I was writing the most miserable songs on Earth. In 'Yer Blues', when I wrote, 'I'm so lonely, I want to die', I'm not kidding. That's how I felt." Lennon's most emotional track on *The White Album* is also a(nother) balance between parody and authenticity. The authenticity is rather overt – as he stated above, Lennon was emotionally distraught in India. John's wife, Cynthia, accompanied The Beatles to India, but John was longing for Yoko. Most references to a female in John's writing from this period were references to Yoko, including "Yer Blues."

The parody, though, is a bit veiled. Beatle historians point to letters and interviews that indicate John was intent on writing a traditional Blues song. However, John quickly discovered that he lacked the innate tools to replicate the Blues. Sure, The Beatles had utilized a Blues backbone on most tracks pre-*Help*, but those tracks were a unique combination of Blues and Pop. Lennon sought the Blues of Robert Johnson, Sleepy John Estes and Muddy Waters.

Lennon concluded that as a White kid from Liverpool, he lacked the authenticity to create a traditional Blues track steeped in the tradition of the American South. Of course, Lennon didn't stop there. Surveying the current music landscape in 1967 and 1968, Lennon observed dozens of bands – White bands – many from the UK – recording and releasing a version of the Blues that intended to convey authenticity, but rather, according to Lennon, conveyed a meager, unthoughtful effort.

Thus, Lennon created "Yer Blues" as an attempt to parody such meager attempts – by including ubiquitous and stereotypical components of a traditional Blues song, including a 12-bar Blues chord structure, the key of E, a bridge, stop and start rhythm and common lyrical themes. The problem, though? The Beatles crushed on "Yer Blues" – and the track seems less like a parody and more a successful representation of traditional Blues. Parody became irony. That's the kind of thing that happened in 1968.

> *Yes I'm lonely*
> *Want to die*
> *Yes I'm lonely*
> *Want to die*
> *If I ain't dead already*
> *Ohhh girl you know the reason why.*

Jonathan Gould interpreted the last line as an example of Lennon's parody. Gould stated that the line was a "joke in that nobody knows the reason why – or for that matter, what any of these bluesy poetics are really supposed to mean." I get that, but I would also offer that, given John's emotional struggle surrounding Yoko Ono, perhaps the line is relatively straight-forward. Perhaps, John was so lonely, he wanted to die, and the only reason he wasn't dead already, was because of Yoko? Later on "Yer Blues", Lennon penned a subtle ode to Dylan – well, not really subtle, as he cites Dylan in the lyric. Lennon sings/yells:

> *The eagle picks my eye*
> *The worm he licks my bone*
> *I feel so suicidal*
> *Just like Dylan's Mr. Jones*

The nod to Dylan's "Ballad of a Thin Man" was Lennon's nod to authenticity. For The Beatles, Dylan was the ultimate pillar of authenticity. Quite ironic, though – as Dylan considered himself derivative of the authenticity of Pete Seeger and Woody Guthrie. Truth is, everyone is imitating. Everything is derivative. Authenticity is in the mind of the artist and the critic and the listener. Lennon's ode to Dylan illustrates his pervasive insecurity. Similarly, Dylan's entire catalog, at least pre-1977, is a case study in insecurity.

351

The last verse of "Yer Blues" is again an example of the darkness surrounding Lennon, but also surrounding the world in late-1968. Meditating in India, in search of peace and light, supposedly in a serene landscape, Lennon wrote:

> *Black cloud crossed my mind*
> *Blue mist round my soul*
> *Feel so suicidal*
> *Even hate my rock and roll*

The last line depicts the insecurity, with emphasis on "my." Lennon doesn't hate Rock and Roll – he hates *his* version of Rock and Roll. The lyrics of "Yer Blues" are devastatingly interesting, but definitely require some study. The music, however, is raw and exposed. Borne out of 1966?

The Beatles recorded *The White Album* at Abbey Road Studios in London, which was equipped with every gadget and piece of advanced recording technology available (courtesy of EMI, the band's distributor). However, The Beatles had lost interest in the studio creativity that utilized the advanced recording technology. On several occasions during the recording of *The White Album*, George joked that the music they were making was so simple that the band could record in the tiny control room, adjacent to the actual large studio. John finally replied, "fine, we're recording the next song in the control room."

Was he serious? Lennon was nothing if not serious. The engineers set up the control room with one vocal microphone (for Lennon), a small kit for Ringo, a guitar amp for each of John and George and a bass amp for Paul (who again used the bigger, Fender Jazz bass instead of the Rickenbacker). The sound is raw and powerful – tight and punchy. Clean production was relegated to a secondary concern, perhaps even tertiary. The stripped down production promoted and enhanced Lennon's grungy vocal, suited Paul's deep dark bass line and propelled George's crunchy, distorted guitar riffs and solo at the end of the track. "Yer Blues" is The Beatles going lo-fi. A stark contrast to *Sgt. Pepper's* and 1967.

According to Ringo, "'Yer Blues' on *The White Album*, you can't top it. It was the four of us. That is what I'm saying: it was really because the four of us were in a box, a room about eight by eight, with no separation. It was this group that was together; it was like grunge rock of the Sixties, really – grunge Blues."

As for Ringo, perhaps one of my favorite moments on *The White Album* is at 3:16 on "Yer Blues." George is in the midst of a piercing guitar solo, which runs right into a perfect drum fill by Ringo and then George continues the guitar solo, but returns to the lead lick from earlier in the track. Perfect drum fill. It's nasty and for folks that consider The Beatles a light-hearted Pop band, take a listen to the end of "Yer Blues."

If you would rather see a live performance of "Yer Blues" from 1968, watch Lennon perform "Yer Blues" as part of the short-lived band, Dirty Mac, featuring Clapton on lead guitar, Keith Richards on bass and Mitch Mitchell (Jimi Hendrix Experience) on drums. Dirty Mac performed "Yer Blues" as part of the maligned *Rolling Stones Rock and Roll Circus*, a concert/film aimed at promoting the band's upcoming release, *Beggar's Banquet* (video available on YouTube).

Back to *The White Album* and back to Paul. In many ways, back to insecurity. Paul was notoriously aware of media coverage – both criticism and praise, but mostly praise. After several critics labeled *Magical Mystery Tour* as "childish" and "excessive", favoring harder records by Cream, Jimi Hendrix and Jeff Beck, Paul listened. Paul absorbed. The seed from which "Helter Skelter" grew was not a reaction to a critic, but rather a reaction to a competitor. In the May 1968 issue of *Melody Maker*, Chris Welch interviewed Pete Townshend about the sound of The Who and, in particular, the track "I Can See For Miles." Townshend stated: "We've just made the raunchiest, loudest, most ridiculous Rock and Roll record you've ever heard."

After reading the interview, but before hearing "I Can See For Miles", McCartney recalled telling The Beatles, "I think we should do a song like that; something really wild." Paul immediately began experimenting on lead guitar with intense volume and distortion. Upon hearing "I Can See For Miles" a few weeks later, Paul stated, "It was quite straight, and it was very sort of sophisticated. It wasn't rough and screaming with tape echo at all. So I thought, 'Oh well, we'll do one like that, then.' And I had this song called "Helter Skelter", which is just a ridiculous song. So, we did it like that, 'cuz I like noise." Thus, "Helter Skelter" became the marriage of a ridiculous song that Paul had written and a quest to match The Who. Fortunately, the title of Paul's ridiculous song meshed perfectly with the rage of instrumentation.

What is a Helter Skelter? Well, a "helter skelter" is basically the English version of a roller coaster. Paul used the rise and fall of the roller coaster to symbolize the rise and fall of society, with emphasis on the fall, the demise. In this context, the lyrics really are quite ridiculous:

> When I get to the bottom
> I go back to the top of the slide
> Where I stop and turn
> And I go for a ride
> Till I get to the bottom and I see you again

The simplicity of the lyrics allowed The Beatles to focus on the grander intent – volume and power. In some respects, the hallmark of Punk. Commenting on the recording Paul stated, "You can hear the voices cracking, and we played it so long and so often…we just tried to get it louder. That was really all I wanted to do – to make a very loud, raunchy Rock and Roll record with The Beatles."

The Beatles began recording "Helter Skelter" on July 18, with one version lasting 27 minutes and 11 seconds. Another version lasted 12 minutes and is particularly awesome, settling into a rhythmic Hard Rock jam (an excerpt of this version was released on *Anthology 3*).

354

The Beatles "jammed" the song out relentlessly, mining the composition for the five or six minutes that would eventually appear on the released *The White Album* version.

On all takes of "Helter Skelter", Paul played lead guitar, Lennon played bass and tenor saxophone, George played rhythm guitar and Ringo was on drums. A trumpet player was also added to the mix. Having not arrived at a final take in July, The Beatles returned to "Helter Skelter" on September 9. The Beatles committed to recording only five minute takes of "Helter Skelter" and on the 18th take, the band arrived at the final version heard on *The White Album*. Famously, after the 18th take, Ringo threw his drum sticks across the studio and screamed, "I got blisters on my fingers." Ringo can be heard on the final recording, after the track fades out at 3:40, the noise returns and culminates in Ringo smashing the cymbals three times at 4:24 and shouting about his blisters.

In addition to embracing the hardest, heaviest music of their career, The Beatles embraced the spirit of "Helter Skelter." Ringo recalled, "'Helter Skelter' was a track we did in total madness and hysterics." Several folks remember George at the September 9 session setting fire to an ashtray and placing the ashtray on his head as he ran around the studio. Critics refer to "Helter Skelter" as the "fiercest and most brutal rocker done by anyone" (Unterberger, *AllMusic*). Many consider "Helter Skelter" to be the first proto-Punk track, launching a genre, and generation. Alan W. Pollack was a bit more prescient. Upon the release of "Helter Skelter", Pollack wrote that the song will "scare and unsettle" listeners due to the track's "obsessive nature" and "undercurrent of violence" stemming from McCartney's "savage vocal delivery."

A song about a roller coaster would instill violence? Well, yes – Pollack was precisely correct, at least with respect to one rather deranged individual: Charles Manson. In July and August of 1969, Manson and a group of his disciples (referred to as his "Family") committed a series of nine murders in four locations, including the slaying of actress Sharon Tate. The tragedy sliced the consciousness

355

of American culture. Further evidence of the declining moral compass of young Americans. There were 14,760 murders in the United States in 1969 (not including the 6,249 murders of United States troops in Vietnam, which absolutely should be counted). Despite omnipresent carnage, the media focused on the murders that unfortunately intersected with popular music.

How, though, did the Manson murders connect with music? Manson was a psychopath. Manson was obsessed with death. Manson was also obsessed with The Beatles. Upon hearing "Helter Skelter", Manson became convinced that the song was a "coded prophecy for an apocalyptic race war." At his trial in 1971, Manson explained the motivation behind the killings, which of course centered around "Helter Skelter":

> *"Helter Skelter means confusion. Literally. Confusion is coming down fast. If you don't see the confusion coming down fast, you can call it what you wish. It's not my conspiracy. It's not my music. It says, "Rise!" It says, "Kill!" Why blame it on me? I didn't write the music. I am not the person who projected it into your social consciousness."*

The controversy further split an already fracturing band. A frustrated Lennon stated, "I don't know what "Helter Skelter" has to do with knifing someone." The Manson situation certainly plagued the success of and affinity for "Helter Skelter", but in 1988 – one of the most popular bands in the world saved the track. On December 10, 1988, U2 released *Rattle and Hum*, a live record compiled from various concerts in the United States and the UK. The first track on *Rattle and Hum* was a cover of "Helter Skelter." The song opens with Bono telling the crowd...and the world: "This is a song Charles Manson stole from The Beatles. We're stealing it back."

The last track we'll cover was actually the first track recorded on *The White Album*. "Revolution" (technically, "Revolution 1"). John wrote "Revolution" in India after a meditation session was compromised by thoughts of the student uprising in Paris, the Vietnam War and the assassination of MLK (RFK had not yet been killed). The Beatles were apolitical, both within the context of songwriting and publicly, but young minds can only withstand so much pain. Meditating and thinking for hours in the hills of India, John underwent a "political awakening", directly resulting in the writing of "Revolution." In John's words:

> *"I wanted to put out what I felt about revolution. I thought it was time we fucking spoke about it, the same as I thought it was about time we stopped not answering questions about the Vietnam War."*

Lennon returned from India eager and intent on recording. John entered the studio before Paul, George and Ringo returned from holiday. Such eagerness would precipitate a bit of controversy. Lennon's initial recording was a mid-tempo, Blues arrangement, with focus on Lennon's lyrics and message, perhaps borrowing from Dylan, yet infused with Lennon's leaning towards R&B (and knack for melody). Eventually, this initial arrangement of "Revolution" would appear on *The White Album*, titled "Revolution 1." However, the public would first hear a very different version of "Revolution."

When Paul, George and Ringo returned to London and arrived at the studio, Lennon immediately played them his initial recording of "Revolution." Lennon was supremely proud of "Revolution", which featured acoustic guitar, played by John, as well as bass and drums also recorded by John. Lennon wanted "Revolution" to be released quickly, as a Single. While the recording of *The White Album* would in fact evolve into a series of solo projects, upon return from India, protocol for The Beatles was still to collaborate. John's unilateral recording and announcement of a desire to release a Single exacerbated the palpable tension.

Paul and George declared "Revolution" too slow, at least for a Single. Lennon was furious. The fate of "Revolution" was determined by a vote – good old fashioned democracy. Paul voted "no", Lennon voted "yes." If two Beatles voted "no", then a stalemate was guaranteed and the track would not be released as a Single. George voted "no" and "Revolution" was therefore shelved. Whether bitter about John's autonomy, or a simple artistic decision, Paul and George's vote furthered the rift between the three creative forces in The Beatles.

John, though, was a fairly stubborn mate. "Revolution" is too slow? Fine, let's quicken it up a bit. Too docile? Let's energize it a bit. John reversed the psychology and challenged Paul and George to orchestrate an arrangement that suited release as a Single. Was John negotiating or did John just want his message surfaced?

Whether Lennon was compliant in his conformity to the energized pace sought by Paul and George, or rather – intent on exaggerating the desire of Paul and George – regardless, the product, the Single version of "Revolution", is quite great. After a distorted and fuzzy guitar lead intro by George, John begins the track with a scream. John scrapped the acoustic guitar and played electric guitar along with George. After the first two verses and a refrain of the chorus, George and John both unleash guitar solos that push the limits of distortion.

The tone of the electric guitar on "Revolution" was nothing like anything recorded by The Beatles previously. Studio engineer, Geoff Emerick, ran both guitars through two microphone pre-amplifiers while also ramping up the overload to a point just below a massive overheat on the console. Another sign of The Beatles adapting, or conforming, to the rage of 1968 – John and George demanded the most violent guitar noise possible. Notably, the Single version was arranged in a key higher than John's initial recording, resulting in a more piercing tone.

Substantively, though – despite the upbeat pace, John delivers the lyrics with clarity and focus. Arguably, the message is more poignant in the fast version. More passion and more energy and a consistent context for the lyrics. The Beatles included a rave up at the end of "Revolution" instead of the mellow fade out at the end of "Revolution

1." Further, the fast version of "Revolution" eliminates the "shoo bee doo wop" backing vocal on "Revolution 1."

The "shoo bee doo wop" was critical to the initial R&B arrangement on the relaxed "Revolution 1." When listening to the versions side by side, the groove of the slow "Revolution 1" is so intoxicating and wonderfully sweet that the listener is almost encouraged to drift away from the anger and importance of the message, as John emphasizes the line, "you know it's gonna be alright." Despite the exact same lyrics in both versions, the versions invoke separate feelings and separate intent.

Whether fast or slow, the focus – our focus – must be on John's message. John's pacifism was yet to fully develop, but the seeds exist in "Revolution." John is critical of government, but the core of "Revolution" is an attack on the revolution, the movement opposing the Vietnam War and any movement that had become radicalized. Controversy epitomized.

Remember, The Beatles were emerging from an immersion in the counterculture movement of 1967, one that they exacerbated. The movement had initially been pure, but as 1968 unfolded, Lennon realized that the movement was as guilty and violent as the government it opposed. Frank Zappa realized this notion ten months prior on *We're Only in it For the Money*, and Dylan realized it immediately in 1966, but Lennon eventually came around. The first verse established the premise.

> *You say you want a revolution*
> *Well, you know*
> *We all want to change the world*
> *You tell me that it's evolution*
> *Well, you know*
> *We all want to change the world*
> *But when you talk about destruction*
> *Don't you know that you can count me out*

The "count me out" lyric caused quite a backlash upon release of "Revolution." Was Lennon siding with the government? If so, which government? Democracy or Communism? The existence of the question was enough to ignite a storm of emotions. Precisely the type controversy that Paul (and EMI) wanted to avoid. The second verse is a classic indictment.

> *You say you got a real solution*
> *Well, you know*
> *We'd all love to see the plan*
> *You ask me for a contribution*
> *Well, you know*
> *We're doing what we can*
> *But if you want money for people with minds that hate*
> *All I can tell is brother you have to wait*

Lastly, the final verse again attacks the revolution, not necessarily in spirit, but rather in organization and execution. While Lennon still espoused remnants of 1967 with the line "you better free you mind instead" and the repeated refrain throughout the song, "you know it's gonna be alright", he remained critical. In the last line of the verse, Lennon gets a bit more granular, invoking the name of "Chairman Mao."

> *You say you'll change the constitution*
> *Well, you know*
> *We all want to change your head*
> *You tell me it's the institution*
> *Well, you know*
> *You better free your mind instead*
> *But if you go carrying pictures of Chairman Mao*
> *You ain't going to make it with anyone anyhow*

Quite incredible lyrics. Of course, uttering "Chairman Mao" in 1968 fueled the storm, but the flames of controversy were commonplace in 1968. The lyrics "Revolution" are as important today as they were in 1968. Movements and "revolutions" must also be diplomatic and reasonable. Movements must not embrace the very attributes they oppose. Lennon articulated a concern, but in 1968, even the concern was radicalized.

The third and final "version" of "Revolution" is titled "Revolution 9", an instrumental noise track created exclusively by John and Yoko. John and Yoko had recorded seven minutes of noise and affixed the segment to the end of the initial slow recording of "Revolution 1." McCartney and Harrison had previously experimented with noise, or sound collages (also referred to as "musique concrete"). McCartney was particularly critical of John and Yoko's attempt, referring to the composition as "amateur." George Martin and the rest of The Beatles management pleaded with John to exclude "Revolution 9" from *The White Album.*

To no avail, as John insisted – and the track was included as the penultimate track, after "Cry Baby Cry" and before "Good Night." Fans and critics generally ignored "Revolution 9." Perhaps, the only noteworthy product of "Revolution 9" was the fuel it provided to the "Paul is dead" myth. When played backward, the repeating line "number 9, number 9" sounded like "turn me on, dead man." Lennon also included the sound effect of a screeching car and subsequent crash and explosion.

The White Album is a massive endeavor. Is it the "best" Beatles album? Is it too long? Should The Beatles have arrived at the 14 best songs from the recording session? Maybe that album would look as follows:

Dear Prudence
While My Guitar Gently Weeps
Happiness Is A Warm Gun
I'm So Tired
Blackbird
Don't Pass Me By
Yer Blues
Mother Nature's Son

Everybody's Got Something to Hide
Sexy Sadie
Helter Skelter
Revolution 1
Savoy Shuffle
Cry Baby Cry

That album/group of songs might actually rival any other Beatles recording. The more the better, though. The tension between the band members, aggravated by the tension in the world, fueled a creative process that resulted in the second best double album ever recorded (I'm still partial to Dylan's *Blonde on Blonde*). *The White Album* not only depicts a critical juncture in the life of The Beatles, but the stripped down nature of the record – production, arrangements, songwriting – profoundly illustrates the effect of 1968 on The Beatles. As we'll see in the next chapter, many bands were more overt in terms of commentary, but The Beatles very much influenced through style and musical choice.

In retrospect, Paul stated, "I think it is a very good album. It [stands] up, but it wasn't a pleasant one to make. Then, again, sometimes those things work out for your art. The fact that it's got so much on it is what's cool about it." If that feels a bit luke warm, it is. Lennon stated, "Paul was always upset about *The White Album*. He never liked it because, on that one, I did my music, he did his, and George did his. And first, he didn't like George having so many tracks, and second, he wanted it to be more a group thing, which really meant more Paul. So, he never liked that album. I always preferred it to all the other albums, including *Pepper*, because I thought the music was better. The *Pepper* myth is bigger, but the music on *The White Album* is far superior, I think."

The Beatles again shifted the narrative in 1968, not by inventing a new sound or aesthetic, but rather solidifying the prevailing shift. By embracing Rock and leaving behind Psychedelic Pop, The Beatles dragged the mainstream into the discussion. No longer could a Beatles fan ignore the chaos and tragedy of 1968. John stated, reflecting on 1968 and *The White Album*, "Rock and Roll then was real, everything else was unreal."

We'll leave it there.

December

December

HISTORY

The Vietnam War

MUSIC

The Rolling Stones – *Beggar's Banquet*
James Taylor – S/T
Neil Young – S/T
Frank Zappa/The Mothers of Invention – *Cruising With Ruben & the Jets*

HISTORY

The Vietnam War

Americans began 1968 plagued with conflict. A horrific, tragic political impasse that resulted in over 11,000 casualties in 1967. Yet, most Americans believed the United States was prevailing – most Americans believed the United States would win the Vietnam War. Of course, this sentiment was facilitated by an untrustworthy government that insisted on misleading the American people, controlling message and rhetoric in an attempt to misdirect and misguide citizens, allowing American military forces time to slaughter the enemy and thwart Communism.

Politically, in 1966 and 1967, the United States had a Democrat-dominated Congress, with a Democrat securely in the White House. President Johnson championed progressive social programs benefiting lower class Americans and minorities. However, Johnson drifted. Johnson abandoned social progress in favor of military domination. Americans had yet to give up on President Johnson, though. Race was an issue in 1967, but tensions had subsided a bit – certainly quieter than the incidents in Selma and Watts in 1965. President Johnson might not have been trusted by African American leaders, but President Johnson was a figure that African American leaders could work with and achieve stability, if not progress.

Then, change. In a span of a few weeks, Americans awoke to evidence that the United States was actually losing the Vietnam War (the Tet Offensive on January 31), followed by the resignation – or election not to run – of the incumbent President of the United States in March, resulting in pervasive political instability. The strings of America further frayed upon the assassination of MLK (April) and the slaying of RFK (June). The sea change in spirit and emotion was massive. America wasn't simply unhinged, the door was blown clear off the frame. Madness.

Change is inherent in the evolution of culture and progress. Change is necessary and a culture's ability to accept change might just be the critical aspect of domestic sustainability. However, the change in culture is typically slow – often glacially slow. When change is precipitated or forced by specific incidents – incidents of grief – the consequence can be erratic, polarizing and radical. If change manifests too quickly, the result can be dramatic, if not tragic. According to John Green, "Grief does not change you...it reveals you."

The United States is not immune to grief. In 1963, Americans reacted to the murder of President Kennedy by mourning, then rallying – rallying around a government and a belief in the United States of America – fueled by a post-World War II generation of young adults. The grief of 1963 revealed a unified America. The grief of 1968 revealed a fractured America.

The reveal not only uncovered emotional pain – the reveal uncovered aspects of American government that had always existed. The United States sacrificed Democracy in the United States in pursuit of Democracy in Vietnam. The United States supported, and possibly created, a Democratic government in South Vietnam simply to prevent the spread of Communism. Yet, the United States government deprived the people of South Vietnam the democratic choice of government.

Maybe the people of South Vietnam would have voted to align with North Vietnam? Not a popular outcome for the United States, geopolitically, but still a democratic choice. The United States favored democracy when democracy suited the United States. At what cost?

The consequence of America's military pursuit was enormously tragic. First and foremost, approximately 60,000 American soldiers died in Vietnam, with hundreds of thousands more permanently disabled (and forgotten). Perhaps more significant, politically, the Vietnam War fostered a mistrust, and distrust, of the American government. Opposition of government had always existed, but skepticism of government was limited to a small pocket of academics and progressives. The decisions of the American government concerning Vietnam, and particularly the events of 1968, forever established skepticism of government as mainstream tenets of the American political psyche. Today, our government tells us that America is pursuing a militaristic cause, to better a society – whether an American society or a foreign society. However, most Americans no longer believe such a communication. The American people now require evidence – we now require logical reasoning. Perhaps this outcome or remnant is positive? Perhaps, but in 1968 – nothing was positive.

Along with the Civil War, the Vietnam War remains a dark cloud – an indelible stain on a wonderful historic resume. The Vietnam War was senseless, unnecessary and unfortunately ruined the lives of hundreds of thousands of Americans. Our challenge, our mission, should be to ensure that such a tragedy never happens again.

Perhaps, though, there is one true positive outcome from the turbulence of 1968: the music of 1968. The scars of 1968 remain. Families suffered the loss of children and parents. The wounds never really heal. The music doesn't cure the pain. In some way, I feel bad about celebrating music created from such misery. I believe that celebrating the music is a way to remember those lost.

<u>MUSIC</u>

This final chapter focuses on one of the foremost expressions of change in 1968 – *Beggar's Banquet* by The Rolling Stones. While The Beatles were typically reticent to include overt political comment in their lyrics, The Rolling Stones became reticent not to do so in 1968. *Beggar's Banquet* now serves as the soundtrack for 1968 – the clearest, rawest illustration of political, artistic and cultural expression in 1968.

368

The Rolling Stones – *Beggar's Banquet*

Reflecting on music 50 years after release isn't perfect. Time cures shortcomings, and illuminates triviality. Time also amplifies greatness and utilizing perspective, immortalizes certain achievements. *Beggar's Banquet* is a perfect record and is justly immortalized as the preeminent example of Rock. Overstatement? Yes, of course. The music on *Beggar's Banquet* is hardly fixed to a time period, the music is generationally agnostic. However, *Beggar's Banquet* uniquely is also historically relevant, lyrically and musically.

This passage will borrow heavily from the words of well-known critics, as the leading voices in music journalism commented on *Beggar's Banquet* in 1968, and thereafter. These comments are too precious and too relevant to mimic. The rawness of the commentary reflected the subject and echoed the noise and lack of color of 1968. In *Rolling Stone*, Jon Landau stated:

> *"Violence. The Rolling Stones are violence. Their music penetrates the raw nerve endings of their listeners and finds its way into the groove marked 'release of frustration.' Their violence has always been a surrogate for the larger violence their audience is so obviously capable of."*

Is there a more perfect quote? Before launching into *Beggar's Banquet*, let's quickly position the record in relation to the career of The Rolling Stones. The Rolling Stones released their first album in 1964, consisting largely of Blues covers. In 1965, emulating The Beatles, and therefore Bob Dylan, The Rolling Stones focused on original compositions. Initially trading predominantly on sex appeal and youth, The Rolling Stones turned out to be magnificent songwriters and musicians.

Over the course of 1965, Mick Jagger and Keith Richards wrote "Satisfaction", "The Last Time" and "Get Off of My Cloud." Each track an international hit. The Rolling Stones were legitimized, among fans and critics (and the record industry). The aforementioned tracks were followed by "Paint It Black" in 1966, a sufficiently darker composition, and yet still another international hit. In January 1967, The Rolling Stones released *Between the Buttons.*

The album again featured a few successful Singles, including "Let's Spend the Night Together" and "Ruby Tuesday", but as a whole, *Between the Buttons* was not considered in the league of The Beatles, Jimi Hendrix and Cream. The Rolling Stone were not considered to be a band that could produce a complete album. The Rolling Stones were a Blues band, a group that produced hits, but lacked the creative intuition and skill to craft an "album" – a cohesive set of songs that communicated an overall purpose or message.

In 1967, The Rolling Stones took their shot. Embracing the Psychedelic Rock of 1967, and chasing the success of *Sgt. Pepper's*, The Rolling Stones released *Their Satanic Majesties Request* in December 1967. The Rolling Stones utilized studio effects, incorporated string arrangements, unusual time signatures, abstract lyrics and even packaged the record with a trippy album cover design – replete with each band member dressed in a costume, reproduced in an animated resolution. The result was failure. Critics crushed the record, musically and personally – meaning, the media chastised The Rolling Stones for abandoning their roots in exchange for commercial success and economic gain.

The clash or rivalry between The Beatles and The Rolling Stones was largely a media fiction. The band members were friendly and reportedly admired each other's work. Each band, though, had an image. In addition to recording and releasing, or selling, music – the bands sold their image. The Beatles had represented "good" while The Rolling Stones represented "evil." However, between 1966 and 1968, The Beatles were trending away from "good" and more towards – maybe not "evil", but controversial – relating largely to drugs, but as we discussed in the last chapter, substantively and politically.

Their Satanic Majesties Request represented The Rolling Stones moving in the other direction, trending back towards "good." No longer a bunch of long-haired, working class kids from England fusing sex and drugs with traditional Blues. The Rolling Stones attempted to be Pop stars. Fortunately, the misguided foray that was *Their Satanic Majesties Request* was only an aberration.

Beggar's Banquet not only marked the triumphant return of The Rolling Stones in terms of musical style, relevance and popularity, *Beggar's Banquet* marked the start of a classic four album streak. After releasing *Beggar's Banquet* in 1968, the band released *Let It Bleed* in 1969, *Sticky Fingers* in 1971 and *Exile on Main Street* in 1972. And, some (including, Chris Jones) would argue that the streak is actually five albums, as *Goat's Head Soup*, released in 1973, is a classic (*Goat's Head Soup* did reach #1 in both the US and UK). The rivalry between The Beatles and The Rolling Stones was not coterminous.

The Beatles peaked between 1965 and 1970, whereas The Rolling Stones peaked between 1968 and 1973. The historical events of 1968 not only influenced the release of *Beggar's Banquet*, but the evil and darkness in 1968 changed the course of music given the renewed disposition of The Rolling Stones. In his review of *Beggar's Banquet*, John Landau penned a terrific line to describe the music of The Rolling Stones:

> *"The Rolling Stones are constantly being reborn, but somehow the baby always looks like its parents."*

Because the songwriting of The Rolling Stones bloomed a bit later than The Beatles (and the Kinks for that matter), when The Rolling Stones hit their peak in 1968, they were more experienced musicians and arrangers, but most importantly – more mature, more aware and conscious. Possibly more important, the timing aligned with the marketplace, as the hallmark attitude of The Rolling Stones was suddenly mainstream. This perspective enabled Jagger and Richards to masterfully intertwine social unrest and the Blues. Landau stated:

"The people who are turning to political themes in their music now are different. They don't do it as a luxury, or for moral reasons. They are doing it because it is part of their lives and they have to express themselves in terms of how what is happening in the streets is affecting their lives…there is no way they can separate themselves as human beings from what is going on out there."

Beggar's Banquet opens with "Sympathy for the Devil." Credited to Jagger/Richards, Jagger wrote all of the lyrics. Initially arranged as a slow, Folk tune on acoustic guitar. Jagger commented that he "wrote it as sort of like a Bob Dylan song." Yet another Dylan disciple. Ultimately, Keith Richards re-arranged "Sympathy for the Devil", infusing percussion and unique rhythm, but the analysis must first be on the narrative, the substance – the lyrics are nothing short of brilliant. Let's break it down. The track opens with the following verse:

> *Please allow me to introduce myself*
> *I'm a man of wealth and taste*
> *I've been around for a long, long year*
> *Stole many a man's soul to waste*

"Sympathy for the Devil" is a first person narrative, told from the perspective of Satan, or the Devil. The first verse hides the identity of the protagonist, but given the song's title, the notion is quite obvious. The third line is critical. Jagger establishes that the Devil has been around for a long, long time – which will be the basis for the song as Jagger recounts historical events from the past two thousand years – but, instead, using the word "time" – Jagger wrote "long, long *year*", in reference to 1968.

Each subsequent verse abrasively depicts the historical presence of evil, through a series of vignettes that expose atrocities and death. In the second verse, Jagger begins his assault.

And I was 'round when Jesus Christ
Had his moment of doubt and pain
Made damn sure that Pilate
Washed his hands and sealed his fate

Taking credit for the murder of Jesus Christ was quite a bit controversial in 1968. Religious organizations condemned The Rolling Stones, labeling the band "devil worshippers." The label only fueled the brand. Sure, parents preferred their kids listen to The Beatles rather than The Rolling Stones, but given the daily violence unfolding on the evening news, on the cover of newspapers and on college campuses, even parents were unable to argue that The Rolling Stones were the cause of such violence.

The third verse features Jagger, or the Devil, assuming responsibility for the deadly Russian Revolution in 1917. Why did Jagger focus on the Russian Revolution? The uprising in St. Petersburg was the inflection point that ended the Tsarist government structure – paving the way for Communism. The reference indicts Communism as evil, but remember – evil is the work of the Devil. And, who is the Devil? Who is responsible for pervasive evil? We are...all of us.

I stuck around St. Petersburg
When I saw it was time for a change
Killed the czar and his ministers
Anastasia screamed in vain

After another verse referencing World War II, the chorus in "Sympathy for the Devil" enters (the chorus is refrained four times throughout the song). The chorus functions as a question – asked of the listener, by Jagger.

Pleased to meet you
Hope you guess my name
But what's puzzling you is
The nature of my game

Two questions, really. The first is easy: "Hope you guess my name." Again, the song invokes sympathy for the Devil, and the first verse introduces the character of the Devil. So, we know his name. The second question, though is the tough question: "What's puzzling you is the nature of my game." What is the Devil's motive? Can it be to just wreak havoc? As Jagger recounts instances of man-induced atrocities, he's asking, "What's the point?" He's asking, "Why are we doing these things to each other?"

Jagger's approach is creative and a massive leap forward in terms of songwriting. The premise is unique and powerful, but the next two verses are even more special. Jagger first attacks Western civilization's proclivity to kill in the name of religion.

> *I watched with glee*
> *While your kings and queens*
> *Fought for ten decades*
> *For the gods they made*

Jagger exposes religion as a platform for violence. This expression was highly unpopular, yet continues to be a truism of modern culture.

The recording of "Sympathy for the Devil" began on June 4. Transforming Jagger's acoustic Folk version into a full band composition was not immediately ascertainable. The band concurred that the lyrics should remain front and center, but crafting a rhythm was a challenge. The verses conveyed a certain consistency, no real climax – a series of stories. The band wanted the musical context to echo the consistency.

Charlie Watts (drums) recalls the band "trying everything." Keith Richards, as he often did when challenged with rhythm, gravitated to the bass. Richards crafted a Samba that Jagger immediately embraced. Commenting on the rhythm in *Rolling Stone*, Jagger stated "it has a very hypnotic groove, a samba, which has a tremendous hypnotic power…it doesn't speed up or slow down. It keeps this constant groove."

The instrumentation is striking and somehow conveys evil. Jagger explained that the track is "primitive" in context and substance and therefore the rhythm is primitive, featuring an "African, South American, Afro-whatever-you-call-that rhythm." These rhythms are perceived as "evil" because they are unfamiliar to the mainstream listener. Jagger continued, "So, to white people, it has a very sinister thing about it."

Further, Richards eliminated the rhythm guitar and included a bongo intro. The bongos, along with Jagger howling in the background, provided a jungle, almost bestial, element. After settling on the rhythmic structure (or lack thereof), Jagger and Richards began orchestrating the timing and phrasing of the lyrics. On June 6, Jagger had finally nailed the delivery and the band began finalizing the track. Except, one very critical lyric change was made by Jagger.

As The Rolling Stones arrived at the studio on June 6, they were informed of the assassination of Robert F. Kennedy. Jagger immediately revised the second line of the sixth verse

> *I shouted out,*
> *Who killed the Kennedys?*
> *When after all*
> *It was you and me*

By pluralizing Kennedys and incorporating a current event into the lyrics, Jagger reinforced the premise that "Sympathy for the Devil" was not just a recitation of past horrors. The statement is that tragedy continues to exist, especially in 1968. The venom in Jagger's voice as he sings, "I shouted out/Who killed the Kennedys?" is severed by his answering of the question. To this point, the Devil has claimed responsibility for the historical atrocities. Good versus Evil. The Devil is Evil and presumably, the listener is Good. Not so fast. Who killed the Kennedys? After all, "it was you and me." The listener is now indicted.

Perhaps "the Kennedys" refers to something broader than Jack and Bobby. Perhaps "the Kennedys" refers to a simpler time, Camelot – a certain innocence and naivety. The simpler time, the innocence was shattered – and who is to blame? We all are to blame. That's the point. The Kennedys, as well as innocence and peace, had perished due to a dangerous divide of political ideology. The fear of Communism had fueled instability and war. No longer could we assure we are "Good." We are complicit in the current historical atrocity.

Jagger's ability to thread that concept is impressive. The line "It was you and me" also introduced the concept of "who actually is the Devil?" The answer is – we really don't know. It might be the Russians. It might be Lee Harvey Oswald. It might be Hitler. It might be a mythical beast in a red outfit with a pitchfork. Point is, it could be anyone. The Devil might just be a man of "wealth and taste." The Devil might approach you and with impeccable manners say, "Let me please introduce myself" and "pleased to meet you." The Devil might not be who you think it is. Be skeptical. Question everyone.

Tough to follow the sixth verse with another verse, so the band adeptly included a guitar solo by Richards. At 2:49, Richards enters with a crunchy, high pitched tone, but doesn't unleash a fluid, typical guitar solo. The notes are sharp and short, sporadic and menacing. This guitar solo has been described as "erotic" and "sexual." Not sure if Richards heard McCartney's solo on "Helter Skelter" prior to recording "Sympathy for the Devil", as the two albums were recorded contemporaneously, but the two solos are similar in tone and context. After the solo, Jagger follows with an assault on authority and finally declares his identity.

> *Just as every cop is a criminal*
> *And all the sinners saints*
> *As heads is tails*
> *Just call me Lucifer*

Indicting religion, criticizing a political ideology – these are hallmarks of free speech – but, calling every cop a criminal? Many believed the line bordered on inciting violence. I'm sure Jagger chose his words very carefully, but I suggest that the line is less an indictment of cops and more a phrase intended to display the chaos caused by the Devil, by evil. Each of the first three lines set forth opposites. Cops and criminals. Sinners and saints. Heads and tails. The first line certainly grabs attention, but when read together with the rest of the verse, there is a larger motive. Either way, Jagger completes the verse by declaring he is "Lucifer."

Before the fadeout and conglomerate of "woo hoo" screams provided by Brian Jones, Bill Wyman, Marian Faithful and Anita Pallenberg, Jagger again speaks directly to the listener. His message is frightening. Not all of the verses rhyme, but pairing "taste" and "waste" is an excellent stroke.

> *So if you meet me*
> *Have some courtesy*
> *Have some sympathy, and some taste*
> *Use all your well-learned politesse*
> *Or I'll lay your soul to waste*

After the verse and subsequent chorus, at 4:32, the band embarks on an extended (mostly) instrumental fadeout, lasting for just under two minutes (the total track length of "Sympathy for the Devil is 6:18). The "jam" begins with Richards laying back and allowing the piano to take the lead. Played by Nicky Hopkins, the piano accentuates the groove and when Richards does join, the instrumental is euphoric yet dark. Richards again fires a series of short, heavily distorted guitar licks, while Jagger scats and grunts in front of the chorus of backing "woo hoos." Not as "hard" and messy as "Helter Skelter", but certainly chaotic.

Reacting to the criticism after the release of "Sympathy for the Devil", Keith Richards stated in *Rolling Stone*, "Before, we were just innocent kids out for a good time…[now they're saying we're] evil?

Oh, I'm evil, really? So, that makes you start thinking about evil…what is evil? Everybody's Lucifer." This quote by Richards is not only the core of "Sympathy for the Devil", but the core of 1968. Evil has always existed – and to some extent, may exist in everyone and everything – however, evil is fortunately often suppressed by positivity, righteousness – and good. In 1968, The Rolling Stones observed that evil had breached the consciousness, surfacing and manifesting as violence. Evil was winning.

Given the uproar surrounding the release of "Sympathy for the Devil", one might think The Rolling Stones would follow with a more accessible, less controversial track? Not so. Ahead of the release of *Beggar's Banquet*, The Rolling Stones released "Street Fighting Man." Given the nexus of "Sympathy For the Devil" and "Street Fighting Man" in terms of release and content, we'll cover the tracks back-to-back, then discuss the remaining tracks on *Beggar's Banquet*.

A peculiar ambiguity exists between the *perceived message* of "Street Fighting Man" and the *actual intent* of Mick Jagger, the song's author. Analyzing the lyrics, Jagger's intent is quite clear – but, ambiguity surfaces as a result of the song's overwhelming title and dominant first two lines. Whether the ambiguity was intentional, such is not clear – but, interestingly – the legacy of "Street Fighting Man", the reputation of "Street Fighting Man" and the symbolic significance of "Street Fighting Man" is the perceived message, rather than the actual intent.

Jagger opens "Street Fighting Man" with the lines:

> *Everywhere I hear the sound of*
> *marching, charging feet, boy*
> *Cause summer's here and the time is right*
> *for fighting in the street, boy*

After public demonstrations of violence in Chicago and, before that, chaos in the streets of Paris, the lyrics quite clearly reference the current state of turmoil and instability in 1968. However, read the lyrics again – Jagger does not endorse violence in the streets, or even condone the expression of frustration. The phrase, "the time is right for fighting in the street" endeavors a bit close, but Jagger is merely observing.

Politicians, police and the institution of "law and order" disagreed. "Street Fighting Man" was banned from most radio stations in the United States, as well as Paris and several UK territories (yet, not London). The Rolling Stones were criticized for attempting to incite violence. Was the band devastated that their new Single was met with a negative governmental reaction?

Hardly. The Rolling Stones had been down this path. As mentioned, "Sympathy for the Devil" was banned and criticized by governments, religious organizations, the Left, the Right, parents, grandparents. Before that, in 1965, the band's hit, "Satisfaction", was criticized due to sexual overtones – and banned from several radio stations and television programs.

In each case, the "negative" attention elevated the profile of the banned track and elevated the profile of The Rolling Stones, resulting in commercial success for each of the "banned" songs and a reinforcement of the image of The Rolling Stones as the nastiest, dirtiest, raunchiest, and perhaps best, Rock band in the world. When told of the song's banishment, Jagger stated, "I'm rather pleased to hear they have banned [the song]. The last time they banned one of our records in America, it sold a million copies."

Back to the ambiguity. After the "time is right for fighting in the street" line, Jagger inserts a key word, "But." Grammatically, the word "but" is used to connect to phrases that contrast. By including the word "but", Jagger signals a contrast, a change – something other than or opposed to "fighting in the streets." The next four lines have forever been lost in the minds of listeners:

But, what can a poor boy do
Except to sing for a rock 'n' roll band

Cause in sleepy London town
There's just no place for a street fighting man

The cultural revolution that swept through the United States and Paris in 1967 and 1968 had not penetrated London – in terms of altering the fabric of government and policy in the United Kingdom. Referencing "sleepy London", Jagger conveys a Blues archetype – just a couple London mates playing Rock and Blues. Jagger reinforced the position in the following verse:

Think the time is right for a palace revolution
But where I live the game to play is compromise solution

Again, Jagger's use of the word "but" to transition away from the "palace revolution." Yet, most listeners were only moved by the "palace revolution" line, not paying attention to following line's indictment of the governments of the United States and France. Citing "compromise solution" as a compliment to the policies and culture of the parliamentary system in the United Kingdom.

Great songwriters consistently observe. Jagger and Richards are no exception. Observing in 1968 meant witnessing violence on a weekly basis. "Street Fighting Man" is an observation, rather than a statement. The Rolling Stones don't object to the action-oriented response of the movement, but The Rolling Stones certainly don't endorse the movement. Similar to Lennon's disposition in "Revolution" where he sings, "you can count me out", Jagger and Richards convey indifference. Critics differed in terms of interpretation.

Richie Unterberger stated, "Perhaps they were saying they wished they could be on the front lines, but were not in the right place at the right time." This interpretation focuses more on the title of the song and the first few lines. Likewise, Roy Carr called "Street Fighting Man" a "great summer street-corner rock anthem." Again, focusing on the misdirection.

Dave Marsh, an editor of *Creem* magazine, got it right, calling "Street Fighting Man" the "keynote of *Beggar's Banquet*", Marsh noted, "with its teasing admonition to do something and its refusal to admit that doing it will make any difference…the Stones were more correct, if also more faithless philosophers than any of their peers." Marsh diagnosed the indifference of the message. In Jagger's words, "It's stupid to think you can start a revolution with a record. I wish you could."

Landing on indifference as the true core of "Street Fighting Man" is supported by the instrumentation utilized on the track, as well as the instrumentation utilized on most other tracks on *Beggar's Banquet*. Despite it being deemed a "rock anthem", the only electric instrument on "Street Fighting Man" is the electric bass (played by Richards). The opening guitar chords are distinctly acoustic, supported by Nicky Hopkins on piano, Charlie Watts on a stripped-down drum kit and Brian Jones playing a sitar (which exists on the recording, but resides deep in the mix). Why, though, does this instrumentation support the attitude of indifference?

Possibly a stretch, but as discussed throughout this book, between January and December, the music scene in 1968 had largely shifted towards Hard Rock and an energized version of electric Blues. Exceptions existed, of course. *Music From Big Pink* by The Band, *Sweetheart of the Rodeo* by The Byrds and the output from Buffalo Springfield (and later in this chapter, Neil Young). In each case, the musicians "checked out" or went in a "different direction" than the scene. Changed course away from the movement.

In each case, the musicians turned to an acoustic arrangement – traditional Folk, acoustic Blues and, generally, a lack of commentary on social and political issues. Call it "indifference", call it "apathy" or, as we did in the chapter on *Music From Big Pink*, call it "genuine." On *Beggar's Banquet*, rather than trend to Hard Rock after *Their Satanic Majesties Request*, The Rolling Stones turned away – opting for a rustic, yet updated acoustic version of the Blues that would thereafter become their hallmark sound.

While the "other" songs on *Beggar's Banquet* are not as charged as "Sympathy for the Devil" and "Street Fighting Man", each track coalesces around an acoustic Blues spine and a genuine resignation. *Beggar's Banquet* is a return to Rock and Blues after their Psychedelic Rock experiment in 1967, but the variation of Rock and Blues on *Beggar's Banquet* is more primitive than even the initial releases by The Rolling Stones in 1964. Maturity and musicianship allowed the band to strip away the clutter, eliminate the guitar distortion, avoid studio effects, unplug and focus on crafting songs.

Before detailing a few tracks, I must comment on the album's construction. The symmetry of *Beggar's Banquet* is critical. Place yourself back in 1968 – think vinyl. Each side of *Beggar's Banquet* contained 5 songs. Each side began with a statement. "Sympathy for the Devil" on Side 1 and "Street Fighting Man" on Side 2. Each side followed the opening anthem with a stripped-down, acoustic, slow, traditional track – reinforcing the "new" direction of The Rolling Stones. Then, each side closed with the second strongest track on the side – with "Jig-Saw Puzzle" closing Side 1 and "Salt of the Earth" closing Side 2. The construction of the album is thoughtful – hardly a "concept album" in the traditional sense, but a certain equality exists on each side of the album – in terms of song length, song type and power.

After "Sympathy for the Devil" on Side 1, the band drops into "No Expectations." For context, remember that the most recent release from The Rolling Stones had been a disastrous foray into Psychedelic Rock. Hearing "No Expectations" must have been at a minimum, surprising, and more likely, jarring.

The feeling of loneliness is immediate. Beginning with lightly strummed acoustic guitar chords, and then just six seconds into the track, a beautifully solemn slide guitar emerges. In 1968, slide guitar playing was mainly a technique used by acoustic Delta Blues players in Mississippi and endorsed by a few electric Blues guitarists, such as Elmore James. Slide guitarists place an object on one of their fingers (usually the index or pointer finger) and pluck or fingerpick individual notes (usually, the guitar is in an open tuning). The sound has been described as emotive, expressive and downright sad. Sounds like 1968, actually.

The slide guitar part on "No Expectations" was played by Brian Jones. Jones was notoriously absent from the *Beggar's Banquet* sessions, a result of drug and alcohol abuse combined with an undiagnosed mental instability. Jones would miss the first 15 takes of a track, then surface in the studio, grab a non-traditional instrument, such as a tamboura or sitar, then magically contribute. As discussed, Jones can be heard playing tamboura on "Sympathy for the Devil" and sitar on "Street Fighting Man." Jones' slide playing on "No Expectations" was his largest contribution to *Beggar's Banquet*. It would also be his last contribution to The Rolling Stones.

In a 1995 interview with *Rolling Stone*, reflecting on the first time he heard Jones play the lead slide guitar line on "No Expectations", Jagger recalled, "We were sitting around in a circle on the floor, singing and playing, recording with open mikes. That was the last time I remember Brian really being totally involved in something that was really worth doing." The somberness of the slide guitar tone seemed to be a direct reflection of Brian Jones.

Jagger's vocals begin at 0:35 and, while Jagger had tackled ballads on prior releases, his voice had never sounded cleaner and more original than on "No Expectations." Jagger's lyrics lean on traditional Blues themes – trains, train stations, "Once I was a rich man/Now I am so poor", a "weary life" – "No Expectations" is a tale of lost love, but the tale is secondary to the sound. After the third verse, Jones again steps in front with the slide guitar, but at 2:01 he is joined by Nicky Hopkins on piano. The combination of slide guitar and piano is the first, most direct signal that The Rolling Stones had changed. Several bands had leaned Country and traditional Blues, but "No Expectations" was far more raw and desolate than any prior offering, by any band.

383

The next two tracks on Side 1 continue the template of traditional Blues. "Dear Doctor" includes harmonica and is more upbeat, possessing a rollicking, barroom rhythm and the line "Oh help me please doctor/There's a pain where there once was a heart." Next, on "Parachute Woman", Richards plays electric guitar, but the track is a classic 12-bar Blues, evoking a traditional quality. Both tracks are decent and certainly extend the theme of *Beggar's Banquet* in terms of sound and aesthetic, but both tracks pale in comparison to the Side 1 closer, "Jig-Saw Puzzle."

Opening with drums, then the lead electric guitar lick from Richards, "Jig-Saw Puzzle" immediately sounds like The Rolling Stones. As Jagger begins the first verse, the quality of his vocal is dramatically different. As a singer, Mick is often inconsistent, but listen to his voice on "Jig-Saw Puzzle" – it's awesome. Still largely spoken word, but the end of each line includes melody and a smoothness that doesn't often surface.

The second verse is when the listener realizes, "wait, I need to pay attention to these lyrics."

> *Oh, the gangster looks so frightening*
> *With his luger in his hand*
> *When he gets home to his children*
> *He's a family man*
> *But when it comes to the nitty gritty*
> *He can shove in his knife*
> *Yes he really looks quite religious*
> *He's been an outlaw all his life*

The verse is a vignette. "Jig-Saw Puzzle" is a series of vignettes – small, quick stories that are not connected. Jagger writes clearly – presenting a character, presumably an evil character, but one that is also a family man, a good man – even a religious man. Jagger succinctly offers the narrative without laboring through the details of the story. What happens to the gangster? What happens to his family? Does his family know that he's a gangster? Doesn't really matter. Point is, Jagger has the listener thinking, even passively, about a character with two different sides. The theme is a setup for the next verse.

Jagger proceeds to describe each member of the band. The descriptions continue the theme of duality. The Rolling Stones were already firmly established as the antithesis to The Beatles. Grungier, harder, apathetic – both in appearance and musical disposition. After a lackluster attempt at conformity (*Their Satanic Majesties Request*), The Rolling Stones revolted against their own behavior. The following verse is a biography of the band – allowing the listener a glimpse behind the curtain. Jagger starts by commenting on himself.

> *Oh the singer, he looks angry*
> *At being thrown to the lions*
> *And the bass player, he looks nervous*
> *About the girls outside*
> *And the drummer, he's so shattered*
> *Trying to keep up time*
> *And the guitar players look damaged*
> *They've been outcasts all their lives*

Typically simple, and without context, Jagger laments the responsibility of being the leader of the band. Are the lions he references the fans, the media, the record label? Likely all of the above. The bass player, Bill Wyman, was nervous about the girls outside? Again, no context. Maybe Wyman is an introvert? Maybe "outside" just kind of rhymes (kind of) with "lions" – but the mention of the girls outside certainly lets the girls outside know that they are noticed and also invokes a self-deprecating narrative – Rock stars are not supposed to be nervous about meeting girls?

I've always loved how Jagger emphasizes the word "shattered." Unclear if Charlie Watts was shattered, generally, or shattered because he's just trying to keep up time. Unclear whether "keep up time" is a metaphor for life, or simply a reference to music. Again, doesn't matter, but the duality plainly exists.

Arriving at the guitar players, the purest image of The Rolling Stones – Keith Richards and Brian Jones. Jagger describes the guitar players as "damaged" and closes the verse with "they've been outcasts all their lives." This last line is the essence of The Rolling Stones – and the essence of the shift from 1967 to 1968. Referencing the Prologue, in 1967, young people desired to be in – a part of the mainstream, latching on to fads and styles, driving commercial success by being a part of commercial success. A self-perpetuating cycle of mediocrity.

In 1968, young people desired to be out. Counter to the prevailing culture. If costumes and silly animated movies were in – the cool bands and the cool kids opted not only for no costumes, but band members dressed in drab, pedestrian and almost impoverished attire. If a band released a movie, the movie was simply a filmed concert – raw, basic and focused on the music (not animated).

That said, arguably in 1968, the "outcast" became the leader of the movement.

In the next verse, referencing the Vietnam War, Jagger writes, "There's twenty thousand grandmas/Wave their hankies in the air." Jagger continues, "There's a regiment of soldiers/Standing looking on/The Queen is bravely shouting/What the hell is going on?"

Those last two lines are interesting. Jagger uses the adverb "bravely" to describe the Queen. While most governments were under siege – in the United States as a result of the Vietnam War, in France as a result of the progressive, liberal uprising and in several Soviet Union controlled territories, such as Czechoslovakia – the government of the United Kingdom was relatively stable. The United Kingdom did not outwardly oppose the Vietnam War, but the United Kingdom was hardly supportive.

Jagger paraphrases the Queen's sentiment through the, presumably fictional quote, "What the hell is going on?" There may not have been a better phrase for the entirety of 1968. You could imagine regular folks heading home from work each night, eating dinner with their family, pouring a drink and settling into a chair to watch the evening news – and you could imagine each person repeating in a hushed, almost mumbling voice, "What the hell is going on?" Night after night after night.

Jagger closes the track with a slightly modified version of the chorus, adding a woman – his girlfriend, presumably – to the verse. The image repeats the theme of desperation – lying on the floor, trying to do a jig-saw puzzle – a metaphor for the currently fractured pieces of the world – hoping it's fixed before it rains anymore – with rain symbolizing all the bad shit that seemingly unfolded regularly in 1968. Jagger sings:

> *Me, I'm just waiting so patiently*
> *With my woman on the floor*
> *We're just trying to do this jig-saw puzzle*
> *Before it rains anymore*

As stated, "Street Fighting Man" opened Side 2 of *Beggar's Banquet*. Following the template of Side 1, The Rolling Stones settle into a mid-tempo acoustic-driven traditional Blues song by Reverend Robert Wilkins, "Prodigal Son." Not nearly as wonderful as "No Expectation", but "Prodigal Son" extends the consistency of *Beggar's Banquet*.

Next, the driving, electric Blues rhythm of "Stray Cat Blues" and a run through "Factory Girl." The production on "Factory Girl" seems intentionally lo-fi, with Jagger's vocals a bit distant – the track is dominated by Richards on acoustic guitar, Watts on percussion and session player Ric Grech on violin. Each of "Stray Cat Blues" and "Factory Girl" are solid, definitely not to be skipped, but both serve as a prologue for the standout album closer, "Salt of the Earth."

Written mostly by Jagger, "Salt of the Earth" is a beautifully odd song. Seemingly, a tribute or celebration of the working class citizens of the United Kingdom, upon further review, including comments directly from Jagger, "Salt of the Earth" is an expression of cynicism. First, the musical arrangement, then we'll look at the lyrics.

The track begins with Keith on acoustic guitar, strumming basic, open chords. Pretty standard opening for a song by The Rolling Stones – with one exception, though. Keith also sings the first verse of "Salt of the Earth." Certainly, not as strong as Jagger's vocal, but Keith handles the verse well and when Jagger jumps in on the second verse, the change lends the song a certain unity. Between the Richards verse and Jagger verse, slide guitar can be heard – played by Richards, as Brian Jones was absent during the recording session of "Salt of the Earth" (Richards added the slide via an overdub). Then, as Jagger begins the second verse, Nicky Hopkins joins on piano.

A bridge is utilized after the second verse to lower the key and darken the tone in preparation for the rather triumphant and bright chorus. Charlie Watts enters the arrangement on drums, completing the staged instrumentation and arriving at a full band sound. After the chorus, Richards joins Jagger for another verse, sung over the full band upbeat arrangement.

After another bridge is used to quiet the band, a full gospel choir joins Jagger for two times through the chorus. The mood is absolutely positive and moving. "Salt of the Earth" ends with a fade-out, or a coda, led by Hopkins on piano and the gospel choir on vocals. The coda lasts for about a minute and a half, fading to silence and the end of *Beggar's Banquet*.

The instrumentation of "Salt of the Earth" was an experiment by The Rolling Stones. Each musician joining the arrangement one-by-one, building to a multi-dimensional, full band sound. The strategy works well on "Salt of the Earth", with emphasis on the choir, but The Rolling Stones would perfect the strategy on "You Can't Always Get What You Want", from the 1969 release, *Let It Bleed*. "You Can't Always Get What You Want" doesn't include a bridge, but otherwise – the songs are tracked very similarly, and dominated by the addition of the gospel choir.

So, what was Jagger communicating through "Salt of the Earth." Just a song paying tribute to the hard working people of London? *Beggars Banquet* was a statement by The Rolling Stones, both musically and lyrically. Each of "Sympathy for the Devil" and "Street Fighting Man" contained poignant substantive comment. We must assume that the album's closing song possessed a similar intention.

The first verse, sung by Richards, actually is refrained as the chorus, but we'll call it the first verse:

> *Let's drink to the hard working people*
> *Let's drink to the lowly of birth*
> *Raise your glass to the good and the evil*
> *Let's drink to the salt of the earth*

Seemingly an acknowledgement of the lower class, the hard working people, Jagger acknowledges that these folks were born into their circumstance (lowly of birth). A sense of sadness exists, and even a sense of gratitude. Raising a glass to the good and evil – a thanks to the working class, irrespective of their morality. Bleak, but tenuously positive.

The second verse reinforces the above narrative. Sung by Jagger, and optimism surfaces:

> *Say a prayer for the common foot soldier*
> *Spare a thought for his back breaking work*
> *Say a prayer for his wife and his children*
> *Who burn the fires and who still till the earth*

The listener has no choice but to root for the plight of the hard working people, the common foot soldier. The working class have spouses and children. Those more fortunate should pray that the lower class experience a more fruitful life. Unstated, and likely fueled by the accompanying optimism of the music, the listener believes that a better life is ahead for the lower class. If we all work together and support the effort, a brighter future will arrive.

389

Then, the bridge. As stated, the bridge drops in key, foreshadowing danger. The darkness of the bridge also introduces the darkness of Jagger's statement.

> *And when I search a faceless crowd*
> *A swirling mass of gray and*
> *Black and white*
> *They don't look real to me*
> *In fact, they look so strange*

By describing the lower class as a faceless crowd and a mass of gray and black and white, Jagger conveys cynicism. Jagger knows of the struggle, but acknowledges that the eradication of poverty is likely impossible. He not only states that the working class people "don't look real to me", he uses the word "strange" to describe their appearance.

Tough to interpret, as the bridge lyrics contrast the verse and chorus lyrics, but given the way Jagger states the bridge lyrics – a deeper voice, more spoken – I believe the bridge lyrics are Jagger speaking from his personal viewpoint. The verse and chorus lyrics are the prevailing sentiment – of the movement – and Jagger espoused such views, but when he really thought about the issues, and thought and looked at the working class, the bridge expresses his true thoughts.

After the bridge, Jagger returns to the movement's sentiment, advancing the plight and struggles of the working class by stringing together several wonderful lines:

> *Raise your glass to the hard working people*
> *Let's drink to the uncounted heads*
> *Let's think of the wavering millions*
> *Who need leading but get gamblers instead*
> *Spare a thought for the stay-at-home voter*
> *Empty eyes gaze at strange beauty show*
> *And a parade of the gray suited grafters*
> *A choice of cancer or polio*

Perhaps Jagger is judging himself. He knows that aiding the working class in their plight for justice and economic equality is morally righteous, however, he is honest (in the bridge) about how he actually views the working class. Jagger doesn't endorse the view of the bridge, but portrays an uncommon honesty in communicating what others were likely thinking. Ultimately, given the emphasis on the verse and chorus, both lyrically and instrumentally, we have no choice but to believe that Jagger and The Rolling Stones supported the working class and genuinely prayed for them and raised a glass to them.

Critics in 1968 were equally confused by the lyrics to "Salt of the Earth." Jagger clarified the lyrical statement in 1970, "'Salt of the Earth' is pure cynicism. I am saying...that these people have no power and never will have [any]." Jagger advances a pessimistic, cynical view that the livelihood of the lower class is destined. After the events of 1968, though, it's hard to blame Jagger for such pessimism. "Salt of the Earth" remains a perfect album closer. The track exudes and illuminates the duality existing throughout *Beggar's Banquet* and the music of "Salt of the Earth" is emblematic of the band's return to Rock (and substance).

In Jann Wenner's review of *Beggar's Banquet* in *Rolling Stone*, he stated that The Rolling Stones "are constantly changing but beneath the changes they remain the most formal of rock bands." Somewhat of a basic statement, but wonderfully accurate. The Rolling Stones are commonly referred to as a Blues band, which I certainly understand – but, make no mistake – The Rolling Stones are a Rock band. Describing the band's sound as loud, metallic and trebly, Wenner stated, "The Stones were the first band to say, "Up against the wall, motherfucker", and they said it with class."

A great line by Wenner, but the "up against the wall" attitude may not have been innate. The attitude may have been learned. Focus on the statements within "Sympathy for the Devil" and "Street Fighting Man", as those tracks best illustrate the direct effect of 1968. The events of 1968 spawned the attitude of The Rolling Stones. *Beggar's*

Banquet remains a remarkably consistent and fresh recording – influencing generations of musicians striving to blend Blues, Rock and Country.

The only way to properly close this passage is to refrain – yes, repeat the quote from John Landau, describing The Rolling Stones and contextualizing 1968:

> *"Violence. The Rolling Stones are violence. Their music penetrates the raw nerve endings of their listeners and finds its way into the groover marked "release of frustration." Their violence has always been a surrogate for the larger violence their audience is so obviously capable of."*

James Taylor – S/T

James Taylor was born in Boston, his father a doctor and professor, his mother an accomplished opera singer. The Taylor family are descendants of Scotland, inheriting a fortune that rendered the family of significant wealth. In 1951, James and his family moved to Chapel Hill, North Carolina after James' father took a job as a professor at the University of North Carolina. Taylor attended boarding school throughout middle and high school.

Originally gravitating towards the cello, James began to focus on songwriting and acoustic guitar. Taylor's musical pursuit obscured the responsibility necessary to succeed academically at a fancy boarding school. Thus, Taylor's grades suffered and he experienced extreme pressure from his teachers, family and friends. Just before his junior year in high school, suffering from extreme depression, Taylor checked himself into a psychiatric hospital. The experience would prove therapeutically successful, but also musically successful.

Taylor wrote "Knockin' Round the Zoo" and "Don't Talk Now", two songs referencing his experience in the psychiatric hospital. Writing and playing music seemed to ground Taylor, so upon his release from the psychiatric hospital, he moved to New York in 1966, in search of a career in music.

Most young musicians in 1966, especially in a commercial center like New York, gravitated to Rock, particularly Psychedelic Rock. Taylor, though, was unaffected by the omnipresent trends and themes. He was grounded in Folk and stimulated by the Blues. Unusual for a wealthy kid from Boston and a college town in North Carolina.

Taylor honed his sound and continued to write, eventually impressing Peter Asher, an A&R executive for the brand new label, Apple Records, owned by The Beatles. As discussed, Apple Records was looking to produce non-Beatles records – and Asher was tasked with finding talent. Asher began his search in the coffee houses of New York.

In May 1968, Asher played a demo of "Something in the Way She Moves" for Paul McCartney and George Harrison. Both Paul and George were immediately affected by Taylor's voice and the simplicity of his acoustic guitar playing. The Beatles unanimously decided that James Taylor's debut record would be the first record recorded and released on Apple Records.

Taylor began recording his self-titled debut in July 1968 at Trident Studios in London – at the very same time, down the hall, from where The Beatles were recording *The White Album*. McCartney and Harrison were infatuated with Taylor's voice and songwriting and each of Paul and George watched James record when on break from their own session. However, once Paul and George heard "Carolina In My Mind", they no longer could just sit and watch.

Both McCartney and Harrison play on "Carolina In My Mind", George playing guitar and Paul layering bass parts. Both remain in the background, as Taylor's voice dominates, mixed in front of the instruments. If you are familiar with "Carolina In My Mind", you're likely familiar with the slower version later recorded and re-released by Taylor. The version on *James Taylor* is fast, almost sounding rushed compared to the later recorded version. The track also includes a string section, reminiscent of the string arrangements that George Martin popularized on several Beatles tracks.

While the entire record is pleasant, the standout tracks are clearly "Knockin' Round the Zoo" and "Something in the Way She Moves." After a string section intro, "Knockin' Round the Zoo" takes off with a funky bass line, paired with an acoustic guitar and a trumpet, then a full horn section. The arrangement is bouncy, but again – dominated by Taylor's voice. Not a raspy Blues vocal, Taylor's voice is pure and clean, yet incredibly soulful and genuine. If you can listen to this track and not tap your foot or bob your head, well – I can't believe you're reading this book.

Beginning with a series of chimes, a prepared piano and an organ, "Something in the Way She Moves" is again a bit faster than the version you likely know well. Distinctly a Folk-inspired ballad, Taylor's voice again (fortunately) lacks the weariness of traditional Folk musicians. Pure is really the best adjective.

Taylor's gift is incorporating melody within the confines of traditional instrumentation, primarily using his vocal inflection. Perhaps Taylor's knack for melody is what initially grabbed McCartney's attention. Paul was not the only one enamored with "Something in the Way She Moves." George Harrison admitted that Taylor's song inspired his most revered track on *Abbey Road*, "Something."

In general, James Taylor is an outlier in 1968. The record is more optimistic than most releases in 1968, especially late-1968. Jon Landau, reviewing the record for *Rolling Stone* stated, "this album is the coolest breath of fresh air I've inhaled in a good long while. It knocks me out." Taylor was 22 years old at the time he recorded the record – perhaps he was too young to digest the events of 1968, or perhaps he simply was flattened by the experience of being a kid in the presence of The Beatles, recording a debut record.

Unfortunately, the optimism did not prevail. Taylor was not able to tour in support of the debut release. During the recording session, Taylor began experimenting with heroin, along with marijuana and alcohol. The drugs led to another bout of depression, forcing Taylor to again check into a psychiatric facility. Taylor recovered, but the lack of touring in support of *James Taylor* resulted in a lack of commercial success. "Carolina In My Mind" reached #118 on the *Billboard* Hot 100, primarily due to McCartney and Harrison appearing on the track.

Released from the psychiatric facility, Taylor hit the road in May 1969 – appearing at The Troubadour in Los Angeles for six consecutive sold out shows, then headlining the famed Newport Folk Festival in July. Taylor moved to California, attracted to the Folk-Rock-Country scene facilitated by The Byrds, Buffalo Springfield and the Country music from Bakersfield. In December, Taylor entered the studio to record his follow-up, *Sweet Baby James*.

Joined on several tracks by Carole King, *Sweet Baby James* was a hit. Released in February 1970, *Sweet Baby James* reached #3 on the *Billboard* Top 200 Albums chart, fueled by the lead Single, "Fire and Rain", which reached #3 on the *Billboard* Hot 100. "Fire and Rain" is an account of Taylor's struggle to kick his drug habit, along with his experiences in various psychiatric institutions.

Capitalizing on the success of *Sweet Baby James*, Taylor recorded and released *Mud Slide Slim and the Blue Horizon* in April 1971. The record included the track, "You've Got a Friend", written by Carole King and featuring Joni Mitchell on backing vocals. "You've Got a Friend" reached #1 on the *Billboard* Hot 100. James Taylor was an international star.

James Taylor remains a model of consistency, dignity and talent. As mentioned earlier, James Taylor was not affected or influenced by the Psychedelic Rock of 1967 and he didn't incorporate popular elements of 1968 into his music – likewise, James Taylor never fell prey to the excess and mediocrity of the 1980s or the grunge of the early 1990s.

The music of James Taylor seems to be affected only by the mind of James Taylor. Thankfully.

Neil Young – S/T

The debut solo release from Neil Young is quite simply – underrated. Such is Neil's own doing, though. The follow-up to Neil's self-titled debut was *Everybody Knows This Is Nowhere*, then *After the Gold Rush*, *Harvest*, *On the Beach* and *Tonight's the Night*. The sheer quality of the subsequent releases obscures the beauty of the debut. The debut release, in many respects, sounds more developed than the subsequent releases due to strings, horns and backing vocals. Ultimately, Neil Young would master a rustic, simple presentation of wonderfully written songs.

Fresh off the dismantling of Buffalo Springfield, Neil Young possessed a notebook full of song fragments, some of which had been written years prior. Inherently political, Neil had yet to incorporate progressive views into his lyrics. In 1968, Neil gravitated towards the undercurrent and influence of Country music, much like The Byrds and his former band, Buffalo Springfield. As a result, *Neil Young* leans towards Country and Folk, but Neil includes elements that very much represent 1968.

Possibly a surprise in 1968, but certainly not surprising to a listener today – knowing the evolution of Neil Young, the first solo track recorded and released by Neil Young is a distinctly Country instrumental titled "The Emperor of Wyoming." At just over two minutes, Neil sets the tone for the record, and possibly his career.

Not only is the track Country, but it is distinctly Nashville Country. Between 1965 and 1972, the Nashville Sound utilized string arrangements, multiple (typically female) backup singers, slide guitar or pedal steel and musical interludes or short instrumentals. The tracks on *Neil Young* that include elements of Nashville Country sound distinctly non-Neil Young. Throughout Neil's distinguished recording career, a consistent hallmark has been the lack of over-production, leaning towards the rustic traditions of Bakersfield Country.

"The Last Emperor of Wyoming" opens with the twang of a Fender Telecaster (by Neil) and then a string section part anchored by violin and cello. A second guitar can be heard, an acoustic guitar played by Ry Cooder. The closest comparison is probably Dylan's "Nashville Skyline Rag", which came out later – in 1969.

Other than just being a remarkably titled instrumental, "The Last Emperor of Wyoming" functions as the establishment of a Country aesthetic, then in typical Neil Young fashion, serves as the antithesis to what followed. The opening instrumental track leads right into "The Loner", the first true iteration of Neil Young as we know him today.

A Rock track, "The Loner" features a crunchy electric guitar (played by Neil), but still incorporates a string section. Fortunately, Neil's vocals and the amped-up guitar render the string section secondary. Much of *Neil Young* is drenched in melancholy – understandably, but "The Loner" possesses the venom of 1968 and formulates the character of Neil Young – an outcast, an outsider – and yes, a loner.

The lyrics of "The Loner" can get a bit lost due to the fire of the guitars, but not only do the lyrics advance the concepts and themes of apathy, rage and discontent, but the lyrics are incredibly poetic and wonderfully literary. The track opens with:

> *He's a perfect stranger,*
> *Like a cross*
> *of himself and a fox.*
> *He's a feeling arranger*
> *And a changer*
> *of the ways he talks.*
> *He's the unforeseen danger*
> *The keeper of*
> *the key to the locks.*

Know when you see him,
Nothing can free him.
Step aside, open wide,
It's the loner.

The first verse wreaks of havoc, certainly an illustration of a negative character. Perhaps even a violent character – "He's the unforeseen danger." However, violence is the farthest thing from central in Neil Young's songwriting. By the third verse, we understand that the core of Neil Young's conveyance is sadness, not violence. A sense of loss. Whether speaking about himself or another, Neil crafts emotion and communicates empathy. The sentiment conveyed was likely a familiar feeling among young people in 1968. The second verse redirects attention.

There was a woman he knew
About a year or so ago.
She had something
that he needed
And he pleaded
with her not to go.
On the day that she left,
He died,
but it did not show.
Know when you see him,
Nothing can free him.
Step aside, open wide,
It's the loner.

A woman. Of course a woman is at the heart of the character's lonerism. The story, though, seems secondary. I'd prefer to focus on Neil's word choices and songwriting style. Neil never fixates on rhyming each verse, but his word choice ensures a fluidity that often seems like a rhyming pattern. Listen to his phrasing on the lines, "On the day that she LEFT/He died, but it did not SHOW/Know when you see HIM/Nothing can free HIM." The last words in each line do not rhyme, as would be traditional, yet the use of "he" and "she" in the first two lines links the phrases. Then, he writes "when you SEE him/Nothing can FREE him." A rhyme within the line, rather than at the end of the line. Subtle, but important and evidence of intuition and rhythm.

Side 1 of *Neil Young* ends with a version of "Old Laughing Lady." I use the term "version" because, over the ensuing 50 years, Neil Young would reinvent "Old Laughing Lady" countless times, rearranging the track to fit a live set or live recording ranging from a solo acoustic track to a power ballad electric arrangement. However, the first recording of "Old Laughing Lady" might surprise even devout Neil Young fans.

Most know "Old Laughing Lady" to be a relatively short, solo acoustic effort by Neil – the substance of which is an ode to his wife, Peggi (whose name appears in the first line of the song). The version that concludes Side 1 of *Neil Young*, though, is six minutes, beginning with percussion and then after the first verse, possesses a brief, yet distinct acoustic Jazz rhythm (reminiscent of *Astral Weeks* by Van Morrison, released one month prior).

Neil's vocals reflect his traditional, strained voice – maybe singing a bit more than speaking on this version – but, it's the surrounding sounds that make this version of "Old Laughing Lady" unique, even an outlier. After the second verse, a string section can be heard building in the background, almost swirling around Neil's vocal. No dominant guitar on the track, mainly piano, strings and percussion.

The arrangement is essentially a series of peaks and valleys, with the peaks being round, rolling hills rather than jagged, and the valleys never dropping completely to the canyon floor. In between each verse, additional instrumental elements are added to build a structure, only to be cut when Neil emerges for the next verse. The final piece is a full choir of female gospel vocalists. Quite similar to the use of a choir on "Salt of the Earth" by The Rolling Stones.

At 3:10, a pause leads into a passage dominated by the chorus. Neil disappears as the chorus fades into a faint Jazz-tinged piano/percussion sequence. Neil's closing verse is accompanied by a dominant and traditional string melody, fading directly into a quiet piano passage and a quiet conclusion to Side 1.

Side 2 opens with a strings-only arrangement by Neil's piano player, Jack Nitzsche. The instrumental piece is titled "String Quartet from Whiskey Boot Hill" and at a brisk 57 seconds in length, the track leads right into "Here We Are in the Years." The Neil Young original is decent, certainly not a "skip", but the focus of Side 2 must be on the final two tracks. Both are stunning examples of Neil's talent – and not "early examples of his talent." I believe the two closing tracks should be included in the canon of Neil's greatest work.

"I've Loved Her So Long" is my favorite track on *Neil Young*. Look, before I attempt to describe the song, I should mention that I have long been a massive Neil Young fan – so, when I say that "I've Loved Her So Long" is my favorite track on *Neil Young* – well, that's obviously a loaded statement. Meaning, of course "The Loner" and "Old Laughing Lady" are terrific songs, as is the album's closing track. "I've Loved Her So Long" is just one of those deep cuts that you can kind of feel like is yours, a small little nugget that only you know about. Of course, that's preposterous logic – but, who cares.

The beauty of "I've Loved Her So Long" is the chorus, but the beauty of the chorus is set up by the melancholy of the verse. Opening with two bars of deep, dark bass – Neil's vocals bounce between tenor and falsetto. It's the first time you can hear the voice that Neil perfected on *After the Gold Rush* and *Harvest*. "I've Loved Her So Long" is the song most similar to the material on those classic, later albums.

Only two verses and a chorus, the first verse again illustrates Neil's talent for phrasing:

> *She's a victim of her senses*
> *Do you know her?*

Can you see her in the distance
As she tumbles by?
Veteran of a race
that should be over
Can you hear her sigh?
With wings to fly
She rolls along
Doing it wrong.

Abstract, yet meaningful. Again, look at Neil's use of rhyming words. He uses rhyming techniques, but the pattern is atypical – maybe even devoid of a pattern. Yet, there's enough there in terms of phrasing and pace to provide consistency and fluidity. Neil balances the word-forward texture of the verses with a bright, simple chorus:

Oh, I've loved her so long
Oh, I've loved her so long

Neil is joined on the chorus by a gospel choir – and it sounds perfect. The choir sings behind Neil, mostly scat and oohs and ahhs. As the first iteration of the chorus concludes, Neil returns to the verse, but astutely, not the same template of the first verse – the choir remains and Neil uses the arrangement's energy to drop the following historically relevant lines:

There's a place that I know
We could go
Get away for a while
I can bring her the peace
That she needs
Give her reason to smile.

Escapism, a return to lonerism – the mentality of the musicians making "genuine", traditional, acoustic music. The beauty of those lines lead to a refrain of the chorus and after a perfectly placed drum fill, another run through the chorus, amplifying the choir and emphasizing the beauty of the composition.

401

The album closes the way we all want the album to close. The way we expect the album to close. Neil Young and an acoustic guitar. For nine minutes and thirty-five seconds. Verse after verse after verse. While familiar in 2018, in 1968, Neil Young solo with an acoustic guitar was not common – it was actually a total outlier. A 1969 review of *Neil Young* in *Rolling Stone* commented on the album closer, "The Last Trip to Tulsa":

"'The Last Trip to Tulsa'...is the most stylistic, anti-Springfield piece on the album. Here we have only Young's chameleon voice and guitar – no strings, drums or piano. [T]he vocal gets wider, the guitar more abandoned, more wanton. An innovative close."

Innovative? Neil Young solo with an acoustic guitar? The format accentuates the lyrics and Neil's voice. Period. Neil's primary assets – the lyrics and his voice. The first verse establishes the element of first person narrative, a vintage tactic, but a new construction built on the mind of Neil Young:

> *Well, I used to drive a cab,*
> *you know*
> *I heard a siren scream*
> *Pulled over to the corner*
> *And I fell into a dream*

Now, if you thought this was going to be a story about a cab driver that got pulled over by a cop – well, the next verse dispels that notion. Neil would use this mechanism throughout his career – inserting himself in the song, only to drift away from the first person narrative. "Pocahontas" and "Powderfinger" are two later examples. The second verse:

> *There were*
> *two men eating pennies*
> *And three young girls who cried*
> *The West coast is falling,*
> *I see rocks in the sky.*

The preacher took his bible
And laid it on the stool.
He said: "With
the congregation running,
Why should I play the fool?"

No context – just great line after great line after great line. On the
fourth verse, Neil shifts to substance and attacks the music industry –
painting himself as an instrument of the machine. A classic Dylan
technique, utilized by Dylan most famously in "Desolation Row."

Well, I used to be a folk singer
Keeping managers alive,
When you saw me on a corner
And told me I was jive.
So I unlocked your mind, you know
To see what I could see.
If you guarantee the postage,
I'll mail you back the key.
Well I woke up in the morning
With an arrow through my nose
There was an Indian in the corner
Tryin' on my clothes.

I could read these lyrics over and over again. Poetry? Maybe, but I
relate these lyrics to Kerouac and Ginsberg. Stream of consciousness
but a focus on rhythm and pace. Neil chose words that conveyed
movement. His lyrics are granular – abstract in concept, but
grounded in terms of pronunciation. The musical accompaniment is
lightly strummed acoustic guitar, but two-thirds of the way through
the song, Neil raises the energy and the strumming picks up
considerably, with more volume – leading into the penultimate verse:

Well, I was driving
down the freeway
When my car ran out of gas.
Pulled over to the station

403

But I was afraid to ask.
The servicemen were yellow
And the gasoline was green.
Although I knew I couldn't
I thought that I was gonna scream.
That was on my last trip to Tulsa
Just before the snow.
If you ever need a ride there,
Be sure to let me know.

Perhaps the song is just a series of images or thoughts while Neil was on a drive to Tulsa? His "last trip to Tulsa" – not his final trip to Tulsa, just his last trip – his most recent trip. Neil again speaks in the first person, but he also speaks to the listener. The final verse:

I was chopping down a palm tree
When a friend dropped by to ask
If I would feel less lonely
If he helped me swing the axe.
I said: "No, it's
not a case of being lonely
We have here,
I've been working on this palm tree
For eighty seven years"
He said: "Go get lost!"
And walked towards his Cadillac.
I chopped down the palm tree
And it landed on his back.

Is it just me? There's so much there. We could analyze each line – focusing on the chopping of a palm tree (an indictment of the West Coast and an interesting use of environmentalism), a man thinking that Neil was lonely (the misconception of appearance, the misconception of a generation), the man reacting negatively and then retreating to his Cadillac (materialism) and Neil finally chopping the tree down and the tree falling on the man (evidence of violence and gore in 1968). It's just an awesome little vignette.

404

The closest comparable track to "Last Trip to Tulsa" in Neil's catalog is probably "Ambulance Blues" from *On the Beach* (1974), a nine minute masterpiece featuring just Neil Young and an acoustic guitar. And, while Dylan remains the preeminent influence of the generation, in terms of songwriting, Dylan has been notoriously influenced by Neil Young. Dylan invented the long format, verse-dominated, no chorus structure – for example, "Visions of Johana" and the aforementioned "Desolation Row" – but, Dylan recognized the beauty of Neil Young's iteration.

On the closing track of Dylan's late-career highlight, *Time Out of Mind*, Dylan exceeded all parameters by offering a 20-verse, sixteen minute blueprint of his famed format. Titled "Highlands", Dylan bounced from verse to verse, diving in and out of vignettes, but most surprisingly – invoking the name of...Neil Young. In the fifth verse, Dylan states:

> *I'm listening to Neil Young, I gotta turn up the sound*
> *Someone's always yellin', "Turn him down"*
> *Feel like I'm driftin', driftin' from scene to scene*
> *I'm wondering what in the devil could it all possibly mean.*

Hearing Dylan sing, "I'm listening to Neil Young, I gotta turn up the sound" – well, that's just one of the most memorable lines in music – but, hey – that's just me. And, notice Dylan's more traditional style of rhyming – consistent, last word in each line, almost predictable, yet rhythmic and pure.

Neil Young's talent is the dichotomy between madness and sadness. The two traits often materialize within a single song, sometimes a single verse. On *Neil Young*, we see the birth of the dichotomy. The madness of "The Loner" compared to the sadness of "I've Loved Her So Long." The consistent thread is Neil's scowl. The passion exerted on each and every track. The songs on *Neil Young* provide the framework for Neil to break down the frame and venture on a singular path.

While critics flocked to *Neil Young*, the record did not perform well commercially. Fans wanted Buffalo Springfield, not Neil Young. Fans wouldn't get Buffalo Springfield, though. Neil joined forces with Crosby, Stills and Nash to become Crosby, Stills, Nash & Young. The combination would result in the most popular band of the era, both in terms of record sales and live shows.

Of course, though – Neil could not be contained. He quit the conglomerate and continued to record and release under his own name, amassing a collection of recordings that rival any musician in the 21st Century.

Frank Zappa/The Mothers of Invention – *Cruising with Ruben & the Jets*

In a year dominated by turbulence, death, negativity and loss, it is only natural to conclude this book with satire. The premier satirist in music was, of course, Frank Zappa. We covered *We're Only in it For the Money* in March, an assault on the commercialistic tendencies and misplaced excess of The Beatles and their 1967 release, *Sgt. Pepper's Lonely Hearts Club Band*. While the message of *We're Only in it For the Money* is brilliant, the music crafted around the satire was difficult to digest. Frank Zappa's second attempt in 1968 would be the opposite.

Released on December 2, *Cruising with Ruben & the Jets* was the fourth album released by Frank Zappa and the Mothers of Invention. Each of the previous three releases were loosely conceived as a singular concept. Not necessarily a narrative, like *Tommy*, but the songs are certainly held together by a common theme. *Ruben & the Jets* is the story of a fictitious doo-wop band, Ruben & the Jets. Each track on *Ruben & the Jets* is composed and arranged as a classic doo-wop song from the Fifties. Because Zappa and his mates were such talented musicians, the songs are wonderful replicas of the Fifties sound. Maybe, too wonderful.

The liner notes told the story of Ruben Sano, the lead singer of Ruben & the Jets. The story discussed how Ruben met the members of the Jets and the genesis of the band. The story also spoke of Ruben's relationship with his girlfriend, ending in the pair breaking up (giving thousands of young women listeners hope of intimacy with the lead singer). Of course, the entire narrative was a rouse. Zappa intentionally included every trope. Mocking the fandom of mainstream Pop fans.

Along with the fictitious narrative and the perfect replica of classic doo-wop, the public bought it. The lyrics of each song, though, were not about love or cars or girls. That was the point. The mainstream ignored the lyrics. The songs were dark in message, but the public was influenced more by the narrative and the song arrangements. Zappa was proving a point. Don't be obscured by what corporations feed you – take the time to understand true meaning and true intent. Be genuine.

Zappa described the lyrics on *Ruben & the Jets*: "I detest love lyrics...the lyrics on *Ruben & the Jets* are intentionally sub-Mongoloid." Zappa also weaved in quotes of several Igor Stravinsky compositions. The lyrics were not meant to influence the public – rather, Zappa hoped that the lyrics were actually overlooked, underscoring his overall purpose. Zappa would achieve his goal.

The album cover looked as though the band releasing the record was in fact Ruben & the Jets. However, for legal purposes, Zappa was instructed that the band's name must appear somewhere on the record cover. As a result, Zappa approved the inclusion of a small thought bubble on the record cover that included the text: "Is this the Mothers of Invention recording under a different name in a last ditch attempt to get their cruddy music on the radio." As expected, nobody focused on the small thought bubble. Zappa was beautifully insane.

A Single was released ("Deseri") and credited to *Ruben & the Jets*. *Ruben & the Jets* was immediately popular with national radio stations. Accompanied by a rumor that the record was an unearthed doo-wop band from the Fifties, the public bought the narrative. As radio stations sought interviews with the band and venues reached out to management to book live shows, the ploy was uncovered.

Fans abandoned the record and critics felt deceived. Musicians in the underground scenes of New York, Los Angeles and San Francisco, though, loved every aspect of *Ruben & the Jets*. Zappa's mocking of the institution of music was viewed as intellectually seminal. Likewise, authors and film producers, as well as progressive academics, lauded the record as a literary triumph – declaring Zappa a genius satirist.

Time has certainly been kind to Zappa, as many of his releases are held in the highest regard. However, Zappa's music is largely inaccessible, musically. Odd time signatures, raging distortion, feedback, chaotic vocals – characteristically and intentionally unpleasant in terms of traditional Rock music. But, that's the beauty of *Ruben & the Jets*. Fifty years after its release, with knowledge of the rouse, the fake narrative – we can choose to either investigate and understand the satirist motive – or, we can listen to the great Frank Zappa play a bunch of doo-wop songs. I thoroughly enjoy doing both, actually.

Of course, I poured through the lyrics and considered reprising several verses in this passage, but ultimately – I gravitated more to the music. Am I falling prey to the very commercialistic tendency that Zappa abhorred? Maybe, but mostly – I fault Zappa. His replication of the genre he was satirizing was just too good.

Now that you understand Zappa's intention – embrace it, think about it – then queue up *Ruben & the Jets* on your back porch when the warm sun is shining or when you're entertaining a bunch of Baby Boomers. Trust me, you'll get several questions of, "Who is this...it sounds really familiar, but I can't place it." You can then make Frank happy by smiling and saying with distinction, "Oh, it's Frank Zappa."

Epilogue

The pages preceding this Epilogue were a study to determine why the landscape of music changed so drastically from 1967 to 1968. What caused such a sweeping change? Typically, commercialism motivates change in music, but not so much in 1968. Here are two examples of commercialism as the instigator of change.

In 1956, Elvis Presley was shown on television shaking his knees, wearing a sharp suit and playing Rock & Roll. Record labels, other musicians and the consuming public devoured the trend. A generation of musicians followed Elvis, ushering a change in style and sound. Elvis didn't invent Rock & Roll. Chuck Berry, Jerry Lee Lewis and Little Richard invented Rock & Roll. Elvis commercialized Rock & Roll.

When The Beatles "landed" in the United States in 1963 and debuted on *The Ed Sullivan Show* – hairstyles and teenage fandom changed instantly. Likewise, the music created thereafter changed dramatically. A fleet of bands adopted the style and sound of The Beatles. However, The Beatles didn't invent the Pop-centric brand of Rock & Roll. Bill Haley and the Comets, Elvis Presley and Carl Perkins invented the Pop-centric brand of Rock & Roll. The Beatles commercialized the sound.

While commercialism had been the typical motivator of change, on July 25, 1965, at the sacred Newport Folk Festival, Bob Dylan introduced a brash, loud and turbulent version of Rock that included substantive commentary. Dylan fused history with music. Dylan fused message with Rock. Dylan also lit a fuse. Musicians effected change in the name of purpose, civility, peace and righteousness – not commercialism.

Arguably, change derived from purpose and message, rather than commercialism, results in greater waves, taller peaks and bolder statements of freedom and expression. Nobody, though, could predict the magnitude of chaos in 1968, possibly the darkest year in American history. How could a musician write lyrics in 1968 and not reflect, or project, the omnipresent tragedy? How could one write a piece of music in 1968 and not contemplate rage? And, if not rage, then overwhelming sadness. Music is the consequence. Music is the output. However, music is hardly static. Music exists as interpretation and, in the case of 1968, music serves as instruction – a template for future generations to express and effect change.

As you listen to current music – and please, you should be listening to the music made currently – it's terrific and ideas are absolutely being conveyed through Rock, Hip Hop and sometimes, even Country. Consider intent and contemplate how politics and injustice are affecting society. Was the music of 2002 affected by the events and aftermath of September 11, 2001? Was the music of 2015 affected by the racial uprisings in Ferguson, Missouri and the death of Freddie Gray in Baltimore? Was the music of 2017 and 2018 affected by the election of Donald Trump?

Maybe this book just recounts facts. Maybe this book is simply a list of events that took place in 1968. Maybe this book only regurgitates the albums and songs released each month in 1968. Maybe reading a book about a time period in American history by an author that wasn't even alive during that period – well, maybe that's just a waste of time? Maybe this book sucks? I really don't know

Ultimately, my hope is that this book presented a path, or a map, from which you may travel. Explore the music discussed in this book, then traverse. Travel forward and meander backward. Venture through the catalogs of the musicians discussed. Consider motive. Listen with intent.

Above all else, though, support the musicians making music today. Musicians are often the voice of society. Often, musicians are the voice that checks authority, contains oppression and balances the system. In times of trouble, in times of darkness, in time of instability, music remains an avenue for freedom.

This book began with a quote from Harry Belafonte, an activist and musician. Belafonte stated, "When the movement is strong, the music

411

is strong." I believe that a twist on Belafonte's quote is also true and incredibly important. I believe that when the music is strong, the movement is strong. We must support musicians to ensure that the movement remains strong.

19786305R00253

Made in the USA
Lexington, KY
29 November 2018